Edward Duffield Neill

Virginia Carolorum

The Colony under the Rule of Charles the First and Second, A. D. 1625-A...

Edward Duffield Neill

Virginia Carolorum

The Colony under the Rule of Charles the First and Second, A. D. 1625-A...

ISBN/EAN: 9783744756686

Printed in Europe, USA, Canada, Australia, Japan

Cover: Foto ©ninafisch / pixelio.de

More available books at **www.hansebooks.com**

Neill's Series of Virginia History.

VIRGINIA CAROLORUM:

THE COLONY UNDER THE RULE OF CHARLES THE FIRST AND SECOND
A. D. 1625—A. D. 1685,

BASED UPON

MANUSCRIPTS AND DOCUMENTS OF THE PERIOD.

BY

EDWARD D. NEILL.

NEC FALSA DICERE, NEC VERA RETICERE.

ALBANY, N. Y.:
JOEL MUNSELL'S SONS, 82 STATE ST.
1886.

PREFACE.

The student of the English colonization of America has regretted that there has been so little published, upon the development of the Virginia Colony, during the Carolan period.

With the hope, that it might lead to a more intelligent comprehension of the motives, and social surroundings, of the chief men of the era, this work has been prepared.

The writer has had no political theory, nor religious party, nor provincial prejudice to sustain. As far as possible those who were prominent in shaping the destinies of the Colony, have been permitted to express their views, in their own words, as found in letters to their friends, or in communications to the English Government.

Their revelations conflict with some traditions, and "old wives' fables," and may not be acceptable to those who dislike

"Records, on a page,
Whence many a pleasant tale is swept away."

PREFACE.

The duty of the historian is to be careful not to distort facts, nor to conceal that which is true.

In the preparation of the volume, use has been made of some unpublished papers, in the British Museum, and Her Majesty's Public Record Office in London; and of the records in possession of the Virginia Historical Society, and the counties of Accomac, and Northampton. Rare printed documents of the period have been freely cited, and the quotations, from the early laws, have been taken from Hening's Statutes.

It is a pleasure to acknowledge the courtesies extended to me, by Secretary Brock of the Virginia Historical Society, Mr. Gilmore Kendall, Clerk of Northampton County Court, and Mr. W. H. B. Custis of the Accomac Court, while searching the records in their keeping.

SAINT PAUL, MINNESOTA,

September, 1886.

CONTENTS.

CHAPTER I.
FROM THE ABROGATION OF THE LONDON COMPANY'S CHARTER TO THE DEATH OF GOVERNOR YEARDLEY - - 8–48

CHAPTER II.
PRINCIPAL EVENTS FROM A.D. 1628 TO A.D. 1630 - 49–76

CHAPTER III.
TRANSACTIONS FROM A.D. 1630 TO A.D. 1634 - - 77–93

CHAPTER IV.
AFFAIRS FROM A.D. 1634 TO A.D. 1638 - - - 98–137

CHAPTER V.
OCCURRENCES FROM A.D. 1638 TO A.D. 1642 - - 138–156

CHAPTER VI.
FROM THE ARRIVAL OF GOVERNOR BERKELEY TO THE APPOINTMENT OF PARLIAMENT COMMISSIONERS - 154–217

CONTENTS.

CHAPTER VII.

AFFAIRS UNDER THE COMMONWEALTH OF ENGLAND - 217–279

CHAPTER VIII.

FROM THE ACCESSION OF CHARLES THE SECOND TO A.D. 1671 - - - - - - - - - 280–338

CHAPTER IX.

FROM A.D. 1671 TO THE DEATH OF CHARLES THE SECOND 339–401

APPENDIX.

ADDITIONAL NOTES - - - - - - - 403–421

INDEX AND ERRATA - - - - - - - 423

Virginia Carolorum.

CHAPTER I.

FROM THE ABROGATION OF THE LONDON COMPANY'S CHARTER TO THE DEATH OF GOVERNOR YEARDLEY.

PROCLAMATION OF CHARLES THE FIRST. GOVERNOR AND COUNCILLORS A.D 1624–5. WILLIAM CLAIBORNE. SECRETARY CHRISTOPHER DAVISON. JOHN MARTIN SUSPENDED FROM THE COUNCIL. YEARDLEY VISITS ENGLAND. LETTERS OF GOV. BUTLER OF BERMUDAS. COMPANION OF POCAHONTAS MARRIED. MATE AND CAPTAIN OF THE MAY FLOWER. INTRODUCTION OF NEGROES. FEAR OF SPANIARDS. DEATH OF EX-GOV. ARGALL. RE-APPOINTMENT OF GOV. YEARDLEY. DOCTOR POTT. CAPT. W. TUCKER. EDWARD BLANEY. WILLIAM FERRAR. CLAIBORNE ANCESTRY. OVID TRANSLATED BY SANDYS. ARRIVAL AND DEPARTURE OF SHIPS. TOBACCO MONOPOLY. DEATH OF GOV. YEARDLEY.

AMONG the earliest acts of Charles the First, after his coronation, was a proclamation concerning Virginia. Sir Thomas Smith, the enterprising East India merchant, and Alderman Robert Johnson, the London grocer, with their associates, were entirely satisfied with the victory over the Earl of Southampton, Sir Edwin Sandys, and the large majority of the members of the London Company, resulting from the declaration of Chief Justice Ley (Leigh), in June, 1624, that the Company's charter was null and void. Toward the colonists in Virginia they had no harsh feelings, but their influence was used with the King so to order the tobacco trade, that their friends in London might derive some profit.

The ship which brought the news of the death of James the First, also conveyed the views of his successor, as to the Plantation. In a communication of the thirteenth day of May, A.D. 1625, from Whitehall, Charles alludes to the "Collonie of Virginia, planted by the hands of our most deere Father of blessed memorie, for the propagation of Christian religion, the increase of trade, and the enlarging of his Royal empire." He thought that it "had not hitherto prospered soe happilly as was hoped and desired for, that the government of that Collonie was comytted to the Companie of Virginia, incorporated of a multitude of persons of severall dispositions, amongst whome the affaires of greatest moment were and must be ruled by the greater number of votes and voyces, and therefore his late Majestie, out of his great wisedome and depth of judgment, did desire to resume that popular government, and accordingly the letters patentes of that Incorporation were, by his Highnes' direction, in a legal course questioned, and therefore judicially repealed and adjudged to be voyd, wherein his Majestye's ayme was onlie to reduce that Government into such a right course as might best agree with that forme which was held in the rest of his Royal Monarchie, and was not intended by him to take awaie or ympeach the particular interest of anie private planter or adventurer, nor to alter the same otherwise than should be of necessitie for the good of the publique."

He also declared : "Our full resolution is, that there maie be one uniforme course of government in and through our whole Monarchie : that the government of the Collonie of Virginia shall ymediately depend upon ourselfe, and not be commytted to anie Companie or Corporation to whom it maie be proper to trust matters of trade or commerce, but cannott be fit or safe to communicate the ordering of State affaires, be they of never so mean consequence : And that therefore we have determyned that our Commissioners[1] for

---

[1] On the 15th of July, 1624, King James had appointed the following Commissioners for Virginia to receive the charters, seals, and letters of the Virginia Company, and attend to the affaires of the Colony:

Henry, Viscount Mandeville, Lord President of the Privy Council.
William, Lord Pagett.
Arthur, Lord Chichester, Baron of Belfast.
Sir Thomas Edwards, Knight, Treasurer.
" John Suckling, " Comptroller.
" George Calvert, " Secretary of State.
" Edward Conway, " "
" Richard Weston, " Chancellor of Exchequer.
" Julius Cæsar, " Master of Rolls.
" Humphrey May, " Chancellor of Lancaster.
" Baptist Hickes, " and Baronet.
" Thomas Smith, "
Sir Henry Mildmay, Knight, Master of Jewels.
" Thomas Coventry, " Attorney General.
" Robert Heath, " Solicitor General.
" Ferdinand Gorges, "
" Robert Killigrew, "
" Charles Montague, "
" Philip Cary, "
" Francis Gaston, "
" Thomas Wroth, "

those affaires shall proceede accordinge to the tenor of our commissions directed unto them, until we shall declare our further pleasure therein ; nevertheless we doe hereby declare that we are resolved with as much convenyent expedition as our affaires of greater importance will give leeve, to establish a Counsell consistinge of a few persons of understanding and quallitie, to whom wee will give trust for the ymediate care of the affaires of that Collonie, and whoe shall be answerable to us for their proceedings, and in matters of great moment shall be subordinate and attendant unto our Privie Counsell here; and that wee will alsoe establish another Counsell to be resident in Virginia, who shall be subordinate to our Counsell here for that Collonie, and that att our owne charge we will maynteyne those publique officers."

" John Wolstenholme, "
" Nathaniel Rich, "
" Samuel Argall, "
" Humphrey Handford, "
Matthew Sutcliffe, D.D., Dean of Exeter.
Francis White, D.D., Dean of Carlisle.
Thomas Fanshaw, Clerk of the Crown.
Robert Johnson, Alderman of London.
James Campbell, " "
Ralph Freeman, " "
Maurice Abbot, Esquire,
Nathaniel Butler, "
George Wilmore, "
Philip Jermayne, "
Edward Johnson, "
Thomas Gibbs, "
Samuel Wrote, "
John Porey, "
Michael Hawes, "

In conclusion, he wrote that he wished to bring the tobacco trade into one hand, and exclude that raised in foreign lands, and to fix his own price upon that raised in Virginia.[1]

After the charter of the Virginia Company had been dissolved, James the First continued Sir Francis Wyatt[2] as

    Edward Pallavacine, Esquire.
    Robert Bateman, Merchant.
    Martin Bonde, "
    Thomas Styles, "
    Nicholas Leate, "
    Robert Bell, "
    Abraham Cartwright, "
    Richard Edwards, "
    John Dyke, "
    Anthony Abdy, "
    William Palmer, "
    Edward Dichfield, Salter.
    George Mole, Merchant.
    Richard Morer, Grocer.

Upon the recommendation of the Commissioners for Virginia, the following Tobacco Inspectors in London were appointed: Edward Dichfield, Salter; Richard Morer, Reuben Bourne, George Bromley, Grocers; William Perkyns, Merchant Tailor; and Edward Bennet, Merchant.

[1] The entire document is printed in Rymer's "Fœdera," Vol. XVIII., pp. 72,73.

[2] Thomas Wyatt, of Allington Castle, Boxley Abbey, married Jane, daughter of Sir William Hawte. His estate was confiscated.

George, his son, had the estate restored in 1570 by Queen Elizabeth. He married Oct. 8, 1582, Jane, daughter of Sir Thomas Finch, Kt., and he was buried about September 1625, at Boxley Abbey, and left five sons and two daughters.

Francis, eldest son of George, in 1618 married Margaret, daughter of Sir Samuel Sandys, of Ombersley, Worcester. He was buried at Boxley Abbey August 24, 1644, and his wife March 27, 1644-5.

Hawte, brother of Francis, was inducted Rector of Boxley October 3, 1632. He died July 31, 1638. He was twice married, and some of his descendants are

Governor. While he had confidence in the motives of those who had directed the affairs of the Company, Wyatt found that their plans were at times impracticable. In a letter to his father he alluded to the "antipathy" caused by the great demands of the Corporation, and the "grumbling obedience" of the colonists, and he wished "that little Mr. Farrar was in Virginia, that he might add zeal to knowledge." His wife, a daughter of Sir Samuel Sandys, who passed some time in Virginia, was a cheerful person, willing to accept the hardships of a new settlement. His deportment was correct, and a captious fellow could only write:[1] "The old smoker, so good, so carefully mild, religious, just, honest, that I protest, I think God hath sent him, in mercy, for good to us."

---

said to have settled in Virginia. There was a Ralph Wyatt who married the widow of Capt. William Button, of Virginia, and Anthony Wyatt a member of an early legislature.

Eleanor, sister of Francis, was the first wife of Sir Thomas Finch, Speaker of House of Commons, 1627.

Hotten in *Lists of Emigrants* gives

THE MUSTER OF SIR THOMAS WYATT, KT., TAKEN IN JANUARY, 1625.

"Sr Francis Wyatt, Kt., Governo' &c., came in the *George*, 1621.
[Wife had gone to England on a visit.]

SERVANTS.

Christopher Cooke, age 25, in the *George*, 1621.
George Hull, age 13, in the *Supply*, 1620.
Jonathan Giles, 21, in the *Triall*, 1619,
John Mathoman, 19, in the *Jonathan*, 1619.
Jane Davis, 24, in the *Abigaile*, 1622"

[1] Letter of William Capps, an old planter, in "Virginia Vetusta," p. 129; Munsell's Sons, Albany, N. Y., 1885.

The Councillors, as their muster-rolls show, were chosen from among the more prosperous and influential.

Francis West[1] preceded his brother, Lord Delaware, and in A.D. 1608 first arrived. In November, 1623, he was appointed Admiral by the Council for New England, and sailed for Plymouth Harbor, but finding that the fishermen insisted that the fisheries should be opened to all, he returned to Virginia.

---

[1] Alexander Brown, in "Mag. of American History," 1883, p. 461, communicates the West Genealogy from the Bennet Roll. From this are gleaned the following facts:

Thomas 3d Lord Delaware, second son of second Lord, " was born the 9th of July, between 2 and 3 o'clock in the afternoon, 1577."

Francis West, fourth son, was born the 28th of October, 1586, between twelve and one o'clock noon.

John West, fifth son, was born the 14th of December, 1590, between five and six o'clock in the afternoon.

Nathaniel West, sixth son, was born November 3, 1592, between two and three o'clock in the morning.

Doyle, in "History of the American Colonies," speaks of Francis, a nephew of Francis, who was drowned.

In January, 1625, Captain Francis West was living on the Company's land at Elizabeth City. The census-roll then taken, printed in Hotten, had the following:

"CAPTAIN FRANCIS WEST, HIS MUSTER.

Capt. Francis West, Counseler, aged 36, in the *Mary Ann Margaret*, 1610.
Mrs. Francis West, Widdowe, in the *Supply*, 1620.
Nathaniel West, born in Virginia.

SERVANTS.

Joane Fairchild, aged 20, in the *George*, 1618.
Benjamin Owin, aged 18, in the *Swan*, 1623.
William Parnell, aged 18, in the *Southampton*, 1622.
Walter Couper, aged 22, in the *Neptune*, 1618.
Reinould Godwin, aged 30, in the *Abigall*, 1620.
John Pedro, a Neger, aged 30, in the *Swan*, 1623."

Sir George Yeardley[1] had always been recognized for his executive ability and business capacity. John Pory had written of him, in 1619, as "the Governor here, who at his

---

[1] "MUSTER OF SIR GEORGE YEARDLEY, KT.
Sr George Yeardley, Kt., &c.. came in the *Deliverance*, 1609.
Temperance, Lady. Yeardley, came in the *Faulcon*, 1608.
Mr. Argall Yeardley, aged 4 yeares, ⎫
Mr. Francis Yeardley, aged 1 yeare, ⎬ Children borne heare.
M's. Elizabeth Yeardley, aged 6 years, ⎭

SERVANTS AT JAMES CITY.

Richard Gregory, aged 40, ⎫
Anthony Jones, 26,   ⎬ came in the *Temperance*, 1620.
Thomas Dunn, 14,   ⎪
Thomas Phildust, 15,   ⎭
Thomas Hatch, 17, in the *Duty*, 1619.
Robert Peake, 22, in the *Margrett & John*, 1623.
William Strange, 18, in the *George*, 1619.
Roger Thompson, 40, *London Merchant*, 1620.
Ann, his wife.
Richard Arundell, in the *Abigall*, 1620.
Georg Deverill, 18, in the *Temperance*, 1620.
Thomas Barnett, 16, in the *Elsabeth*, 1620.
Theophilus Bereston, in the *Treasuror*, 1614.
Negro Men, 3.
Negro Women, 5.
Susan Hall, in the *William & Thomas*, 1608.
Ann Willis, in the *Temperance*, 1620.
Elizabeth Arundell, in the *Abigall*, 1620.

SERVANTS AT HOG ISLAND.

Maximillian Stone, aged 36, came in the *Temperance*, 1620.
Elizabeth, his wife, in the same shipp.
Maximillian, his son, aged 9 months.
Robert Guy, 22, in the *Swann*, 1619.
Edward Yates, 18, in the *Duty*, 1619.
Cesar Pugget, 20, in the *Diana*, 1619.
William Strachey, 17, in the *Temperance*.
Alexander Sanders, 24, in the *True love*, 1623.
George Whitehand, 24, in the *Temperance*, 1620.

first coming, besides a great deal of worth in his person, brought only his sword with him, was at his late being in London, together with his lady, out of his mere gettings here, able to disburse very near three thousand pounds to furnish him with the voyage." In another paragraph he is called "a soldier truly bred in the University of War in the Low Countries."

George Sandys[1] had been a Colonial Treasurer, and as the brother of the head of the Virginia Company in London, at one time exercised a great influence.

---

[1] "Henry King, 22. in the *Jonathan*, 1620.
John Day, 24, in the *London Merchant*, 1620.
The wife of John Day in the same Shipp."

"MUSTER OF M'S GEORGE SAND'S, ESQUIRE.
Servants.

Martin Turner,
George Bailife,
John Sparks,
John Dancy, } came in the *George*, 1621.
John Edwards,
Nicholas Tompson,
Rosamus Carter,
John Stone, a boy,
Nicholas Comon, } in the *Guift*, 1622.
Nicholas Eyres, a boy,
David Mansfeild, } in the *Bona Nova*, hired servants.
John Claxon,
Thomas Swifte, } in the *Tyger*, freemen, 1622.
John Baldwine,
hired, Daniel Poole, a french man.
his wife, a young child of theires.

MUSTER OF THOSE THAT LIVE IN YE TREASURORS PLANT.
Robert Sheaperd, came in the *George*, 1621.
James Chambers, in the *Dutie*, 1620.

Captain Roger Smith[1] had served twelve years in the wars of the Netherlands, and is supposed to have been the

> John Parsons,
> William Benge,
> John Evans,
> Robert Edmunds,   } in the *Marygold*, 1619.
> John Comes,
> John Tyos.
>
> William Pilkington,
> Elias Longo,   } in the *Bona Nova*, 1620.
> Thomas Hall,
>
> Margaret Pilkington,
> Jane Long,   } weomen.
>
> M'Vincencio, the Italian.
> M' Bernardo.
> his wife.
> A child."

[1] "MUSTER OF CAPT. ROGER SMITH.
Capt. Roger Smith, came in the *Abigaile*, 1620.
M's Joane Smith, came in the *Blessinge*.
Elizabeth Salter, aged 7 yeares, came in the *Seafloure*.
Elizabeth Rolfe, aged 4 yeares,
Sarah Macock, aged 2 yeares,   } born in Virginia.

SERVANTS.

Charles Waller, aged 22, came in the *Abigaile*, 1620.
Christopher Bankus, aged 19 yeares, in the *Abigaile*, 1622.
Henery Booth, aged 20, in the *Dutie*.
Henery Lacton, aged 18 yeares, in the *Hopwell*, 1623.

[Plantation over the water.]

> Francis Fowler, aged 23 yeres.
> Christopher Lawson.
> Alce, his wife.
> Christopher Redhead, aged 24.
> Stephen Webb, aged 25 yeres.
> John Butterfield, aged 23 yeres.
> William Baker, aged 24 yeres.
> Richard Alford, aged 26 yeres.
> Thomas Molton, aged 25 yeres."

second son of John Smith,[1] of Nibley, in Gloucestershire. In January, 1625, there resided with him Elizabeth Rolfe, whose widowed mother, Jane, appears to have been absent, perhaps with her father, Capt. William Peirce, in England. In "Virginia Vetusta," published by the Munsells, of Albany, this child, by a slip of the pen, is called Jane.

Ralph Hamor[2] is supposed to have been the son of Ralph Hamor, of London. In 1615 he published a Description of

---

[1] Among the "Cholmondely Papers," are letters of Richard Berkeley and John Smith, of Nibley, on Virginia affairs. Yates' account of a voyage to Virginia in the *Margarete*, of Bristol, which left England on 16th of September, and on the 20th of November arrived at Point Comfort or Elizabeth City, is addressed to George Thorpe, of Wanswell, afterwards killed by the Indians, and John Smith, Esq., of Nibley. On December 19, 1620, George Smith, then in Virginia, writes to John Smith, at North Nibley, Gloucestershire, "is busy examining witnesses concerning Capt. Argall," and then recommends that he should send over his second son to the plantation.

[2] "MUSTER OF CAPT. RAPH HAMOR.

Capt. Raph Hamor.
M's Elizabeth Hamor.
Jeremy Clement, } her children.
Elizabeth Clement,

SERVANTS.
John Lightfoote, in the *Scarenture*.
Francis Gibbs, a boy, in the *Seaflower*.
Ann Addams, a maid servant.

AT HOG ISLAND.

Jeffrey Hull, came in the *George*.
Mordecay Knight, in the *William & John*.
Thomas Doleman, in the *Returne*.
Elkinton Ratliffe, in the *Seafloure*.
Thomas Powell, in the *Seafloure*
Thomas Cooper, in the *Returne*.
John Davies, in the *Guifte*.

Virginia. Returned with Argall from England in May, 1617, and was described by Sandys as one whose extreme poverty forced him to "shifts."

John Martin was one of the earliest settlers, supposed to have been the brother-in-law of Sir Julius Cæsar,[1] and was positive in his convictions, and generally in opposition to the majority. At the meeting of the first legislative assembly, in 1619, he insisted that by a special clause in his patent he was exempt from local authority, except in time of war. He returned from England in 1624 with an increased grant of land. Governor Wyatt and Council, on February 4, 1625, wrote to the Earl of Southampton, and the Company, of which he was the head, that while they could "but praise the Company's charity in forgiving the many foul injuries of Captain Martin," they did not like his appointment as Councillor.[2]

Samuel Mathews had not come to the colony until A.D. 1622, in the ship "Southampton," but was destined to be-

---

[1] The following manuscripts in the collection of Sir Julius Cæsar, Judge of High Court of Admiralty, and Master of the Rolls, in the British Museum, are attributed to his brother-in-law, Thomas Martin, and evidently John is meant.

"Proposals of Thomas Martin, respecting the question between the Virginia Company and himself," Dec. 9, 1622.

"The manner howe Virginia may be used as a royall plantation," by Thomas Martin.

"Letter of Thomas Martin, in Virginia, to Sir Julius Cæsar," March 8, 1626.

[2] "MUSTER OF CAPT. JOHN MARTIN.

Capt. John Martin,
Sackford Wetherill,
John Smith, aged 31,   } in the *Swan*, 1624."
John Howard, aged 24,
John Anthonie, aged 23,

come a leader. He had influence in London. He married
the daughter of Sir Thomas Hinton by his first wife. Hinton afterwards married the rich widow of Sir Sebastian
Harvey, Lord Mayor of London.[1] Her only daughter, Mary,
the King wished to marry the brother of the Duke of Buckingham. A letter written on May 31, 1619, told a friend
"The Lord Mayor is ill because the King wishes him to
marry his only daughter, a child of fourteen, to Christopher
Villiers, which he refuses." Harvey, in February, 1622,
died, and Mary, his daughter, married John, son of Sir Francis Popham.[2]

---

[1] The following marriage is entered on the Register of Stratford le Bowe Church, London, under date of October 1, 1622: "Sir Thomas Hynton of Chilton Foliot, Kt., and the Lady Mary wife of Sir Sebastian Harvey."

[2] "MUSTER OF CAPT. SAMUEL MATHEWS, JAMES CITY.

Capt. Samuell Mathews, came in the *Southampton*, 1622.
M' David Sand's, Minister, came in the *Bonaventura*, 1620.

SERVANTS.

Robert Mathews, aged 24,
Roger Williams, 20,
Samuell Davies, 18,
Henery Jones, 25, } came in the *Southampton*, 1622.
Aaron Conaway, 20,
John Thomas, 18,
Michaell Lapworth, 16,
William Lusam, 27,
William Feild, 23, } in the *Charles*, 1621.
Peter Montecue, 21,
Robert Fernall, 31, in the *London Merchant*, 1619.
Walter Coop[er], 33, in the *Jonathan*, 1619.
William Walters, 27, in the *Bona Nova*.
Nicholas Chapman, 31, in the *Jonathan*, 1619.
Gregory Spicer, 22, in the *Triall*, 1618.

John Harvey, of Lyme Regis, Dorsetshire, had been the Captain of a ship in the East Indies,[1] and one of the Commissioners of A.D. 1624, who reported upon the condition of the Colony to the King, and Admiral of New England after West and Argall. He was absent from Virginia, from the beginning of 1624, for several years.

Abraham Perscy, Merchant, also written Peirsey, was a merchant, and, in 1616, first arrived in the ship "Susan,"[2] and about 1628, died. His will is in the Appendix.

Nicholas Peirse, 23, in the *Falcon*, 1619.
Robert Penn, 22, in the *Abigaile*, 1620.
William Dalby, 28, in the *Furtherance*, 1622.
Thomas Hopson, 12, in the *Bona Nova*, 1618.
Abraham Wood, 10, in the *Margrett & John*, 1620.
William Kingsley, 24, in the *Marmaduk*, 1623.
Thomas Bridges, 12, " " " "
Arthur Goldsmith, 26, in the *Diana*, 1618."

[1] The East India Company ordered, in November, 1617, that "Security for 2000*l* or 3000*l* be taken from Capt. Harvey, who is suspected to be about to sail to the East Indies with a ship well victualled and furnished with twenty pieces of ordnance," and on the 16th of January, 1617-18, they were informed that "Sir Thomas Bromley and Captain Harvye were making a voyage from Flushing to the East Indies in a great ship," and that they had been stayed.— *Col. of State Papers, East Indies*, 1617-1621. Upon giving security to the States General the vessel was released. John Chamberlain, in a letter to Dudley Carlton, describes Harvey as "somewhat choleric and impatient."

[2] "MUSTER OF M' ABRAHAM PEIRSEY, MERCHANNT.

M' Abraham Peirsey, came in the *Susan*, 1616.
Elizabeth, his daughter, aged]15, } came in the *Southampton*, 1623.
Mary, his daughter, aged 11,

SERVANTS.

Christopher Lee, aged 30 yeres,
Richard Serieant, aged 36 yeres,
Alice Chambers, } maid servants, } in the *Southampton*, 1623.
Annis Shaw,

VIRGINIA CAROLORUM. 23

Isaac Madison, of Charles City, died in 1624, before notice of his appointment arrived. His widow, Mary,[1] who arrived

AT PEIRSEY'S HUNDRED.

Thomas Lea, aged 50,
Anthony Paggit, 35,
Solomon Jackman, 30,
John Davies, 45,
Clement Roper, 25,
John Bates, 24,
Thomas Abbe, 20,
Thomas Brooks, 23,
Nathan Jones, 23,
Peter Jones, 24, } *Southampton*, 1623.
Pierce Williams, 23,
Robert Graues, 30,
Edward Hubberstead, 26,
John Lathrop, 25,
Thomas Chambers, 24,
Walter Jackson, 24,
Henry Sanders, 20,
William Allen, 22,
Georg Dawson, 24,

John Upton, aged 26, in the *Bona Nova*, 1622.
John Banıford, aged 23, in the *James*, 1622.
William Garrett, aged 22, in the *George*, 1619.
Thomas Sawell, 26, " " " "
Henery Rowinge, 25, " " *Temperance*, 1621.
Nathaniel Thomas, 23, " " " "
Richard Broadshaw, 20, " " " "
Robert Okley, 19, in *William & Thomas*, 1618.
Negroes, 4."

[1] " MUSTER OF M'S MARY MADDISON, WIDDOW.

West and Shirley Hundred.

Mary Maddison, aged 30, in the *Treasurer*, 1618.
Katherine Layden, aged 7.

SERVANTS.

James Watson, aged 20 yeares, in the *George*, 1623.
Roger Lewes, " 19 " " " *Edwin*, May, 1617."

in the "Treasurer" in A.D. 1618, and was about thirty years of age, was living. Madison was a brave man, and a street ballad was printed and sung in the streets of London, in 1624, in which his attack upon the Indians was noted,—

> "And Captain Middisone likewise,
>   with honor did proceed
> Who coming, tooke not all their corne,
>   but likewise tooke their King
> And unto James his Citty, he
>   did these rich trophies bring."

William Claiborne,[1] also written Clayborne, Cleyborne, Cleburne. The Virginia Company, in a letter dated July 25, 1621, sent by the ship "George," write, "It is our expresse will that the Tenants belonging to every office be fixed to his certaine place uppon the lands sett out for itt, for which Mr Cleyburne is chosen to be our Surveyor, who att the Companies very great charge is sett out, as by his condition of agreement you may perceive."[2]

Too little has been written of Christopher Davison,[3] the last Secretary of the Colony before the death of King James. His father was William Davison, of Stepney, Middlesex, Secretary of State under Queen Elizabeth, and in whose service, for a time, was William Brewster, the leader of the Leyden Puritans, who had landed at Plymouth Rock but a

---

[1] So written in Rymer.

[2] Neill's "Virginia Company," Joel Munsell, Albany, p. 225.

[3] The mother of the Secretary was Catherine Spelman, a relative of Sir Henry Spelman. He was born about A. D. 1577, and is said to have been a student of Gray's Inn. His younger brother, Walter, was also a poet.— *Life of Davison*, by Nicholas.

few months before Christopher Davison arrived at Jamestown. In the will of William Davison, made in A.D. 1608, Christopher is called his second son, and Francis, the poet, his eldest.

At a meeting of the Virginia Company, held June 11, 1621, as John Pory, Secretary under Yeardley, had not carried himself well, it was decided to choose a successor, and on the 13th, Mr. Parramore, Mr. Waterhouse, and Mr. Davison were balloted for the office, and "choice was made of Mr. Davison, he having the major part of balls, who being called in to take notice that the Secretary's place was fallen upon him, did declare his thankful acknowledgment unto the Company." He arrived in October, 1621, at Jamestown, but did not have good health. In a letter of April 8, 1623, to Deputy Ferrar, of the Company, he alludes to his sickness and absence from business, and promises to send a list of inhabitants. He also mentions that his "brother," perhaps brother-in-law, Thomas Finch, had died soon after his arrival.

When Pory and other Commissioners from England came, in 1624, Edward Sharpless was appointed clerk, in consequence of a vacancy in the Secretaryship, caused by Davison's death. Among the poems of Francis, the eldest brother, was published the following paraphrase of one of the Psalms by Christopher:

> "Lord, in thy house, who shall forever bide?
> To whom shall rest in sacred mount betide?
> Ev'n unto him that leads a life unstained,
> Doth good, and speaks the truth from heart unfeigned.
> Who with his tongue, deceit hath never used;
> Nor neighbor hurt, nor slandered, nor accus'd;

> Who loving good men, is from bad estranged,
> Who keeps his word, though to his loss, unchanged,
> To usury, who hath no money lent,
> Nor taken bribes against the innocent,
> Who in this course doth constantly persevere,
> In holy hill, unmoved, shall dwell for ever."

The condition of the Colony was not prosperous, but it had been improved by the abrogation of the charter of the old Company. While there had been a disposition upon the part of its officers and stockholders to promote a Christian civilization, yet the people did not feel that they were a commonwealth, but, subject to the ordinances of those who were anxious to receive some pecuniary return from their investments. The first of January, A.D. 1625, found a population of only about twelve hundred persons, one horse, one mare, five hundred hogs, and five hundred neat cattle in the valley of the James River, and on the eastern shore of the Chesapeake Bay. There was not a public inn, nor was there a church edifice, nor a residence of brick or stone at Jamestown.

On the 15th of June, 1625, Governor Wyatt and Council notified the Privy Council in England, that they had been forced to suspend Captain John Martin from their body, and that the reason they had taken the Secretaryship from, and cut off the ears of Edward Sharpless, was, because he had violated his oath[1] and "delivered papers, committed to his charge, which greatly concerned" them.

---

[1] After Secretary Davison's death, in 1623-4, an oath was administered to Edward Sharpless, acting as Secretary, in these words:

"You shall keep secret all matters committed unto you, with all things that shall be treated secretly at the Counsell table until such tyme as by the consent of his Maiestie's Gouernor and Captayn Generall and the full Councel of the

The monopoly of the tobacco trade tended to produce stagnation in business and discontent, and Yeardley was appointed to visit England and secure, if possible, a modification of the pernicious contract.

On the 4th of October, Yeardley was in England, and wrote to the King how utterly disheartened the Virginia planters were, by the enforced sale of their tobacco, and asking that he might have a hearing before the Privy Council. When the opportunity offered, he asked for the liberty of holding a General Assembly for local legislation and the election of officers by the people, also that there should be no tax on staple commodities, and free trade in all things.

Small vessels were constantly seen trading with the Indians toward the Falls of the Potomac and the mouth of the Susquehanna River for corn and beaver-skins, and at Palmer's Island in that stream, named after Edward Palmer, who had, in 1624, projected a University and School of Arts for Virginia.[1]

Intercourse had been established with the feeble settlements at Cape Cod and Bermudas. Fish was brought from the former and fruits from the latter.[2]

State then resydent, or the maior part of them, publication shall be made thereof.

"And you shall most exactly and faithfully do your utmost, record all acts and matters to be recorded and kept from time to time which shall be resolued upon by the Gouernour and Counsell of State or the maior part of them and you shall not deliuer any thing concerninge the affayres of the Counsell to any other person to be copied out or engrossed without first making the Gouernour acquainted and pleasure obtained. So help you God and the contents of this Boke."— *Virginia MS. Records*, Library of Congress.

[1] Neill's "Virginia Vetusta," pages 183, 184.

[2] The beginning of the trade in fruits was in A.D. 1621. In a treatise on the

Some of the leading men longed to see the parish and town organization of England introduced, and lamented

---

Bermudas written in 1623, it is supposed by Capt. Butler, edited by Lefroy, and published in A.D. 1882, by Hakluyt Society, are the following letters:

"To my worthy friend Sir Francis Wiatt, Gouernor of Virginia.

"Sir: If your name deceaue me not we knowe one another. Howsoeuer your neighbourhoode and affinitie of command, inuite me to wellcome you, and to wish you all happiness in this your onerous Honnour.

"Our plantation commenceth a commerce vnto you, for by this shipp I haue sent vnto you suche of our prime fruicts as I heare you haue not, but assure myself you would haue, nor is ther ought els with vs but (during my tearme here) you shall as brethren command it. And (although your own climate giues a beliefe you can haue noe badd aire) I cannot chuse but wish you the temperature and salubritie of ours, the which I dare pronounce to be equall with the best of the world, and with it also communicated our bothe natural and artificial strength.

"I doubt not but that you haue your good wishes for vs, likewise as a participation with you of a spatious continent, goodly pasture, fayre riuers, necessary yron mines, and perhaps some other secret hopes: We are glad and thank you for it, and let vs still iointly goe on to wish one another's good, and to act it, and God second our honest endeauors.

"And thus (noble Sir) you haue hastily and heartily recommended the true and faithful affection of

"Your assured friend,
"NATH. BUTLER.

"SAINT GEORGES, IN THE
"SUMMER ISLANDS,
"December 2, 1621."

A second chest of cedar, well filled, was sent

"To my worthy friend Sir George Yardley, in Virginia, giue these.

"Worthy Sir,—This bearer (who loues you well) assureth me that you meant so well the last yeare, and that you sent out a ship of purpose to let vs knowe it, of which however we were depriued by the ignorance of the pilote, yet your noble entention ought to be esteemed as an act done to encrease my thancks. I haue now sent you some of our countrey's fruicts, and I wish they may multiplie with you, they are of our choice ones, and such as giue vs much content here, wher and everywher els I shall by all means expresse myself

"Your affectionate friend,
"NATH. BUTLER.

"ST. GEORGES, IN SUMMER IDS.,
"Dec. 2, 1621."

that their plantations were scattered, and, from the lack of bridges over the many inlets, only accessible by boats on

The fruits and plants were so acceptable that, in March, 1622, a bark came from Virginia to obtain another supply. While this vessel was in port, the writer of the manuscript about A.D. 1623, refers to the

MARRIAGE OF A COMPANION OF POCAHONTAS.

Sir Edwin Sandys, at a meeting of the London Company, on June 11, 1621, (O. S.), remarked that experience had taught that the Indians brought over by Sir Thomas Dale, was "far from the Christian work intended." Dale arrived with Pocahontas and her companions in England, early in June, 1616, but London life did not improve their health or morals. On the 6th of August, the dead body of a Virginian named Abraham was borne from the fair house of Sir Thomas Smith, in Philpot Lane, Langborne Ward, and buried at St. Dionis Church at the north-west corner of Lime street in the same ward. On the 18th of October another native of Virginia died, and was taken from the same house to the same church, and on the 15th of November there was a third burial of an Indian. In May, 1620, one of the Indian girls was dying of consumption, who had been a servant with a mercer in Cheapside. The remaining maid in England was sent back. The words of the Hakluyt Society narrative, are : " Her ladeinge was aqua vitæ, sack, oyle, and bricks, in exchange whereof she desired plants and herbs of all sortes, potatoes, duck, turkeys, and lime-stone . . . In the interim of this shyps abode here the marriage of the Virginia mayde recommended vnto the Gouernour by the Virginian Company resident in London, the shypeinge before was consumated : she being there married to as fitt and agreeable an husband as the place would afford, and the weddinge feste kept in the Gouernour's newe house, and at his charge, whereto not only the master of the new come shypp and some other strangers were inuited, but not fewer than one hundred persons wer made guests, and dined with all sortes of prouisions that the Islands could afford, in a very plentifull manner.

" And it was thought to be done in a more fashionable and full manner that the strangers returned to Virginia might find reason to carry a good testimony with them of the welfare and plenty of the plantation : as also, that the kindred and friends of the Virginian bride who were proud commandours, and not less than Viceroyes might receive a knowledge of the well being of their kinds woman [kinswoman], and by the good respect and kind vsage shewed vnto her among the English be encouraged both to continue and augment their former friendshyp, and to become Christians themselves, to which ende also, the Gouernour wrote of aduice to the Gouernour in Virginia, and caused the mayde herselfe likewise to doe as much to her brother, who by her father's late death had succeeded in all his roialties and commande."

Powhatan died in 1618, and the Indian maiden appears to have been one of the sisters of Pocahontas.

the James River, and that they were "bereft of friendly communion" as well as the "mutual Societie of one another in religious duties, the first fruit of civility."[1]

During the year 1625, Giles Beaumont, a Frenchman, arrived with some colonists, authorized to claim the privileges of an English subject and establish a plantation.

It is worthy of note that the Captain and Mate of the May Flower both died in the valley of the James River. John Clark, who piloted the Puritans of Leyden to the coast of Massachusetts, was a resident of Virginia as early as A.D. 1612. One day, when Sir Thomas Dale was Deputy Governor, a Spanish ship appeared off Point Comfort and asked for a pilot. Captain James Davies, the commander there, acceded to the request, and the Spaniard sailed away with him, leaving three of their company on shore, one of whom was discovered to be an English traitor who, in A.D. 1588, had piloted the Spanish Armada to the coasts of England and Ireland, and was subsequently hung by Dale.[2]

Clark was taken to Spain and confined for some time in the galleys, and after a long time released.

Cushman writes to Pastor Robinson on June 20, 1620: "We have hired another pilote here, one Mr. Clarke, who went last year to Virginia with a ship of Kine." This pilot, John Clark, was the first to land upon the island in Plymouth Harbor, where the Puritans from Leyden, on December 20 (N. S.), kept their first Christian Sabbath. Clark returned in the May Flower to England, and on February 13,

---

[1] Commission to Yeardley to settle a colony, in "Virginia MS Records," Library of Congress.

[2] Purchas, IV. Part, p. 1713.

1621-2 (O. S.), Deputy Ferrar acquainted the Virginia Company[1] "that one, Mr. Jo. Clarke, being taken from Virginia long since by a Spanish shippe that came to discouer that plantacon, that forasmuch as he hath since that time doun the Companie good service in many voidges to Virginia, and of late went into Ireland for the transportation of cattle to Virginia, he was an humble suitor to this Court that he might be admitted a free brother of the Companie, and have some shares of land bestowed upon him." In 1623 he was employed by Daniel Gookin to carry some cattle in the ship "Providence" to Virginia and there died.

Captain Thomas Jones, in 1625, died, after an eventful if not honorable career. In 1617 he was sent out to the East Indies by Sir Robert Rich, afterwards Earl of Warwick, in command of a ship called the "Lion." Patrick Copland, Chaplain of the "Royal James," of which Martin Pring was the Captain, wrote to Sir Thomas Smith that "two English pirates had been taken in chasing a junk at Gogo." Sir Thomas Roe, Ambassador to the Great Mogul, sent a despatch "that Sir Robert Rich and one Philip Bernardoe set out two ships to take pirates, which is generally a pretence for being pirates, and that near the end of the Red Sea they had chased the Queen Mother's junk." Early in 1619, Jones came home under arrest, and in the "Transactions of the East India Company," under date of January 31, 1619-20, is this entry: "Thomas Jones, a servant of Lord Warwick, arrested by the Company for hiring away their men, but now being employed to go to Virginia, with cattle, by his Lordship, who desires his release, order is given to set him

---

[1] Neill's "Virginia Company," p. 132.

at liberty, Lord Warwick engaging to answer for what shall be objected against him."

On the 2d of February of the same year the Virginia Company allowed a commission to Captain Jones, of the "Falcon," to go to Virginia with fifty-two kine, four mares, and thirty passengers.

His voyage to the New England coast in the latter part of 1620, as captain of the "May Flower," is well known. On the 21st of November, 1621 (O. S.), he was commissioned by the Virginia Company as master of the "Discovery," a vessel of sixty tons, to trade for furs in the Delaware and Hudson Rivers. Upon the 18th of April, 1622, he arrived at Jamestown. On the 17th of July, in the Virginia Company of London, "a motion was made in the behaffe of Captaine Thomas Jones, Captaine of the 'Discovery,' nowe imployed in Virginia fur trade and ffishinge, that he might be admitted a ffreeman of this Companie." The Council of New England, in London, on December 22, complained to the Virginia Company that during the summer Captain Jones had robbed some Indians of furs, and taken others captives, who, however, escaped by the ship running aground. In August, Jones visited the Puritans, at Plymouth. Bradford, in his "History of the Plymouth Plantation," writes: "Behold another providence of God; a ship comes into ye harbor, one Captain Jones being cheefe therin. They were set out by some marchants to discovere all ye harbors betweene Virginia and ye shoulds of Cape Cod, and to trade along ye coast wher they could. This ship had store of English beads, which were then good trade, and some knives, but would sell none but at dear rates, and also a good quantie togather. Yet they were glad of yᵉ occasion, and faine to buy at any rate; they were faine to give after yᵉ rate of cente per cente if not more, and yet pay away coat-beaver at 3s. per lb., which in a few yeares after yielded 20s. By this means they were fitted againe to trade for beaver & other things, and intended to buy whatever they could.

"But I will here take liberty to make a little digression. There was in this ship a gentleman by name Mr. John Poory; he had been Secretarie in Virginia, and was now going home, passenger in this ship."

Winslow wrote: Captain Jones "used us kindly, he made us pay largely for the things we had."

The Governor and Council of Virginia, on the 20th of January, 1622-3 (O. S.). wrote[1] to the London Company: "And as for the fur voiadge we cannott resolue you, Capt. Jhones being nott yett retorned."

In 1625 he entered the Chesapeake Bay with a Spanish frigate, which he declared he had taken under a commission from the United Provinces, which had been given to Captain Powell. He brought with him a negro named Brass, and soon after died. The first question as to the legal status of the negro in North America arose in connection with Brass, and when there were not thirty persons of African descent in Virginia. Thomas Jefferson refers to the case in a small volume of reports published at Charlottesville, Va. The General Court in October, 1625, ordered that he should belong to Sir Francis Wyatt, Governor, notwithstanding any

---

[1] Neill's "Virginia Company," p. 273.

rule by Captain Jones, or any challenge by the ship's company.

Manuscripts recently printed give additional particulars as to the landing of negroes in Virginia.

The "Treasurer," Captain Daniel Elfrith, arrived at Bermudas just as the "Blessing" was leaving the harbor for England with Governor Daniel Tucker. In a "History of the Bermudas," printed from manuscript written about A.D. 1623, by the Hakluyt Society in 1882, and edited by Lefroy, the following occurs concerning the "Treasurer:" "Sent out she was by Captaine Argoll from Virginia, where he was then Gouernor, under a pretence of tradeinge all alongst the coast for skinnes, and at the Virgin and Sauuage Ilands for goates, but some of his people comeing abord the 'Blessinge,' by some speeches unaduisedly let falne, begett a suspicion in Captaine Tucker of a farther project than was openly pretended."

The captain was kindly entertained by Kendall, Governor Tucker's successor, remained six weeks, and received a large supply of corn.

About the last of July, 1619, a frigate appeared at Bermudas, "knowen to be a good fellowe, manned for the most part with English, who haueing played some slie partes in the West Indies, and so gotten some purchase, part whereof consisted of negroes, a welcome for a most necessary commoditie for thes Ilands, she offered to leaue and giue them to the Gouernour, so he would be pleased to admit her ingresse and egresse."¹ Kendall received fourteen negroes for privileges granted.²

Fourteen days after another "handsome pinnace, manned for the most part with Dutch, and some two or three English," entered the Bermudas harbor. Shortly after this, after the middle of August, 1619, the "Treasurer," for the second time, enters the harbor.

The Hakluyt Society Publication also mentions "how the 'Treasorour,' hauevinge bin upon the coast at Captain Tucker goeinge awaye, was admitted by Kendall, and so went to the West Indies, from whence she returned to Virginia, when, not likeinge her entertainment, she conveyeth herselfe awaye secretly, and shapeth her course for the Ilands a second time, and arriveth extremely poore, hauing all her upper works so rotten as she was utterly unable" to go to sea again.

The Dutch or Flemish frigate was at Jamestown during the month of September, 1619, and was recognized as the consort of the "Treasurer," both holding commissions from the Duke of Savoy. The first negroes were said to have been all landed from this vessel, although in the census of 1624-25, Angelo, a negro woman belonging to Captain William Pierce or Peirce, the father-in-law of the late John Rolfe, is marked³ as having arrived in the "Treasurer."

During the year 1625, before the Earl of Essex sailed for Cadiz, there was fear that sympathizers with Spain might be

---

¹ Hakluyt Society Publications.
² See "Virginia Vetusta," p. 113.
³ Hotten, p. 224.

among the sailors who arrived in the James River. Upon January 11, 1624-5 (O. S.), the Governor and Council of Virginia[1] wrote to England that Simon Tuchin, the Master of the ship "Due Returne," who had been banished out of Ireland because he was strongly affected to Popery, had been examined, and that they thought he would be dangerous to the Colony should he become a pilot to the foreign country, and they suspected he would go to the Spaniards in the West Indies. In England, in June, 1625, he declared to the Privy Council that he had not taken soundings of the rivers and harbors of Virginia as had been charged, and asked for release.[2]

In the fleet that appeared before Cadiz in November, 1625, were two captains who had been identified with the settlement of Virginia. John Harvey was captain of the "Friendship," of three hundred and eleven tons, with fifty-seven sailors and one hundred and sixty-four landsmen. Sir Samuel Argall, knighted in 1622, was captain of the "Swift Sure," a large vessel of about nine hundred tons, and carrying two hundred and fifty men, with also the Earl of Essex on board.[3] The large fleet to which they belonged was un-

---

[1] Sainsbury, p. 72.

[2] There had always been a few arrivals from Ireland. As early as August 1609, a proposition was made to the Earl of Salisbury by Sir Richard Moryson to send Irish pirates to Virginia. His words were: "Should his Lordship please to allow of them employed in the intended plantation of Virginia, which he has not yet motioned to them, he thinks good use might be made of them for the present there, both in defending them now in the beginning, and if they be disturbed in their first setling in relieving their wants from time to time."— *Cal. State Papers, Ireland*, 1608-1610.

[3] Glanville's Cadiz, Camden Soc. Pub., 1883.

successful, and on December 11, 1625, had returned to Kinsale harbor. A letter written on January 28, 1626, has the following :[1] "The Master of the 'Swift Sure,' very backward and very cross, as the report goes, to his captain, Sir Samuel Argoll,[2] which broke his heart, and a few days since he died."

The father of Governor Wyatt died in September, 1625, and he asked permission to return to England, which was granted. The commission of his successor, dated March 4, 1625-6, uses this language :[3] " Whereas our late royal Father upon information that George Wyatt, Esquire, the father of the said Sir Francis Wyatt, was then lately deceased in the realm of Ireland, whereof happily the said Sir Francis Wyatt might desire to return into England about his own private occasions, which our said Father, notwithstanding the great and weighty importance of his affairs in that country, was graciously inclined to yield unto, if himself should so desire, as occasions shall require." The commission then continues, "Now know ye that We, Taking into our princely consideration the care and providence of our late Royal Father having respect to the good of that Plantation so happily begun, which we conceive to be a business of that consequence which we ought to encourage, and by all good means to bring to perfection, we being forced by many other urgent occasions in respect of our late access

---

[1] Cal. State Papers, Domestic.

[2] His daughter Ann, married Samuel Perceval. On June 25, 1641, he and his wife complain to the House of Commons that they have been deprived by John Woodhall, of property in Virginia, left by the father, Sir Samuel Argall.

[3] Rymer, vol. xviii. The spelling modernized.

unto the Crown to continue the same means that was formerly thought fit for the maintenance of the Plantation, until we would find some more convenient means upon mature advice to give more ample directions for the same, and reposing assured trust and confidence in the understanding, care, fidelity, experience, and circumspection of you, the said Sir Yardley [Yeardley], Francis West, John Harvey, George Sandys, John Pott, Roger Smith, Ralph Hamor, Samuel Matthews, Abraham Percy [Piersey], William Clayborne, William Tucker, Jabez Whitacres, Edward Blaney, and William Ferrar, have nominated and assigned, and by these presents do nominate and assign you, the said Sir George Yardley, to be the present Governor, and you, the said John Harvey, and the rest before mentioned, to be the present Council of and for the said Colony and Plantation in Virginia, giving, and by these presents granting unto you, and the greater number of you respectively, full power and authority to perform and execute the places, powers, and authorities incident to a Governor and Council of Virginia respectively, and to direct and govern, correct and punish our subjects now inhabiting, or which shall hereafter inhabit, or be in Virginia, . . . and to execute and perform all and everything concerning that Plantation as fully and amply as every Governor and Council resident there at any time within the space of five years now last past. And because by the discovery of industrious and well-experienced men, the limits of the said Plantation may be augmented," they were authorized to grant commissions for discovery.

Provision was also made in the document, that in the case of the death of Yeardley, John Harvey should be Governor,

VIRGINIA CAROLORUM. 39

and if he should also die, that then Francis West and fellow-councillors to choose one of their own number.

Yeardley and Harvey, who had already taken the oaths before the Privy Council in England, were empowered to administer the same to Francis West, John Pott, William Tucker, Jabez Whitacre, Edward Blaney, and William Farrow, [Ferrar.] Pott, Tucker, Whitacre, Blaney, and Ferrar had never before been in the Council.

Dr. John Pott was recommended to the London Company by Theodore Gulston, the founder of the Gulstonian Lectureship of the London College of Physicians. In the minutes of the Virginia Company of July 16, 1621 (O. S.), is this entry : " For so much as the Phisicons place to the Company was now become voyde by reason of the untimely death of Dr. Bohune, slaine in the fight with two Spanish Shipps of Warr the 19th of March last, Doctor Gulstone did now take occasion to recommend unto the Company for the said place one Mr Potts, a Mr of Artes, well practised in Chirurgerie and Physique, and expert allso in distillinge of waters."

Upon his arrival in Virginia, he soon showed a great fondness for company and distilled waters, if George Sandys is to be credited.[1]

---

[1] "MUSTER OF DOCTOR JOHN POTT, JAMES CITY.

Doctor John Pott, } arrived in the *George.*
Mrs Elizabeth Pott, }

SERVANTS.

Richard Townshend, aged 19,   in the *Abigaile,* 1620.
Thomas Wilson,   " 27, " "   "   "
Osmond Smith,   " 17, " " *Bona Nova,*"
Susan Blackwood, maide servant" " *Abigaile,* "

William Tucker had represented Kiccowtan, afterwards Elizabeth City, in the Legislature of 1619, and in the winter of 1623 led an expedition against the Rappahannock Indians.[1]

Edward Blaney came in 1621 as the factor of the London Company. He married the widow of Captain William

Men in the Maine.

Thomas Leister,	aged 33 yeares,	⎫
Roger Stanley,	" 27,	⎪
Thomas Pritchard,	" 28,	⎬ in *Abigaile*, 1620.
Henry Crocker,	" 34,	⎪
Thomas Crosse,	" 22,	⎪
John Trye,	" 20,	⎭
Randall Holt,	" 18, in the *George*, 1620."	

[1] "MUSTER OF CAPT. WILLIAM TUCKER, ELIZABETH CITY.

Capt. William Tucker, aged 36, in *Mary & James*, 1610.
Mrs. Mary Tucker, aged 26, in the *George*, 1623.
Elizabeth, borne in Virginia in August.

SERVANTS.

George Tomson,	aged 17,	⎫
Paule Tomson,	" 14,	⎬ in the *George*, 1623.
William Thomson,	" 11,	⎭
Pascoe Champion,	" 28,	⎱ in the *Ellonor*, 1621.
Strenght Sheere,	" 23,	⎰
Thomas Evands,	" 23,	⎫
Stephen Collowe,	" 23,	⎬ in the *George*, 1623.
Robert Munday,	" 18,	⎭

Matthew Robinson, aged 24, in *Greate Hopewell*, 1623.
Richard Appleton, " 19, in the *James*, 1622.
John Morris, " 24, " " *Bona Nova*, 1619.
Mary Morris, " 22, " " *George*, 1623.
William Hutchinson, " 21, " " *Diana*, 1618.
Peeter Porter, " 20, " " *Tyger*, 1621
William Crawshaw, an Indean, baptised.
Antoney, Negro.
Isabell, "
William, theire child, baptised."

Powell, who in 1619 represented James City in the Legislature.[1]

William Ferrar, also written Farrar, was a brother of Nicholas, the Deputy Governor of Virginia Company, and resided near the plantation of Cecilia, the widow of Samuel Jordan, to whom he was attentive after the minister Greville Pooley had received, as he alleged, a promise of marriage. In the Company's "Transactions," under the date of April 21, 1624 (O. S.), is the following: "Papers were read whereof one containing certain examinations touching a difference between Mr. Pooley and Mrs. Jordan, referred unto the Company for answer, and the Court entreated Mr. Purchas[2] to confer with some civilians and advise what answer was fit to be returned in such a case."

---

[1] In the list published by Hotton is
"THE MUSTER OF M' EDWARD BLANEY.
M' Edward Blaney came in the *Francis Bonaventure*.
SERVANTS.

Robert Bew,	aged 20,	came in the	*Dutie*.
John Russell,	" 19,	"	"	*Bona Nova*.
Rice Watkins,	" 30,	"	"	*Francis Bonaventure*.
Nathaniel Floid,	" 24,	"	"	*Bona Nova*.
George Rogers,	" 23,	"	"	"	"
John Shelley,	" 23,	"	"	"	"
Thomas Ottowell,	" 40,	"	"	"	"
Thomas Crouch,	" 40,	"	"	"	"
Robert Sheppeard,	" 20,	"	"	*Hopwell*.
William Sawier,	" 18,	"	"	"	"
Robert Chauntrie,	" 19,	"	"	*George*.
William Hartley,	" 23,	"	"	*Charles*.
Lawley Damport,	" 29,	"	"	*Duty*.
William Ward.	" 20,	"	"	*Jonathan*,
Jeremy White,	" 20,	"	"	*Tyger*.
John Hacker,	" 17,	"	"	*Hopwell*.
Robert Whitmore,	" 22,	"	"	*Duty*.

[2] Samuel Purchas, a learned London divine, called the English Ptolemy, the author of the *Pilgrimage* and *Purchas his Pilgrimes*.

A few months later the Governor of Virginia issued the following order concerning flirts: "Whereas, to the great contempt of the majesty of God and ill example to others, certain women within this Colony have, of late, contrary to the laws ecclesiastical of the realm of England, contracted themselves to two several men at one time, whereby much trouble doth grow between parties, and the Governor and Council of State much disquieted: To prevent the like offense to others, it is by the Governor and Council ordered in Court that every minister give notice in his church, to his parishioners, that what man or woman soever shall use any words or speech tending to the contract of marriage though not right and legal, yet may so entangle and breed struggle in their consciences, shall for the third offense undergo either corporal punishment, or the punishment by fine or otherwise according to the guilt of the persons so offending."[1]

In Yeardley's commission was also this clause: "And forasmuch as the affairs of the said Colony and Plantation

---

"[1] MUSTER OF M' WILLIAM FERRAR, & M'S JORDAN, JORDANS JORNEY, CHARLES CITTIE.

William Ferrar, aged 31, in the *Neptune*, August, 1618.
Sisley Jordan, " 24, " *Swan*, August, 1610.
Mary Jordan, aged 3 years, ⎫
Margrett Jordan, aged 1, ⎬ borne heare.
Temperance Baley, " 7, ⎭

SERVANTS.
William Dawson, aged 25, in the *Discouery*, March, 1621 [O. S.]
Robert Turner, " 26 " *Tryall*, June, 1619.
John Hely, " 24, " *Charles*, November, 1621.
Robert Manuell, " 25, " *Charles*, November, 1621.
Roger Preston, " 21, " *Discouerie*, March, 1621.
Thomas Williams, " 24, " *Dutie*, May, 1618.

may necessarily require some person of quality and trust to be employed as Secretary for the writing and answering of such letters as shall be from time to time directed or sent from the said Governor and Council of the Colony aforesaid, our will and pleasure is, and we do by these presents nominate and assign you, the said William Clayborne,[1] to become Secretary of State, and for the said Colony and Plantation of Virginia, residing in those parts."

Upon the 6th of April, 1626, Wyatt was still at Jamestown, and signed with his councillors, Francis West, Hamor, Roger Smith, Abraham Peirsey, and Clayborne (Claiborne), a communication to the Commissioners in England, in which a mention is made of the arrival of the ship "Virgin" of Southampton, on the 23d of March, with letters of the 24th of October. It also refers to the Colony in these words: "Nothing hath bine longe more earnestly desired than the setling of the affaires of the Colony as well for the government as other wayes, neither could there haue bine a greater incouragement to the Planter than to understand it to be his Maiestie's gratious pleasure that no person of whom they have heretofore iustlie complayned should have any hand in the gouerment, either here or there. And wee humbly desire your Lordshipps to solicitt his Maiestie (if it bee not alreadie done) for the speedie accomplishment

---

[1] Cleborne, Cleyborne, Clayborne, Claiborne. William, the 2d son of Edward Clybourne, of Westmoreland, was born 1587, married Jane Buller, of London, died 1676. Had three sons. William, of Romancock, Thomas, Leonard, died in the West Indies 1694, and a daughter, Mary. See O'Hart.

Claiborne was the first Secretary in Virginia appointed by the King. Pory and Davison, his predecessors, had been elected by the London Company. On a brass memorial tablet in Cliburn Church, near Penrith, Westmorelandshire, is the following: "Insuper et in memoriam Gulielmi de Cleyborne seu Claiborne primi e Secretis Coloniæ Virginiensis qui anno vixit MDCXXVII."

thereof, the rather because the Gouerner's necessary occasions require his present retourne."

The letter also expresses pleasure at the intelligence that every man will have his rights preserved and request was made for five hundred soldiers, with a year's provisions for discovery and protection.

Instructions were issued to Yeardley, as the successor of Wyatt, to see that new-comers were properly entertained, that merchants were not to be forced to take tobacco at 3s. per pound for their goods, and that Indians were not allowed to enter planters' houses without license.

It was not, however, until after the middle of May that Wyatt sailed for England.[1]

On the 24th of April, 1626, King Charles issued a concession, in which he relates that "our trusty and well-beloved George Sandys, Esquier, hath with great care and industry translated into English verse the fifteen books of Ovid's Metamorphoses, which he hath to his great charge caused to be imprinted and made ready to be published in print, rather for the delight and profit of our living subjects, than for the hope of any great benefit to be by him reaped thereby, and hath humbly besought us to vouchsafe him a privilege for the sole printing of the said work for such term of years as we should think fit and convenient, the better to encourage him and others to employ their labors and studies in good literature," and then grants him the privilege to print and sell the same for twenty-one years.

---

[1] In August he was in England, and a warrant was ordered "to Sir Francis Wyat, late Governor in Virginia, to import 10,000 weight of tobacco custom free."— *Cal. State Papers, Dom.*, pp. 408, 409.

Sandys had been engaged on this translation for several years. Drayton's poem to George Sandys, Treasurer of the Colony of Virginia, would seem to indicate that five books had been prepared before he went to Jamestown.

> "Go on with Ovid as you have begun
> With the first five books; let your numbers run
> Glib as the former, so shall it live long,
> And do much honour to the English tongue.
> * * * * * *
> If you vouchsafe rescription, stuff your quill
> With natural bounties, and impart your skill
> In the description of the place, that I
> May become learned in the soil thereby:
> Of noble Wyat's health, let me hear
> The Governor; and how our people there
> Increase and labour, and what supplies are sent,
> Which I confess shall give me much content;
> But you may save your labour, if you please,
> To write to me aught of your savages,
> As savage slaves be in Great Britain here,
> As any one you can show me there.
> And though for this I'll say I do not thirst,
> Yet I should like it well to be the first,
> Whose numbers hence into Virginia flew,
> So, noble Sandys for this time, adieu."

In a letter[1] to Samuel Wrote, Esq., of London, dated March 28, 1623, Sandys alludes to the completion of two more books of Ovid, in these words: "If I could be proud, your censure had so made me, for that slothfull worke wch I was ashamed to father, notwithstanding it begot a desire to proceed, but heare my own Author.[2]

'—— nec plura sinit tempusque pudorque
Dicere; majus opus magni certaminis urget.'

---

[1] Neill's "Virginia Vetusta," Munsell's, 1885, pp. 124, 125.

[2] Ovid. Book VIII., lines 388, 389.
"Neither time and glory allow more,
A greater work of great importance impels."

Yet amongst the roreing of these as, the rustling of the shrowdes, and clamour of Saylers I translated two books, and will perhaps, when the sweltering heat of the day confines me to my Chamber, give a further essaye, for which if I be taxt I have noe other excuse but that it was the recreacon of my idle howers, and say with Alciat,—[1].

> " Dum pueras inquilanas invenes dum tessera fallit,
> Desinet et segnes chartula picta vires
> Hæc nos festivis emblemata adimus horis."

In the fall of 1626, Capt. John Preen, in the ship "Peter and John," arrived with provisions and passengers, and also brought ten barrels of powder for defence of the plantation, sent over by the Commissioners. Among the passengers were Thomas Willoughby and John Pollington, old colonists returning from a visit to England. Willoughby, when a boy nine years old, in 1610, first arrived in Virginia, and Pollington had been a member of the first legislature, which, in 1619, met at Jamestown. The next year Preen made another voyage to Virginia. In 1627, the ship "Temperance," Capt. Marmaduke Rayner, sailed for England, with Samuel Sharpe, who had been in the colony since 1610, and twelve other passengers. A letter written in England, dated August 18th of this year, mentions that "there are many ships going to Virginia, and with them fourteen or fifteen

---

[1] Andreas Alciati, born in Milan, A.D. 1492, died at Pavia, A.D. 1550, was the author of "Sacra Emblemata," published in Venice, in 1546, by the Sons of Aldus. Andrew Willet, a Puritan, was born in Ely, Cambridgeshire, a fellow of Cambridge, and chaplain to Prince Henry, died Dec. 4, 1621, aged 59 years, and was buried at Barley. He was the author of "Sacrorum Emblematum Centuria una," chiefly from Andrew Alciatus. To this Sandys refers.

hundred children, w'ch they have gathered up in divers places."

In April, 1627, Gov. Yeardley and Council[1] wrote to the Privy Council that the people are disheartened by the intelligence that a Mr. Anis has made a contract for their tobacco, and "they earnestly entreat that free trade and the sole importation of tobacco may be continued, and Spanish tobacco excluded. They ask the Commissioners not to let them fall into the hands of avaricious and cruel men, whose exorbitant and wide consciences project and digest the ruin of the plantation for profit and gain to themselves."

The King sent back by William Capps, an old planter, a letter in which he urged varied planting, and told them "that this plantation is wholly built upon smoke, tobacco being the only means it hath produced."

On the 9th of August, 1627; Charles the First declared "his final resolution touching all sorts of tobacco." All plants in England, Wales, and Ireland were to be destroyed, and no tobacco imported from Spain. To prevent the planters of Virginia and Bermudas giving "themselves over to the planting of tobacco only to make a present return of profit, and neglect to apply themselves to solid commodities fit for the establishing of colonies will utterly destroy these colonies" the King ordered that no tobacco should be imported into England without a special license.[2]

In November, Governor Yeardley passed from earth. Although the hangers-on at Court were vexed at his promo-

---
[1] Sanisbury, I. 84.
[2] Rymer, Vol. XVIII. pp. 921, 922.

tion, and called him "a mean fellow" because he had no title, and was the brother of Ralph the London Apothecary, he proved a good man, an enterprising citizen, and loyal subject. His will was made October 12, 1627; Abraham Peirsey, of the Council, William Claiborne, Secretary of the Colony, and Susanna Hall, a servant, being witnesses.[1]

To his wife, Temperance, he left his plate, linen, and all household stuff, and ordered his notes, debts, servants, and " negars" to be sold, and the moneys therefrom to be divided into three parts : one for the widow, one for elder son Argoll, and the third to be divided between his son Francis, and daughter Elizabeth.

---

[1] N. E. Hist. Gen. Register, January, 1884.

CHAPTER II.

AFFAIRS FROM A. D., 1628 TO 1630.

Death of Abraham Piersey. Rossingham, Yeardley's nephew. Francis West acting Governor. Capt. Henry Fleet, explorer of the Potomac River. Immigrant ship wrecked. Ship Temperance. Legislature of A.D., 1628, Condition of White Servants. Arrival of Negroes. Narrative of William Peirce. Lord Baltimore's visit. Virginia Council's letter about Lord Baltimore. Wife of Baltimore. Jamestown, in A.D., 1629. Indian hostility. Grant of Carolana to Sir. Robert Heath.

ABRAHAM Piersey, also spelled Peirsey, of Piersey's Hundred, councillor, who had signed Governor Yeardley's will as a witness, in a few months, also, departed from earth. He came to Virginia a widower, and in 1623, his two daughters came out from England. This year Nathaniel West, a brother of Lord Delaware, died at West and Shirley Hundred, leaving a widow Frances, and infant Nathaniel. After January, 1625, the widow West became the wife of Piersey. By his will, she became sole executrix, and his "well beloved friends Mr. Grevill Pooley Mynister, and Mr. Richard Kingsmill of James Citty Island gentellmen" were

7

made overseers "to be as helpefull and aydinge unto my executrix in all things to the uttermost of theire power."

He directed that his body should be "decently buryed without any pompe or vayne glorie in the garden plote where my new frame doth stand."[1]

Governor Yeardley in 1618, brought his nephew, Edmund Rossingham, to Virginia, and that year sent him to trade for corn, for three months with the Indians of Chesapeake Bay. He was accompanied by John Martin, and the voyage was profitable. The next year, his uncle sent him to New Foundland, for fish, and in 1621, he was sent to Holland, to dispose of the Governor's tobacco, and in 1623, went again to that country, as factor for Governor Yeardley. After his uncle's death, he demanded that Ralph Yeardley, the brother of the Governor, residing in London, should pay him for certain of his cattle in Virginia which he alleged his uncle had used. The matter was referred, by the Privy Council of England, to Thomas Gibbs and Samuel Wrote. In their report they write that Ralph Yeardley "the Deft'e delyvered his answeare in writinge which he desired might be presented to yo' Lor'pps and therefore wee have annexed the originale itself, wherein the Defte pretends himselfe to be ignorante of any buisinesses the peticoner was ymployed in by Sir George Yardeley, or of any stock of cattle of the peticoners remayninge in Sir George Yardley's handes. Notwithstandinge it appeared by l'res under the

---

[1] A copy of the will, in 1634, was sent to England attested by, "Ben. Harryson" Clerk of the Council. The will in full is printed in the Appendix.

Deft"s owne handes directed to the peticoner in Zealande to dispatch Sir George Yardley's affayres there, and to come over to follow them there. And the Def't further alleadged that Sir George Yardley payde the Def^{ts} himselfe £ i j for a cowe of the peticoners before his last going over in 1626; and offered to make proof of it to us the Referrees, whereuppon wee gave him a new meetinge to produce his proofes, but before the tyme appointed hee came to us, and wayved his proofes, and sayde he would make us no other proofes, nor defences but what hee had formerly delyvered in writeinge. The Def^{te} and wee the Referees pressed the peticoner to render a reason why hee did not legally question Sir George Yardley for a perfect accompte at his last beinge in Englande to which the peticoner answered: That Sir George Yardeley had no means then in Englande to make him satisfaccon, and further that he was protected by your Lor^{pps} for one whole yeare before the end of which tyme he went for Virginia."

The referees decided that the nephew could recover nothing under the law of England.¹

In the commission issued to Yeardley it was provided that in case of his death, John Harvey, should be acting Governor, and after him, Francis West. Harvey, when the news of Yeardley's death was received in England, was in the naval service under the Duke of Buckingham, and therefore Francis West, a brother of the late Lord Delaware, became Governor. He had long been identified with

---

¹ Colonial Papers, Public Record Office, London, Vol. V., No. 15.

the Colony and by birth, education, and experience was adapted for the office.[1]

During the year 1627, the London Merchants were surprised by the arrival of Henry Fleet from Virginia, who had been in captivity for several years among the Indians of the Potomac, the site of whose former dwelling place is not far from the monument of Washington, in the capital of the Republic. He was one of the expedition of twenty six men, who under Henry Spelman, early in 1623, went to trade for beaver and corn with the Anacostan and other Indian bands between Potomac Creek, and the Falls of the Potomac. The pinnance in which they sailed, belonged to John Pountis, a well known colonist. Spelman, Fleet, and twenty of their companions went ashore, presuming on the

---

[1] Henry Spelman in his *Relation of Virginia*, a manuscript first published by James F. Hunnewell at the Chiswick Press, London, in 1872, gives incidents of West's early career in Virginia. He writes: "I was caried by Capt. Smith our President to ye litell Powhatan where unknowne to me he sould me to him for a towne called Powhatan and leavinge me wth him, he made knowne to Capt. Weste, how he had bought a toune for them to dwell in * * * desiringe that Captaine West would come & settle himself there, but Captaine Weste hauing bestowed cost to begine a toune in another place misliked it; and unkindness thereuppon ariseing between them Capt. Smith at that time replied litell but afterward conspired wth the Powhatan to kill Capt. Weste, wch plott took but small effect, for in ye meantime Capt. Smith was aprehended, and send abord for England."

Edward Winslow in a Relation published in 1624, in London, wrote: "Captain Francis West ben in New England about the latter end of May past [1623], sailed from thence to Virginia, nd returned in August. In September, the same ship and Company being discharged by him at Damarins Cove came to New Plymouth, whereupon our earnest inquiry after the state of Virginia since that bloody slaughter committed by the Indians upon our friends and countrymen, the whole ship's company agreed that upon all occasion they chased the Indians to and fro, insomuch as they sued daily into the English for peace, who for the present would not admit of any, that Sir George Early [Yeardley] was at that present employed upon service against them."

friendship of the savages, and while absent, the vessel with only five on board, was surrounded by Indians in canoes, some of whom clambered on to the deck, to the surprise of the sailors, one of whom, at random, fired a cannon, which frightened the assailants, who jumped overboard and went ashore. The sailors then heard the noise of conflict, and soon saw a man's head roll down the bank when they weighed anchor and returned to Jamestown.[1] Spelman was among the slain, and Fleet was taken prisoner.

Edward Hill of Elizabeth City on the 14th of April, 1623, wrote[2] to his brother John, a mercer of Lombard street, London,[3] that "more than 400 persons had perished in the first massacre [March, 1621], more than 20 in the second; and a pinance, shallop, and a small boat, with twenty-six men had been cut off on March 23, by the Indians, and that a great famine was imminent, for the colonists had not been "suffered to plant as much corn as they would," and were afraid "to step out of doors either for wood or water."

Mede, the great scholar at Cambridge University, on the eighth of June, 1627, received a letter from London, with these words: "Here is one, whose name is Fleet, newly come from Virginia, who being lately ransomed from the Indians, with whom he hath long lived, till he hath left his own language, reputeth he hath often times been within

---

[1] Smith's *General History*.

[2] Eighth Report Royal Commission on Historical Manuscripts. *Appendix*, p. 41.

[3] Richard Boyle of London married his sister. He was probably the Edward Hill of Elizabeth City, buried on May 15, 1624.

sight of the South Sea; that he hath seen Indians besprinkle their paintings with powder of gold; that he had likewise seen rare precious stones among them, and plenty of black fox, which of all others is the richest fur."

Quick witted, fond of trade, and adventure, Fleet's residence among the savages for several years, made him useful to London merchants disposed to send goods to the Indian tribes, and valuable as an interpreter, to the colonists. William Cloberry and associates, were impressed by his description, and gave him in September, 1627, the command of the 'Paramour,' a vessel of one hundred tons. By his exertions, a trade was opened between the Massachusetts settlement and Potomac river.

A ship containing some planters, and their servants, chiefly Irish, on their way to Virginia after a boisterous voyage in the beginning of winter, 1626-7, ran aground in Barnstable Bay. The principal persons were Fell and Sibsie or Silsby.

The Governor of Plymouth Colony visited the wreck, provided for the sufferers, and until they could make arrangements to go to Virginia, they were allowed land to cultivate for their benefit. Puritan sentiment was shocked when common rumour charged Fell with living with one of his servants, and treating her as a concubine, and he to avoid arrest ran away with her, in a small boat to Cape Ann, and from thence to Massachusetts Bay. Toward the latter end of summer the whole party were carried in two barks to Virginia, and, writes Bradford, "have acknowledged their thankfulness since."

Private planters began to take their tobacco to England. The ship "Temperance" probably built in Virginia and named in compliment to the wife of Governor Yeardley, commanded by Marmaduke Rayner, who had piloted in 1619, to Jamestown, the Dutch vessel which brought the first negroes, in 1628, arrived at Southampton, with the old planter Samuel Sharpe, who had come to Virginia in 1610, with Gates and Somers, and twelve other colonists. As they were unable to pay the duty on their tobacco, they begged, that it might be admitted free.

King Charles made a kind response to the memorial of the Virginia authorities, in 1627, and by William Capps, an old settler, who had been on a visit to England, he sent over instructions allowing a General Assembly, and urging the cultivation of staple commodities, as heretofore they had depended too much "upon smoke." To Capps also was given the privilege of erecting salt works. He arrived in Virginia on the 22d of February 1627-8 (O. S.), and on the 26th of the next month, the colonial legislature met[1] the first during the reign of Charles, and four or five days after, Governor West left, on a visit to England.

During Governor Wests' term of office the principal topic of discussion was the tobacco trade. The legislature of 1628, asked the king to take 500,000 pounds of tobacco, properly inspected, at 3s 6d. per pound delivered in Virginia clear of freight and customs, or at four shillings delivered in England, the contract to continue for seven years, with the privilege of disposing of their surplus in New England, West Indies or Turkey, by paying the usual duty.

---

[1] Thirty-one representatives were present.

The Colony was supposed at that time to contain a population of three thousand, and it was estimated that every family could raise 200 pounds of tobacco, and each servant 125 pounds, in the aggregate 412, 500 pounds. It is quite remarkable that the authorities should refer to the want of pitch and tar. While near one of the best pine forest districts in the world, they were without horses, had opened no roads, depending upon boats for intercourse with the plantations, and fearing to go far into the woods, lest they should be attacked by Indians.

Henry the Fourth, Lord Delaware, was written to, asking his influence, as his deceased father's had been given, and the Earl of Dorset was thanked for the aid he had rendered in annulling the contract of tobacco, and their friends in England induced the House of Commons to write a letter to the King* dated June 25, 1628, in which he was informed that "by the patent granted by the late King the colonists were free of customs except taxes upon their commodities 1£ per centum, but of late years these privileges had been disregarded and that now 3£ per centum was imposed."

The demand for laborers in the tobacco fields continued to increase. Any person going to Virginia, at his own charges, and declared his intention to reside there, was entitled to fifty acres of land, and an additional fifty for each member of his family. If he brought other persons into the colony at his own cost, he was also entitled to fifty acres for each immigrant. He was liable to pay an annual quit rent of a shilling for every fifty acres, and required to plant thereon within three years from the date of the grant. Planters,

---

* 4th Report *Royal Historical Commission.*

under these conditions, brought over a large number of indentured white servants,[1] while some of these were treated

---

[1] The following is a servant's indenture which was printed in the *Richmond Standard* by R. A. Brock, Secretary of Virginia Historical Society, from a transcript of the original, owned by W. Bushell of Philadelphia, Pa.

"THIS writing indented made the ffirst day of July Anno dom 1628 And in the yare of the regne of our sovraigne Lord Charles by the grace of god King of England Scotland ffrance and Ireland defender of the faith Etc. Betweene John Logward of Bling in the County of Surry husbandman of th one party And Edward hurd Cittizein and Ironmonger of London of the other party. WITNESSETH that the said John Logward hath hired himselfe and is become and by theis prste doth Covenant and agree and bind himselfe to be remayne and Continue the Obedient Servant of him the said Edward hurd his heires and assignes and to be by him or them sente transported unto to the Countrey and land of Virginia in the parts beyond the seas to be by him or them employde upon his plantation there for and dureing the space of ffour yeares to begin from the day of the date of theis prste dureing ye said terme the said John Logward shall and will truely employ and endeavor himselfe to the uttermost by his power knowledge and skill to doe and pforme true and faithful service unto ye said Edward hurd his heires or essignes in for and concenteing all such Laboures and businesses at he or they shall think good to use and ymploy him ye said John Logward in And shall and wilbe tractable and obedient and a good and a faithful servant onyst to be in all such thinge at shall be Comanded him by the said Edward hurd his heires or assignes in Virginia aforesaid or elsewhere dureing the said service In consideracon whereof the said Edward hurd for himselfe his heires executours and administrators and assignes and for any of them doth Covenant p-mise and graunt To and for ye said John Logward his heires executours administrators and assignes by theis prste that he the said Edward hurd his heires executours administrators or assignes shall and will (att his and their one charge) transporte and furnishe to the said John Logward to and for Virginia aforesaid and these find p-vide and allowe unto him sustenance meate drink apparnell and other necessaryes for his livelyhood and sustenance during the said service In Witnesse whereof the said pties to this writing have indented interchangeably have sett their handes and seales unto this bond above written.

"Ye marke of X John Logward

[seal.]

"Sealed and deliverede
in ye prsnce of
  "Tho. Thomnson servt
  and Jo Davies his servant"

with kindness, others received no more consideration than "dumb, driven cattle."[1]

During the summer of 1619, the consort of the ship "Treasurer" landed about twenty "negars" in the language of a document of the period. When the census was

---

[1] The sufferings of these white and occasionally intelligent servants were often intense. In the appendix to the Eighth Report of Royal Historical Commission is the following abstract of a letter from Martin's Hundred written in April, 1623, by Richard Frethorne to his parents, every word of which seems to weep. He wrote that since he landed he had eaten nothing "but pease and lobbolly" "and had to work both early and late for a mess of water gruel and a mouthful of bread and beef, a mouthful of bread, for a penny loaf must serve for four men." The people cried out day and night "Oh that they were in England without their limbs * * * * though they begged from door to door."

"He had nothing at all, not a shirt to his back but two rags, nor no clothes, but one poor suit, nor but one pair of shoes, but one pair of stockings, but one cap, but two bands." His cloak had been stolen by one of his fellows, he had not a penny to help him to " spice or sugar, or strong waters." He had " eaten more in a day, at home" than was now allowed him for a week, and his parents had often given more than his present day's allowance, to a beggar at the door. Goodman Jackson had been very kind to him, and marvelled much that he had been sent "a servant to the Company." He begged his father to " redeem " him, or at least send over provisions which might be sold at a profit especially cheese that might be bought for 2¼ or 2½ d. If his father could not afford this, he might " get a gathering, and entreat some good folks to lay out some little money" for the purpose. Unless the ship Sea Flower came shortly with provisions his masters' men would have but half a penny loaf each for a day's food and might be " turned up to the land, and eat barks of the trees, or moulds of the ground. Oh! that you did see my daily and hourly sighs, groans, tears and thumps that I afford mine own breast, and rue and curse the time of my birth with holy Job. I thought no head had been able to hold so much water as hath, and doth daily flow from mine eyes "

The Goodman Jackson was probably the John Jackson of Martin's Hundred who with his wife and infant arrived in 1621, in the ship "Warwick." A few months after this letter was written the unhappy writer died. In a list of persons who died at Martins Hundred between April, 1623, and February, 1624, appears the name of Richard Fethram evidently a misprint for Frethorne. Loblolly referred to in Frethorne's letter was a word in use among sailors for gruel, chowder, or spoon meat

taken in January, 1625, there were only twenty persons of the African race in Virginia, but during the government of West, there was a large increase. Captain Arthur Guy, in the ship "Fortune" of London, met and captured a slaver, from the Angola coast, and brought many negroes to Virginia, and exchanged them for tobacco.[1]

During the year 1629, Governor West and several prominent Virginians visited England, one of whom was the old planter and prominent colonist, William Pierce or Peirce, whose daughter Jane, was the widow of the well known John Rolfe.

Among the manuscripts of the Public Record office, in London, is "A relation in generall of the present state of his M^ties Colony in Virginia, by Capt. William Perse, an antient planter of twenty yeares standing there." The relation is brief and in these words: "First for quantity ye people, men, women & children, there are to the number of between fower and five thousand English, being generally well housed in every plantation, most plantations being well stored wth head cattle, as likewise wth goates and swine in abundance, and great store of poultry, the land abounding all the year long wth Deer and wilde Turkeyes, and the rivers

---

[1] Nicholas, Secretary of State, received a letter, dated May 13, 1628, informing him, that there had arrived at Cowes, a frigate from the "West India," taken by Arthur Guy, of the "Fortune" of London, with 900 or 1000 hides, 30 tons and upward of ebony, and some Indian wax, and that the "Fortune" hath also taken an Angola man with many negroes, which the captain bartered in Virginia for tobacco, which was sent home in a ship called the "Plantation." As Winthrop was leaving England, on Easter Monday, March 29, 1630, over against Yarmouth, he "met with a ship, the "Plantation," newly come from Virginia."—Savages Winthrop, Vol. 1., p. 8.

in winter wth many sortes of wilde fowle, and in summer wth great variety of wholesome fishe. And the soile is so fertile as by the industry of our people they may raise great crops of corne both Indian and English. Besides, all fruits, rootes, and herbes, out of England soe wonderfully prosper there. The Colony under the favor of God, and of his Ma^ty hath bine raised to this heighth of people, and provisions especially by the means of Tobacco, by which also they must subsist for awhile untill by degrees they may fall upon more stable comodiies, as upon salte, fishe, hempe for cordage[1] flaxe for linnen and others. And as touching timber for building of ships of all sortes, and mastes I have heard many good Masters and Shipwrights affirm there can not be found better in all the worlde, the Countrey affourding also great quantity of pine trees for making of pitche & tarre, and so may in short time abound with all materials for building & rigging of ships. For our defense against the natives every plantation is armed with convenient number of muskettiers to the number of two thousand shott, and upwards, but against a forrein enemy there is no manner of fortification (wch is our greatest wante) wee of ourselves not beeing able to under take the chardge thereof. As for the natives Sasapen is the chief, over all those people inhabiting upon the rivers next unto us, who hath been the prime movver of all them, that since the massacre have made war upon us. But nowe this last Somer, by his great importunity for himselfe, and the neighbouring Indians hee hath obtained a truce for the present, from the Govr and Councell of Virginia being forced to seeke it by our con-

---

[1] Colonial papers, Vol. V, 624.

tinuall incursions upon him, and them by yearley cutting downe, and spoiling their corne.

"This being the summe of the present state of thinges in Virginia."

A letter writer of the period alludes to his wife in these words "Mistress Pearce, a honest and industrous woman hath been there near twenty years, and now returned, saith she hath a garden at Jamestown containing three or four acres, where in one year she hath gathered near a hundred bushels of excellent figs and that she can keep a better house[1] in Virginia for three or four hundred pounds than in London, yet went there with little or nothing."

After West's departure for England, Doctor John Pott was chosen temporary Governor. During this period the Virginians were surprised by the arrival of George Calvert the first Lord Baltimore, the proprietor of Avalon in New Foundland. Born in Yorkshire, of comparatively humble parentage, a graduate of Oxford, a good scholar, able writer, and of pleasant address, he entered upon a public career, as the private Secretary to Sir Robert Cecil, afterwards the Earl of Salisbury. His efficiency was recognized by his appointment as clerk of the Privy Council. In 1613, he was associated with Sir Charles Cornwallis the grandfather of Thomas Cornwallis, one of the earliest Maryland councillors, as a Commissioner to Ireland[1], to inquire into cer-

---

[1] George Sandys when Treasurer of the Colony lived in Pierce's house and on April 8, 1623, wrote to John Ferrar of "his own chamber at Lieut. Peirce's, the fairest in Virginia."—*Sainsbury*

[1] August 24, 1613, Sir Humphrey Wynd, Kt., Sir Roger Wilbraham, Kt, Sir C. Cornwallis, Kt, and George Calvert, Esq., were chosen Commissioners for Ireland to hear complaints.

tain grievances, four years later he was knighted by King James, and after two years was commissioned as principal Secretary of State.

By education and temperament he was fitted to be a courtier, and none of the sycophants of King James were more successful than he, in pandering to the tastes and prejudices of the coarse, and pedantic monarch.[1]. He was a firm defender of the King's position, in the speech at the opening of a Parliament, "it is the king that makes laws, and ye are to advise him to make such as will be best for the commonwealth," and the active opponent of the people's party, which was yearly increasing.

Confident that it would promote his advancement, he was enthusiastic in the advocacy of the marriage of Prince Charles with the Infanta of Spain, and to the displeasure of the House of Commons kept up an intimacy with Gondomar, the Spanish ambassador; and then, with the Duchess, the mother of Buckingham, entered the church of Rome.

Feb. 22, 1613-14, John Latham and William Peasley, servants of George Calvert, Esq., Commissioner to Ireland, were given £50 by way of reward for "their travail and pains in engrossing all the business, using twenty-six quires of paper, besides vellum."

Peasley subsequently married Anna, the daughter of Secretary Calvert, who was at the above period a girl of about seven years of age.

[1] On Dec 4, 1621, he writes to Buckingham "There are many pasquils abroad and seditious sermons are printed. An alarm has been given to Gondomar of an intended attack upon his family. A strong watch was appointed and his house has been guarded. It may be only a design to frighten him."

His wife died in August 1622, and eight months later he was the life of the party at the king's festival at Windsor in honor of St. George. In a letter he is described as "very gay, and gallant, all in white, cap a pie even to his white hat and white feather"

After the match failed, he lost standing with Buckingham,[1] his fortune, began to decline,[2] and he retired from the Secretaryship, but, just before the king's death, was ennobled as Baron of Baltimore in the county of Longford, Ireland. While Charles, upon ascending the throne, retained his friendship for him, and would have kept him in the Privy Council, yet as he refused to take the required oath of office it was impossible. Retiring to Ireland, Calvert soon determined to visit Avalon, in New Foundland, a colony which he had planted some years before he left the church of England, not from any religious motive, but in the hope that it would yield pecuniary profit. In May, 1627, just before he sailed, he wrote to his old friend Wentworth, soon made the Earl of Strafford that he had, "rather be esteemed a fool, by some, for the hazard of one month's journey, than to prove myself one certainly, for six years by-past, if the business be now lost, for the want of a little pain's and care."

In the autumn he returned from America, but the next spring, went again to Avalon, and made an effort to remain, but the climate, sickness, and opposition made him faint-

---

[1] Buckingham, in 1624, wrote to King James: "I hope to have the happiness to-morrow, to kiss your hands, therefore I will not send you the letter you wrote to the Pope, which I have got from Secretary Calvert. When he delivered it to me, he made the request that your Majesty would as well trust him, in a letter, you were now to write, as you had heretofore in the former. I did, what I could, to dissemble it, but when there was no means to do it, I though best to seem to trust him absolutely, thereby, the better to tie him to secrecy. If this be a lie, as I am sure it is, you may bear to think, that with little more stock he may cry quittance."—*Hardwick Papers.*

[2] Archbishop Abbott wrote about this time: "Secretary Calvert hath never looked merrily since the prince's coming out of Spain. It was thought he was much interested in the Spanish affair."

hearted, and on the 19th of August, 1629, he wrote from his residence at Ferryland to King Charles: "I have had strong temptations, to leave all proceedings in plantations, and being much decayed in my strength, to retire myself to my former quiet, but my inclination carrying me naturally to these kind of works, and not knowing how better to employ the poor remainder of my days, than with other good subjects, to further the best I may, the enlarging your Majesty's Empire in this part of the world. I am determined to commit this place to fishermen that are able to encounter storms and hard weather, and to remove myself, with some forty persons to your Majesty's dominion in Virginia, where, if your Majesty will please to grant me a precinct of land, with such privileges, as the King your father, my gracious Majesty was pleased to grant me here, I shall endeavour to the utmost of my power to deserve it."

Without awaiting a reply, or notifying the authorities of Virginia of his intended visit, early in October, he appeared at Jamestown, and while they were disposed to treat him with kindness, they could not break the law which required the administration of the oaths of allegiance and supremacy to every person arriving in the colony. As he refused to obey the laws, he was requested to depart by the first ship, which he did, leaving there, for a time, his wife and servants.

Capps left for England, without permission of the Governor and Council, about the last of October, and as he sailed probably in the first ship that departed after Baltimore was requested to leave, the latter may have been his fellow passenger.

The communication of the Council in Virginia, to the Privy Council, in England, relative to their action is a calm, reasonable, and courteous paper, worthy of being preserved.

It is dated November 30, 1629, and is as follows: "May it please yo' Lord'pps to understand that about the beginninge of October last, there arrived in this Colony, the Lord Baltimore from his plantation in New Foundland, wth an intention as we are informed rather to plant himself to the Southward, than settle here, although since, he hath seemed well affected to this place, and willing to make his residence therein wth his whole family.

"We were read'ly inclined to render unto his lordship all those respects wh'ch were due unto the honor of his person or wch might testifie wth how much gladness we desired to receive and entertain him, as being of that eminence and degree, whose presence and affection might give greater advancements to this plantation. Whereupon, according to the instruction from y^{r} Lord'hipps, and the which course¹ held in this place, were tendered the oaths of

---

¹ Governor Wyatt on the 24th of July, 1621, Governor Yeardley on the 19th of April, 1626, Governor Harvey, on the 6th of August, 1628, were directed to see that every person who arrived in the Colony, took the oath of allegiance and supremacy. The last history of Maryland by William Hand Browne published in 1884, by Houghton, Mifflin and Company, Boston, makes this erroneous statement:

"Of course Baltimore believing the Pope to be the spiritual head of the church neither could nor would take this oath. He might very well have challenged their rights to offer it, since while it is true that the President and Council of the Virginia Company had been empowered to administer this oath, no such power was given to Pott, or to any authority in the Province, after the Company's dissolution, and in offering it, they incurred the penalties of a high court." P. 16.

supremicie and aleidgiance to his lordship, and some of his followers, who making profession of the Romishe religion, utterly refused to take the same, a thing wch we would not have doubted in him, whose former employm'ts under his late mat'y might have endeared to us a persuasion he could not have made denyall of that, in poynt, whereof consisteth the legaltie and fidelitie wch every true subject oweth unto his soveraigne. His lord'hip then offered to take this oath, a copy whereof is included, but in true discharge of the trust imposed on by his Ma'tie, wee could not imagine that soe much latitude was left for us to decline from the prescribed forms so strictly exacted and soe well justified and defended, by the pen of our late Soveraigne Lord, King James, of happy memory.

"And among the many blessings and favors for w'ch wee are bound to blesse God, and wch the colony has received from his most gratious ma'tie, there is none whereby it hath been made more happy than in the freedome of our religion, w'ch we have enjoyed, and that no Papists have beene suffered to settle their aboade amongst us. The continuance whereof wee most humbly implore from his most sacred ma'tie, and earnestly beseech y^{or} lord'hps, that by your meditations and councells the same may be established, and confirmed unto us. And wee as our duety is with the whole colony, shall always pray for his ma'ties long life and eternall felicity, from whose royal hands the plantation must expect her establishment, and for whose honor God hath so reserved so glorious a worke by p'fection thereof."

Before Lord Baltimore arrived in England, Charles the First on the 22d of November, 1629, in a reply to his letter of the following August, wrote: "We out of our princely care of you and well weighing that men of y^{or} condition and breeding are fitted for other employment than the forming of new plantations, which commonly have rugged and laborious beginnings, and require much greater meanes in managing them than usually the power of one private subject can reach unto, have thought fit hereby to advise you to desist from further prosecuting y^{or} designs that way, and with your first conveniency to returne back to y^{or} native countrie."

In a letter[1] to Lord Dorchester, Secretary of State, written after his arrival in England, he asked that the Governor of Virginia might be instructed to assist his wife in coming home, in recovering debts due to him, and in disposing of her servants, and then he requested permission to choose a portion of land not already granted, with a charter like that of Avalon, and he with the assistance of gentlemen and others, though he did not go in person, would found a colony.

John Pory late Secretary of Virginia wrote to Joseph Mede the distinguished scholar and theologian upon February 12, 1629-30, that Baltimore was "preparing a bark to send to fetch his Lady[2] and servants from thence, because the king will not permit him to go back again."

---

[1] The letter in full was first printed in *Founders of Maryland*, Albany N. Y., Joel Munsell, 1876.

[2] Lord Baltimore's first wife was a most charming woman, a devoted wife and exemplary mother of many children. Her maiden name was Ann Myone. Her death occurred on August 18, 1622, and Camden the Annalist in noting it, calls her "modestissima mulier." But there is no record of his second marriage. It must have occurred after he ceased to be Secretary of State, and retired to Ireland. This wife is never mentioned in books on the Baronetage. Lord Baltimore's most intimate friend Thomas Wentworth, Earl of Strafford, lost his

Jamestown, during the administration of Governors West and Pott, was an insignificant hamlet. The houses of the colonists were small wooden buildings with not the faintest resemblance to the baronial halls of England, and the place for God's worship was of the same material as the dwellings and quite as plain.

Sir George Yeardley's residence was in an enclosure of seven acres, which on the north abutted on the river, and his neighbor on the south was Captain Roger Smith. Easterly he was bounded by a fence which separated him from the land of the main island, and westerly by the Park. Captain Roger Smith had a lot of four acres, which upon the south touched the Governor's garden, and eastward it was bounded by a bridge which led across the marsh to the island, and the yard of Capt. William Peirce. Ralph Warner, a member of the council, in 1624, built in the new town, upon one acre and a half of ground which on the south, was bounded by the James River, and on the east was a highway which separated it from the grounds of George Manefie

---

first wife, the daughter of the Earl of Cumberland, about the same time in the summer of 1622, as Baltimore lost his first wife. The Earl of Strafford's second wife a daughter of the Earl of Clare, died in October, 1631.

Lord Baltimore wrote from Lincoln's Inn Fields London, where he was then lodging, on the 11th of the month, in which he alludes to Strafford's loss and adds " There are few perhaps can judge of it better than I, who have been a long time a man of sorrows." In less than a year Strafford was living with Elizabeth Rhodes whom he did not for some time publicly acknowledge as a wife. *Forsters Statesmen of the British Commonwealth.* Baltimore in his letter seems to be alluding to the loss of his wife who died in the year 1622, and it is possible that his wife who left Virginia in 1630, and is said only in a sketch of Baltimore among the Ayscough Manuscripts to have been lost at sea, may have been one, to whom he was privately married. Philip Calvert, Secretary and Governor of Maryland, Governor Stuyvesant calls his illegitimate son.

merchant, and on the west was the grounds of Richard Stephens, merchant, and John Chew, merchant. East of the house built by Stephens, upon a lot which lay south upon the bay along the river, was the residence of Capt. Ralph Hamor.

The brick church whose ruins are still seen, was not erected until about a half century after this period, although often represented as the church in which the first colonists worshipped.

The minister at this time was the Rev. Francis Bolton who, in 1621, upon the recommendation of the Earl of Southampton, had come to Virginia. After preaching for a period at Elizabeth City, and on the Eastern Shore[1] of the Chesapeake he became the minister at Jamestown, where Richard Buck, and Hawte Wyatt, had been his predecessors in the parish.

The principal merchant was Thoma_ Southwark, London, son of John Wa_ Sussex. He died in February, 1629-30, a few weeks, before

---

[1] In a book of manuscript records in the Library of Congress is the following which shows the salary Bolton received as the first minister on the Eastern shore of Virginia.

"WHEREAS, It is ordered by the Governor and Council that Mr. Bolton shall receive for his salary, this year throughout all the plantations all the Eastern shore, ten pound of tobacco, and one bushel of corn, for every planter and tradesman, above the age of sixteen years, alive at the crop. These are to require Captain William Eps, commander of the said plantation, to raise the said ten pounds of tobacco, one bushel of corn, to be levied accordingly throughout all the said plantations, charging all persons there residing, to yield ready obedience, and to be aiding and assisting unto the said Captain William Eps in the execution of the warrant as they will answer the contrary at their peril. Given at James City, November 21, 1623."

"FRANCIS WYATT."

the arrival of Governor Harvey. His will[1] witnessed by Bolton the minister, and John Southerne indicates that he was a prominent man in social life and gives an idea of the style of dress, of the period. To Dr. John Pott, acting governor, he bequeathed five thousand pounds of nails, of great value to one commencing a plantation; to Elizabeth Potts, his wife, he gave one corfe, and cross cloth of wrought gold, and to Francis Pott his brother, a debt of eighty pounds of tobacco. The minister Francis Bolton received very useful supplies; a firkin of butter, a bushel of salt, six pounds of candles, a pound of pepper, a pound of ginger, two bushels of meal, a rundlett of ink, six quires of letter paper, and a pair of silk stockings. The wife of John Johnson was given six pounds of soap, six pounds of blue, and a pound of white starch. To the wife of John Browning was bequeathed a thousand pins, a pair of knives carved with two images upon them, twelve pounds of white, and two pounds of blue starch. The wife of Mr. John Upton's was remembered by the present of a sea green scarf, edged with gold lace, two pounds of blue, and twelve of white starch. To his friend Thomas Burges he gave his best felt hat, and his second best sword, and to the wife of John Grevett a pair of sheets, six table napkins, three towels, and a table cloth, six pounds of soap, a pound of blue, and six pounds of white starch. The wife of Sergeant John Wane received four bushels of meal, four gallons of vinegar, a half pound of different colored thread, twenty needles, six dozen silk and thread buttons, a pewter candlestick, and a pewter pot de chambre. The wife of Thomas Key was left a gilded

---

[1] See Gleanings of H. F. Waters in *N. E. Hist. Gen. Register*, April, 1884.

VIRGINIA CAROLORUM. 71

looking glass ; and of Roger Thompson, a jar of oil, a pound of pepper, and a half bushel of salt. Benjamin Symes who became the first American benefactor to the cause of education, received a weeding hoe, the wife of Michael Batt two bushels of meal. His own wife Thomasine, daughter of William Hall, of Woodalling county Norfolk, England, received the rest of his estate, and John Southern, and James Stormes were overseers of the will. Southerne received a black beaver hat, and gold band, a doublet of black camlet, a pair of black hose, a Polander cap furred, and a pair of red slippers, and Stormes his best sword and a gold belt. Warnet certainly loved his neighbors. John Browning whose wife is mentioned, in October, 1629, represented Elizabeth City in the legislature, and in that of 1630, sat John Southerne, Thomas Key, John Upton, Thomas Burges.

The only legislature which assembled during the period Doctor John Pott, acted as governor, met in October, and was largely composed of the earlier colonists.[1] The Assem-

---

[1] BURGESSES OF THE ASSEMBLY CONVENED AT JAMESTOWN, OCTOBER 16, 1629.

College Plantation or Henrico.

Lt. Thomas Osborne.	Arrived in 1619, in *Bona Nora*, and was now 35 years old Justice in 1632.
Mathew Edlowe.	Came in 1618 in *Neptune*, died in 1668, his wife Tabitha in 1670. His son John was under the guardianship of Col. Robert Wynne.

Neck of Land, Charles City Corporation.

Serg't. Sharpe.	Samuel Sharpe came in 1610, with Gates and Somers, and had been a member of the first legislature in 1619. He married a girl who came in 1621.
Chene Boise.	Arrived in 1617, in the *George*, and was now 35 years old.

VIRGINIA CAROLORUM.

Shirley Hundred Island.

Mr. Thomas Palmer.   He, and his wife, and daughter seven years old, came in 1621, in the *Tiger*. Justice in 1632.

John Harris.   Had been several years in Virginia.

Henry Throgmorton's Plantation.

William Allen.   Came in 1623, in *Southampton*.

Jordan's Journey Charles City.

William Popleton.   Came in 1622, in the *James* as a servant of John Davies.

Chaplain's Choice Charles City.

Walter Price.   Came in 1618, in *William and Thomas*.

Westover, Charles City.

Christopher Woodward.   Aged 35 came in 1620 in *Trial*.

Fleur Dieu Hundred.

Anthony Pagett.   Aged 40, came in 1623, a servant in *Southampton*.

James City.

Mr. Menefie.   Arrived in July 1623, in the *Samuel*. A merchant.

Mr. Kingsmell.   Perhaps Kingswell came in the *Delaware*. His wife in the *Susan*.

Paces Pains, James City.

Lt. William Perry.
John Smyth.   Came in 1611, in *Elizabeth*.

Over the River.

Capt. John West.   Brother of the late Lord Delaware, and Gov. Francis West.

Capt. Rob't Fellgate.

Pasbehay, James City.

Thomas Bagwell.   An old settler.

Neck of Land, James City.

Richard Brewster.

bly authorized the beginning of a plantation on the York, then called Pamunky River. As early as 1624, the King's Commissioners had recommended the planting of "Chis-

Archer's Hope, James City.

Theodore Moyses,	Came in *London Merchant*.
Thomas Doe.	

Between Archer's Hope, and Martin's Hundred.

Mr. John Utie.	Came in the *Francis Bona Ventura*. A man of influence.
Richard Townsend.	Now about 24 years old. Came in the *Abigail*, 1620, had been a servant of Dr. John Pott.

Hog Island.

John Chew.	Came in the *Charity*. A merchant.
Richard Tree.	Arrived in the *George*, with his son twelve years old.

Martin's Hundred.

Thomas Kingston.	In the colony several years.
Thomas Fawcett.	In the colony several years.

Mulberry Island.

Thomas Harwood.	Came in 1622, in *Margaret and John*.
Phettiplace Close.	An old settler, who came in the *Star*.

Warwick River.

Christopher Stokes.	Had been five years in colony.
Thomas Ceeley.	A county justice in 1632.
Thomas Flint.	Came in 1618, in *Diana*, a county justice in 1632.
Zachary Cripps.	Came in 1621 in *Marg't and John*, a county justice in 1632.

Warosquoyake.

Capt. Natt Basse.	Was about 40 years old and came in 1622, in *Furtherance*.
Richard Bennett.	Afterwards Councillor.
Robert Savin.	
Thomas Jordan.	Justice in 1632.

kiake situated upon Pamunky" and to build a pale across from thence to Martin's Hundred, seven miles below James City.

Joseph Mede in a letter[1] to Sir Martin Stuteville in January, 1629-30, after referring to Lord Baltimore's return to London, from Virginia, continues: "About the time of his being there, a certain Indian, dwelling some four or five days journey off, came and offered himself his wife, and four children," and "to ensure them of his fidelity he conducted them against the Indians, their enemies upon whose persons, by his guidance" they obtained "more spoil and revenge than they had done since the great massacre there." And this action had so much the more of justice in it, by reason, that of late, those treacherous savages assailed the house of one Mr. Poole,[2] a minister and slew him, his wife, and all his family."

Nutmeg Quarter.

William Cole.	Now about 31 years old, came in 1618 in *Neptune*. His wife came in 1616, in *Susan*.
William Bentley.	About 41 years of age, came as a hired man in 1624, in the *Jacob*.

Elizabeth City.

Lt. Thompson.	
Adam Thorowgood.	Came in 1621, when 18 years old.
Mr. Rowlston	Came in 1623 in *God's Gift*.
John Browning.	About 27 years old, came in 1621, in *Abigail*.
John Downeman.	When a boy, came in 1611, married a maid sent out in 1621, in *Warwick*.

[1] *Court and Times of Charles the First.*

[2] Greville Pooley, minister, came, in 1622, in the ship James, and was a friend of Abraham Piersey. See p. 49.

The action referred to was probably that of Captain Claiborne who attacked and defeated the Indians at Candayak, now West Point, at the junction of the York and Pamunky Rivers.

Sir Robert Heath, formerly Recorder of London, when Attorney General of England, on the 10th of February, 1629-30, a few weeks after Lord Baltimore's return, for himself and associates, asked that two degrees of land, upon which to settle a colony, with power "to create, and establish or confirm for ever, officers, ministers, and agents of all qualities and conditions, touching as well the church, as the military, and political part of the government, according to the general orders and laws of the whole province; paying and causing to be paid to these officers, ministers, and agents, all their entertainment and wages."

Antoine Rideoute, the Baron de Sancé a French refugee, and his son George, were made subjects of England, at this time, with the intention of planting a colony, of members of the Reformed Church in France, south of the James River. A charter was granted to Heath and the usual phraseology relative to zeal for Christianity, and desire to enlarge the bounds, and increase the trade of the kingdom, and the region ceded between the 31st and 36th degrees of north latitude in compliment to the king was called Carolana a few years later written Carolina. On the 15th of April, 1630, the proprietor was informed that those who settled in that country must acknowledge the church of England. The next month under this charter, an agreement was made with George, Lord Berkeley, Sir William Boswell, Samuel

Vassall, Hugh L'Amy and Peter de Licques,[1] by which they could form a settlement in Carolana, with power to appoint a Governor, and other officers, and that no appeal should be taken from the General Assembly of the province. This plan was not carried out, and in 1631, the charter was modified, in which Heath is referred to in these words: "He beeing about to lead thither a Colonye of men large and plentifull, professing the true Religion, sedulously and industriously applying themselves to the culture of y*e* sayd land, and to merchandising, to be performed by industrye at his own charges and others by his example." By this instrument he was made "sole Lord Proprietor in chiefley Knight's service, and by paying for it, to us, our heirs, and successors, one circle of Gold in the fashion of a crown of the weight of twenty ounces with the inscription ingraved upon it: '*Deus coronet opus suum.*'"

---

[1] Peter de Licques of Picardy had been naturalized.

CHAPTER III.

EVENTS FROM A.D. 1630 TO A.D., 1684.

Governor Harvey's Arrival. Assembly of 1630. Doctor Pott's Trial. Claiborne Trades with Boston. Daniel Gookin at Newport News. Death of Capt. John Smith. Social ties of Massachusetts and Virginia. Henry Fleet, Potomac Trader. Assembly of February, 1631–2. Sunday Legislation. Monthly Courts. Assembly of September, 1632. Wreck of the Warwick. William Bolton Agent for Planters. Capt. De Vries at Jamestown. John Stone a rough Sea-captain.

JOHN Harvey when commissioned as Governor of Virginia, was knighted, in accordance with the custom commenced, at the appointment of Governor Yeardley. He remained in England for some time, and applied for an increase of the emoluments and privileges of his office. He also requested that the city of London, as before, might be permitted to send over one hundred friendless boys, and girls, and that six ministers conformable to the church of England, might also be procured for the Colony.

The Privy Council, in reply to the petitions presented, allowed the colonists to hold a legislative assembly, whose ordinances would not be valid without the King's approval and agreed that Christian ministers could go to Virginia, provided, the settlements which invited them would assume their support.

Early in the year 1630, after a tedious voyage, by way of Cape Verd, Governor Harvey reached Jamestown, but on account of unusual sickness among the planters, he did not convene the General Assembly, until the week before Easter Sunday. At this time Francis West, late acting Governor, William Claiborne, and William Tucker, Councillors, were in England. The Assembly met on March 24, 1629-30 (O. S.), and as had been the custom, the oath of allegiance and supremacy was taken by the delegates.[1]

Harvey did not manifest the conciliatory spirit of his immediate predecessors, Yeardley and Wyatt. He walked among the colonists, as he did the quarter-deck of a ship of war, and desired to impress the settlers with the idea that he was a vice-roy. His arrogancy and arbitrary course immediately engendered opposition, and a people's party was the result. His unpopularity was increased by the alacrity displayed, in assisting Lord Baltimore, in establishing a province, out of a large and fertile portion of Virginia. The day after the Assembly convened there appears to have been some discussion as to the propriety of Lord Baltimore's project, and Thomas Tindall for calling Lord Balti-

---

[1] The councillors present at this Assembly, were Dr. John Pott, William Ferrar and Samuel Mathews. A few weeks later Capt. John West, Hen. Finch, Christopher Cowling, Capt. Richard Stephens, Capt. John Utie, and Capt. Nath. Basse were members of his council.

more a liar, and threatening to knock him down was placed in the pillory for two hours.[1]

John Pott the acting Governor, at the time of Harvey's arrival, was an educated physician, careless in business, fond of good living, and a jovial companion.[2]

He had pardoned Edward Wallis who had been convicted of murder and restored his privileges. He was also charged with keeping some cattle which did not belong to him. Harvey had not been at Jamestown but a few weeks, when he ordered Potts' arrest, who was at his plantation called Harrope, seven miles from Jamestown. He appeared before the General Court on the ninth of July, 1630, and before a jury of thirteen was tried for stealing cattle. The first day was occupied in pleading and Kingswell[3] an old planter testified adversely. The next day Pott declared that the witness was unreliable and hypocritical, and told the story of Gusman of Alfrach, the rogue.[4]

---

[1] Hening, 1, 552.

[2] George Sandys on April 9, 1623, in a letter to Samuel Wrote, of London, alluding to Pott, writes: "I have given from time to time the best councell I am able, at the first, he kept companie too much with his inferiours, who hung upon him, while his good liquor lasted. After, he consorted with Captaine Whitacres, a man of no good example, with whom he is gone into Kicotan, yet wheresoever he bee, he shall not bee without reach of my care, nor want for any thing that I or my credit can procure him "— *Virginia Vetusta*, p. 127.

[3] A Richard Kingswell, a planter on the neck of land, near Jamestown, came in 1610, in the ship "Delaware;" his wife Jane, in 1616, arrived in the "Susan."

[4] Reference may be had to the hypocrite and Spanish spy, Don Juan of the house of Gusman, who with Captain Henry Duffield was employed, by the King of Spain, to go to England, and burn ships with wild fire.

Don Juan Gusman in his narrative declared that he reached Ireland in a ship, and was seized by the servants of Mahona, and taken to his castle and from

The jury declared him guilty, but Governor Harvey declined to pronounce judgment, until he consulted the king, and he wrote to England that Pott "was the only physician in the colony, skilled in epidemical diseases," and suggested that his estate should be restored in view of his long residence, and the value of his services. Elizabeth, the doctor's wife, impelled by affection, after a dangerous voyage, reached London, in September, after an absence of ten years, and with earnestness pleaded for her husband. The case was referred to commissioners who reported that the condemning of Doctor Pott " for felony " was very rigorous, if not erroneous, and recommended his pardon which the king granted. During the autumn of this year an expedition of two hundred men under Captain Mathews was sent to search for mines beyond the Falls of James River, but overtaken by winter, returned without important results.

William Claiborne continued during the whole of this year in England. John Winthrop, and associates, in 1630, entered Massachusetts Bay, and settled Boston, and the next spring his friends in London, contracted with Claiborne still there, to bring to Boston, from Virginia, forty tons of Indian wheat. A son of Winthrop writes from London, to his father; "This corne we understand they buy of the natives there, for trucke, there is great store all alongst

---

thence was sent to the Earl of Desmond, where he was examined by a legate of the Pope and escaped suspicion by a forged passport, and then went to Limerick, where he attended the church of England, and assisted to expel cattle stealers. This story was a tissue of falsehoods. In April, 1594, his companion Henry Duffield, and a son of the Earl of Desmond, were confined in the Tower of London, charged with burning her Majesty's ships at Chatham, at the instigation of the K. of Spain.

the coast, from a little to the southward of you, to Florida beyond, to be had for toyes, beades, coper, tools, knives, glass, and such like."¹

On the 16th of May, 1631, the king issued a commission to his "trusty and well beloved William Cleyborne one of the council, and Secretary of State for our Colony of Virginia, and some other adventurers," to keep an interchange of trade with Nova Scotia and New England, and to trade for furs and corn in any region for which there is not already a patent granted to others for sole trade." Under this permit Claiborne returned to Virginia, and established trading posts at Kent Island in Chesapeake Bay, and at Palmers Island in Susquehanna River. Among those prominent at this period in colonizing Virginia, was Daniel Gookin² of Cariggaline, a few miles south of Cork, on the shores of Cork Harbor, Ireland. In 1621, he determined to begin a plantation, in Virginia, near that of his friend Sir William Newce,³ and his brother Thomas Newce.

In August of that year, the London Company wrote to the Governor of Virginia that he was about to transport cattle from Ireland and used these words, "Let him have very good Tobacco for his cowes now at his first voiadge, for if he makes a good return it may be the occasion of a trade with

---

¹ John Winthrop, Jr., in Mass. His. Soc. Coll., 5th Series, Vol., VIII, p. 20.

² He was the son of John Gookin of Ripple Court, Kent County, England, and with his brother Sir Vincent, settled in Ireland; Vincent settled at Bandon, Cork County.

³ Captain, afterwards Sir William Newce, laid out a suburb of Bandon called Newce's Town, and in 1613, was mayor of Bandon. He was appointed marshal of Virginia, and in October, 1622, arrived there at Newport News, and soon died.

you from those parts [Ireland] not only with cattle, but with most of those commodities you want att better, and easier rates, than we from hence, shall be able." Gookin in November,[1] arrived at Newport News in the ship Flying Hart, Cornelius Johnson, a Dutchman, being master thereof, and established a plantation where he made a brave stand against the Indians the following March. Soon after the massacre Governor Wyatt and wife paid him a visit, and he returned to England in the ship, which brought the news of the slaughter of more than three hundred of the settlers. In 1623, the ship "Providence" again brought more servants for his land, and he may have been a passenger, but after this time he does not appear to have been a resident, for any long period. It is probable his son Daniel, attended to affairs in Virginia, while he looked after his interests in England and Ireland. In a petition dated March 11, 1631, he mentioned that he has been "for many years a great well wisher to new plantations, and a planter and adventurer in most of them" and asks for a grant of a certain island which he "is credible informed lies between the

---

[1] The Governor and Council of Virginia under date of January, 1622, wrote to the London Company: "There arrived here about the 22 of November, a shipp from Mr. Gookin out of Ireland wholy uppon his owne Adventure, withoute any returne at all to his contract wth you in England, w'ch was soe well furnished with all sortes of p'visiones as well as with Cattle as we could wyshe all men would follow theire example, hee hath also brought with him about 50 men upon that Adventure, besides some 30 other Passengers, we haue according to their desire sented them at Newport's News, and we doe conceive great hope yff the Irish Plantation p'sper, yt from Ireland greate multitude of people will be like to come hither * * * * * * * Mr. Pountis hath had some, conference with ye Mr. of the Irish shipp, a Dutchman, whose name ys Cornelius Johnson of Horne in Hollande, who is soe farr in loue with this Countrey, as he intendeth to returne hither."

50th and 65th degree of north latitude, named St. Brandon or Isle de Verd, about three leagues, from the Blasques of Ireland." De Vries, the Dutch captain, writes that on the 20th of March, 1633, he "anchored at evening, before Newport Snuw, where lived a gentleman of the name of Goegen" [Gookin].

On the 21st of June, 1631, died the great adventurer Captain John Smith, whose stories were as wonderful as those of the traveler Coryat. During the brief period he lived in Virginia, he quarreled with Francis West, brother of Lord Delaware, and others, and was sent home in disgrace.[1] In a letter to Earl of Salisbury, Lord High Treasurer, dated October 4, 1609, from Captain John Ratcliff is the following: "We heard yt all the counsell, were dead, but Captain Smith the President who reigned sole governor without assistants and would at first admitt of no councill but himself. This man is sent home to answer some misdeamenors whereof I persuade me, he can scarcely clear himself from great imputations of blame." Wingfield mentions that he had been a beggar in Ireland, and in a letter to Lord Bacon, in 1618, Smith writes relative to some scheme:[2] "Should I present it to the Biskayers, French, or Hollanders, they have made me large offers, but Nature doth binde me thus to begge at home, whom strangers have pleased to make a commander abroad." In a description of New England, which accompanied this letter, he also wrote: "Lett not the povertie of the author cause the action to be less re-

---

[1] Spelman's Relation quoted p. 52.

[2] The entire letter from the original, in the British Public Record Office, has been published in the American Antiquarian Society Proceedings for 1870.

spected who desyres no better fortune than he would find there. In the interim, I humbly desyre y^{or} Honor would be pleased to grace me with the title of y^{or} Ld'ps servant. Not that I desyre to strut upp the rest of my days in the chamber of ease and idleness, but that thereby I may be the better countenance for this my most desyred voyage." After Smith had published a book on Virginia, George Percey who had lived more than five years in the colony, wrote[1] to his brother the Earl of Northumberland, of a work containing "many untreuthes," wherein the Author "hathe nott spared to apropiate many deserts to himselfe which he never p'formed and stuffed his relacyons wth so many falseties and malycyous detractyons." George, Earl of Kildare, wrote to the Secretary of State, on April 21, 1630, that he had chosen a Captain Smith to live with him, "who through unfortunate disasters in his Majesty's service is a subject of pity." The Virginia Company, after he came back from Jamestown, never gave him their confidence, and he was used for a time by the New England companies. In his last days, he was befriended by Sir Samuel Saltonstall, Kt., a relative of Sir Richard Saltonstall, Kt., one of the founders of Massachusetts. Wye, the son of Samuel, a graduate of Oxford, in a translation of a History of the World by Hondius, published in 1635, inserted a portrait of Smith. The quaint historian Thomas Fuller who knew Smith gave the following estimate of his General History : "From the Turks in Europe, he passed to the Pagans in America, where such his perils, preservations, dangers, deliverances

---

[1] See **Virginia Vetusta**, published by Munsell's Sons, Albany, N. Y., 1885.

they seem to most men, above belief, to some, beyond truth. Yet we have two witnesses to attest them, the prose and the pictures both in his own book, and it soundeth much to the diminution of his deeds that he alone is the herald to publish and proclaim them." The remains of Smith were interred in Saint Sepulchre's church, chiefly erected by the ancestors of the Popham family, next to a fair and large inn, without Newgate, called the Saracen's Head, where an old chronicler mentions that "the carriers of Oxford do lodge, and are there on Wednesday or almost any day " and here Smith in the poverty of his last days may have often lounged, an appropriate place to tell the story of his taking three Turks' heads. But a few days after his burial the Privy Council appointed a new commission to consider how the plantation of Virginia now standeth, and to consider what commodity may be raised, in those parts." The commissioners[1] were chiefly members of the old London Company and George Sandys who had returned from Jamestown wished to be Secretary of the body. A vigorous effort was made to restore the charter of the old Virginia Com-

---

[1] Rymer, Vol. XIX, p. 301.
The commissioners were:

—Earl of Dorset,
Earl of Danby,
Sir John Coke, Knight,
" Robert Killigrew, Kt.,
" Thos. Roe,
" Robert Heath, Kt.,
" Heneage Finch, Kt.
" Duddley Diggs, Kt.
" John Wolstenholme, Kt.
" Francis Wyatt, Kt.,
" John Brooke, Kt.

Sir Kenelm Digby, Knight.
" John Zouch, Kt.
" John Davis, Kt.
" John Banks, Esq.
" Samuel Wrote.
" George Sandys, Esq.
" John Wolstenholme, Esq.
" Nicholas Ferrar, Esq.
" Gabriel Barber, Esq.
" John Ferrar, Esq.,
" Thomas Gibb, Esq.

pany, by the Ferrars and others, but the colonists, who at the time of its abrogation preferred the officers appointed by the London corporation, to the place hunters sent over by the king, had begun to reap the fruit of their own industry and were more independent, and they were opposed to any step that would again make them the serfs of London merchants. While a new charter was prepared, the king at the last wisely refused his approval.[1]

Some of the founders of Boston and the adjacent towns in Massachusetts, were connected by social and family ties with the leading planters in the valley of the James River. Richard, the eldest son of Sir Richard Saltonstall, Kt., in November, 1631, visited Virginia, on his way to England to be married.[2] Herbert Pelham born in 1546, married the sister of Lord Delaware, the Governor General, and of Francis West, Deputy Governor of Virginia. His son Herbert, by his first wife, in 1599, married Penelope, another daughter. Her daughter also named Penelope, married in Boston the well known Governor, Richard Dillingham, and her son Herbert, born in 1600, was the first treasurer of Harvard College. The daughter of Herbert married Governor Josiah Winslow of Boston.

William Brewster, the leader of the Plymouth seperatists when a young man was in the service of William Davison,

---

[1] On March 2, 1632, a communication from Whitehall was received by the Attorney General that the old Virginia adventurers having accepted a new charter of restitution, he should not pass any grant or patent without a proviso or exception of all formerly granted to the late Virginia Company.

[2] In Hotten's List of Passengers in the "Suzan and Ellin" for New England, appear the names of Richard Saltonstall 23 years, his wife Merriall 22 years, and babe Merriall 9 months old; also the following: "May 15, 1635, Penelopy Pelham 16 years to passe to her brothers Plantacon."

ambassador of Queen Elizabeth at the Hague, and while there an elder of the Presbyterian church at Delft,[1] and soon after Brewster landed on the New England coast, Christopher, the second son of his employer, arrived at Jamestown, as Secretary of the Virginia Colony.

Before the close of the year 1632, trading vessels frequently passed from Virginia to New England. The bark, Warwick, of about eighty tons burthen, with ten pieces of ordnance under Captain Walter Neale, was sent by London merchants in March, 1630, "for the discovery of the great lake in New England so to have intercepted the trade of beaver" and arrived about the first of June at Piscataqua. After returning to England, the owners sent her again with "a factor to take charge of the trade goods, also a soldier[2] for discovery." The factor was Henry Fleet, whose arrival from Virginia in 1627, had created in London a great interest. The "Warwick," on the 19th of September, 1631, again cast anchor in Piscataqua harbor, and from thence sailed for Virginia, John Dunton being master of the vessel. After a short stay in the James River, the ship entered the Potomac river, and Fleet stopped at the Indian village Yowaccomoco, where he had traded before, and in time, to be the capital of the Province of Maryland, by his advice, a province whose charter had not then been written. Purchasing eight hundred bushels of corn from the natives,

---

[1] William Boswell, then ambassador at the Hague, on March 18, 1633, wrote of the distressed state of church government among the merchant adventures at Delft., that it was entirely Presbyterian, and continued " Mr. Davison, Queen Elizabeth's ambassador was an elder in this church." Cal. State Papers.

[2] N. E. Hist., Gen. Register July, 1867, p. 224.

88   *VIRGINIA CAROLORUM.*

he sailed for New England on the 6th of December, but owing to bad weather, he did not until the 10th of January, 1631-2, leave Point Comfort. On Tuesday, the 7th of February, he arrived at Piscataqua with his acceptable cargo, and on the 6th of March, he went to the Isle of Shoals for a supply of provisions for a return voyage to Virginia. The "Warwick" on the 16th came to the "Winysemett" now Chelsea, where resided the hospitable Samuel Warwick, in a house, built in 1625, "fortified with a pillizado, and flankers and gunnes both, below, and above." Winthrop mentions under date of March 24, 1631-2. "The 'Bark Warwick' arrived at Natescua having been at Piscataquak and Salem to sell corn, brought from Virginia." On the 21st of February, 1631-2, a legislative assembly convened at Jamestown, and the councillors were Francis and John West,[1] Samuel Mathews,[2] William Claiborne,[3] Nathaniel Basse,[4] John Utie,[5] William Tucker,[6] and Richard Stephens.[7]

The councillors Henry Finch, Christopher Cooling, William Peirce and Thomas Purify were absent. For the first

---

[1] Brothers of Lord Delaware.

[2] Samuel Mathews, see p. 20.

[3] See p. 24.

[4] Nathaniel Basse aged 41 years came in 1622, in the ship "Furtherance." After the decease of Capt. Christopher Lawne, he and his associates had Lawne's Plantation called Isle of Wight. *History of Virginia Company,* p. 194.

[5] John Utie came in the "Francis Bonaventura" and settled on Hog Island near Jamestown.

[6] William Tucker, see p. 40.

[7] Richard Stephens arrived in 1623, and soon had a duel with George Harrison who died a few days after, from a wound received. Governor Harvey subsequently had a fight with him and knocked out his teeth with a cudgel. After the death of Stephens, Harvey married his widow.

time, the first day of the week, in one of the acts of this legislature, is called Sunday instead of the Sabbath; the act may have been prepared at the suggestion of Laud then Bishop of London, who was opposed to the use of the latter word. It was enacted "that the Statutes for comminge to Church every Sunday and holy days bee duly executed." These statutes however inclined to the strictness of the Mosaic system. Every one absent from church was fined a pound of tobacco for each absence; if absent for a month, without good reason the penalty was fifty pounds of tobacco. At this session, it was also ordered that "Mynisters shall not give themselves to excesse in drinking or riott, spending their tyme idellye by day or night, playing at dice, cards, or any other unlawfull game; but at all tyme convenient they shall heare or reade somewhat of the Holy Scriptures or shall occupie themselves with some other honest study or exercise always doing the things which shall appertayne to honesty, and endeavour to profit the Church of God always showing in mynd that they ought to excell all others in puritie of life, and should be examples to the people to live well and Christianlike."

As yet the Colony had no State House but the burgesses were required to attend divine service in the room where they held their sessions, at the third beating of the drum, an hour after sunrise, and if absent without proper excuse were fined one shilling.

The increase of population led to the extension of monthly courts, and those appointed justices in March, 1631-2 (O. S.), were among the most prominent citizens, and their names are worthy of preservation.

Monthly Courts.

Upper parts of Charles City and Henrico.

William Ferrar, Quorum,[1] Capt. Francis Epes, Capt. Thomas Pawlett,[2] Capt. Thomas Osborne,[3] Capt. Thomas Palmer,[4] Walter Aston, Gent.

Warwick River.

Capt. Samuel Mathews, Quorum, Capt. Richard Stephens, Capt. Thomas Flint, Zackary Cripps, Gent., John Brewer, Gent., Thomas Seeley, Gent.

Warrosquoyacke.

Capt. Nathaniel Basse, Quorum, Thomas Jordan, Gent., William Hutchinson, Gent., Richard Bennett, John Upton, Gent.

Elizabeth City.

Capt. William Tucker, Quorum, William English, Gent., Capt. Thos. Willoughby, Capt. Thos. Purifrie, Esq., Quorum, John Arundell, Gent., George Downes, Gent., Adam Thoroughgood.

Accawmacke.

Capt. William Claiborne, Quorum, Obedience Robins, Gent., Roger Saunders, Gent., Capt. Thos. Graves, Quorum, Charles Harman, Gent.

---

[1] In commissions when one was designated quorum his presence was necessary to the validity of a meeting.

[2] Pawlett was 48 years of age, in 1618, came in the "Neptune."

[3] Came in November, 1619, in the "Bona Nova."

[4] Arrived in the "Tiger," in November, 1621, with his wife Joane, and child Priscilla, eleven years old.

Three of these persons could form a legal court provided two were quorums. Appeal could be taken to the General Court at Jamestown, composed of the members of the Council.

Councillor Basse, in March, was authorized to invite those of New England who disliked " coldness of climate or barreness of soil " to emigrate to the shore of Delaware Bay.

On Monday, April 9, 1632 (O. S.), the bark " Warwick " left Boston, with a pinnace of twenty tons belonging to Samuel Maverick. The pinnace proceeded up the Potomac River, but Fleet in the " Warwick " stopped at Accomac, and on the 16th of May, accompanied by Claiborne in another small vessel, also sailed for the Potomac River. When he reached Yowocomaco he learned that Charles Harman of Accomac had been in the region, but three days before, and obtained three hundred pounds of beaver. Ascending the stream, Fleet on the 26th of May arrived at an Indian village on Potomac creek, in what is now Stafford county, Virginia.[1] and here he found Maverick's pinnace laden with corn, which on the first of June, departed for

---

[1] This village for years had been a point at which the English had traded. On the 20th of June, 1640, Capt. Claiborne was granted 3000 acres at the town of Potomack, bounded on each side, by the place were this fort was formerly built by the English, anno 1622. In Harpers Magazine for January, 1886, Moncure Conway describes an old tombstone in this vicinity which a few years ago had the following rude inscription, in letters 1½ inches long.

    HERE LIES INTERED
    THE BODY OF EDMOND
    HELDER PRECTIONER IN
    PHYSICK AND CHYRURGE
    RY. BORN IN BEDFORDE
    SHIRE   OBIIT MARCH 11
    1618. S ATATIS SUA Y6.

New England. Fleet remained and obtained a large amount of beaver from the Nacostines or Anacostans who resided where, now, is the city of Washington.

On the 26th of June, his vessel anchored two leagues below the Falls of the Potomac. He passed several weeks in trading with the Indians, and on the 28th of August met a pinnace, with eight persons, one of whom was Charles Harman, a rival trader, and another John Utie of the Virginia Council. The latter arrested him, by order of the Council, and on the 7th of September, the "Warwick" anchored at Jamestown.

Governor Harvey, always fond of money, saw that Fleet might be a profitable acquaintance. Fleet, in his Journal writes: The Governor bearing himself like a noble gentleman showed me very much favor and used me with unexpected courtesy. Captain Utye (Utie) did acquaint the Council with the success of the voyage, and every man seemed to be desirous to be a partner with me, in these employments, I made as fair weather as might be with them, to the end in question, and what they would or could object, that I might see what issue it would come to. The Court was called the 14th of September, when an order was made and I find the Governor hath favoured me therein. After this day, I had free power to dispose of myself."

The owners of the "Warwick"[1] in London, two years after made legal complaint that by authority of Governor Harvey, Henry Fleet had retained the ship, to their great loss.

---

[1] The "Warwick" never returned to London. Winthrop under date of June 30, 1636, wrote; "Warrant to the constable of Dorchester to inventory and apprize the rigging of bark Warwick, cast away." Harris in 1804, wrote "Near

The legislature was in session when Utie returned to Jamestown with Fleet, and Charles Harman sat as a burgess from Accomac, and Nicholas Martain from the new plantation of Kiskeyake.

To restrain trade among the Indians of the Potomac River it was enacted that all vessels coming into Virginia waters should report at Jamestown. About this time, a small vessel was sent from Virginia to explore the valley of the Delaware River, and trade with the natives, and Capt. De Vries was told by the Indians, that they had killed all on board.

The year 1633, witnessed a large increase of population, a larger tobacco crop, with more attention to the cultivation of corn, and raising of cattle, and the colony was becoming a granary for New England.[1]

Among those who arrived as a planter, was William Button, supposed to have been the nephew of Captain Button, the Hudson Bay explorer, the name of whose pilot, Nelson, was given to that river whose waters flow from Lake Winnepeg, into which also flow those of the Red River of Minnesota. He had been the captain of a ship in the expedition against Rochelle and was not a stranger to Governor Harvey. At the request of the planters, in February 1634,

---

this place [Commercial Point, Dorchester] is a small creek which bears the name of 'Barque Warwick' from a small vessel which ran aground here, two or three years after the first settlement of the town, the remains of which are still to be seen." W. B. T., in N. E. Hist. Gen. Register, July, 1867, writes: " My father's estate was bounded southerly on this same creek, and the street in front of the house, in which I was born, now Commercial Street, was in my younger days ' Barque Warwick' Street."

In 1632, there were 5000 bushels of corn raised and in 1634, 10,000 bushels.

he went to England, and presented their wants, to the Privy Council. His mission was successful, and it was ordered that the planters should "enjoy all the privileges they had before the Virginia Company's patent was abrogated, and that the Governor and Council, as was the custom before 1625, might grant lands to freemen."

For his services Button was allowed to select lands on either side of the Appomattox River. He died before 1639, and his widow became the wife of Ralph Wyatt, who had been wounded in the expedition against the Isle of Rhé.[1]

The tobacco trade had now become so extensive that Dutch as well as English ships sought the landings of the planters. De Vries, an experienced Dutch captain, on the 9th of March, 1633, in a vessel from Manhattan now New York city, reached the frail fort that had been erected by Capt. Samuel Mathews at Point Comfort, by direction of the legislature. When he went to Jamestown he found Governor Harvey at the wharf, with an escort of "some halberdeers and musketeers," by whom he was cordially received, taken to his home, proffered a glass of sack, and invited to stay all night. In conversation the Governor discovered that he had known De Vries in the East Indies. The Dutch captain was astonished at finding so many of the planters inveterate gamblers, even staking their servants, and told them he had "never seen such work in Turkey or Barbary."

---

[1] Children of Hawte Wyatt, minister of Jamestown, and brother of the Governor, are said to have settled in Virginia.

On the 15th of June, Captain Stone, whom De Vries had met at the Governor's table, sailed into the beautiful harbor of Manhattan. His relatives in England were said to have been respectable and influential people, but his bearing was that of a pirate. He strutted, swaggered, swore horribly, indulged in lewd conversation, and ignored the ten commandments, which he had read in childhood on the tablets of parish churches. While on a carouse with Governor Von Twiller of Manhattan, he persuaded him to permit the seizing of a vessel from Plymouth colony, in charge of a member of its Council who had finished trading, and was about to return with a good cargo. Alleging that some of the Plymouth sailors had spoken reproachfully of Virginia, while the merchant and several of the chief men, were on shore, Stone went aboard, with some of his crew, and compelled those in the Plymouth vessel to steer for Virginia. Several Dutch sailors who had been to Plymouth, and kindly treated there, said, "shall we suffer our friends to be thus abused before our faces, while our Governor is drunk?" and procuring a pinnace sailed after, and brought the vessel back.

The next day Captain Stone, and Governor Von Twiller were sober, and asked the captain of the Plymouth vessel not to take legal steps, to which he consented, but when Stone arrived in Massachusetts Bay to sell some cows, and salt, the Plymouth Colony sent brave Miles Standish to prosecute him, in the General Court of Massachusetts, and he was also bound over to appear in the Admiralty Court of England, but the Plymouth people discovering that they could not make good the charge of piracy, his sureties were released.

While in Boston, his conduct was boisterous, and he sneeringly called Roger Ludlow, one of the General Court, *a just ass*, a play upon the word justice, which office he held. Found in bed, one night, with another man's wife, he was brought before the Governor, and "though it appeared he was in drink, and no act to be proved, yet it was thought fit he should abide his trial," and his pinnace was stayed,[1] but he refused to obey the warrant, and fled. Command was given to the soldiers to take him dead or alive, and he was found in a corn field near Dorchester.[2] Brought before the Boston court, the Grand Jury did not find sufficient evidence to sustain the charge of adultery.[3] The court however, in September, made this order:[4] "Captain John Stone for his outrage committed in confronting authority, abuseing Mr. Ludlowe both in words and behaviour, assaulting him, calling him a iust [just] ass is fined C*l* and p'hibited comeing within this pattent wth out leave from the Gou'rm't under the penalty of death."

After this, with some gentlemen, he visited Plymouth, and was courteously received, but soon quarreled with the Governor, and drew his dagger.[5] On his return to Virginia, he sailed into the Connecticut River to trade with the

---

[1] Winthrop.
[2] Clapp.
[3] Winthrop.
[4] Massachusetts Bay Records, Vol. 1, p. 108.
[5] Bradford.

Pequods, and his company, eight in all, were killed. Three of his men while on shore, hunting, were first slain; then the chief with other Indians came into the cabin, and stayed until Stone fell asleep, when they killed him with a tomahawk. The rest of the crew were in the cook's room, which the Indians entering, the powder exploded by accident. The Indians jumped overboard, but soon returned and killed those on board, took their clothes and goods, and burned the pinnace. Governor Winthrop of Massachusetts, wrote to Governor Harvey of Virginia, that the Indians should be punished, and thus began the Pequod war.[1]

In the autumn of 1633, a ship arrived at Jamestown with Edward Kingsmell and family, and a Mr. Wingate, wife, child, and forty other passengers on their way to begin a settlement in Carolana, now written Carolina, but owing to some misunderstanding they were carried to, and left in Virginia. Kingsmell instituted a suit against Samuel Vassal of London for breach of contract, and he was imprisoned for some time.

---

[1] Jonathan Brewster the son of the Plymouth leader, in 1636, had a trading post on the shores of the Connecticut River, and he wrote that it was the Pequod chief, Sassacus who killed Stone.

CHAPTER IV.

AFFAIRS OF THE COLONY FROM A.D. 1634 to A.D. 1638.

SETTLERS OF MARYLAND ARRIVE. THOMAS CORNWALLIS CHIEF COUNCILLOR, AND THREE-FOURTHS OF MARYLAND COLONISTS PROTESTANT IN FAITH. ANCESTRY OF CORNWALLIS. FIRST COMMISSIONERS FOR PLANTATIONS. WOODHOUSE ASKS TO BE GOVERNOR. ROUTE TO WESTERN OCEAN. EXPLORATION OF DELAWARE RIVER. MODE OF IMMIGRATION. SIR EDWARD VERNEY'S SON. PLANTATIONS OF MATHEWS AND MENEFIE. NOTICES OF STONER, KEMP, AND LIDCOTT. CENSUS A. D., 1635. DISPUTE WITH GOV. HARVEY. LETTER TO SIR JOHN ZOUCH. GOV. HARVEY GOES TO ENGLAND. SETTLERS NEAR PHILADELPHIA. NARRATIVE OF GOV. JOHN WEST. VISIT OF MAVERICK OF BOSTON. GOV. HARVEY'S RETURN. SERGEANT MAJOR DONNE. NORFOLK COUNTY NAMED. CAPT. THOMAS STEGG, GEORGE LUDLOW MERCHANT. BENONI BUCK THE FIRST IDIOT BORN IN VIRGINIA.

UNDER the charter granted, in 1632, to George Calvert, the first Lord Baltimore, his son and successor Cecil, helped by some friends, sent out a Colony to the Province of Maryland, in a ship and pinnace, which on the 24th of February, 1633-34, arrived at the mouth of the James River.

While Leonard Calvert, the brother of the second Lord Baltimore, was the ostensible Governor of Maryland, the leading spirit was the chief councillor Thomas Cornwallis,[1] a man of more distinguished ancestry, and an adherent of the church of England.

More than three-fourths of the first settlers of Maryland were Protestants[2] while those who adhered to the Church of Rome were "for the most part poor."

---

[1] Thomas Cornwallis, a merchant, and sheriff of London in the days of Richard the Second, was a remote ancestor of the Maryland councillor, and also of the Lord Cornwallis who surrendered to Washington at Yorktown, Virginia. The great grandfather of the Maryland councillor was Sir Thomas, knighted by Queen Mary, and builder of Browne Hall. The following pasquinades appeared in his time:

"Who built Brown Hall? Sir Thomas Cornwallis.
How did he build it? By selling of Calais."

Another was

"Sir Thomas Cornwallis what got you for Calais?
Browne Hall, Browne Hall, as large as a palace."

His tombstone is oblong, of black and white marble, and upon it is a recumbent statue with feet resting on a stag, the family crest, and on it is inscribed "Sir Thomas Cornwallis, son of Sir John, Comptroller of the Household to Queen Mary, Treasurer of Calleys, dyed 26 Dec., 1604, aged 86."

The grandfather of Thomas of Maryland was Charles, knighted by King James, and ambassador to Spain. His father was Sir William, and his mother Catherine, daughter of Sir Philip of Erwarton Suffolk. His uncle Thomas married Anna, daughter of Samuel Bevercott, the predecessor of William Brewster, who became leader of the Plymouth Colonists, as postmaster at Scrooby.

A son of the Maryland councillor, Thomas, born 1662, was Rector of Erwarton, and afterward of Bradley Parva in Suffolk, England.

A grandson of the Councillor William born in 1708, was Rector of Wenham Mag. and Chelmondester Suffolk.

A great grandson, also named William born in 1751, was Rector of Whitersham and Elam in Kent and his daughter Caroline Frances, was a talented woman, scholar and authoress, who died January 8, 1858.

[2] This fact is mentioned in a letter written by a Jesuit, to his Superior in England. The whole letter was first published in the third volume of "Records of the English Province of the Society Jesus," Burns and Oates, London. It was reprinted in this country, by the writer of this note, in Pennsylvania Historical Society Magazine, Volume V, 1881. Reference also, to it will be found in

The arrival of the Baltimore Colony to take possession of lands, already cultivated, and settled by Virginians, led to years of controversy. On the 14th of March, 1634, at a meeting of the Governor and Council of Virginia, Capt. William Claiborne, "requested the opinion of the Board how he should demean himself in respect of the Lord Baltimore's Plantations Patent, and his deputies, now seated in the Bay, for that they had signified unto Captain Claiborne, that he was now a member of their plantation, and therefore, should relinquish all relations and dependence on this Colony. It was answered, by the Board, that they wondered why there should be any such question made, that they knew no reason why they should render up the Right of that Place of the Isle of Kent more than any other formerly given to the Colony, by his Maties Patent, and that the right of my Lord's Grant being yet undetermined in England, we are bound in duty and by our Oaths to maintain the Rights and Privileges of the Colony. Nevertheless in all humble Submission to his Majestie's Pleasure we resolve to keep and observe all good Correspondency with them, no way doubting that they on their parts will intrench upon his the Interest of this, his Majestys Plantation."

Governor Harvey, in a letter to Secretary Windebank, a friend of Lord Baltimore, vividly described the situation.

"SIR: I shall put the daye wherein I did that service to my Lord Baltimore which deserved thankes from your

---

Bradley Johnson's "Foundation of Maryland" published in 1888, by Maryland Historical Society, and in Neill's "Maryland in the Beginning," Cushings and Bailey, Baltimore, 1884

Honor, into the accompt of my happie days, next unto that day wherein I was designed to doe his Majestie service in this place; and for the respect I owe to your Honor, and for the Noblenes I know to be in my Lord Baltimore and his designes I doe promise your Honor to do him, and his, all the service I am able, but I must sincerely let your Honor know that my power heere is not greate, it being limited by my Commission to the greater number of Voyces at the Councell Table, and there I have almost all against me in whatever I can propose, especially, if it concerns Maryland; and these proceedings of the Councell do so embolden others, that notwithstanding the obligation of Christianitie and his Maj^{ties} commands to be assisting to them, in their first beginning; many are so averse as that they crye and make it their familiar talk, that they would rather knock their Cattell in the heads than sell them to Maryland.

"I am sorry it is not in my power to rule these exorbitant courses, but for their present accommodation I sent unto them some Cowes of myne owne, and will do my best to procure them more, or anything else they stand in need of.

"This faction I find great cause to suspect is nourished from England, for this summer came letters to Capt. Mathewes who is the patron of disorder, as your Honor will understand by the bearer hereof, Lieutenant Evelin (and by his comportment in other matters as your Honor will find in these papers) upon the reading whereof hee threw his hatt upon the ground, scratching his head, and in a fury stamping, cryed a pox upon Maryland; many letters and secrett intelligences hee and the rest of the Councell have, especially Clayborne, and many meetings and consultations for which Letters if I had power to search and examine their Consultations, I doubt not but to find notable combinations. I have written at large of the estate of the Colonie to the Lords in generall, to which I remitt your Honor, humbly craving pardon for my brevity which is enforced by my indisposition of health at this tyme, so humbly presenting to your Honor, my best service and respects I take my leave and still will rest.

"Your Humble, very affectionate servant,
"JOHN HARVEY."
"Virginia, 16th December, 1634."

In April, 1634, the King appointed Commissioners for Plantations[1], and among other powers, were authorized to make laws, ordinances, and constitutions, to provide for the support of the clergy with the advice of two or three bishops, to remove any Governor and appoint a successor, to choose bishop's suffragan with the advice of the Archbishop of Canterbury, and to revoke any grant of land surreptitiously obtained.

Henry Woodhouse, who had been Governor of Bermuda, and served in the Isle of Rhé and Rochelle expeditions, this year, applied to be Governor of Virginia, and it was rumored that he had been appointed. A friend of Governor

---

[1] The commissioners designated in the proclamation were William Laud, Archbishop of Canterbury; Thomas, Lord Coventry, the keeper of the Great Seal; Richard Neile, Archbishop of Yorke; Richard, Earl of Portland, the High Treasurer; Henry, Earl of Manchester, keeper of Privy Seal; Thomas, Earl of Arundel, and Surrey, Marshal of England; Edward, Earl of Dorset, Chamberlain to the Queen; Francis, Lord Cottington, the Chancellor; Thomas Edmonds, Kt., Treasurer of the Household; Henry Vane, Kt., Comptroller of the Household; John Cooke Kt., Secretary; Francis Widebank, Kt., Secretary.

Winthrop of Massachusetts, wrote from London, "that there were ships and soldiers provided, and given out as carrying the new Governor, Captain Woodhouse,[1] to Virginia." In his petition, Woodhouse urged that Harvey had already served more than the usual term of three years. The appointment for some reason was delayed, and the next year the petitioner again applied.

The occupation of Quebec by the English led to information of seas to the westward, and renewed the desire to discover an inland passage to Asia, through North America. In the days of Queen Elizabeth, Apsley, a London dealer in gew-gaws and playing cards, wrote to a friend, that he expected to live long enough to see a letter in three months carried from London, to China, across the American conti-

---

[1] Woodhouse was Governor of Bermudas from 1623 to 1626. He was a member of the Virginia Assembly in 1647, and also in 1652, from Lower Norfolk.

Among the papers in Her Majestys' Public Record office, London, is the following.

"To the King's Most Excellent Matie
　　　The humble peticon of
　　　　　　　　　　　　HENRY WOODHOUSE.

Humbly sheweth that whereas your Matie hath been graciously pleased neere four yeares past to promise your Peticoner the Governor's place of Virginia the settling of wch Plantacon hath bene of suche long continuance that yor peticoner starveth with the expectation. And having lost £600 of his arrears, and £60 of yearly intertainment in Suffolk, never having received one penny for his employment on the Isle of Rey and Rochell. Captain Talbott enjoying the command of Tillbury Fort given by your Matie bee pleased to give a final end to his tedious suite.

"Hee, therefore humbly prayeth your Matie will graciously declare your pleasure, and make your peticoner enjoy the happiness of your Maties favour by giveing your warrant for the drawing of his Commission whereby your Peticoner shall avoid further troubling of your Matie who is absolutely undone without yor Maties immediate dispatch. And hee shall (as in duty ever bound) daily continue his prayers for your Maties long and most prosperous raigne."

nent, between the forty-third and forty-sixth parallels of north latitude. In the days of King Charles, one wrote: "Now all the question is only how broad the land may be at that place from the James River above the Falls, but all men conclude it to be not narrow, yet, that there is, and will be found the like rivers issuing in a South Sea or a West Sea, on the other side of these hills, as there is on this side where they run from the West, down into the East, after a course of one hundred and fifty miles, but of this certainty Mr. Henri Briggs, that most judicious and learned mathematician wrote a small tractate, and presented it, to that most noble Earl of Southampton, the Governor of the Virginia Company in England, Anno, 1623, to which I refer for full information. And by such a discovery the planters of Virginia shall gain the rich trade of the East Indies, and so cause it to be drawn through the continent of Virginia, part by land, and part by water, in a most gainful way, and safe and far less expenseful and dangerous than it now is. And yet they doubt not to find some rich and beneficial country and commodities not yet known to the world that lies west and by south now from the Plantation." Joseph Mede on Sept. 14, 1623, wrote to Sir Martin Stuteville;[1] "It is said that Capt. Button hath discovered the Hudson's passage so far, as it is supposed, he came up to the Virginian Bay."

In 1630 the bark "Warwick" arrived at the mouth of the Piscataqua River, New England, with a party sent for "discovery of the great Lake" and in 1633, Thomas Young, born in London, more than fifty years of age, petitioned

---
[1] Court and Times of Charles the First.

the King to be allowed at his own charges, to discover and search the unexplored parts of Virginia and adjacent regions, and that he would "graciously be pleased to signifie by His royall letters to all the colonies of America, and in very particular manner the Governor and Councell of Virginia, and to let them understand that he is well satisfied of the fidelitie, allegiance, loyall proceeding, and great devotion of Mr. Young, to his Majesties Service[1] and that therefore he hath employed him, together with his nephew, Mr. Robert Evelin."[2]

On the 23d of September, 1633, a special commission[3] was issued to Young, authorizing him to fit out ships, appoint officers, and make explorations without molestation from any of the colonial authorities of America. Among his assistants were a surgeon named Scott, and Alexander Baker, of St. Holborn's Parish, Middlesex, who had been confined "in regard of some questions which occurred long ago concerning conscience, but now at liberty," who was to be the cosmographer, examiner of mines and trier of metals.[4]

In April, 1634, Young wrote to Secretary Windebank, that he wished to sail as soon as possible and "that he be pleased to send for Mr. Robinson, the King's searcher at Gravesend, and to signifie to him, in his Majesties name that Mr. Young, his nephew Mr. Evelin, Mr. Baker his Cosmographer, and Mr. Scott his Phisition, have already

---

[1] Young's letter is given in full in Scull's *Evelyns in America*, pp. 55, 56.

[2] Robert Evelyn, second son of Robert of Goodstone, Surrey, and wife Susanna, daughter of Gregory Young, of London, was born about A. D. 1595.

[3] Rymer, Vol. XIX.

[4] Scull's Evelyns, p. 57.

given satisfaction to his Majestie, in swearing their allegiance, and that therefore, they are not more to be questioned in that point. * * * * Mr. Young humbly desires that some verie particular order may be given by His Majestie to my Lord Keeper for the pressing and keeping private of these articles from being seene or knowne by any. Pray, Sir, remember to ask if their be anie new Governor shortly to be made in Virginia.'"[1]

On the 16th of May, 1634, he was able to sail from Falmouth, with two vessels, but on the voyage was exposed to storms, and the larger ship became leaky. On the 4th of of July he had reached Point Comfort, and Captain Claiborne of the Isle of Kent, in a small bark, arrived about the same time and passed the night on board his ship. The next day he had an interview with Governor Harvey, and Thomas Cornwallis, the chief councillor of the new province of Maryland, and then visited Jamestown.

On the 20th of July, his ship being repaired and provisioned and shallop built, he proceeded on his exploration of the Delaware River. On the 23d of August, he reached a lesser river which fell into the Delaware, supposed to have been the Schuylkill, and remained five days trading with the Indians, and then continued his ascent, and on the 29th reached shallow water. On the 1st of September, Lieutenant Robert Evelin went up in the shallop to the Falls of the Delaware. While the Dutch at Manhattan occasionally traded with the Indians, their post, Fort Nassau, was not then occupied. In a report written from the shores

---

[1] Scull's Evelyns, p. 58.

of the Delaware River on the 20th of October, to Windebank, Secretary of State, he discloses his hope of finding a passage to the Pacific ocean. His words are: "I passed by the great river, which I mention to your Honour, with purpose to have pursued the discovery thereof till I had found the great lake, from which I am informed this great river issueth, and from thence I have particular reason to believe there doth also issue some branch, one or more, by which I might have passed into that Mediterranean Sea, which the Indian relateth to be four days journey beyond the mountains; but, having passed near fifteen leagues of the river, I was stopped from further proceeding by a ledge of rocks which crosseth the river over, so as I could not get over with my vessel, by reason of the shallowness of the water, which at high water riseth not above a foot and a half over the rocks, and at low water the rocks are discovered five or six foot deep, so that I determined against the next summer to build a vessel which I will launch above the rocks, in which I propose to go up to the lake [Lake Erie?], from whence I hope to find a way that leadeth into the Mediterranean Sea [Lake Superior?]; and from the lake, I judge, that it cannot be less than 150 or 200 leagues to the North Ocean; and from thence I propose to discover the mouths thereof, which discharge themselves both into the North and South Seas. But if I fail in arriving at the lake, which I am confident I shall not, I will then take with me out of my vessel both workmen, and provisions which shall be portable, for the building of a small vessel, which I will carry those four days journey over land, with a competent number of men, and then I propose to cut down wood, and fit up a vessel upon the banks of that sea, and from thence make my discovery."[1]

Evelin left Jamestown, with this letter about the middle of December, and during the last week of May, 1635, he sailed again for America to join his uncle Young upon "special and very important service."

The exploration of the Delaware River above the Falls appears to have been abandoned, and an attempt to reach the great inland lake was made by the Kennebec River. Maverick, in his description of New England, writes :[2] "This is a great and spreading River, and runes very neer into Canada. One Captaine Young and three men with him, in the yeare 1636, went up the River upon discovery, and only by Carying their canoes some few times, and not farr by Land came into Canada River, very neare Kebeck Fort, where by the French, Capt. Young was taken, and carried for ffrance, but his Company returned safe."

The Secretary of the Colony, under Harvey, in a report, to the King's Secretary, mentions that "of hundreds of people who arrived in the colony, scarce any but are brought in as merchandize, to make sale." Agencies were established in London, to procure servants for persons disposed to invest money in tobacco plantations. Amid the meaner sort of immigrants, occasionally landed some man of family, and education, broken in fortune and reputation, or some youth under the displeasure of parents, sent away from home. Thomas, a son of Sir Edward Verney, in 1634, fell in love with one, whom his parents did not wish

---

[1] Aspinwall Papers.

[2] First printed in *New England Hist. and Gen. Register*, January, 1885.

that he should marry, as he was only about nineteen years of age, and the girl lower in social rank. After anxious deliberation it was decided to send him to Virginia, and the mother opened a correspondence with an immigration agent who lived in Bucklesbury, Cheapward, London, a street at that time on both sides occupied by grocers, apothecaries, and dealers in small wares. His reply is worthy of preservation, as it contains the best description of the mode of procuring servants and their transportation to Virginia, at that period. He writes with the directness of one experienced in his business: "If it will please Sir Edmond and your ladyshipp to bee ruled by my aduise your sonne should haue with him iij servants, at least, which may bee had heare, at a dayes warninge; but indede I desiered if it were possible to have him bring a cooper out of the countrey, which wee cannot get soe redily here.

"Every seruant hee sends ouer will stand him in xij^{li} his passage, and apparel fit for him, with other charges. After his cumming into Virginia I doubt nott but my frends, I haue there, hee shall bee well acomodated for his owne person, and at a resonable rate, and his men maye likewise be taken off his hande, and dyated for theyre worke, for the first yeare, and with some advantage to your sonne besides; then, the next yeare, if hee shall like the country and be mynded to staye, and settel a plantation himselfe, these servants will bee seasoned, and bee enabled to direct such others as shall bee sent vnto him, from hence, hearafter; or if hee shall nott like the country then he may sell theyre tyme they haue to Serve him, vnto other men that have neede of servants, and make a good beneffitt of them, as alsoe of all such things as he shall carry with him, for ther is nothing that we carry from thence, but if it cost 20s. heare, they doe goue there for it 30s.

"Now, for his owne proper acomodation I must intreat your Ladiship that he maye bring up with him a fether bed, bolster, pillow, blanketts, rugg, and 3 payre of sheets vnless you will please they shall bee bought heare; it is but a spare horse the more to bring them up. And let not his staye be longer. If hee had come up nowe I had then bespoake for him that accommodation (in regard to the intimasie I haue with the owners of this ship) which he cannot haue in every ship, that goeth thether; for he should have layne in the greate cabbin, but I am afeared if wynde fayre for them to be gone, they will not staye past iij or iiij days longer at most. But howeeuer ther shal bee nothinge wantinge in mee to doe the best I can to get him the best acomodation I maye in some other shipp, if hee doe cum too late.

"Madam, the reason why I intreat your ladyshipp that hee may haue with him, for his own particular vse a fether bed, bolster, blanquetts, rugg, curtaynes, and vallance, is that although many howsholds in Verginia are soe well prouided as to entertayne a stranger with all thinges necessary for the belly, yet few or none better prouided for the back as yeat them to serve theyre own turnes; therefore 'tis necessary that hee bee prouided.

"Now, if it will please your ladiship that he maye haue ij men with him, I haue hear inclosed, and he might cum time enough to goe awaye in this shipp which I soe much desier hee should goe, for the good acomodation that I am suer he wold haue there.

"The charge for himself and ij men, with the provisions which is needfull for him to carry will come toe 56 li, more or less, and if you shall think fit toe lett him haue a third man, it is but xll^{li} more, and truly it is the opinion of all that I haue conferred with that it is a greate deale better for him to haue som seasoned men of his owne, when he goes to settell a plantation, than to haue all fresh men, because these men maye bee inabled to direct others that hee shall haue hereafter."[1]

In August, young Verney, with his men, barrels, and baggage[2] was received on board the good ship called the "Merchants Hope" of London, whereof was "master[3] under God, Robert Payge," then "riding at anchor in the river Thames and bound to Virginia."

In 1634, there were two planters in Virginia that were surrounded with many comforts and some of the luxuries of life. Above Newport News, at Blunt Point, was the home of Samuel Mathews, perhaps the wealthiest man in the colony. His wife was the daughter of Sir Thomas Hinton, now one of the Council in Virginia. His wife's brother William Hinton, was a gentleman of the King's Privy Chamber. Sir Thomas Hinton had married a second time

---

[1] Verney Papers, *Camden Society Publication*.

[2] His freight bill was £117 18s. 6d.

[3] Robert Page was a well known ship captain in the Virginia trade. Verney ultimately settled in the West Indies.

in 1622, the rich widow[1] of Sir Sebastian Harvey, Lord Mayor of London.

His house was comfortable, and he employed many servants. His plantation was a miniature village, flax and hemp were there woven, cattle and swine were raised for the ships outward bound, hides were tanned and leather made into shoes. His dairy was large, and poultry was abundant. He was known as one who "lived bravely, kept a good house, and was a true lover of Virginia."

A few hours sail from Blunt Point and nearer Jamestown, was the next most attractive place owned by an enterprizing merchant, George Menefie. His large garden contained the fruits of Holland, and the roses of Provence, and his orchard was planted with apple, pear, and cherry trees, and here the peach was cultivated for the first time in North America. Around the house were rosemary, thyme and majoram, favorites of that age.[2]

Four years before John Harvard bequeathed his estate to the college near Boston, which bears his name, Benjamin Symmes of Virginia, left the first legacy by a resident of the American plantations of England, for the promotion of education. By his will made Feb. 12th, 1634–5, he gave two

---

[1] See page 21.

[2] Perdita in Shakespeare's Winter's Tale, says:
"Give me those flowers there, Dorcas. Reverend Sirs
For you there's rosemary and rue, these keep
Seeming, and favour all the winter long."
In the same Act, again
"Here's flowers for you
Hot lavender, mint, savory, majoram."

hundred acres on the Poquoson, a small stream which enters the Chesapeake Bay between Yorktown and Point Comfort, "with the milk and increase of eight cows for the maintenance of a learned and honest man to keep upon the said ground a free school, for the education and instruction of the children of the adjoining parishes of Elizabeth city and Kingston, from Mary's Mount[1] downward to the Poquosen river."

A few years after his death, in a little pamphlet,[2] the author wrote: "I may not forget to tell you we have a free school, with two hundred acres of land, a fine house[3] upon it, forty milch kine, and other accommodations. The benefactor deserveth perpetual mention, Mr. Benjamin Symmes,[4] worthy to be chronicled. Other petty schools we have."

---

[1] Capt. Wollaston of "Maire Mount" now Quincy, Mass., about 1626, writes, Bradford "transports a great part of ye servants to Virginia, and goes himself." Did he settle on the shores of James River, at Mary's Mount near Elizabeth city?

[2] "A Perfect Description of Virginia," 1649.

[3] By the provisions of the will, the moneys arising from the first increase of cattle were to be used to build a school house. The profits from the subsequent sales of cattle, for the support of poor children.

[4] Benjamin Syms, written also Symmes and Simes was probably the same person, who in 1623, was living at Basse's Choice, and about 33 years of age. In 1624, at this point died a Margaret Symes. In 1629, Thomas Warnet the merchant of Jamestown, bequeathed Benjamin Symes a weeding hoe. He was evidently a honest, religious, and childless planter. In March, 1642–3, the Virginia Assembly, passed the following: "Be it enacted and confirmed, upon consideration, had of the godly disposition and good intent of Benjamin Symms deceased, in founding by his last will and testament a free school in Elizabeth county, for the incouragement of all others, in the like pious performance, that the said will and testament with all donations therein contained concerning the free school and the situation thereof in the said county, and the land appertaining to the same, shall be confirmed according to the godly intent of the said testator without any alienation or conversion thereof to any place or county."

John Stoner was sent by the King, in the autumn of 1634, to act as agent in making a contract concerning tobacco, and to be one of the Virginia Council, but died on the voyage.

In December, 1634, Richard Kemp, who had been appointed Secretary through the influence of the Earl of Pembroke, arrived, and he sent the answer of the colony to the proposition that the King should have the sole preémption of tobacco. Robert Lidcott,[1] a son of Sir John, was at this time in Virginia. He was connected with Edward Palmer,[2] the benevolent man who before 1625, projected a college and art school, to be situated on Palmer's Island in the Susquehanna near its mouth.

Francis Pott, the brother of Governor Pott, early in 1635, was removed from the command of the fort at Point Comfort, and Capt. Francis Hook, a naval officer who had been on duty with his ship upon the Irish coast, was appointed. By a census taken about February of this year[3] there were

---

[1] Sir John Lidcott was the brother-in-law of Sir Thomas Overbury, the victim of intrigue poisoned in the Tower of London. The wife of Sir Thomas Overbury, was the aunt of Edward Palmer.

[2] For a notice of Edward Palmer and proposed School of Art, see *Virginia Vetusta*, Munsell's Sons, Albany, 1885, pages, 182–184.

[3] CENSUS of A. D. 1634–5.

"*A list of the number of men, women, and children Inhabitinge in the severall counties wth in the Collony of Virginia Anno Dmi* 1634.

Imprimis from Arrowhattock to Shirley Hundred, on both sides the river, being within the Countie of Henrico. 419

Item, from Shirley hundred Iland to Weysnoake on both sides the River, being wthin the countie of Charles Citty. 511

found to be five thousand men, women and children in Virginia.

The relations between Governor Harvey and his Councillors became less pleasant every year.¹ In open court he would revile them "and tell them they were to give their attendance as assistants to advise with him," but that "the power lay in himself to dispose of all matters as his Majesty's substitute." During the month of January, he received a letter from the King, which he acknowledged and wrote that on the 20th of February he would communicate it to the General Assembly. He however, detained certain letters to the King, which had been prepared by the planters,

Item, from Upper Cheppeake Creek to Lawne's Creeke on the Southward side and from Checohominey River to Creeke on the northward side of the river, being wth in the countie of James City.	886
Item, from Lawne's Creek to Warrosquyoake Creeke on the southward side of the river, being within the Countye of Warrosquyoake.	522
Item, from Ketches [Keith's] Creeke & Mulbury Iland to Marie's Mount on the northward side of the river being wth the countie of Warrick River.	811
Item, from Maires Mount to Foxhill wth the Plantations of the Back river & the old Pocoson river on the Northward side, and from Elizabeth river to Chesepeake River on the Southward side of the river being wth in the countie of Elizabeth Citty.	859
Item, in the Plantations of Kiskyake, Yorke & the new Pocoson, being within the countie of Charles River.	510
Item, in the Plantations on the Esterlie side of Chessepeake Bay, being within the countie of Accowmack.	396
The whole number is	4,914

"After this list was brought in, there arrived a ship of Holand with 145 from the Bermudas.

"And since that 60 more in a English shipp wch likewise came from the Bermudas." *State Papers Colonial,* Vol. VIII, 35.

¹ See Appendix, for letter of Mathews, to Sir John Wolstenholm.

and a petition was presented to the Council asking some redress from the evils they suffered.

Late on the night of the 27th of April, 1635, Governor Harvey was informed that there had been a meeting at York, in the house of William Warren, which had been addressed by Francis Pott, Capt. Martin, and William English, sheriff of the county, severely commenting on the course of the Governor. The next day the speakers were arrested, brought to Jamestown and ironed. During the day Francis Pott was before the Council, and produced the paper mentioning the grievances of the Colony which he had sent on to York.

On the 29th the Council again met, and the Governor wished that those under arrest should be tried by martial law, but most of the Councillors insisted that the case belonged to the civil law.

The Governor sat in a chair with a "frowning countenance," and ordered the Councillors to be seated. He then drew a paper from his pocket, and said he was about to propose a question, and required each one, without consulting with his colleagues, to give an answer in writing.

The query was "What do you think they deserve, that have gone about, to persuade the people, from their obedience to his Majesty's substitute?" Mr. Menefie was the first Councillor addressed, who replied that he was "but a young lawyer and dare not upon the sudden deliver his opinion." William Farrar began then to make some remarks as to the unreasonableness of the request, when he was silenced, and told not to speak out of his turn. Samuel Mathews said there was no precedent for his strange course.

Others also expressed their disapproval, and after criminations and recriminations the session of the Council closed. When they again met he sternly demanded why they had procured a petition against him.

Menefie answered that a chief cause of the displeasure was his detaining certain letters that had been addressed to the King and the Lords. "Do you say so?" quickly said the Governor. "Yes." was the cool, but firm reply. Harvey angrily moving toward him struck him on the shoulder and said, " I arrest you on the suspicion of treason." Captain Utie in return, being near, said, " We, the like to you, Sir." Mathews seeing that the Governor had lost control of himself firmly placed his arms around him and said, "There is no harm intended against you, sit down in your chair, and listen to the complaints of the colonists." Harvey insisted that they had no grievances and this meeting ended.

After this, Capt. Purfury, a Councillor friendly to the Governor, wrote that he feared the people would proceed to violent measures. The Governor then held another conference with his Council, on the 30th, and his commission was read, when the Councillors who had opposed him, agreed that they would assist him, if he would conform to his Majesty's pleasure as expressed in his commission and instructions. The Council deeming it expedient, issued a call for the Burgesses to assemble and consider grievances, and adjourned for six days. A guard was left for the protection of the Governor. Three days after, he left Jamestown, "and went unto the Mills, to the house of one William Brockas, whose wife was generally suspected to have more familiarity with him than befitted a modest woman," and here dismissed his guard.

On the 7th of May, the Council and Burgesses assembled, but before they organized, Secretary Kemp exhibited a threatening letter from the Governor, received that day, to which no attention was given. The next morning, the Secretary showed the Council another letter he had received, requesting that he would secretly surrender the commission of the King appointing him Governor, which the Council had already placed for safe keeping with one of their number, George Menefie, until differences were settled. After resolving to send their statement of grievances to the King's Commissioners for Virginia in England, the Council until they heard from them, made choice of a temporary Governor, "Captain John West, an ancient inhabitant, a very honest gentleman of noble family, being brother to the Lord Laware sometime Governor of Virginia."

Sir John Zouch, one of the Commissioners for Virginia, and a friend of Mathews, in November, 1634, visited the Colony where he had a son and daughters. Governor Harvey told the Privy Council that he was "of the Puritan Sect." After remaining a few months, he and Captain Button returned to England. His son writes to his "deare and loving father" this letter now first printed.

"Sr, I perceive that if the Gov' could haue done you any dispight hee would haue pursued it to the utermost, for one of the 2 Kine shot I was to receive for you; being but a shrimpe I left at Capt. Brownes who promised to procure a letter, but was stricktly charged to retaine hir, wch command the Councell since have contradicted. The Councellors and Burgesses for the last Assembly haue fained a letter as from the Burgesses and others to the Councell complayning of their manifould aggreevances, and desiring redresse from them.

"The people of the lower parts mett in such troopes to set theire hands to the letter, that it put Capt. Purifie into an affright that caused him to write to the Govern^r of many incident dangers, insoemuch that hee durst not keepe a Courte, untill hee heard from him, or had a letter from his Matie. Hereupon the Govr sendeth warrants for the Councell who soone after they met, consulted about sending the Govr for England, but Capt. Browne went home over night, a paine that hee had in his belly excused him sufficiently by reason hee opposed him, as did the rest. Mr. Manifie did absolutely refuse his aide in arresting him alleadging reasons that it was not fitt to deale soe wth his Maties substitute; hee went not home as hee said, but to the back river where hee debated wth himselfe, desiringe of God to confirme his resolucon or abolish it, but the losse of the Country sticking in his stomacke at last hee came, resolved as the rest, when the Govern^r did arrest him of high treason for the words hee spoke against him, at Kecoughtan, you then present, but hee had no sooner given Mr. Menefie the thumpe on his shoulder, but Capt. Utay tooke him by the middle, and arrested him in his Maties name, the rest stepping and taking hould of him likewise: looking pale, as did Kempe, hee refused to goe till hee saw noe resistance, and then hee desired their leave to chuse a Deputie who though hee spoke very mildely ever since was denyed, they meete, sending him wth all that can object

120   *VIRGINIA CAROLORUM.*

ought against him, himselfe residing at little towne, the intrim, forgetting and laying aside all malice formerly between them. I neede not to bee further impertinent presuming you will bee acquainted with the cause shortlie after you haue wondered att this unlooked for coming. The Maryland men haue boorded Capt. Claiborne, taken all his trade, and trading stuffe, bound his men, and cast them into the hold, besides beating and hurting them in what manner wee are not fully acquainted wth, but I hope wee shall haue a journey to the Pacowomecke. The Countrey prayeth for you both [four words torn away] you come Governor. My sisters, and all your friends are very well who haue obleidged mee to them by infinit curticies. Soe wth my honest humble dutie I rest, desiring you to salute all my friends, as from mee."

At the time of Harvey's deposition by the Assembly, there was a ship[1] about to sail for England, and after he went aboard, Capt. Claiborne arrived from the Isle of Kent with the news of the encounter between his men and the Maryland people in the Pocomoke River, and also in another tributary of Chesapeake Bay.

A boat of Claiborne, under the command of Ratcliff Warner, called the Long Tail, in which was Charles Harney of Accomac with goods for trading with the Indians, was met " in the river of Pocomoque[2] on the Eastern Shore "

---

[1] The Dutch Captain De Vries, wrote in his journal under date of May 17, 1635, " 4 o'clock at Point Comfort, where we found a ship from London, in which was Sir John Harvey, Governor on behalf of the King of England. He was sent to England by his Council, and the people, who made a new Governor."

[2] Language of Bill presented to the Grand Jury at Saint Mary, Maryland.

by two pinnaces of the Marylanders under Councillor Thomas Cornwallis, on the twenty-third of April, and a skirmish took place, resulting in the killing of Warren and two of his party, John Bellson, and William Dawson; also one of the men of Cornwallis, William Ashmore, and an apprentice, of Saint Mary. Not far from Claiborne's Island[1] of seven hundred acres, near Hudson's River, in the harbor of Great Wighcomoco, on the 10th of May, Cornwallis met Thomas Smith, Gent. of Kent Island with Philip Tailor, Thomas Duffill, and Richard Hancock. Smith was charged with felony, and piracy, and after a long delay was sentenced to be hung.

Claiborne sent the following account of the affair to John Coke, one of the Secretaries of State.

"EVER HONOURED SIR : How unhappy is this Colony to returne to his friends and welwishers a yearlly increase of infelicities, which though they seem ever at the height, yet new addition arises by some unfortunate accident. And behold now, tumults and broyles, wrongs and oppressions perpetrated with a high hand, and not without undue courses in alteration of Government, and such violence acted as hath

---

[1] In Harrison's Memoir of Christison, published by Maryland Historical Society, referring to Peter Sharpe a physician, and member of the Society of Friends, he writes : " This Peter Sharpe is the same person from whom the island in the mouth of Great Choptank river takes the name it now very improperly bears. This island has been known by several names according as it has belonged to this or that person, but the name of the Quaker physician of Culvert has clung to it, and will ever be used to designate a little patch of earth, originally 700 acres, diminishing year by year. * * * But, if purity of designation should be allowed to govern, the proper name of this island is *Claiborne*. In the deed of Will. Sharpe, son and heir of Peter, to John Eaton, Sept. 10, 1675, it is expressly stated that this island " was formerly known by the name of *Claiborne's Island*."

shewed itself in the effusion of native bloud, undoubtedly God will make a way for his glory, through the injustice of men, and the end will be an establishment of this long languishing Colony.

"These actions here befell in a time while I at home was alsoe sett upon all sides by my cruell neighbours who have not only trampled upon all right, but contemned the express command of his Majestie under the protection whereof I deemed myself soe safe that I provided not enough against their malice, and soe perished by security, not deeming that I had such enemies or such men to deale with as would spurne at the Kings Royall commands upon them.

"The particulars I need not trouble you with, these inclosed papers and relations will be too much testimony of the misfortunes that swallow us. It seems a wonder to me that Sir John Harvey always left to himselfe without violence should not gaine a power to reestablish himself but all men were wronged, and even good and bad had forsaken him. A strange thing a Governor should so demeane himself, for my part I am ignorant of all these things, and my own brothers are weight enough to presse down my thoughts. In which I shall possess patience untill it shall please God to move his May[ties] Royall heart, and the Lords minds to relieve and support as men wronged with as greivous pressures as ever Englishmen endured at the hands of their Countrymen.

"For the future I advise as little innovation may be done as the nature of the affaires *   *   *   and that they expect redress from the means his May[tie] shall please to appoint. I desire your Candor may excuse my lynes which I desire to abreviate rather than to enlarge with the sad events of unhappy affaires rather coveting to mourne with in our own bossome,.than to transfer to the eares of others. We beseech a speedy signification of his Majesties pleasure to * * the fury of our adversaries. In the interim we put up a supplication to the King of Kings to deliver us from them. I humbly take my leave and remaine.

"Eliz. Citty   "Your most humble servant,

"23ᵈ May, 1635.   " W. CLAYBORNE."

In the same ship, with Harvey, sailed Francis Pott, and Thomas Harwood, representatives of the Assembly to present their complaints, and reasons for sending the Governor home. Upon the 14th of July the ship reached Plymouth and upon complaint to the Mayor,[1] the representatives of the Virginians were arrested, and Governor Harvey, the same day wrote to his friend, Secretary Windebank:

"RIGHT HONOURABLE: I doubt not not but that your Honor will admire at my coming, from my charge without any licence or other direction from his May⁽ᵈᵉ⁾ or the Lords. But it may please your Honor to calle to mynde howe that in my last Letter concerning the affayres of Virginia, I signified that the Assemblies being composed of a rude, ignorant, and ill-conditionede people were more lykelye to

---

[1] Plymouth officers made this report:

"John Martyne, Mayor of Plymouth, Robert Trelawny and John Clement to the Privy Council:

"Arrival that morning of Sir John Harvey, Governor of Virginia, who gave information of a late munity and rebellion in the colony. Francis Pott having been charged as a principal author and actor they have detained . . . . from some letters sealed up in a trunk from the mutineers, in charge of Thoˢ Harwood and desires to know what shall be done with Francis Pott."

effect mutinye than good lawes, and orders especially whilst the Councell gave them such examples; what I then feared, I soon after founde (but I must confess) their exorbitance, have by much exceeded my expectations; for presently after the departure of the ships (having received an information of some mutinous Assemblies,) I sent sent for the Councell as also warrants for the apprehending of the chieff mutineers, the Councell I called for theyr Advice in so dangerous a business: But I found them so farre from intending any good, that they came armed with a strength to surprise mee, and laying violent hands upon mee charged mee with Treason, for going about (as they saide) to betray theyr Forte into the hands of theyr Enemies of Marylande, telling mee I must resolve myselfe to goe presently into Englande, theare to make answer to the Countries Complaynts against mee, forthwith setting at libertie such of the mutiny menne I had caused to be layed fast in irons.

"In the next place they called an Assembly of the Burgesses, and some five days after made a new Governor, myself being yet resident in the Countrie; a large account of all theyre proceeds I shall with all convenient speed in person render unto your Honor, in the mean tyme I thought these but of Dutye.

"As also to signifie to your Honor that landing at Plimouth the 24th of the month, I have made use of the Authoritie of the Mayor of the Place to fasten upon the two persons which came in the shipp with mee; the one a person principally employed up and downe the Collonie to persuade the Inhabitants to subscribe to a cabbal of pretended grievance agaynst mee, the other, expressly sent with

Letters for the Councell and their unlawful Assemblies to their Agents and abettors in Englande. I have also used the same means to fasten upon theyr Letters which being brought to view no doubt already the malice of theyr rebellious Action's and Intentions may be discovered and it is to be feared that they intend no less then the subjection of Maryland for whilst I was aboard the ship, and readie to depart the Collonie theare arrived Capt. Claborne from the Isle of Kent with the news of a hostile encounter twixt some of his people and those of Maryland and Capt. Francis Hooke tould mee that by the relation of some of Capt. Claybornes owne companye it was they who sought out the Maryland Boates which were trading among the Indians, and twice assaulted them, and that theare were some hurt and slayne on bothe sydes, and at Captain Clabornes' request two of the Councell were dispatched for Maryland unto which, if those of Maryland condiscend not, they intend to supplant them and send them home as they have don mee, I presume Mr. Kemps' letter will more fully inform your Honor therein. After many troubles, and a wearisome passage I am bound to repose a day or two. I will hasten up to sende an account to your Honor of all matters concerning my Trust, in the mean tyme I rest.

    " Most readie to obey
     "your Honor's commands
      " JOHN HARVEY."
" Plimouth, the 14th of July, 1635."

It was not until the 11th of December, that the case of Harvey was formally discussed by the King and Privy Council.

After the letter of the Virginia Councillors and Burgesses had been read, the King thought it was necessary to send Harvey back, even if he should remain but a day, that it was "an assumption of regal power to send hither the Governor."

To the charge that he had not administered the usual oaths to all who arrived in Virginia, Harvey made a denial. He also declared that while a minister named Williams had charged that one Rabent had said it was lawful to kill a heretic, that he had not shown deference to Williams because he had married without a license, and that he had silenced White, another minister, because he had preached two years and had never exhibited any orders.

The Archbishop of Canterbury, who was present, said that no minister ought to be allowed to go on board a ship to Virginia, unless he showed orders from the Bishop of a diocese. The Governor admitted that he had retired Sir Thomas Hinton from the Council, because his language was not respectful, and that in a fight with Richard Stephens, a councillor who had insulted him, he had knocked out some of his teeth " with a cudgel."

During the summer of 1635, a number of persons under the leadership of George Holmes, went to the valley of the Delaware River, and occupied the deserted Fort Nassau, "obliquely opposite," where the city of Philadelphia was laid out, about half a century afterwards, by William Penn. Thomas Hall, one of the party, for some reason ran away from Holmes,[1] and reaching Manhattan, informed the

---

[1] Secretary Windebank on May 22, 1685, wrote to Earl of Lindsey to give every assistance to the bearer, Lieut. Robert Evelyn, about to return in th

Dutch authorities, of the design of the Virginians. A vessel was sent and they were arrested during the summer, and on the first of September, returned to Manhattan, with Holmes and fourteen or fifteen Virginians. Captain De Vries was employed to take them in his vessel to Virginia, and on the 10th of September landed at Kiquotan now Hampton, where he found twenty men in a pinnace about to sail and settle with those who had so unexpectedly returned.[1]

During the autumn of 1635, there were thirty-six ships[2] in the James River, each carrying from twenty to twenty-

---

"Plain Joan," to Capt. Young "on special and very important business."— *Sainsbury.*

[1] Thomas Hall and George Holmes became leading citizens in New Netherland. On the 23d of March, 1639, they were both living in a house belonging to Governor Von Twiller. Calling themselves tobacco planters, in November they obtained a grant of land on East River, that portion of New York City between 47th and 52d street. In 1640, Hall sells his interest to Holmes. In 1643, Hall had become one of the "Eight Men" of Manhattan or New Amsterdam, and was prominent for a quarter of a century. In 1649, Hall and Holmes bought lots in Lady Moody's settlement at Gravesend. In 1664, when the English took New Amsterdam now New York, Hall gave in his allegiance.

[2] Among the ships that sailed from London in 1635, with passengers for Virginia, were:

Names	Time.	Master.
Bona Ventura,	January,	James Ricroft.
Plain Joan,	May,	Richard Buckam.
Speedwell,	"	John Chappell.
Thomas and John,	June,	Richard Lambard.
Philip,	"	Richard Morgan.
America,	"	William Barker.
Transport,	July,	Edward Walker.
Paul,	"	Leonard Betts.
Alice,	"	Richard Orchard.
Assurance,	"	Isaac Brownell.
Primrose,	"	Capt. Douglass.
Merchants Hope,	"	Hugh Weston.

four guns awaiting cargoes of tobacco. The season was unusually sickly and fifteen captains died. During the following winter great mortality prevailed among the colonists, and as the tobacco crop had been poor, one half of the ships were obliged to leave without freight.[1]

The popular sovereignty exercised in Virginia found no favor with Charles the First; and John West, Samuel Mathews, and William Pierce were ordered to be sent for,[2] and Francis Pott was kept a close prisoner in the Fleet. During the year ending March 25, 1636, sixteen hundred immigrants settled in Virginia and twenty-one ships laden with tobacco had sailed from London, the customs of one vessel being estimated at 3334 pounds sterling. Governor West did not come to England, but in March,

Elizabeth,	August,	Christopher Browne.
Globe,	"	Jeremy Blackman.
Safety,	"	John Grant.
George,	"	John Severne
Thomas,	"	Henry Taverner.
David.	"	John Hogg.
Constance,	October,	Clement Campion.
Abraham,	"	John Barker.

[1] De Vries.

[2] The Privy Council on Dec. 22, 1635, issued the following:

"That his Maytie will be pleased to give order that Capt. John West, Samuel Mathews, and William Pearce bee sent for, into England, to answer theyre misdemeanours, they being the prime actors in the late Mutenye in Virginia.

"To give warrant to the Attorney Generall to have a newe Commission for Sir. John Harvey as shall be for his Mayties service in Virginia. The Lord Baltimore desires that Mr. Secretary Windebank will be pleased if any Petition or Question should bee made touching Maryland to gett it referred to bee examined in the Countrye, in regard noe proofe can heare be made of the truthe. But if that cannot be done, then to move the Kinge to heare itt."

1636 wrote to the Commissioners of Plantations the following account of his election :

"Wth in few days after Sir John Harvey had expressed his intent to the Counsell heere of departinge the Colonye, Wee opened his Maties Commission wherein wee found ourselves enjoyned in case of vacancye whither by death or occasioned by publiq or private affayres to elect among our number, one to supply the place, with further command eyther from his Matie or your Lord^{pps} received, wch choice made by pluralitye of voyces his Ma^{tyes} Commission expressly ratifyes.

"The Counsell with one consent were so pleased as to fasten their votes on mee to wch the peoples suffrages as willingly condiscended. Neyther was presumption the cause of soe hasty a choyce, before Sir John Harvey was out of the Capes, as it is injuriously objected by some but I hope your Honours will conceive a truer and a more direct reason necessitated it, for wee deferred the election untill the last day, and houre of the Counsell's sitting after wch tyme it was impossible to effect it wth a full conformitye to his Ma^{tyes} commission, and reserving our duetie of informaçon to your Lo^{pps}, the dwellings of some of the Counsell being remote, one hundred miles from the other of them, and from the place of the shipps ridinge, that one ship being the last of that yeare left in the river, soe that onles we had then made our choyce we could not for want of the full number of the Counsell haue daly preferred it, neyther could we have given y^{or} Lor^{pps} a satisfaction that we had still preserved the old forme of Governm^t prescribed by his Ma^{tye} which we are resolved soe punctually to observe that (as formerly we have engaged ourselves to y^or Lor^pps) we shall not until further instruction swerve from thence, though but in things indifferent. If by y^or Lor^pps favourable mediation it shall please his Ma^tye to confirme the act of the countrye, I shall to my uttmost expresse myself a faythfull and zealous servant, or otherwise wth as devoted a submission be ready to give up my charge where his M^tye shall place it.

"Y^or Lor^pps may please to be informed that the Colonie hath this yeare received an increase of one thousand six hundred and six persons, but I find with all that muche imputation indeservedly lyeth upon the Countrye, by the Merchants crime whoe soe pester their shipps wth passengers, that though throng and noysomeness they bring noe lesse than infection among us wch is soe easily to be distinguished from any cause in the malignitie of the clymate, that where the most pestered shipps vent their passengers they carry wth them almost a general mortallitye wch my ductye therefor prefers to y^or Lor^pp serious consideracon. Without infringing his Ma^tyes Grant to the Lord Baltimore we have taken the nearest course for avoiding of further unnaturall broiles between them of Maryland, and those of the Isle of Kent, as we find those of Maryland in o^r limits we bind them in deep bondes to keep the Kinges peace towards those of the Isle of Kent, as also Capt. Clayborne the Commander of the Isle of Kent, to those of Maryland. As further cause shall require your Honours shall receive an accompt."[1]

---

[1] This letter was dated "Point Comfort, this 28th of March, 1636," and it was received on the 19th of June, at Hampton Court.

Mathews, Menefie, and Peirce went to England to answer the charges against them, and remained several months.

Samuel Maverick of Massachusetts, passed about a year in Virginia while Harvey was absent, and in October, 1636, returned to Boston with two pinnaces, and brought fourteen heifers and eighty goats. Owing to a drought there had been a failure in the crop, and corn in Virginia this year, sold at 20 shillings a bushel, and most of the people had been obliged to live on purslane and other plants. One of his pinnaces, of about forty tons, was built of cedar at Barbadoes, and was brought to Virginia by Captain Powell, who died, and was bought for a small sum.

He interested men of science in Boston, by his narrative, as to the geology of the James River, and mentioned that there was a place about sixty miles above its mouth where the ground was full of shells and bones, and that he had seen a whale bone, but probably that of a mastodon, which had been found while digging a well, eighteen feet below the surface.

Jerome Hawley, a friend of Harvey, who had been one of the gentlemen sewers to Queen Henrietta Maria, and a councillor of the Maryland Province, arrived in March, 1637, in the "Friendship" and not long after was commissioned by the King as Treasurer for Virginia, provided he took the oath of allegiance and supremacy, and also councillor with the authority to collect 12 pence annual rent due on each fifty acres, which had not been collected since the dissolution of the Virginia Company.[1]

---

[1] Jerome Hawley was a brother of Henry, for so many years Governor of Barbadoes, and of William, the signer in 1650, of the Protestant Declaration in Maryland.

This year there was recommended to the King as members of the Council, John Sibsie,[1] Richard Townsend, Robert Evelyn,[2] and Christopher Wormeley. Wormeley had gone in 1631, to Association or Tortuga Island, and, while acting as Governor owing to his negligence the Spaniards seized it, and he, making his escape, arrived in 1635, in Virginia, about the time that Governor Harvey sailed for England.

Captain Walter Neale, who had been an officer of the army, in 1630 arrived at Piscataqua, New Hampshire, to seek for a great lake toward the west, but in three years returned to London, when at the request of the King he was chosen Captain of the Artillery Company of the city. After carefully drilling the company for four years, he applied to be Sergeant Major of Virginia; but George Donne, now thirty-two years old,[3] obtained the appointment.

Donne was the second son of the celebrated divine, John Donne, Dean of Saint Paul Cathedral, London, and led an eventful life. He had been associated with Sir Thomas Warner, in the settlement of the Isle of Saint Christopher, in the 17th degree of north latitude, and when the Spaniards under Don Frederic de Toledo captured the place, Donne was carried as hostage to Madrid, where he remained for a long time. In a letter written from London, on the 6th of

---

[1] John Sybsie or Sibsie was probably the same person who had made trouble in the Massachusetts Colony. John Sipsey was a delegate in September, 1632, to the House of Burgesses from the upper precinct Elizabeth City.

[2] Robert Evelyn came in 1634, with Capt. Young the explorer, visited England, returned in 1637, as Surveyor General with the rank of Lieutenant, in place of Gabriel Hawley, deceased.

[3] Baptized May 9, 1605, in Parish Church, Camberwell, Surrey.

December, 1633, to Wentworth, Lord Lieutenant of Ireland, are these words: "George Donne hath broken prison, and is come into England, My Lord of Carlile was so slow in getting him off, that he was constrained to take this course, to corrupt his keepers, and get away."

Governor Harvey, on the 18th of January, 1636-7, read his new commission in the church of Elizabeth City, and called an Assembly to meet on 20th of the next month, at Jamestown. His chief councillors were Secretary Richard Kemp, Sergeant Major George Donne, Thomas Purifye,[1] Henry Browne,[2] John Hobson,[3] Adam Thoroughgood,[4]

---

[1] Purifye came in 1623, settled at Elizabeth City, and at this time was about 55 years old. Capt. Thomas Young the explorer of the Delaware River, and a friend of Harvey, in a letter to Sir Toby Mathew, dated July 13, 1634, wrote that the Governor had incurred the "extreme hazard and malice from all the rest of the country, to whom I can find only two of his Council indifferent; the one of them Captain Purfree, a soldier, and a man of open heart, honest and free, hating for aught I can perceive all kind of dissimulations and baseness; the other an honest and plain man, but of small capacity and less power."

[2] Henry Brown or Browne was the man referred to in the last sentence of the above foot note. On July 14, 1637, he entered 2250 acres in James City County, and in November, 1643, 2459 acres.

[3] John Hobson, with Nathaniel Basse and others, was associated with Christopher Lawne in establishing the Isle of Wight plantation. He returned from a visit to England, in the summer of 1637, in the ship "Unity," Capt. William Upton.

[4] Adam Thoroughgood when a boy, in 1621, came in the ship "Charles," and in 1625, was a servant of Edward Waters, who remained in Bermudas for several years after the wreck in 1609 of the "Sea Venture" and then migrated to Elizabeth City. In 1626, he bought of John Gundry of Kiquotan, now Hampton, 152 acres, adjoining land of William Capps and William Claiborne, in Elizabeth City County. In 1629, 1630, and 1632, he was a member of the House of Burgesses, and a member of the Monthly Court. He moved to Lynn Haven in Lower Norfolk, and on June 20, 1635, a patent was issued to him of 5350 acres, and on the 18th of December, a patent for 600 acres, and on February 8, 1637, a patent for 200 acres, all these lying on Chesapeake Bay, fronting northerly, and on Lynn Haven River. During the year 1637, he was the President of the Court of Lower Nor-

William Brocas[1], and Francis Hooke.[2]

About this time George Menefie returned from England with many servants and soon regained his influence.

The Earl Arundel and Surrey[3] being one of the Commissioners of Plantations, on the 18th of April, 1637, his son

---

folk. His will was dated February 17, 1639-40, and probated April 27, 1640. Among other items is this : " My will and desire is that my beloved friend Captain Thomas Willoughbie, and Mr. Henry Seawell here in Virginia, and my dearly beloved brother Sir John Thoroughgood, of Kensington, near London, and Mr. Alexander Harris, my wife's uncle living on Tower Hill, shall be overseers of this my last will and testament."

John Thoroughgood was knighted, about the 1630, had been Secretary of the Earl of Pembroke, and in the service of the Duke of Buckingham. The widow of Adam Thoroughgood married Captain John Gookin of Nansemond, a member of the Assembly of 1639, and probably a relation of Daniel Gookin who in 1642, was the presiding officer of the court of Upper Norfolk. John Gookin died, and on the 22d of November, 1643, letters of administration were granted to Mrs. Sarah Gookin, on the estate of her husband. At a General Court held at Jamestown, October 8, 1644, the following judgment was rendered : " Whereas, it appeareth to the Court by the confession of James Lopham, that he hath in a most beastial and uncivil manner, by most scandalous and false suggestions, defamed Sarah, the daughter of Captain Adam Thoroughgood, deceased, to her great disparagement and defamation.

" It is therefore ordered, that the said Lopham shall receive fifty lashes, at the mulberry tree, well applied to his naked back, and stand committed till he put in security for his good behavior."

" Whereas it appeareth to the Court, that John Farnehough hath in a most scandalous manner defamed the daughter of Mrs Gookin, to her discredit though most vilely and falsely suggested.

" It is therefore ordered, that the said Farnehough shall publicly in the parish church of Lynn Haven, in the time of divine service, ask the said Mrs. Gookin, and her children's forgiveness, put in security for good behavior, and pay unto the said Mrs. Gookin eight hundred and fifteen pounds of tobacco, for her charges herein expended."

[1] William Brocas in 1649, had a fine vineyard, and in the *Perfect Description of Virginia* he is mentioned as having been a " great traveler."

[2] The successor of Francis Pott in charge of fort at Pt. Comfort.

[3] Thomas Howard, Earl Arundel and Surry born July 7, 1592, was the seventh in descent from John Howard, Duke of Norfolk. In 1616, he conformed to the

Henry, Lord Maltravers, obtained a grant of land north of James River, with the order, that it should be known as Norfolk County.

On the 22d of January, 1638, the Governor and Council of Virginia did assign[1] to Henry, Lord Maltravers, his heirs, and assigns, the territory on the south side of James River, on a tributary to be called "Maltravers River toward the head of ye s'd Nanzimum, als Maltravers being bounded from that point of Nanzimum als Maltravers River where it divides itself into branches, one degree in longitude on either side of the River, and in latitude to the height of 35 degrees Northerly Latitude, by ye name and appellation of ye County of Norfolk."

Among the principal traders now in Virginia, was Thomas Stegge, also written Stegg and Stagg. His daughter was the wife of John Byrd, a goldsmith of London, and the mother of William Byrd, the founder of the family of that name in Virginia. He was a correspondent of Mathew Cradock[2] one of the founders of the Massachusetts Colony, residing in London.

Church of England, and on Christmas day received the communion. Sir Horace Vere on January 8, 1616–17, wrote to Sir Thomas Roe: "The Earl Arundel has received the sacrament with his Majesty, and talks sharply against the Papists." He was on August 29, 1621, made Earl Marshal of England. His latter years were passed in traveling, and in 1646, he died at Padua. He was described as one who "was a Protestant but no bigot or Puritan," and was a patron of scholars, painters, and sculptors. The celebrated Arundel Marbles of the University of Oxford were a part of his valuable collection. His son Henry Frederick, Lord Maltravers, succeeded to the Earldom, and died in 1652, at his house in Arundel Street, London.

[1] A full copy of the indenture is in the Appendix

[2] The following letter from Cradock to John Jolifie, dated Feb. 21, 1636–7, is in the *Winthrop Papers*, Mass. Hist. Soc. Col. 4 s Vol. 6.

Among the other merchants of note at this time, were John Chew, Thomas Burbage and George Ludlow. Ludlow, in 1630, at the same time as Samuel Maverick and Edward Gibbons, had applied to be admitted as a freeman of the Massachusetts Colony. When Roger Williams, the great divine, came to America, he sold to Ludlow the better clothes of himself and wife, as they were not needed, and Ludlow moved to Virginia without making payment, and "telling many falsehoods." On the 15th of July, 1637, Williams wrote to Governor Winthrop of Massachusetts, concerning his "vagrant debtor from whom he had much suffered."[1] The next year when Ludlow was on a visit to Boston, he told Winthrop that he would send Williams eight hundred pounds of tobacco, but afterwards failed to keep his promise.[2] His plantation in Virginia, was situated near the York River, adjoining that of Ralph Wormeley.

"ffayle not to send the shipp "Rebecka" victualled for three monthes to Virginea to Mr. Thomas Steggs, with some commodditty such as you vnderstand to be there most vendable, for valleue of 120l or 150l at most. Leaue the Ship wholey to Mr. Tho. Steggs disposing & if he send ought, back in her, to you & Rich. Hoare (for so is our advise) ffolowe his order therewith & with the shipp as neare you can. I wish Mr. John Hodges * * * command & goe Master in her & that he obserue Mr. Stegg's order in further ymployment. She is to be victualled, for three months & to haue all her ordynance belonging to her with other necessaries whereof; all I desire is an Inventory may be sent me & the Master's hand to it."

[1] On the 12th of September, 1637, he writes again: "It is now an old debt, especially my cows left behind four years ago, for me in Virginia and some goats."

[2] Williams on Dec. 30, 1638, wrote to Gov. Winthrop: "I am bold to request a little helpe and I hope the last concerning my old and bad debtour about whom I had formerly troubled your Worship, Mr. George Ludlow. I heare of a pinnace to put in to Newport, bound for Virginia, and I understand that if you please to testifie that you remember in the case, I may have some hope at least to get something. You were pleased, after dealing with him, in Boston, to certifie me that he had promised 800 li of tobacco."

By a statute enacted in the days of Queen Elizabeth, the monarch was the custodian of all born fools, and the courts decided that an idiot or natural fool, was a child who could not count to twenty, rightly name the days of the week, or measure a yard of cloth. The first idiot born in Virginia was the son of Richard Buck, the early minister of the Colony, who came to Virginia, in 1610, with Sir Thomas Gates and who had been commended by Bishop Ravis of London, a prelate of mildness and liberality. He was born in 1616, and appropriately christened Benoni, a child of sorrow. Ambrose Harman, who had been his guardian for thirteen years, in 1637, sent a petition to England relative to his estate, which was referred to the Court of Wards, but before judicial action was had in the case, the poor boy died.

The year after Buck's arrival in the Colony, in 1611, his wife had a daughter born during a period of great want and she was in remembrance of the language of Naomi, in the book of Ruth, named Mara; three years later a son was born and baptized as Gershom, a stranger in a strange land. After the birth of Benoni another son was born, to whom was given the name of Peleg. Both parents before the year 1624, had died.

The first grant of land Ludlow obtained was Aug. 31, 1638, in the Puritan district, the upper county of New Norfolk, and amounted to 500 acres. Subsequently he entered other lands.

July 26, 1646, in York County, 1947 acres.
March 14, 1646-7, in York County, 1452 acres.
Oct. 18, 1650, in Northumberland County, 1000 acres.
Mc'h 10, 1652-3, in Gloucester, 2000 acres.
October 10, 1653, in Northumberland, 1000 acres.
October 25, 1652, in Gloucester, 2000 acres.
October, 1654, in Piankatanck Neck 186 acres.
May 12, 1661, South side of Rappahanock, 1000 acres.

CHAPTER V.

PRINCIPAL OCCURRENCES FROM A.D. 1638 TO A. D., 1642.

LEGISLATURE OF 1637-8. RICHARD MORISON IN COMMAND AT POINT COMFORT. LETTER OF TREASURER HAWLEY. SWEDISH VESSEL ARRIVES. NOTICE OF HAWLEY. PANTON, A CLERGYMAN, BANISHED. EATON OF HARVARD COLLEGE FLEES TO THE COLONY. FIRST BRICK CHURCH COMMENCED. GOV. WYATT REAPPOINTED. ROGER WINGATE, TREASURER. DONNE'S ESSAY ON VIRGINIA. CRITICISM OF NEW ENGLAND PURITANS. DONNE'S PETITION. PANTON'S COMPLAINT TO HOUSE OF COMMONS. ROBERT EVELIN SURVEYOR OF VIRGINIA, AND WRITES UPON NEW ALBION.

LEGISLATIVE assembly was convened on the 20th of March, 1637-8, and remained in session a month. The burgesses as the representatives of the people expressed their disapprobation of the duty on tobacco, and petitioned the King for free trade. The fort which had been erected during the first years of Harvey's administration, situated at Point Comfort and mounted with eight pieces of ordinance, was ordered to be repaired. Until this time the meetings of the Council for the want of a better place was held at the Governor's residence, and he was

obliged to entertain them. To remedy this the Assembly also resolved to build a house for state purposes, and George Menefie was appointed the agent of the Colony to go to England, and sell tobacco to obtain moneys and also to employ suitable workmen.

Richard Morison[1] the brother of Francis, afterwards Governor, on the 29th of March, 1638, was appointed by the King, to succeed Francis Hooke, deceased, as commander of the fort. The Colonists now demurred to the fee of sixpence charged by the commander for registering each immigrant, and administering the oath of allegiance and supremacy; but the Commissioners for Plantations declined to relieve them of this tax.

In the spring of 1638, the sloop Griffin from Sweden touched at Jamestown, Jerome Hawley, the Colonial Treasurer, wrote to Windebank, Secretary of the King: " Uppon the 20th of March last, I took the bouldness to p'sent you wth my letters wherein I gave only a tuch of the business of our Assembly, referring y^{or} Hon^{or} to the general letters sent by Mr. Kemp from the govern^{r} and Councell. Since wch tyme heare arrived a Dutch shipp' wth comission from the

---

[1] In Rymer's Foedera Vol XX, p. 306, is the following:

"Rex, vicesino nono die Martii concedit Richardo Morison, Armigero, officium Capitanei sive Custodis castri sive Propugnaculi de Point Comfort infra Dominium de Virginia, durante bene placits in reversione."

[2] A Swedish Dutch company, in 1637, was organized to trade on the banks of the Delaware River. An expedition under Minuits late in the fall sailed from Gottenberg in a large ship of war Kalmar Nyckel (Key of Kalmar) and in the sloop Gripen (Griffin.) During March, 1638, the Swedes had reached their destination, and it is supposed that the sloop Griffin came to Jamestown from the Delaware River.

young Queene of Sweaden, and signed by eight of the Chief Lords of Sweden, the coppe whereof I would have taken to send to yo' Hono' but the Captayne would not p'mitt me to take any coppe thereof, except hee might have free trade for tobacco to carry to Sweaden, wch being contrary to his Ma^ts instructions, the Govern' excused himself thereof.

"The shipp remayned heare about 10 days to refresh wth wood and water, during wch tyme the M^r. of the said shipp made knowne that both himself and another shipp of his company were bound for Delaware Baye wch is the confines of Virginia and New England, and there they p'tend to make a plantation, and to plant tobacco, wch the Dutch do allso already in Hudson's River, wch is the very next river, northard from Delaware Baye. All wch being his Ma^ts territorys I humbly conceive it may be done by his Ma^ts subjects of these parts, making use only of some English ships that resort heather for trade yearly, and be no charge at all to His Ma^te.

"I am not able yet to give your Honour so good an accompt of the estate of his Majesties revenewe heare as I desire in regard it was late in the yeare before I arrived and the business of our Assembly hathe taken up all my tyme hitherto, but by the next returne of shipping I shall endeavor to bring things into better order than heretofore they have bein, and by that tyme I hoape to make it appeare that your Honour, hath done his Majestie service in giving him notice of the estate of his reveneue in those parts; which although I cannot now say it will be great, yet I presume it is so farr considerable as that his Matie will not think it fitt to be lost; for I doubt not but it will serve to defray the pension which his Matie is pleased to allow the Governour yearly, which is £1000 per annum, yf his Majestie be pleased to imploy itt that waye, and I hoape to improve it dayly, as new comers do encrease the plantation, besides his Majesties customes from hence wil-be much better understood, than heretofore they have bein.

"Since my comeing to the place of Treasurer, I have decerned some underhand oppositions made against me, but littell hathe appeared in publick, therefore I can not particularly laye it to any man's charge. And because I finde that it chiefly aimed at the hindering me in making any benefitte of my place (whereof I assure your Honour I have not yet made the value of five pounds toward my charges.) I doe therefore make it my humble sute unto your Honour that you wilbe pleased to move the King in my behalfe, and procure His Majesties warrant for my fees, to the effect of this I send enclosed, which being added to your former favours, will much encrease my obligations to your Honour, and I shall still remayne, Your Honours much devoted servant."[1]

Jerome Hawley, and Thomas Cornwallis, were the two councillors of the Maryland Colony, which in 1634, had settled at Saint Mary. Hawley returned to England in the summer of 1635, and came back to Virginia, early in 1638, as Colonial Treasurer, an office which had not been filled since the dissolution of the Virginia Company. He soon

---

[1] Secretary Kemp wrote from Jamestown, February 26, 1637-8: "George Menefie has arrived with a great many servants but Hawley is away in Maryland."

visited Maryland where he had large interests, and was present at a meeting of the Legislative assembly on February 8th, 1637-8, at Saint Mary.

George Reade wrote from Jamestown on the 26th of February, to his brother Robert, a clerk of Secretary Windebank: "Mr. Hawley has not proven the man he took him for, having never given satisfaction for money received of him, nor brought him any servants."

Hawley, then in Jamestown, on May 17th, wrote to Robert Reade, of London, to excuse his delinquency, and urged that his brother lives in the Governor's house, and wants for nothing." In less than three months after this note was written, Hawley died deeply in debt to Cornwallis and Lord Baltimore.[1]

Upon the solicitation of the merchant George Menefie, Anthony Panton became rector in the new plantations of York and Cheskiack.[2] Richard Kemp, Secretary of the Colony in 1639, acting as accuser and judge, charged the minister with having called him "a jackanapes," and say-

---

[1] Jerome Hawley was the brother of James Hawley of Brentford, Middlesex, England, of Henry Hawley, long Governor or Councillor of Barbadoes, and of William Hawley, who came from Barbadoes to Maryland after the death of Jerome, and in 1650, was one of the signers of the Protestant Declaration.

On the 14th of August, 1638, the Maryland authorities appointed Thomas Cornwallis, as the administrator of Jerome Hawley, "late of St. Maries." Five pounds were paid to the surgeon who attended him, three pounds for mourning clothes, and five pounds for funeral expenses.

[2] Some times called Cheese Cake, "Kiskynke" or Cheskinck, by the Legislative assembly of January, 1639-40, was recognized as a parish situated between Williamsburg and York. In 1642, it became Hampton Parish, afterwards known as York Hampton.

ing, that he was "unfit for the place of Secretary," that his hair-lock was "tied up with ribbon as old as Pauls," also complained that he had spoken slightingly of Lord Archbishop of Canterbury, and Harvey banished him from the Colony "for mutinous, rebellious, and riotous actions."

The person selected to superintend the building of the school at Cambridge endowed by Harvard, and to be its first head, was the brother of the pure and high minded Governor of the New Haven Colony, but, Nathaniel Eaton proved the widest contrast, and a mortification to his relatives. For barbarously beating his usher Briscoe, on a Sabbath morning, with a walnut cudgel "big enough to have killed a horse" and for giving the scholars of Harvard fare not equal to that, which Dickens has described, as the diet at Dotheboys Hall, such as half-cleansed mackerel, and "goats' dung in the hasty pudding" he was fined and debarred from teaching in the Massachusetts Colony.

Cotton Mather, with some Attic wit, wrote: "he was a blade who marvellously deceived the expectations of good men concerning him, for he was one fitter to be a master of a Bridewell, than a college. He was a *rare* scholar himself, and he made many more such, but their education truly was in the school of Tyrannus." Dishonest in his dealings he fled from Cambridge, and Endecott, a deputy, wrote to Governor Winthrop, on the 10th of October, 1639, inquiring whether it was "not needful to send after him where hee is gone in Nele's bark to Virginia, * * * If you think meete to send him back, * * * Mr. Younge his shipp is like to staye these two or three dayes yet, who is bound for Virginea." It was not thought expedient to bring him back. His good wife and children sailed to meet him, but the ship and all on board were lost.

About this time, Winthrop mentions that Thomas Graves, a member of the Dorchester church, "and a very understanding man," contrary to the advice of his friends determined to go to Virginia to live. The climate proved unfavorable, and soon he and his whole family, with the exception of a daughter, died. As she was left with a good estate, the renegade Eaton married her, and spent her patrimony in riotous living, and then, about the year 1646, deserted her, and went back to England.

It was not till the year 1639, that any solid buildings[1] were erected at Jamestown. An impetus had resulted from a law passed, the year before, giving a portion of land, in the town, to any one who would build a house. During the year twelve houses and stores were erected, one of which was of brick, belonging to Secretary Kemp, "the fairest ever known in the country for substance and uniformity." Heretofore the places of worship had been barn-like structures framed of wood, but now the first brick[2] church in Virginia, was commenced. The raising of silk worms received more attention, and the Governor sent to the King, a quantity of silk.

---

[1] Secretary Kemp, on April 6, 1638, wrote that people began to think about good buildings, "scarce any but hath his garden and orchard."

[2] Lord Delaware in 1610, completed a rude wooden church at Jamestown, 24×60 ft. in dimensions which soon decayed.

In 1619, there was a wooden church 20×50 ft. built at the expense of the people of Jamestown.

The foundations of the brick church of 1639, were 28×56 ft. which were visible a few years ago. The present dilapidated church so often sketched is a later and larger edifice, and should not be called the church of the first settlers.

It was not until the autumn of 1639, that Sir Francis Wyatt arrived at Jamestown as the successor of Governor Harvey. By the influence of Lord Baltimore and Secretary of State Windebank, Kemp was retained as Secretary of the Colony. Of the hundreds of white people who now arrived in the ships, Secretary Kemp wrote that "scarce any, but are brought in as merchandise to make sale of." Under Wyatt's commission there was a concession, by which, when, there was a vacancy in the Council, it could be filled, by the majority of the votes of the remaining councillors. Among the earliest acts of the Governor was a strict inspection of tobacco, and the burning of all below a certain grade. He wrote: "Though the physic seems sharp, yet I hope it will bring the body of the colony to a sounder constitution of health than it ever yet enjoyed before."

At an Assembly which convened on January 6th, 1639-40, there was legislation which showed an improving condition. Hitherto an inn-keeper was authorized to charge eighteen pence, or six pounds of tobacco for a meal, but it was then enacted, that "on account of plenty provisions" only twelve pence should be the price. Ministers of the Gospel were allowed ten pounds of tobacco per poll, each to pay the clerk, and sexton; the Muster Master General three pounds per poll, the Captain of the Fort and Point Comfort was allowed ten guards, and three pounds of tobacco per poll. A levy of two pounds per poll was made for a new fort, and also two pounds per poll to build a state house. Cattle had so increased, that it was made lawful to export to New England, the seventh head of neat cattle. Benjamin Harrison, who had been clerk of the Council for some years, was allowed £7, 10s. for his services. The boundaries of the Isle of Wight, Upper, and Lower Norfolk counties were defined, and the parish of Lawne's Creek was created. The first minister in Norfolk County is said to have arrived about this time, named John Wilson.

Roger Wingate was appointed by the King, Treasurer in the place of Jerome Hawley, deceased.

On the 10th of August, 1639, the case of Panton was referred to the new Governor Wyatt, about to sail for Virginia, and the Council there, and his sentence suspended, and Governor Harvey ordered to deliver up his estate. It was further ordered, that if upon examination he should be found innocent, he should be restored to the rectorship of York and Chiskiack.

Secretary Kemp, and Sergeant Major Donne, were in England the early part of the year 1640, in the interest of Governor Harvey, and the latter addressed a labored treatise to Charles the First, entitled "Virginia Reviewed," which is still preserved among the Harleian Manuscripts of the British Museum.

After mentioning that a settled government in Virginia was just beginning, and "that till of very late, every man's own particular profit hath been the most earnestly pursued" he continues "How this assercon findes warrant is evident by the late action of some pticulers, fiery and head strong in their disorders and conspiracy against yor Maj^{ties} commissioned Governo^r, at this present, in that Country, of whose condition an officer neither I nor any und^r y^{or} sacred authority can, if justly, but speack honorablie, he being according to his place ready to accompt, able to justifie, discreet to mannage every circumstance of his proceedings, in that deputation, as in y^or roiall presence, at the Councell table y^or Maj^tie with y^or Lords allowed.[1]

"But in this poynt I will content my satisfaction, with a calmness of silence, by reason that if any Tempest threaten the Delinquents to y^or Maj^ties High Court of Starre Chamber, is the power of qualification by y^or gracious mercy referred.

"From the convenience (most likely) of some former Govr their easinesse of nature, or uncertainty of appeals (the Plantation then wholly depending on the wills and counsails of Men and Trade,) hath this enormity drawn p'sump on. Out of such p'sumpc̄on (we doubt long in plotting though lately practised) during the licence of this aristocracie, those of that councell have used to eye authority, and to dispute power with their Govern^or whom certainly they always find readie to assent with them, rather looking after their own thrift, than the dignity of their trust, or els the successe of their discrec̄ons was more fortunate than their fortunes.

"Cases in descases of desperate quallitye are not allwaies lenative, for had this insolence bene passed over, the defects of this colonie, had still lyen asleep, untill a second sudden mischance, I might say, a mischiefe, had for ever disheartened a third attempt of Peopling it, casting a dishono^r upon our Nation, lessning and diminishing yor possession, cutting of a greater number of yor subjects, had it not apparently bene proved that it is better to dye, noblie

---

[1] See page 126.

mayntencing the justice of hono‍ʳ, the honoʳ of justice, than to comply with a multitude whose policy is gayne, whose gravitye is giddinesse, whose discretion is noyse and tumult."

After several pages devoted to the condition of Virginia, he writes the following sharp criticism of New England.

"On the Northern part of the Virginian Continent lieth New England. In that Countrye it is a question undecided though yoʳ Majᵗⁱᵉˢ hath a firm interest whether the Inhabitants acknowledge you their King, or whether they by yoʳ Majesty are worthy to be acknowledged subjects.

"New England it is styled, supposed in the same Latitude wᵗʰ Nova Albion, whose discoverer was Sir Francis Drake * * * * Much available for comfort, for assistance (if occasion should bee) might such a complantation prove, were not the people themselves in their manners and lives both infectious and pestilent. They, in religion, their country, in its Barronnesse and not unequallie fruitfull. So heartily they hate conformity that they detest order, ambitious of a new Creation of ridiculous novelty, most ridiculous schisme by Sepačon. They are in a manner desprate Enthusiasticks, for whereas all men are moved (as a heathen noted) by Religion, the p'swasion whereof is the chief in pollicy, a good historian granteth, these Fanaticks choose, rather without pollicy or religion, to be misled by their lay elders, than be guided by the true Pastors of their selves, or governed by their naturall Soveraigne.

"Allmost, it exceeds a wonder howe manye of faire quallitye alien and sell their whole estates in their Old age to shuffle themselves, Wives, and Children, into their New England Blind zeale, and more blinde Seaducers doe so gull and cheat their consciences, that willingly they make exchange of their Reason, and knowledge for credulous simplicitye, willfull Ignorance. The antick prancks, the strange unheard of Vanityes which are constantly brought for Newes, that these men in New England doe, and studdy to doe, gives more and more as much occasion of pitty as of laughter.

"Dissembled Sanctity is a double Iniquity sayd the Proverbial speech, verefyed in these seperatists of New England, all pretend, none professe Religion as they ought. * * * * * What a Comonwealth amongst such Precisians is likely to flourish where zeale is preposteroous, Cruelty in Justice, Confusion in Law, is not difficult to be resolved. A Colony there can be none; it were dishon' to the name so to entitle it, a Plantation not to be expected, the people themselves so slouthfull that had not Virginia lately supplyed and relieved them their Calamitye had beene remedilesse."[1]

While in England Donne presented the following petition to the King.

"That y^{or} Pet^r goeing over wth Sir John Harvey Govr for yor Matie in the Province of Virginia was by him recommended to yor Matie who was graciously pleased to appoint him for one of his Councells, when following yor Maties orders and directions by yor letters in speedy appointing a Muster Mas-

---

[1] A full abstract of Donne's essay, is given in the Appendix.

ter General & Marshall by choyce both of Sir John Harvey & the rest of the Councell then, yor pet^r was thought well fitt to execute the aforesaid places, and soe did, untill the Govr & Counsell employed him as Agent for the Collonye to prosecute a suite against those persons y^t were lately seditious and disturb'd the peaceable Government & were by yor Royall commands sent to answeare theyre contempt & misdemeanor which service to his power he has effected & is now returninge to his charge.

"May it therefore please yor Royall Matie to give order that yor humble pet^r may have a confirmacōn under ye Great Seale of ye foresaide places of Muster Master Generall and Marshall whereof theis two yeares y^or Pet^r hath been possest and executed without excepcōn."

The dispute begun in Virginia between Anthony Panton, clergyman, and Secretary Kemp, was continued in England, and on the 30th of October, 1641, the following was presented to the Privy Council and the House of Commons. "Anthony Panton, clerk, Minister of God's word in Virginia, and agent for the Colony and clergy complaineth of the conduct of Sir John Harvie late Governor, of Mr. Richard Kempe the Secretary, of Captain Wormeley late commander of Charles County, and others, at whose hands the colonists have suffered many arbitary and illegal proceedings in judgment, tyranny, extortion, and most cruel oppression which have extended to unjust whippings, cutting of ears, fining and confiscation of honest mens' goods, converting fines to their own profit and use, supporting Popery, and in many other ways."

The petition further mentioned that Kemp privately ran out of Virginia[1] carrying the charter and records, and that he and his associates had slandered Governor Wyatt, and "obtained surreptitiously a new Governor, and a new charter without any just cause shown against the former Governor [Wyatt] who has only exercised his authority for a year and a half," he prayed for the stopping of the Governor elect and his commission till matters and rectified, and that order may be taken for the forthcoming of Sir John Harvie, Richard Kemp, and Christopher Wormeley[2] to answer the charges against them."

His request received attention, as the following counter petition of Kemp and Wormeley indicates, which on November 3, 1641, was presented; "In August last, upon the unjust complaint of Anthony Panton a turbulent person petitioners were by order of the House of Commons stayed, when about to return to their families in Virginia. The House of Commons by an order of the 8th of September, allowed them to depart, but on the 1st of October, when on board of the ship, were again stayed. Berkeley the Governor elect presented a similiar petition. George Donne never returned to Virginia and soon died, John West taking

[1] Thomas Stegg, the influential merchant of Westover, was fined fifty pounds sterling and to be imprisoned during the Governor's pleasure, for furnishing money to Kemp and assisting him to leave the colony with some of its important records.

[2] Christopher Wormeley does not appear to have returned to Virginia, while his son Ralph, was a prominent planter. In the Sixth Report of the Royal Historical Commission, p. 414, there is the following: "4 May, 1640, two copies of an award made by Richard Washington and Christopher Wormely, Esquires (acting as arbitrators at the request of certain dissentients) respecting a dispute about a right of way from Carcrofte to Ousten Co., York."

his place as Marshall and Muster Master General. The power of Governor Harvey was completely broken. In a letter to Secretary of State, Windebank, on May 8th, 1640, he wrote, "that he was so narrowly watched that he had scarce time of privacy to write, his estate had been torn from him, his return to England had been denied, notwithstanding his many bodily infirmities, which were beyond the skill of the Colony." During his last years he had married the widow of the Richard Stephens, merchant and councillor, with whom he once had an altercation. Captain De Vries, the Dutch trader, in September, 1642, instituted a suit to recover £4, 14s. due from the estate of Richard Stephens, "for goods sold to Lady Harvey, who was at the time wife of said Stevens."

---

[1] George Evelyn, also written Evelin, his brother, ceased to be commander of Kent Island, Maryland, on April 22, 1638, and on May 30th of this year he acknowledges a debt to "his brother Lieut. Robert Evelin, fourteen hundred pounds of tobacco and fifty-two pounds of beaver, for so much received of him upon the account of William Clobery and Company;" and for his security assigns to him all the right, title, and interest, of the said Clobery and Company in the service of Andrew Baker, Thos. Baker, and John Hatch, and all the profits and use of said servants until the debt shall be satisfied. He also in another entry acknowledges himself to owe " to his dear brother Robert Evelin " a hundred weight of beaver and as security assigns to him his Manor of Evelinton or Piny Point on the Maryland shore of the Potomac. Captain George Evelyn, on August 3, 1649, purchased of Thomas Grendon, certain land in James City County, which on April 28, 1650, he gave to his second son, Mountjoy. On June 20, 1651, Governor Berkeley granted to Mountjoy Evelyn 600 acres of land in the county of James City, on the south side of the river.

Scull, in "The Evelyns of America," mentions that Robert Evelyn's uncle, Captain Thomas Young, also purchased a farm in James City County, and that his son Thomas served in the Parliament Army, under General Monk. In later years this son was an officer in Bacon's rebellion in Virginia and known as " Captain Young of Chickahominy." In January, 1675-6, he was hung in York County under a sentence of a Court Martial.

After a long visit to England, Robert Evelin[1] in 1637, in the ship "Plain Joane" returned to Virginia, and after the death of Gabriel Hawley, was appointed by the Governor, and duly confirmed Surveyor General of Virginia.

About the year 1640, he made another voyage to England, and printed a little book of directions for immigrants to America, which has become very rare, with the following title:

A

Direction

for Adventurers

With small stock to get two for one
and good land freely:
And for Gentlemen, and all Servants, Laborers, and
Artificers to live plentifully.
And the true Description of the healthiest, pleasantest and richest
plantation of new Albion
in North Virginia, proved by thirteen witnesses.
Together with
A Letter from Master Robert Evelin who lived there many
yeares, showing the particularities, and excellency thereof.
With a briefe of the charge of victuall, and necessaries to transport
and buy stocke for each Planter and Laborer there, to get his
Master 50*l* or more in twelve trades and
at 10*l* charges onely a man.

Printed in the yeare 1641.

[1] See note preceding page.

CHAPTER VI.

AFFAIRS FROM A.D., 1642 TO A.D., 1651.

ARRIVAL OF GOV. BERKELEY. GEORGE SANDYS COLONIAL AGENT. ATTEMPT TO RESTORE THE LONDON COMPANY. REMONSTRANCE OF ASSEMBLY. VISIT OF NEW ENGLAND MINISTERS. SUPPORT FOR GOV. BERKELEY. ASSEMBLY OF 1642-3. LORD BALTIMORE SEEKS VIRGINIA REVENUE. LETTERS OF MARQUE. CAPT. RICHARD INGLE. DE VRIES VISITS JAMESTOWN. FIGHT BETWEEN SHIPS. RISING OF THE INDIANS. CAPTAIN STEGG CAPTURES A BRISTOL SHIP IN BOSTON HARBOR. ROBERT EVELIN. SIR EDMUND PLOWDON. DANIEL GOOKIN. ASSEMBLY OF 1644. CRUEL STRIFE IN MARYLAND. LEGISLATION OF 1645 HENRY BISHOP VISITS ENGLAND. OPECHANCANOUGH DEFEATED. LT. THOMAS ROLFE. THOMAS HARRISON AND PATRICK COPLAND NONCONFORMIST MINISTERS. PUBLIC MARKET. COLONY IN 1649. ARRIVAL OF NORWOOD, STEVENS, AND FRANCIS MORYSON. THE CUSTIS FAMILY. GOVERNOR BERKELEY'S SPEECH AGAINST THE NAVIGATION ACT.

SIR William Berkeley,[1] Knight, in February, 1642, arrived at Jamestown as the successor of Governor Francis Wyatt. In the prime of life, a graduate of Merton College, Oxford, accustomed to travel, a

---

[1] His father was Sir Maurice Berkeley Kt., of Hamworth Middlesex. He was born in July, 1608, and matriculated at Merton College, Oxford, in 1623, and in 1629, received the degree of A.M.

favorite of the King, and once a Gentlemen of the Privy Chamber, his administration, from the first, was energetic and progressive.

Taught to believe that no commonwealth could exist without a King, and that there could be no church without a bishop, he could not separate disloyalty and non-conformity. By his commission, it was provided, that he and Secretary Kemp, then in England, should take the oaths of allegiance and supremacy before sailing, and after arrival in Virginia, administer the oath to the following Councillors, Sir Francis Wyatt, Kt.,[1] John West,

---

His brother, Charles Henry, born in December, 1600; Maurice born in April, 1603; and John in February, 1607, were men of distinction. The latter led the army of King Charles, in 1638, against the Scotch and was created Baron Berkeley of Stratton. Charles was knighted in 1623, and after the restoration, Treasurer of the Household of Charles the Second.

[1] Gov. Wyatt seems to have remained in the colony several months after the arrival of Berkeley. In 1613, his wife was a widow, living at Baxley, Kent, England. He had several sons, one, named George, was in 1653, a Lieutenant in the Navy and when in that year he was offered the command of the "Sampson" he declined for "he did not think himself fit for command, as he had received many wounds in the late wars, especially in his head." G. D. Scull in his memoir of Dorothea Scott prints a letter from King James' daughter Elizabeth, Queen of Bohemia, dated from the Hague, March 4, 1655, and addressed to Lord Finch, whose first wife was the sister of Governor Wyatt, in which there is a reference to the Governor's son The words are: "As for the "Countess" I can tell you heavie news of her, for she is turned quaker, and preaches every day in a tubb. Your nephew George [Wyatt] can tell you of her quaking, but her tubb preaching is come since he went, I believe."

Governor Wyatt's aunt, Jane Wyatt, married a Scott, whose grand-daughter Dorothea Scott, married Major Daniel Gotherson of Cromwells' Army, and about 1655, became a Quaker preacher. Her husband died in 1655, when she again married Joseph Hogben, of Kent, and about 1680, she settled on Long Island, New York.

Esq.,[1] Samuel Mathews, Esq.,[2] Nathaniel Littleton, Esq.,[3] Christopher Wormeley,[4] Esq., William Peirce, Esq.,[5] Roger Wingate, Esq.,[6] John Hobson,[7] Thomas Powlett,[8] George Menefie,[9] Henry Brown, Esq., William Brocas, Esq., Argall

---

Francis Wyatt, son of the Governor, in 1641, was enrolled as a student of the Inner Temple. Brock gives the following from the Virginia Land Records:

Henry Wyatt, Esq., eldest son of Sir Francis Wyatt, Dec. 26, 1641, lease for 21 years of 50 acres in Pasbyhay, James City county for the raising of corn, for the better protection of the plantation. George Wyatt, April 21, 1642, in James City County 250 acres. Thomas Wyatt, Sept. 24, 1643, " twenty miles up " on the south side of Rappahannock, 2000 acres.

Richard Wyatt, Aug 20, 1645, in Mobyack Bay, 500 acres.
Ralph Wyatt in 1636 lease to Abraham Wood and others of certain islands.
William Wyatt April 27, 1653, in Gloucester Co., 400 acres.
William Wyatt March 16, 1663, in Gloucester Co., 400 acres.
Mayor William Wyatt May 20, 1664, in New Kent Co., 1940 acres.
Anthony Wyatt, June 28, 1664, in New Kent Co., 282 acres.
Anthony Wyatt July 24, 1669, in Charles City, 398 acres.

[1] See page 15.

[2] See page 21.

[3] His plantation was on the eastern shore of Chesapeake Bay.

[4] He does not appear to have remained in Virginia, but son Ralph was prominent.

[5] Peirce as early as May, 1623, had been appointed by Governor Wyatt during his first term of office, Captain of his Guard, and commander of James City. For other notices see pages, 59, 128.

[6] Appointed in August, 1639, Treasurer for life.

[7] See Chapter V.

[8] Thomas Powlett or Pawlett, came in the " Neptune" in 1618, and was in 1642, about 57 years old.

[9] See p. 112.

Yeardley,[1] Thomas Pettus, Thomas Willoughby,[2] Richard Bennett,[3] and Humphrey Higginson,[4] George Ludlow,[5] early in 1642, also appeared as one of the Council. Claiborne was appointed by the King, colonial Treasurer.

The first assembly after Berkeley's arrival convened on April 1, 1642, and among the Burgesses were a number of the more enterprising colonists. Benjamin Harrison[6] who had for several years been clerk of the Council, and Richard Townsend, who, in 1629, had represented the planters be-

---

[1] Argall Yeardley was the eldest son of the Governor and now about 21 years old. See page 16.

[2] Thomas Willoughby came in the ship "Prosperous" as early as 1610, and was now about 40 years old and was a merchant.

His only son Thomas born Dec. 25, 1632, was sent to the Merchant Tailors, School, London.

Elizabeth, the wife of Col. William Willoughby, one of the Commissioners of the Navy, about 1652 died in England, and at the time her sister Jane Hammond was living in Virginia, perhaps the wife of Col. Manwaring Hammond, one of Gov. Berkeley's councillors. She had a son Lawrence Hammond.

Francis, the son of the widow Elizabeth, being the Deputy Governor of Massachusetts, died in 1672, and his widow Margaret married Lawrence, son of Jane Hammond of Virginia.

A Willoughby Allerton was in 1711, Deputy Collector of Customs for Potomac River indicating some connection of Isaac Allerton's family with the Willoughbys. A Henry Willoughby, born in 1626, at Stukely, Berkinghamshire, died in November, 1685, at Hill's Creek, Virginia. His son Henry who went with his father to Virginia, married July 28, 1695, Elizabeth daughter of William Pidgeon of Stepney. The relation between these families has not been ascertained.

[3] Governor of Virginia under Cromwell.

[4] Among the passengers for Virginia in the ship "George," Capt. Severn, in 1635, was Humphrey Higginson.

[5] See Chapter IV.

[6] Benjamin Harrison on July 10, 1635, received a grant of 200 acres in Warrosquoyake afterwards Nansemond County.

tween Archer's Hope and Martin's Hundred, John Upton, who had in 1632, been appointed a judge for Warrosquoyoake, Obedience Robins,[1] an old justice in Accomack, Thomas Harwood who had been prominent in the dispute with Governor Harvey, Edward Hill, who was afterwards insurrectionary Governor in Maryland, and John Hill, a sympathizer with the New England Puritans.[2]

Berkeley was often choleric and arbitrary in his measures, yet his hospitality to strangers, outspoken manner, and hearty interest in the general welfare of the Colony, for several years, gave him influence with many. At the outset of his administration he sustained the people, in opposing a measure, which tended to cripple their energies.

The legislative assembly of 1639, had appointed George Sandys[3] who had been Treasurer of the Colony, before the

[1] John Robins, in 1628, in a communication to the colonial authorities, speaks of his father who died on the voyage. In 1632, John Robins, the younger son and heir of John Robins, deceased, received on September 7th, a grant of 300 acres in Elizabeth City County.
In 1640, December 3d, Obedience Robins entered 2000 acres in Accomack County.

[2] In addition to the above, the following, were members of the Assembly, of April, 1642, and signers of the Remonstrance. Thomas Dewe, Ferd. Franklin, John Weale, Nath. Gough, Jos. Johnson, Walter Chiles, Wm. Dacker, W. Butler, Thomas Fallows, George Worleigh, George Hardy, Francis Fowler, Tho's Bernard, Edward Windham.

[3] It is probable that Sandys went to England, and was there when his translation of Ovid's Metamorphosis was elegantly published in 1632, in folio, at Oxford. In 1636, he also published a duodecimo, with this title:
"Paraphrase upon the Psalmes of David and upon the Hymnes dispersed throughout the Old and New Testament."
Four years later he published an 18mo. "Christ's Passion, a Tragedy; with annotations, London, printed by I. L., and are to be sold by William Leake at his shop in Chancery Lane, neere unto the Rowles, 1640."

abrogation of the charter of the Virginia Company of London, to watch over their interest in England, but in disregard of their wishes, he revived the project, which had been pressed ten years before, and presented a petition to the House of Commons, in the name of the adventurers and planters of Virginia, asking a restoration to the old London Company of all the privileges of their old charter, except, that the Crown should reserve the right to appoint a Governor.

The Assembly of April, 1642, after fully debating the matter, "maturely considering the reasons on both sides as well enquiring for, as against the company" with the Governor, and Council, sent a statement to the King in which they set forth sound principles of constitutional liberty.

They declared that their agent had mistaken his instructions, and that they would consider it a calamity to see the charter of the old company revived, and that if it were again to attempt to exercise power, there would come anarchy and unhappiness in the Colony, whose people had not forgotten the intolerable sufferings, illegal proceedings, and barbarous treatment during the period of the said company's sway.

Collins mentions that in the family Bible of Archbishop Sandys, was this record: " George Sandes born the seventh day of March, at six of the Clock in the morning 1577. His godfathers were George, Earl of Cumberland and William, Lord Ewer. His godmother Catharine, Countess of Huntington." He died at the age of 66 years, in the house of his niece, the widow of Governor Wyatt. In the register of Bexley Abbey is this entry: " Georgius Sandys, Poetarum Anglorum sui soeculi facile princeps, sepultus fuit Martii 7 Stilo Anglic, An. Dom., 1643."

The whole trade of the Colony had been monopolized by the company, insomuch that when any person desired to go for England he had not liberty to carry with him the fruits of his own labor, for comfort and support, but was forced to bring it to the Magazine of the company, there to exchange it for unprofitable and useless wares.

That they were now happy by the freedom of annual Assemblies, warranted to them by his Majesty's gracious instructions, by legal trials, by juries in all criminal and civil causes, and by his Majesty's royal encouragement upon all occasions to address him, by humble petitions, which so much distinguisheth our happiness from that of former times when private letters to friends were rarely permitted to be sent to England.

They further argued that the old corporation could not be introduced without proving the illegality of the King's proceedings against them, so that all grants since, upon such a foundation must be void; "and if as they pretend, the King had no right to grant, our lands held by immediate grant from his Majesty must be void, and our possessions must give place to their claim, which is an invincible argument of ruin and desolation to the Colony, as we must be outed of our possessions if their pretence."

"And though it is alleged by them that the charter of orders from the Treasurer and company (Anno 1618) gives us claim and right to be members of the corporation *quatenus* planters, yet it appears by the charter, that planters and adventurers who are members of the company are considered by themselves, and distinguished in privileges, from planters and adventurers not being members; and as the King's grantees we find ourselves condemned in the said Charter one clause of it pronouncing in these words; "we do ordain that all persons as of their own voluntary will and authority shall remove into Virginia without any grant from us, in a great and general Quarter Court, in writing, under our seals shall be declared, as they are, occupiers of our land; that is of the common lands of us the said Treasurer and Company."

Now if persons who remove into this country without license from the Treasurer and company are to be deemed occupiers of the company's land, much more will such grantees be deemed occupiers of their land, who hold their rights under an erroneous judgment as they pretend.

That if the company be revived, and they have leave by virtue of their charter of orders publickly to dispossess us, the wiser world we hope will excuse us if we refuse to depart with what, next to our lives, nearest concerns us (which are our estates, the livelihood of ourselves, our wives and children) to the courtesy and will of such taskmasters, from whom we have already experienced so much oppression.

That we will not admit of so unnatural a distance as a company to interpose between his Sacred Majesty, and us his subjects, from whose immediate protection we have received so many royal favors and gracious blessings.

That by such admission, we shall degenerate from our birthrights, being naturalized under a monarchical and not a popular, or tumultuary government, depending upon the greatest number of votes of persons of several honors and dispositions as that of a company must be granted to be, from whose General Quarter Courts all laws binding the planters here did, and would again, issue.

That we cannot without breach of natural duty and religion, give up and resign the lands we hold by grants from the King upon certain annual rents (fitter as we humbly conceive, if his Majesty shall so please, for a branch of his own royal stem than for a company) to the claim of a corporation; for besides our own births, our possessions enjoin us as a fealty without a *salva fide aliis Dominis.*

That by the admission of a company the freedom of our trade (the blood and life of a commonwealth) will be monopolized, for they who with most secret reservation, and most subtlety argue for a company though they pretend to submit the government to the King, yet reserve to the corporation property to the land, and power of managing the trade; which word managing in every sense of it is convertible to monopolizing, and will subject the trade to the whole control and direction of their Quarter Courts held at so great a distance from us that it is not probable or possible for them to be acquainted with the accidental circumstances of the Colony, so as to form proper rules and regulations for our trade, which our Grand Assembly, acquainted with the clime and accidents thereof, have and may upon better grounds, prescribe, and which in any other way will be destructive to us.

That the pretence that the government shall be made good to the King, that is, that the King shall nominate and appoint the Governor, we take at best, to be but a fallacy and a trap, not of capacity enough to catch men with eyes and forethought ; for upon a supposition that the Governour shall be named and appointed by the King, yet his dependence, so far as respects his continuance or removal, will by reason of their power, and interest with great men, rest in the company, which naturally brings with it conformity to their wills in whatever shall be commanded, and we leave it to the best judgments whether such dependence will not be pernicious to the Colony.

After these reasons, with firmness they make the following positive declaration.

"We the Governour, Council, and Burgesses of this present Grand Assembly having taken into serious consideration these and many other dangerous effects which must be concomitant in and from a company or corporation, have thought fit to declare, and hereby do declare, for ourselves and all the commonality of this Colony, that it was never desired, sought after, or endeavored to be sought for, either directly or indirectly by the consent of any Grand Assembly or the common consent of the people ; and we do hereby further declare and testify to all the World, that we will never admit the restoring the said Company, or any, for, or in their behalf, saving to ourselves herein a most faithful and loyal obedience to his most Sacred Majesty, our dread Sovereign whose royal and gracious protection, allowance, and maintenance of this our just declaration and protestation we doubt not (according to his accustomed clemency and benignity to his subjects) to find.

"And we do farther enact, and be it hereby enacted and manifested by the authority aforesaid, that what person or persons soever either is, or shall be hereafter any planter or adventurer, and shall go about, by any way or means, either directly or indirectly, to sue for, advise, assist, abet, countenance, or contrive the reducing this Colony to a Company or Corporation * * * * shall be held and deemed an enemy to the Colony and shall forfeit his or their whole estate or estates that shall be found within the limits of the Colony, the one half shall be and come to the publick use, the other moity or half to the informer."

After the preparation of their objections, the Assembly postponed all business and adjourned to the second of June. When the protest was received by the King, the civil war had begun in England, and he was in Yorkshire directing troops against the friends of Parliament. Although his approval of their propositions would have no weight with Parliament, yet it was most graciously given, while he was sojourning at York, in these words :

"CHARLES REX

"Trusty and well beloved, we greet you well. Whereas we have received a petition from you, our Governour, Council, and Burgesses of the Grand Assembly in Virginia, together with a declaration and protestation of the first of April, against a petition presented in your names, to the House of Commons in this our Kingdom, for restoring of the letters patent for incorporating of the late treasurer, and Company, contrary to your intent and meaning, and against all such as shall go about to alienate you from our immediate protection; and whereas you desire, by your petition, that we should confirm this your declaration and protestation under our royal signet, and transmit it to that our Colony. These are to signify, that your acknowledgment of our grace, bounty, and favour toward you, and your so earnest desire to continue under our immediate protection is very acceptable unto us; and that as we had not before the least intention to consent to the introduction of any Company over that our Colony, so we are by it much confirmed in our resolution, as thinking it unfit to change a form of government, wherein (besides many other reasons given and to be given) our subjects there having had so long experience of it, received so much contentment and satisfaction. And this our approbation of your petition and protestation we have thought fit to transmit to you, under our royal signet. Given at our Court, at York, the 5th of July, 1642."

During this summer, there was an effort to secure New England ministers for some vacant parishes. Some of the settlers upon the banks of the Nansemond River were from the city of London, and had been under the influence of those Puritan preachers who had opposed the policy of Archbishop Laud. The parish of Upper Norfolk had grown so large that in 1641, the Assembly enacted: "For the better enabling the inhabitants of this colony to the religious worship and service of Almighty God, which is often neglected and slackened by the inconvenient and remote vastness of parishes. *Resolved,* That the county of Upper Norfolk be divided into three distinct parishes, viz: one, on the south side of Nansimon river, from the present glebe to head of said river, on the other side of the river, the bounds to be limited from Cooling's Creek, including both sides of the creek, upward to the head of the western branch, and to be nominated the South Parish. It is also thought, and confirmed that the east side of Nansimun river from present glebe downward to the north of said river, be a peculiar parish, to which the glebe and parsonage house that now is, shall be appropiated and called East Parish ; the third parish, to begin on the west side of Nansimun river, to be limited from Cooling's creek, as aforesaid, and to extend downward to the mouth of the river, including all Chuckatuck, on both sides, and the Ragged Islands, to be known by the West Parish."

During the summer of 1642, Philip Bennett, of the Upper Norfolk district, came in small pinnace, to Boston, with a petition, signed by John Hill, Richard Bennett, an influential merchant, afterwards Governor, and Daniel Gookin, junior, " a Kentish soldier, a very forward man to advance martial discipline," and others, in all, to the number of seventy-one, asking for three able ministers, to occupy parishes in their neighborhood.

At a session of the General Court of Massachusetts Bay on the 8th of September, it was voted relative to "the ministers proposed to be sent to Virginia, that if the churches will consent to have them go, the Magistrates should commend them to the Government there."

The churches selected John Knowles,[1] a ripe scholar who

---

[1] Knowles after a few years left New England and became a preacher at Bristol Cathedral, and then was sixteen years at Pershore, Worcester. On April 9, 1665, his house was searched, and he imprisoned for sedition because he had collected money for suffering Polanders, which, in his petition for release he quaintly says, " he did not know was unlawful, but thought them an object of pity." After his release, he devoted himself to the sufferers from the plague in London. He lived to the ripe age of 85 years, and in 1685 died.

had been educated at old Cambridge University, William Tompson,[1] a graduate of Oxford, and Thomas James, who had been two years preacher at Charlestown, Massachusetts, but then at New Haven, Connecticut.

Their voyage was long, and stormy, occupying several weeks. As they passed Hell Gate in Long Island Sound, their pinnace was "bilged upon the rocks," but Mr. Allerton, the son-in-law of William Brewster, the leader of the Plymouth Colony, who was then at Manhattan, obtained for them another vessel, in which in mid-winter they sailed for Virginia.

Soon after they reached their destination, on March 1st, 1642-3 (O. S.), the Assembly[2] convened at Jamestown, when

---

[1] William Tompson, as the name was written, was born in Lancashire, Eng., in 1598, and in 1619, left Oxford, and before coming to New England, preached at Winwick. In "Terra Mariæ," J. B. Lippincott & Co., he is erroneously mentioned as the cordial friend of Lord Baltimore. That William Tompson was a Maryland settler and the only Roman Catholic that sided with Ingle and the friends of Parliament, but afterward came back to Lord Baltimore's party.

[2] HOUSE OF BURGESSES MARCH 1, 1642-3.

Henrico County	Capt. Mathew Gough.
	Mr. Arthur Bayley.
	Mr. Dan. Luellin.
Charles City Co.	Walter Ashton.
	Thomas Stegg, Speaker.
	Mr. Walter Chiles.
	Capt. Rob't Hutchinson.
	Mr. Rowland Sadler.
James City Co.	Mr. Henry Filmer.
	Capt. John Fludd.
	Mr. Stephen Webb.
	Mr. Wm. Davis.
Warwick River Co.	Capt. Thomas Flint.
	Mr. Toby Smith.
Elizabeth City Co.	Mr. John Branch.
	Mr. John Hoddin.

under Governor Berkeley's influence, it was enacted "for the preservation of the puritie of doctrine, and vnitie of the church, that all men whatsoever, which shall reside in the collony are to be conformable to the orders and constitution, of the Church of England, and the laws therein established, and not otherwise to be admitted to teach publickly or privately. And that the Grand Counsel do take care that all non-conformists upon notice of shall be compelled to depart the collony with all convenience."

It was also re-enacted that no popish recusants should at any time hold office unless they had taken the oaths of allegiance and supremacy, and that no popish priest could remain in the Colony longer than five days, after receiving notice to leave from the Governor, or the authority of the place.

The church polity determined upon for the parishes was quite peculiar. In New England civil affairs were subject to the vote of the church, but the reverse was the order in Virginia, and spiritual concerns were under the supervision of officers chosen by the body politic. Each parish was independent. The law passed, declared : "That the vestrie of

Isle of Wight Co.	Mr. Arthur Jones.
	Mr. Richard Denth.
Upper Norfolk Co.	Mr. John Carter.
	Mr. Randall Crew.
Lower Norfolk Co.	Mr. Cornelius Lloyd.
	Mr. Edward Windham.
York County.	Mr. John Chew.
	Capt. Chesman.
	Mr. Wm. Tayler.
Northampton Co.	Mr. Phil. Tayler.
	Mr. Edward Scarborough.

evrie parish, with the allowance of the commander, and comr's of the county living, and resideing within the said parish, or the vestrie alone, in case of their non-residence, shall from henceforward, have power to elect, make choyce of their ministers, and he or they so elected by the commander and com'rs, or by the vestrie, in case of non-residence as aforesaid, to be recommended and presented to the said commander, and com'rs or vestrie alone, to the Governor, and so by him admitted, Provided, that it shall be lawfull for the Gov' for the time being to admit and elect such a minister as he shall allow of in James Citty parish. And in any parish where the Governour and his successors shall have a plantation, provided he or they enjoy not that privilege but in one parish, where he or they have such a plantation, And vpon the neglect, or misbecoming of the ministers or any of them compl't thereof being made by the vestrie, The Governour and Council are requested so to proceed against such minister or ministers, by suspension, or other punishment as they shall think fitt and the offence require, Removall of such ministers, to be left to the Grand Assembly." With a vestry elected by a community of godless planters, the most orthodox minister was liable to be complained of, suspended or removed, by the secular power, while a wine bibbing and horse racing parson could be retained for years by a vestry of jolly and loose living parishioners. As yet the rancor of civil war had not separated neighbors, and while Stegg the speaker of the House, Bennett of the Council, and others, sympathized with Parliament, they were disposed to support their royalist Governor as the following legislation shows.

22

"Whereas the vnkind differences now in England, It may be with great reason be assured to the most scrupolous that the severall pension & allowance from his Ma'tie to the Governour of this place is for the present withdrawn and suspended & that therefore for sustentation and support of the honour of this place of Governour in accomodation from the plantation in cleare and absolute terms of necessitie is required and inforced;

"Yet nevertheles this present Grand Assembly together and eye to the honour of the place, having alsoe entered into a deep sense and consideration of the duty and trust which the publique votes and suffrages have cast vpon them vnder which is comprehended as the most speciall and binding obligation the preservation of the rights and properties of the people, to which this course now intended may seem to threaten violence however, rather innovated in the manner and circumstance, then in value and substance; Yet as well for the silencing of pretences as for answearing arguments of weight.

"*It is thought fitt* hereby to declare that as from the infancy of the colony there never was the like concurrence and pressure of affairs which they likewise hope and pray to Almighty God to [avert] from his Ma'tie and his ma'ties kingdom, soe they have recorded to the posteritie, with this ensueing president of accommodation for the Governour, that the aforesaid instance, and motives removed, they will never yield or consent to receive [renew ?] the same" and it was ordered that a levy of two shillings upon each tithable person, payable in provisions[1], be made for the support of the Governor, and a house with a lot of two acres was also presented, as "a free and voluntary gift, in consideration of many worthy favours manifested toward the Colony." At this session, persons who fled from England on account of their debts, were exempted from prosecution by creditors, because in the language of the Act, "it might hazard the deserting of the great part of the country."

Several changes were made in names and boundaries. The plantation of "Achomack" was ordered to be called Northampton, and Charles River County was changed to York, and Warwick River to Warwick County. Upper Norfolk was divided into three parishes, and "Chescake" was changed to Hampton Parish. Two parishes were created in Northampton County, one south of Kings Creek, the other between Kings Creek and Naswattocks. The monthly courts were made bi-mensal, and designated as County Courts.

Walter Austin, Rice Hoe, Joseph Johnson and Walter Chiles, were authorized to explore the country west and south of the "Appomattake" river, with the privilege of trading with the Indians for fourteen years.

All old settlers who arrived at the last coming of Sir Thomas Gates, or before, were exempted from military

---

[1] Indian corn was rated at 10 shillings a barrel, two barrels in ear, equivalent to a barrel without cobs; wheat at 4s. a bushel; beef at 3½ pence a pound, pork at 4 pence a pound; good hens at 12 pence, capons at 1s. 6d., calves six weeks old, at 25 shillings; butter at 8d. per pound; good goats at 20s.; pigs to roast three shillings; cheese 6 pence a pound; geese, turkeys and kids each 5 shillings.

service, and public taxes, except those for the support of ministers.

The doctrine of popular sovereignty was set forth in a declaration that an Act of the Assembly was higher than any act of the General Court, or proclamation of the Governor.

The New England ministers received no encouragement from Governor Berkeley. An old chronicler quaintly mentions: "They found loving and liberal entertainment in the country and were bestowed in several places, by the care of some honest minded persons that much desired their company rather than by any care of the Governor. * * * * It fared with them as it had done before with the Apostles in the primitive times, that the people magnified them, and their hearts seemed to be much inflamed with an earnest desire after the Gospel, though the civil rulers of the country did not allow of their public preaching because they did not conform to the orders of the church of England, however, the people resorted to them in private houses as much as before."

Early in the summer of 1643, not wishing to continue preaching in opposition to the authorities, they returned to Massachusetts. Lord Baltimore profiting by the short-sighted policy of the Virginia Governor, was quick to make known through Capt. Edward Gibbons,[1] of Boston, that

---

[1] Gibbons as a young man had been inclined to be wild, but became a sedate and prominent merchant of Boston, having commercial transactions with the planters of Virginia and Maryland. Gov. Winthrop, under date of 10th month 1646, wrote: "But the Lord is still pleased to afflict us in our shipping, for Major Gibbons and Capt. Leverett having sent a new ship of about one hundred

the officers of Maryland would welcome any English nonconformist.

In February, 1636-7, Cecil, Lord Baltimore, presuming upon his powerful court influence, and devoted friendship of Secretary Windebank,[1] applied for the Governorship of

tons to Virginia, and having there freighted her with tobacco, going out of the river, by a sudden storm was forced ashore, and lost her anchor and much of the goods, to the loss (as is estimated) of two thousand pounds."

Lord Baltimore in 1650, " having good experience of the honour, worth, and ability, of Edward Gibbons, Esquire, Major General of New England" appointed him one of the council of State and Admiral of the Province of Maryland. He was present, in 1652, when Maryland surrendered to the Commonwealth of England, and at his death, he owned a wind-mill at Saint Mary.

[1] Francis Windebank, son of Sir Thomas, of Hurst, Berkshire, a graduate of Saint Johns, Oxford, was a trimmer, and trickster. Through the influence of Laud, when Bishop of London, he was in June, 1632, appointed to succeed Sir Dudley Carleton, the Viscount Dorchester, deceased, as Secretary of State, and that month George, Lord Baltimore, obtained the grant of Maryland. When Laud became unpopular, he forsook him, and suspected of being a Roman Catholic he fled in 1640, to France. Charles the First learned to dislike him. In a letter from Paris, dated Feb. 5-15, 1640-1 the Earl of Leicester alludes to him: " I assure you that of all the men in the world, I have the least obligation, and the least affection to the little Ex-Secretarius that is come hither. I never held any other correspondence with him heretofore than that which his office and my employment required ; and since his being here, he hath had no more from me than such civility as is due to a person of his quality, painfully and dangerously accused, I must confess, but not yet condemned for aught I know, and I am sure it doth not belong to me, to judge or to degrade him. He comes often to my chapel, though he find no altars there to bow unto, nor any candles upon them to help a blind devotion." The Secretary, in 1646, died in Paris.

CECIL, BALTIMORE, FEB. 23, 1636-7, TO SECRETARY WINDEBANK.

RIGHT HONORABLE.

Since I waited on you I have (heere in the Country) further considered of the proposition which I made unto your Honor concerning the advancement of his Majties service in Virginia, and I have desired my Brother Peaseley to acquaint you with my resolution in it, which I will infallibly performe if his Majtie please to accept of it, for you may be most assured that I would not ingage my credit in business of such importance, and especially to such persons before I

Virginia, with a salary of two thousand pounds a year, and while it was not obtained, it is probable that by his influence, Gabriel Hawley received the appointment of Surveyor, and Jerome Hawley that of Treasurer of Virginia. Ever anxious

---

was very well assured of my ability to performe with satisfaction what I undertake. I do presume by him, also to propose unto you a way of the King in the business; such a one as I conceive may be most likely to take effect, or in case of his refusall of it, in that way will I conceive be less prejudiciall to me; but this I submit to your better judgment. If the business takes effect as the King will receive a great benefitt by it, so will it be of good consequence to me, which I shall accordingly acknowledge to your honor, and besides I shall thereby be inabled to do you such further service as shall make me to appeare unto you a really grateful man.

I am much your debtor Sir for former favours, and in especiall for your present care of my New Foundland business, that concerns me very much which I shall likewise acknowledge to you, for I know by good experience your noble integrity and favour to me to be such, as that you will by the best of your Endeavors protect me from injury.

Your honors most affectionate
and humble servant,
Warder Castle
25 Feb., 1636.
C. BALTIMORE.

MEMORIAL.

The Lord Baltimore having considered of the discourse that was betwixt us Mr. Secretary and himself, concerning his desire to do his Majestic service in Virginia doth conceive (with submission to Mr. Secretary's better judgment) this to be a fitt way to propound the matter to the King.

That Mr. Secretary may bee pleased to take notice to his Majestic how sensible he hath often found the Lord Baltimore to bee, for the great favours he hath received from the King in his late occasions, and how desirous hee is to do him some acceptable service, wherein hee may express his duty and gratitude to his Majesty. The consideration whereof hath invited him to take some paines to informe himselfe, of the present state of Virginia whereof hee hath acquired so much knowledge as hee will understand the great prejudice the King suffers there by not receiving so much profit from thence, as he ought to have and is due; wherefore he did assure Mr. Secretary that he would undertake to improve his Majesties Revenue further eight thousand pounds yearly more than now he received for, or by revenue of that plantation, and this his Lordship will do without laying any new, or other taxes or imposition on the Planters than what they now do, and will most willingly pay. But because this advancement of the King's revenue in Virginia cannot be effected unless the Lord Baltimore do remove and

for his own aggrandizement at the expense of political and religious scruples, on the 28th of February, 1643-4, he received authority from the King, then at Oxford, authorizing his brother Leonard Calvert, Governor of Maryland, to treat with the General Assembly of Virginia[1] as to duties to be imposed upon goods exported, or imported, and that, when this agreement was effected, that then Lord Baltimore should, with such associates, as he should choose, have a lease of these customs, with power to appoint such collectors as he might desire.

---

reside some time there, which he cannot with his safety, well do except hee be authorized and enabled, by having the government of that country, whereunto, though Mr. Secretary perceives the Lord Baltimore hath no ambition or affection, yet for the advancement and performance of this service hee doth verily thinke that upon his Majesties command the Lord Baltimore would accept of the government, and two thousand pounds per year for the support thereof, payable out of that improvement of Rent, and for that purpose would so accommodate his private occasions heere, as he might bee ready to transport himself thither with as much speede as his Maties service required. And that if his Majtie were pleased to speake with the Lord Baltimore hee would upon signification of his pleasure make his present repayre from the country, to give him particular and perfect satisfaction of the meanes and manner to raise the increase of Revenue.

[1] The following are extracts from a blank commission prepared on April 10, 1644.

"Cecilius, Lord Baltimore, to all to whom these presents come, greeting: Whereas, our Sovereign lord, the King, by his Highness commission, under the great seal of England, bearing date at Oxford, the 28 day of February, now last past, hath authorized Leonard Calvert, brother of me, the said Lord Baltimore, to treat, conclude, and agree, and with the General Assembly of the Colony of Virginia, for and concerning the ascertaining and establishing, by Act of General Assembly there, of customs, and duties, to be paid to his Majesty, his heirs and successors in Virginia, upon exportation of tobacco and other goods and merchandize from thence, and upon all other goods and merchandize brought in and imported there, other than for necessary supply of clothing imported, as by the said commission more at large appeareth.

And, whereas, by a contract or agreement in writing, bearing date the day of the date of the said commission, made between our sovereign Lord, the King, of the one party, and the said Lord Baltimore of the other party, reciting the

The Earl of Warwick as Admiral of the Parliament fleet, gave letters of marque to captains of ships authorizing them to capture all vessels from Bristol, Barnstable, Dartmouth and other places whose merchants supported the King, and during the winter of 1643-4, the Virginians were informed that henceforth they should be free from all taxation not self-imposed, and that whenever there was a vacancy, they might choose their own Governor.

While those in the Governor's presence continued to pray "God save the King," those who had business relations with the merchants of London, were disposed to give heed to the orders of the House of Commons.

Richard Ingle,[1] Captain of a London ship, in January, 1643-4, arrived in the waters of Chesapeake Bay and sailing up to Saint Mary, the capital of the province of Maryland, he

---

said commission hereinbefore recited, our said Sovereign Lord, the King, for the consideration in the said contract or agreement expressed, is pleased, and hath agreed with me, the said Lord Baltimore, that in case a certainty and customs, and duties shall be established by act of General Assembly of the said Colony of Virginia, according to the tenor of said commission; That then his said Majesty will make a lease, or grant to me, and such others as I shall desire to be joyned with me, of the same customs and duties which shall be established as aforesaid, for such term, and under such rents and covenants as in the same contract or agreement are expressed," etc., etc.

[1] Ingle was probably the same person who came to Boston early in the summer of 1642, of whom Winthrop in his History of New England, writes: " The ship Eleanor of London, one Mr. Ingles, master, arrived at Boston. She was laden with tobacco from Virginia, and having been about 11 days at sea, she was taken with such a tempest, as though all her sails were down and made up, yet they were blown from the yards, and she was laid over on one side, two and a half hours, so low as the water stood upon her deck, and the sea over-racking her continually. * * * * * She staid here and was well fitted with masts, sails and rigging, and victuals at such reasonable rates, as the master was much affected with his entertainment, and professed that he had never found the like usage in Virginia, where he had traded these ten years."

was arrested for speeches disloyal to the King, by acting Governor Brent, and the following proclamation issued: "These are to publish & p'claym to all psons as well seamen as others, that Richard Ingle Mr of his ship is arrested upon highe treason to his Ma{ty}; & therefore to require all p'sons to be aiding and assisting to his Lo{ps} officers in seizing of his ship, and not to offer any resistance or contempt hereunto, nor to be any otherwaise aiding or assisting to the said Richard Ingle upon per'l of highe treason to his Ma{ty}."

The chief charges[1] when examined were of no great importance and Thomas Cornwallis, the chief councillor and most prominent man in Maryland "to show his affection to Parliament found means to free Ingle, and restore his ship, and goods, for which, he was fined the highest sum that could, by law, be laid upon him, and for safety of his person was forced to leave his estate in the hands of a servant, and fly with Ingle to England" about the middle of March.

A Rotterdam vessel on the 22d of October, 1643, arrived at Jamestown with a cargo of wine, and in it, was Capt. De Vries as passenger. He remained during the whole winter

---

[1] It was charged that on the 20th of November, 1644, "not having the feare of God before his eies, but instigated thereunto by the instigation of the divill & example of other traitors of his Matie traiterously & as an enemy did levie war and beare arms agst his matie & exercise the command and captainship of the town of Gravesend" in England; that he had said in 1642-3, that in February of that year he had been bidden in the King's name to come ashore at Accomac in Virginia, but he had refused to do so, and had threatened to cut off the head of any one who should come on his ship: that in April, 1643, at Mattapanian St. Clement's Hundred, he said "that Prince Rupert was Prince Traitor & Prince Rogue and if he had him aboard his ship he would whip him at the capstain."

in the Valley of the James River and frequently visited Governor Berkeley, who treated him with great hospitality. The ship in which he came sailed one hundred and seven miles beyond Jamestown and discharged its freight. The planters, as when De Vries was before in Virginia, still lost "their servants by gambling." He wrote that while the Virginians were hospitable, " they are not proper persons to trade with. You must look out when you trade with them Peter is always by Paul or you will be struck in the tail, for if they can deceive any one they account it a Roman action. They say in their language 'He played him an English trick.'"

On the 10th of April, 1644, De Vries, at the suggestion of Governor Berkeley, engaged passage in a London ship of twenty-eight guns, then anchored at Jamestown. When the vessel reached Blunt Point, on the 13th, there was seen a Bristol vessel of twelve guns, pursued by two London ships discharging cannon, but it being of lighter draught sailed into Warwick Creek, and escaped with little injury. De Vries passed the night, after the fight, on board of one of the London vessels, and the next morning, visited the Bristol ship in the Creek, and learned that a planter who was on board to purchase some goods, had been killed. On the 15th of April, he went aboard his own ship, and on the 18th, eleven ships of London, each carrying from eighteen to twenty guns, sailed from the fort, at Point Comfort, for England.

The eighteenth day of April, was Good Friday, of the ecclesiastical calendar, and Governor Berkeley had ordered it to be kept as a special fast day to pray for King Charles, but it was not observed, as it had become a day of unexpected mourning. The Indians observing that the white population was engaged in civil war, determined to gratify their revenge, and the day before Good Friday commenced to kill the settlers and continued their bloody work for two days. They divided themselves into small companies, and beset the English houses a little before the break of day, waiting for the first person who should open the door. Beating out his brains they entered the house, slew all within, and then burned the building with the dead, or wounded women and children.[1] About three hundred whites lost their lives.

Governor Calvert, of Maryland had already gone to Oxford, to confer with King Charles, and Berkeley, perplexed by the demonstration against the King, made Secretary Kemp acting Governor, and sailed for England to take advice. While he was absent, during the summer, Capt. Thomas Stegg, a member of his Council and who had been speaker of the Assembly, in March, 1643, appeared in the waters of Boston with a letter of marque from the Earl of Warwick, and a ship of twenty-four guns, and finding there a Bristol ship with a cargo of fish, he showed the captain his commission and said that he would give him thirty minutes to consider certain terms of surrender. The movement was surprising and there was great excitement, crowds having gathered upon Windmill Hill during the parley. The Bristol captain, after consulting with his sailors, accepted the terms, and the ship was taken

---

[1] Johnson's *Wonder Working Providence*.

by Stegg as a prize The next Sunday some of the Boston ministers denounced the Virginia captain, and urged the magistrates to prevent his taking the ship, but they did not see how they could restrain one acting under a commission from parliament. Majors Gibbons, and Sedgwick, were subsequently ordered not to permit any ships to fight in the harbor.

Robert Evelin after publishing in England in 1641, his small tract on New Albion, returned to America and was in 1642, living on his plantation in Maryland. Some frontier settlers, near Pascatoway, having been murdered by marauding Indians, Governor Calvert, on the 23d of June appointed him to "levy, train, and muster" the people in that region, and protect them from the savages. During the month of July, he sat as a member of the Maryland Assembly[1] from St. George's Hundred, having been summoned by special writ.

Sir Edmund Plowden[2] probably arrived from England with

---

[1] After this Assembly, Gov. Calvert wrote to Gov. Berkeley, asking him to send one hundred men by the first of October, to Kent Island to unite in an expedition against the hostile " Sasquesahanocks, Wicomeses, and Nanticokes." On the 5th of October the Governor and Virginia Council decided that it was "impossible to comply with his request, as many of the inhabitants were about to remove to new plantations, and were hardly able to get arms and ammunition to defend themselves ; and those remaining upon the old plantations not having a supply of military provisions, besides the heavy hand of God's visitation upon the plantations generally, of which few were recovered."

[2] Sir Edmund Plowden, Kt., was the grandson of Edmund Plowden, the learned and honorable pleader, who died in 1584, and whose commentaries on law, Chief Justice Coke called " exquisite and elaborate." His father was Francis Plowden, of Plowden Salop. The Knight was married about the year 1610, to Mabel, daughter of Peter Mariner of Wanstead, Hampshire, who brought him an estate of £300 per annum in land.

Evelin, in 1642, and sailed up the river Delaware.[1] The settlement of English spoken of by the council of Manhattan, this year, as "obliquely opposite Fort Nassau," which is now the site of Philadelphia, may have been fostered by him, and near this spot in 1634, Robert Evelin, and his uncle Capt. Young, had stopped.

The winter of 1642-3, Plowden seems to have passed in Virginia, and Maryland. Printz, the Governor of the settlement of Swedes, on the Delaware, in a letter to the Swedish West India Company, gives some account of Plowden. He mentions: "How last year [1643] in Virginia he desired to sail with his people, sixteen in number, in a barque from Heckemack [Accomac] to Kikathans

---

In 1632, he with other persons petitioned the King for " Manitie or Long Isle " and " thirty miles square of the coast next adjoining, to be erected into a County Palatine called Syon to be held of " " his Majesty's Crown of Ireland without appeal or subjection to the Governor and Company of Virginia," with some modifications, the isle called Plowden, and the country New Albion, the petition was granted at Oatland on July 24th, of this year, and a charter granted and sealed June 21, 1634, at Dublin, Ireland

He was a violent person. In 1635, owing to excessive cruelty his wife was obliged to leave his house. Plowden having professed conformity to the church of England, and giving bond not to use any cruelty, his wife returned to her home, but in March, 1639, she complained that her husband was still cruel and refused to support her, and remained in prison to avoid paying alimony. As late as the 7th of May, 1640, he was in the Fleet Prison, and probably after being released from confinement he sailed for America, where he stayed seven years.

Not only his wife but others suffered from his unbridled temper. Philip Oldfield, Rector of Lasham, Hants, for twenty-five years, in May, 1638, complained that Plowden " threatened his ruin, unjustly detained his body, beat his wife, great with child, and insulted over his weak and declining estate."

[1] In the *Delaware Register*, Vol. I, page 83, a writer mentions that " in 1642, the Dutch proceeded to the Schuylkill, with a view of dispossessing the Marylanders, who had lately seated themselves there."

[Hampton] and when they came to the Bay of Virginia, the captain who had previously conspired with the Knight's people to kill him, directed his course, not to Kikathan, but to Cape Henry passing which, they came to an isle in the high sea called Smith's Island, when they took counsel in what way they should put him to death, and thought it best not to slay him with their hands, but to set him, without food, clothes, or arms, on the above named island, which was not inhabited by men, or animals, save wolves and bears, and this they did. Nevertheless, two young noble retainers, who had been brought up by the Knight, and who knew nothing of that plot, when they beheld this evil fortune of their lord, leaped from the barque into the ocean, swam ashore and remained with their master. The fourth day following, an English sloop sailed by Smith's Island, coming so close, that the young men were able to hail her, when the Knight was taken aboard, half-dead and as black as the ground, and conveyed to Hackemack, where he recovered. The Knight's people, however, arrived with the barque May 6, 1643, at our Fort Elfsborg and asked after ships to old England. Hereupon I demanded their pass, and enquired from whence they came; and as soon as I perceived they were not on a proper errand, I took them with me, with their consent, to Christina, to bargain about flour and other provisions, and questioned them, until a maid servant, who had been the Knight's washerwoman, confessed the truth and betrayed them. I at once caused an inventory to be taken of their goods, in their presence, and held the people prisoners, until the very English sloop which had rescued the Knight arrived, with a letter from him, concerning the matter, not alone addressed to me, but to all the governors and commandants of the whole coast of Florida. Thereupon, I surrendered to him the people, barque, and goods, in precise accordance with the inventory, and he paid me, 425 riksdaler for my expenses. The chief of these traitors the Knight has had executed. He himself is still in Virginia, and as he constantly professes, expects vessels and people from Ireland and England. To all ships and barques that come from thence, he grants free commission to trade here, in the river, with the savages; but I have not permitted any of them to pass, nor shall I do so, until I receive order and command to that effect, from my most gracious Queen, her Royal Majesty of Sweden.'"

While residing in Virginia, in 1643, Plowden bought an interest in a bark,[2] with Draper, of Kickotan, and in May of this year, Margaret Brent, subsequently the executrix of Governor Calvert of Maryland, visited Kent Island accompanied by Anne, his lame maid servant.

In May, 1644, Daniel Gookin, Jr., son of Daniel Gookin, who had become much interested in the preaching of the non-conformist ministers, left Virginia and became one of the most distinguished citizens of Boston.[3]

---

[1] Printz's letter translated by Gregory B. Keen, first appeared in Vol. VII, *Pennsylvania Magazine*.

[2] In N. Y. Colonial Documents Vol. XII, p. 57, is the following:

"I Peter Jansen aged about 22 years declare at the request of Mr. Moor that he when, in 1643, in the River Rapahanick heard one Middeler say that the bark now belonging to Peter Lawerensen and Mr. Throckmorten, when Mr. Middeler was skipper, was the property of Sir Edmund Pleyden, Knight, viz.: one half of the bark & 2 hogsheads of flour, freighted on account of said Knight.

[3] His father was also named Daniel Gookin also written Gookins There is an indenture on record dated Feb. 1, 1630, between Daniel Gookins, Gent. and

On the first of October, an Assembly[1] convened, Richard Kemp the Secretary, acting as Governor, in the absence of Berkeley.

Thos. Addison his servant. In 1637, there was a grant to Daniel Gookins of 2500 acres upon the north-west of Nansemond River. In 1642, Daniel Gookins was President of the Court of Upper Norfolk. From a verse by Cotton Mather he appears to have been influenced by William Tomson's preaching.

> " A constellation of great converts there
> Shone round him, and his heavenly glory wear,
> Gookins was one of them, by Tompson's pains,
> Christ and New England, a dear Gookins gained."

While he did not live there, he owned a plantation near South River, Maryland, and, in 1655, two of his negroes there were killed by Indians. He was a friend of John Eliot, the Indian Missionary, and wrote a history of the Massachusetts tribes. Chief Justice Sewall called to see him when dying, and that day wrote in his journal, "a right good man."

His tombstone is at Cambridge, Mass., with this inscription.

> " Here Lyeth Interred
> Ye body of
> Major-General Daniel Gookins
> aged 75 years
> Who departed this life
> Ye 19th March, 1686-7."

[1] COUNCIL AT ASSEMBLY CONVENED OCTOBER 1, 1644.

Capt. Wm. Claiborne, Capt. Wm. Peirce, Capt. Henry Browne, Capt. W. Brocas, Mr. George Menifie, Mr. Richard Bennett, Capt. Humphrey Higginson, Capt. Thos. Bernard, Mr. George Ludlow, Capt. Richard Townsend.

BURGESSES, OCTOBER, 1644.

James City County.

Capt. Robert Hutchinson.
Mr. Stephen Webb.
Mr. Edward Travis.
Mr. Tho's Loveing.

Mr. George Jordan.
Mr. John Shepherd.
Mr. Tho's Warren.

York County.

Mr. John Chew.
Mr. Rowland Burnham.

Capt. X'pher Caulthropp.

The increased consumption of liquor led to some prohibitory enactments. It was ordered that no one should keep an inn unless he had the approval of the county court, and a license from the Governor, and that he should not "sell or utter wine, or strong liquor," but might dispose of strong beer at the rate of eight pounds of tobacco a gallon, and that no "debts for wines or strong liquors" could be recovered by law. The price of a meal at a public house was fixed at ten pounds of tobacco.

Isle of Wight Co.

Mr. Peter Hull.   Mr. Richard Death.
Mr. George Hardy.

Lower Norfolk Co.

Mr. Cornelius Lloyd.   Mr. John Sydney.

Elizabeth City Co.

Lt. Wm. Wos.   Mr. John Hodin.

Warwick County.

Capt. Tho's Bernard.   Mr. John Hoyrick.
Mr. John Walker.

Northampton County.

Mr Obedience Robins.   Mr. Edward Douglas.

Upper Norfolk Co.

Mr. Randall Crew.   Mr. Moore Fontleroy.

Charles City Co.

Capt. Edward Hill, Speaker.   Mr. John Westrop.
Mr. Francis Poythers.   Mr. Dan. Lewellin.
Mr. John Bishop.

Henrico County.

Mr. Richard Cocker.   Mr. Wm. Hatcher.
Mr. Abraham Wood.

Acting Governor Kemp, on February, 17, 1644-45 convened another Assembly,¹ which authorized George Mene-

---

¹COUNCILLORS PRESENT AT ASSEMBLY FEBRUARY 17, 1644-5.

John West, William Claiborne, William Peirce, Thomas Willoughbie, Thomas Pettys, Richard Bennett, Henry Brown, Argoll Yeardley, Capt. Humphrey Higginson, Capt. Bernard, Mr. George Ludlow, Capt. Rich. Townsend.

BURGESSES.

James City Co.

Mr. Ambrose Harmor.   Mr. John Corker.
Capt. Rob't Hutchinson.   Mr. Geo. Stephens.
Mr. Wm. Barrett.   Mr. John Rogers.

Henrico County.

Mr. John Baugh.   Mr. Ab. Wood.

Charles City Co.

Capt. Ed. Hill, Speaker.   L't. Francis Poythers.
Mr. Rice Hoe.   Mr. Edward Prince.

Lower Norfolk Co.

Mr. Edward Lloyd.   Mr. X'pher Burroughs.
Mr. Tho's Meares.

Warwick Co.

Capt. Harwood.   Mr. Henry Heyricke.
Mr. Tho's Bernard.

Isle of Wight Co.

Mr. Arthur Smith.   Mr. George Hardy.

Upper Norfolk Co.

Mr. Philip Bennett.   Mr. Moore Fontleroy

Elizabeth City Co.

Capt. Yeo.   Mr. Arthur Price.
Capt X'pher Calthropp.

Northampton Co.

Mr. Edm'd Scarborough.   Mr. Stephen Charlton.

fie' and Richard Bennett, to purchase powder and shot for the use of the Colony against the Indians, and enacted "for God's glory and the publick benefitt of the Collony to the end that God might avert his heavie judgments that are now vpon us, that the last Wednesday of everie month be sett apart for a day of ffast and humiliation, and that it be wholly dedicated to prayers and preaching," and also "that the eighteenth day of April be yearly celebrated by thanksgivinge for our deliverance from the hands of the Salvages."

Captain Claiborne, Henry Fleet, and Argall Yeardley were invited to be at Jamestown, in October, 1644, at a meeting of the General Court, to give their advice as to an expedition against the Rappahannock Indians, and in February, 1645, the Assembly authorized the erection of a fort, at Pamunkey, to be called Fort Royal ; one at Falls of James River to be named Fort Charles ; and a third on the ridge of Chickahominy to be known as Fort James. Arrangements were made to send sixty men, and a piece of ordinance to each post, and supplies for three months, and in April, Captain Fleet was sent "to trade witlf the Rappahannocks, or any Indians not in amity with Opechancanough" to obtain the necessary corn.

While these preparations were being made, in February, 1645, Richard Ingle in the ship "Reformation" with a commission from Parliament appeared again before Saint Mary, Maryland, aided in an uprising in favor of Parliament, carried the zealous Jesuits Andrew White and Philip Fisher, prisoners to England, and compelled Governor Calvert to flee to Virginia. The action of the Virginia Assembly in

---

[1] Menefie was now the leading merchant. On April 19, 1638, he entered 3000 acres of land on account of 69 transport, of whom 23 were, as he asserts, "*negroes, I brought out of England.*"

March, 1645-6, showed that some in that colony, were friendly to those opposed to Lord Baltimore. The following appears among the transactions of the session: "whereas Lieutenant Nicholas Stillwell and others of the colony, have secretly conveyed themselves to Maryland or Kent, and divers others engaged to follow, if timely prevention is not had therein. Be it therefore enacted that Capt. Thos. Willoughby, Esq., and Capt. Edward Hill be hereby authorized to go to Maryland, or Kent, to demand, the return of such persons, who are already departed from the colony." Hill had been speaker of the Assembly in 1644, and after he arrived in Maryland was commissioned as Governor and in January, 1646, called an Assembly whose members, with two or three exceptions, were unfriendly to Lord Baltimore[1]. In December, Governor Calvert returned from Virginia with an armed force, and took Hill, and the Assembly then in session, prisoners. Claiborne who had occupied Kent Island then returned to Virginia.

It was not until the 7th of June, 1645, that Governor Berkeley returned from his visit to England, and nine days after, at a meeting of the Council, at Jamestown, a letter was read from Margaret Worleigh, a prisoner in the hands of the great chief Opechancanough, in which, she mentioned that he desired a redemption of captives and a treaty of peace. It was agreed that there should be an armistice and that Margaret Worleigh should be informed that the Governor would soon come to Rickahock, or Fort Royal, on the Pamunkey River, and would be pleased there

---

[1] Lord Baltimore in a letter of 1649, mentions that "with the exception of two or three, of the rebelled party" were the members of the Assembly.

to confer with twelve of the chief's principal men. Captain Henry Fleet was engaged as interpreter, to meet the Governor at his estate, the Middle Plantation, not far from Jamestown. The conference does not appear to have taken place, for the legislature of March, 1645-6, authorized the erection of Fort Henry at the Falls of Appommatox, and Lieut. Francis Poythers was empowered to raise sixty men, and act under the advice of Captain Henry Fleet. Fleet had been instructed to gather, by the 20th of April, at Kiquotan, now Hampton, boats, provisions for six weeks, three hundred pounds of powder, twelve hundred of shot and bullets, and a company of sixty men. It was understood that if Fleet did not conquer, a peace with Opechancanough and his allies, that the Colony would not pay for the supplies.

The first legislature,[1] after Berkeley's return, convened on November 20, 1645, and some changes were made in the method of raising revenue, for the support of the Colony. Hitherto, the expenses of government had been met by a

---

[1] BURGESSES OF THE ASSEMBLY, CONVENED NOV. 20, 1645.

James City Co.

John Flood.	Ambrose Harmer.
Walter Chiles.	Tho's Warne.
Thomas Swan.	Peter Ridley.
Robert Wethrall.	George Stevens.

York County.

Capt. Xpher Caulthrope.	Arthur Price.
Rowland Burnham	

Isle of Wight Co.

Capt. John Upton.	John Seward.
George Hardin.	

Lower Norfolk Co.

Cornelius Lloyd.	X'pher Burrows.

general poll tax which proved "insupportable for the poorer sorte," and it was now ordered that each owner of one hundred acres of land should annually pay four pounds of tobacco; each three years old cow and breeding sheep was taxed three pounds of tobacco, each horse, mare or gelding, thirty-two pounds, each goat, two pounds, and every tithable person twenty pounds of tobacco. It was also enacted that not more than thirty pounds of tobacco should be charged for a gallon of "Canary, Malaga, Sherry, Muskadine and Allegant" wines, nor more than twenty pounds for "Maderea, and Fyall," nor more than forty, for "Aqua Vitæ or Brandy," nor more than eighty pounds for "English Strong Waters," and that "no merchant of Jamestown whatsoever shall retayle wine or strong

Elizabeth City County.

Capt. Leonard Yeo.   John Chandler.

Warwick County.

Capt. Tho's Bernard.   Randall Crew.
John Walker.

Northampton Co.

Edmund Scarborough.   Tho's Johnson.

Upper Norfolk Co.

Philip Bennett.   Richard Wells.
Edward Major.

Charles City Co.

Capt. Francis Eps.   William Barker.
Capt. Edward Hill.   Charles Sparrow.
Edward Prince.   Anthony Wyatt.
Rice Hoe.

Henrico County.   Abraham Wood.
Northumberland Co.   John Matrum.

waters," and that tavern keepers, shall not charge above the established price.

As many troublesome suits had been multiplied by the unskillfulness and covetousness of attorneys for their own profit, "and inordinate lucre" rather than "the good and benefit of their clients," it was ordered that "all mercenary attorneys, be wholly expelled from such office," except in those cases which had already been commenced.

Excessive doctors' fees had led planters to allow their servants to die, rather than to "fall into the hands, of griping and avaricious men," and it was also provided, that a physician, or chirurgeon, could be brought before the court and be made to testify as to the value of his drugs, and medicines, when complaint had been made of his exorbitant bill.

The Assembly was prorogued by the Governor to the first of March, 1645-6, and on the 17th, the House of Burgesses transmitted the following, which showed that they now acknowledged Parliament: "We desire to thank the House of Commons for all its favours, but especially for informing us by letter of the 18th of October, 1644, that all sequestrations upon the goods of planters and others of Virginia was taken off; in return the merchants of London have enjoyed trade with the Colony, and free admission to her courts of Justice.

"The savage King, who contrived the massacre of our people, is so abandoned by his people, and they so routed and dispersed, that they are no longer a nation, and we now suffer only from robbery by a few starved outlaws whom by God's assistance, we doubt not to root out in another year.

"We send this by Mr. Henry Bishop[1], who formerly served the King, in these unhappy wars in England, but is now a member of our Colony, and actually engaged by plantation, and servants upon the place. His lands are in sequestration and we humbly pray that the sequestration may be taken off, that he may be enabled to strengthen his plantation with people, and supply those already seated there."

At this session measures were adopted for a vigorous prosecution of the war against the Indians, and for the defence of the inhabitants south of James River, and to prevent the savages from "fishing in the Bristoll or Appomattocke River," and from cutting down their corn, and other services against them, forty-five soldiers were ordered to be raised from Bass's Choice, and the country upward, and a

---

[1] Henry Bishop of Henfield, Sussex, entered on October 20, 1640, in Lower Chipoak, south side of James River, 1200 acres, but he did not return to Virginia. Charles the Second on August 14, 1660, commissioned him for seven years as Postmaster General of England. His enemies complained that during the days of the Commonwealth he had been accustomed to meet Major John Wildman, Praise God Barebones, and other Republicans, at the Commonwealth Club House in Bow Street, Covent Garden, and that he also employed disaffected persons in the Post Office. In consequence of these charges he was obliged in March, 1663, to surrender his commission, and Daniel O'Neale who had been groom of the King's bed-chamber, was his successor. O'Neale died in 1664, but his wife the Countess of Chesterfield continued to carry out the postal contracts. Her maiden name was Katherine Wooton, and her first husband was Henry, Lord Stanhope. As his widow she was the governess in Holland of the Princess Mary, the sister of Charles the Second. Her second husband was John Poliander Kirckhoven of Holland.

Charles the Second created her Countess of Chesterfield on June 5, 1660, for services to his sister. Her third husband was O'Neale groom of the King's bed-chamber. She died April 9, 1667, and was buried at Becton, Malherbe, Kent.

O'Neale's successor as Postmaster General was Henry, Lord Arlington.

fort erected at the Falls of the Appomattox. The campaign of the summer of 1646, was successful. The writer of the "Description of New Albion" alludes to the 'Indian war ended, first, by the valour, courage, and hot charge of Captain Marshall, and valiant Stillwell, and finished by the personal and resolute march and victory of Sir William Berkeley, Governor there, taking the old King Ope Chankino prisoner." On an early map[1] between the Falls of Appomattox and the James River is this sentence, " Hereabout Sir Will. Barkley conquered and took prisoner the great Indian Emperour, Abatschakia, after the massacre in Virginia."

At the Assembly[2] held in October of that year, Nictowance the new chief, made a treaty of peace by which the

---

[1] Heerman's.

[2] ASSEMBLY HELD OCTOBER, 1646.

Councillors present Capt. John West, Secretary Richard Kemp, Capt. William Brocas, Capt. Tho's Pettus, Capt. Thomas Willoughby, Capt. W. Bernard, Capt. Henry Browne, Mr. Richard Bennett, George Ludlowe.

BURGESSES.

James City Co.

Ambrose Harmer Speaker.	George Jordon.
Walter Chiles.	Thomas Lovinge.
Capt. Rob't Shepheard.	Wm. Barrett.

Henrico Co.

Capt. Ab. Wood.	William Cocke.

Charles City Co.

Rice Hoe.	Dan Lluellen.

Isle of Wight Co.

Mr. Fawdowne.	James Bagnall.

Elizabeth City Co.

John Robins.	Henry Ball.

Indians agreed to abandon the land below the Falls of the James, and those of Pamunkey, and confine their hunting to the region between the York and Rappahannock Rivers.

Fort Henry, on the Appomattox, with six hundred acres of land was granted to Capt. Abraham Wood, on condition that he would keep there, ten men, for three years, each person, to be exempted from taxation; Fort James on the Chickahominy was granted to Lieut. Thomas Rolfe[1] with

	York County.
Hugh ———.	Wm. Luddington.
	Warwick Co.
Tho's Taylor.	John Walker.
Randall Crew.	
	Lower Norfolk Co.
Edward Lloyd.	Robert Eyres.
Tho's Mears.	
	Northampton Co.
Edward Douglas.	Tho's Johnson.
	Nansemond Co.
Edward Major.	Sam. Stoughton.

[1] In " Virginia Vestusta " it was mentioned that Capt. John Rolfe's last wife was Jane, daughter of Capt. William Peirce of Jamestown, and that John Rolfe made a will dated March 10, 1621-2, in which he speaks of Thomas and Elizabeth " two small children of tender age," and it was assumed that Thomas " of tender age," was the son of Jane Peirce. Some have taken exception to this position, and think that the Thomas of the will, was the son by Powhatan's daughter.

Thomas Rolfe the son of John had a daughter Jane, which was also the name of his father's last white wife. At Sculthorpe Rectory, Norfolk, England, there is a portrait of a wife of Capt. John Rolfe with a lad by her side. Her hair is parted in the middle, without ornaments, and her dress is that of a civilized woman.

In " Virginia Vetusta," Munsell's Sons, Albany, 1885, page 141, Rolfe's daughter Elizabeth, is erroneously called Jane; and in " Virginia Company of London," Joel Munsell, Albany, page 91, there is a misleading typographical

four hundred acres, provided he held it, for the same time with six men; Fort Royal or Rickahock on the Pamunkey, with six hundred acres was given to Capt. Roger Marshall, on condition he held it with ten men.

While Daniel Gookin removed from Nansemond, after the non-conformist ministers were silenced, quite a congregation in that region maintained services without the Book of Common Prayer. Thomas Harrison, a minister who had been a friend of Governor Berkeley and approved of the act which had been passed requiring services to be held according to the canons of the church of England, after the Indian massacre repented of the course he had pursued, and went and preached to the Nansemond people, and avowed his sympathy with Puritanism.

It is worthy of notice that Patrick Copland,[1] also written Copeland the friend of the Ferrars, projector of the first

---

error. Quoting from Hamor are these words, "two of *her* sons to see the marriage," the *her* should have been printed *his*, referring to Powhatan.

The following grants of land to Thomas Rolfe are on record:

August 8th, 1653, 525 acres north side of Chickahominy River called Fort James.
April 25, 1656, 325 acres in James City County.
Sept. 26, 1658, 50 acres, an angle in Chickahominy River.
Sept. 25, 1663, 750 acres S. W. side of Paspetank River.

[1] In 1614, Copland was chaplain of one of the ships of the East India Company, and in 1616, returned to England with an East Indian lad whom he had taught to read and write. At his suggestion, on Dec. 22d, 1616, the youth was publicly baptized in St. Dionis church, London, "as the first fruits of India." In 1617, Copland returned to the Indian Ocean in the "Royal James," and on the 2d of December, 1618, preached to the commanders of the English Fleet, the Admiral of whom was Sir Thomas Dale, formerly Governor of Virginia. Leaving Java in February, 1621, the "Royal James," begun the return voyage to England, and near Cape Good Hope, Copland collected £70 for the good of

English free school in North America, a building for which was commenced, at Charles City, and also in 1621, President elect of the College at Henrico, should at the Bermudas, on January 31, 1643-4, have left the church of England, and joined an Independent, non-liturgical body. A peti-

---

Virginia. On the 18th of April, 1622, he preached before the Virginia Company a thanksgiving sermon, and in it he speaks of "This noble Plantation tending so highly to the advancement of the Gospel, and to the honoring of our dread Sovereign, by enlarging of his kingdoms, and adding a fifth crown into his other four: for '*En dat Virginia quintum*,' is the motto of the legal seal of Virginia."

In the Mask of Flowers played by gentlemen of Grays' Inn upon Twelfth Night 1613-14, Kawasha, a God of the Virginians appears, and says:

"But now is Britannie fit to be
A seat for a fifth Monarchie."

On the 24th of October, 1621, the London Company, after conferring with Copland, determined to use the money raised on board the "Royal James" to the building of a free school in Virginia, at Charles City, and in March, 1622, a Mr. Dike or Dilke was selected as teacher. Richard Downes, bred a scholar, went over about 1619, in search of work at the Indian college in Henrico, as rector of which, in July, 1622, Copland was appointed, but owing to the Indian troubles and other difficulties, did not go to Virginia.

In June, 1622, Leonard Hudson, a carpenter, with wife and five apprentices left England to build the East Indian school at Charles city. In December, 1623, a collection was made for this school by the East India company both on shore, and on board their ships in port. This was not immediately called for, and on October 20, 1624, Sir John Wolstenholme moved that the Council of Virginia should receive the moneys collected. A Mr. Caroloff was sent over to look after the school, of whom the Governor and Council of Virginia, wrote under date of June 15, 1625. "We should be ready with our utmost endeavours to assist the pious work of the East India free school, but we must not dissemble that besides the unseasonable arrival, we thought the acts of Mr. Caroloff will overbalance all his other sufficiency though exceeding good."

Copland was induced to leave London in 1625, as a minister for Bermudas at a salary of 100 marks, and to have "a free school erected for the bringing up of youth in literature and good learning." He was accompanied by his wife and daughter. On the 20th of November, 1626, at a meeting of Bermudas Council was urged the support of the free school. The Governor who did not like free schools wrote to London that Copland had purchased land, and erected a

tion from this body, received the favorable consideration of the House of Commons in October, 1645, and on the 4th of the next November, Lord Admiral, the Earl of Warwick, with the Commissioners for Plantations, issued a proclamation ordering the petitioners "and all others in that part of the world" freedom of worship without "trouble and molestation," with permission to remove "their goods to any other part of America." In 1646, Governor Sayle of Bermudas, one of Copland's associates, on his way to England, in the interest of the free church, visited the non-conformists of Virginia, and proposed that they should unite with the movement to form a free church on the isle of the sea. Governor Winthrop of Massachusetts when he heard of this project seems to have written in disapproval, to which Harrison writing from Elizabeth river November 2d, 1646, replies "Had your propositions found us risen up, and in a posture of removal, there is weight and worth, and force enough in them to have staked us down again, but the good hand of the Lord hath put the same care and consideration into the hearts of some amongst us, and since you have permitted and encouraged us, to give an account of our matters we

---

building, and had "a project to train up children to be preachers, to send abroad to convert the Indians, and adds " I wish we had ministers contented to preach the gospel, and let this Free School alone, until we are free from debt." In 1634, Copland is spoken of, as having purchased four acres of land, on which he had built, and disbursed £1000 sterling. "Father Copland" as he was now called, on December 4, 1639, wrote to Governor Winthrop of Massachusetts, relative to the training of Indian children, and asks that he will send to him an Indian boy and a girl to be educated, whose passage he will pay.

Early in 1644, Copland left the Church of England. In 1647, he was imprisoned as a non-conformist, and was then a widower. In 1649, he went with an independent church to Eleuthera Isle, and was then about eighty years old. Before 1655, he was dead.

shall be bold to do it, when the mind of the Lord shall be made out unto us, and to seek, and take directions, (if you please commands), from you, for such shall all your advices be unto us, which are dictated, and breathed from so much goodness, sweetness, affection, experience, prudence, piety."

This letter was borne to Boston in the vessel of Captain Edward Gibbons, whom Scottow calls "the younger brother of the house of an honourable extraction" and the same person to whom Lord Baltimore, in 1650, tendered a commission as Councillor and Admiral of the Province of Maryland.

Governor Berkeley called an Assembly[1] which on the 3d of November, 1647, convened and took notice of the non-

---

[1] MEMBERS OF ASSEMBLY NOVEMBER 3, 1647,

Councillors present, John West, Richard Kempe, William Brocas, Thomas Petters, William Bernard, Henry Browne, George Ludlowe.

BURGESSES.

James City Co.

Capt. R. Hutchinson.	George Jordan.
Capt. Bridges Freeman.	William Davis.
Capt. Robert Shepheard.	Peter Ridley.

Charles City Co.

Capt. Edward Hill.	Capt. Francis Poythers.

Elizabeth City Co.

Anthony Elliot.	Henry Poole.
John Chandler.	

York County.

Richard Lee.	Francis Morgan.
Capt. W. Tayler.	

Upper Norfolk Co.

Moore Fantleroy.	Richard Wells.
Sam. Stoughton.	

VIRGINIA CAROLORUM. 199

conformists by the passage of the following: "Vpon divers informations presented to the Assembly against severall ministers for their neglect and refractory refusing, after warning given them to read common prayer, or divine service vpon the Sabbath days, contrary to the canons of the church, and acts of Parliament therein established, for future remedie thereof; Be it enacted, by the Governour, Council and Burgesses of this Grand Assembly that all ministers in the several cures throughout the colony doe duly vpon every Sabboth day read such prayers as are appointed and prescribed vnto them by the said booke of common prayer; And be it further enacted as a penaltie to such as have neglected, or shall neglect their duty herein, That no parishioner shall be compelled either by distresse, or otherwise to pay any manner of tythes or duties to any unconformist as aforesaid."

Supported by the House of Commons, and the Earl of Warwick, Harrison continued to worship according to the liberty permitted by Parliament, and in February, 1648,

Warwick County.

| Capt. Tho's Flint. | Randall Crew. |

Isle of Wight Co.

| Capt. John Upton. | John George. |

Lower Norfolk Co.

| Lt. John Sidney. | Cornelius Lloyd. |
| Henry Woodhouse. | Thos. Meares. |

Northampton Co.

| Edmund Scarborough. | Stephen Charlton. |

Northumberland Co.

| | William Presley. |

Henrico County.

| | Capt. Thos. Harris. |

wrote from Nansemond, to Governor Winthrop: "That golden apple, the ordinance of toleration is now fairly fallen into the lap of the saints, no more compelling men to go to the parish churches, or to sacrifice the abomination of their souls, or to offer up the sacrifice of fools; and yet all such as preach, print, or practice any thing, contrary to the known fundamentals of religion, the peace of the State, or power of godliness, are excluded from the sweetness of this indulgence. Concerning ourselves we have received letters full of of life, and love, from the Earl of Warwick, who engageth himself to the uttermost to advance the things of peace and welfare, and the Prince of Peace himself hath hitherto been so tender to us, that He hath not suffered any opposition yet to fall amongst us, a matter of no small admiration, considering where we dwell, even where Satan's throne is. Seventy-four have joined here in fellowship, and nineteen stand propounded, and many more, of great hopes and expectations."

In February, 1648, he again writes to Winthrop and gives much information of the state of parties in England, and mentions "that part of this news, I had from the mouth of an old Jesuit who wanted neither information to know the truth, nor malice to misreport and misrepresent."

About this time Philip Fisher,[1] a Jesuit who had been taken prisoner with Andrew White, by Ingle and carried to

---

[1] Fisher was born in Madrid, Spain, in 1595-6, entered the Jesuit order 1616-17, and in 1636 was superior of Maryland Mission; with Andrew White he was taken prisoner in 1645, by Ingle, and brought to England. After being confined some time in Newgate Prison, by the influence of Secretary Windebank he was released. He died in 1652. His letter in 1648 to Carrara, General of the Jesuits, is in Foley's *Records of English Jesuits*.

England, returned to Maryland, by way of Virginia, and is probably the person to whom Harrison refers.

A letter of Fisher has been preserved, dated March 1, 1648, in which he writes: "At length my companion and myself reached Virginia in the month of January, after a terrible journey of seven weeks. There I left my companion, and awaited myself the opportunity of proceeding to Maryland where I arrived in the month of February. * * * A road, by land, through the forest has just been opened from Maryland to Virginia. This will make it but a two days journey, and both countries can be united in one mission. After Easter, I shall wait upon the Governor of Virginia on important business.

In 1648, arrangements were completed by which the Virginia non-conformists removed to the shores of Chesapeake Bay, in sight of where is now the capitol of Maryland. Captain William Stone of Hungar's Neck, on the Eastern shore of the Chesapeake Bay in Virginia, a nephew of Thomas Stone, a haberdasher of London, a Protestant in faith and in sympathy with Parliament, was the agent who carried on the negotiations relative to removal, and was in August, 1648, commissioned Governor of Maryland.

One of the first to arrive in Maryland was William Durand[1] of Upper Norfolk. Richard Bennett also went to Maryland and remained for a short time.

---

[1] William Durand had listened to John Davenport, the first minister at New Haven, Ct., when he was the Vicar of St. Stephens, London. He brought with him late in 1648 or early in 1649, to Maryland his wife, daughter, four children, two freemen, Pell and Archer, and servants Thomas Marsh, Margaret Marsh, William Warren, William Hogg, and Ann Coles. In 1652, he was one of the Commissioners who made treaty with the Susquehannas at the Severn River,

Harrison visited Boston, in October, 1648, and awaited there the action of the House of Commons in England, on Berkeley's conduct toward the Nansemond congregation. Before the close of the year he married Dorothy, a daughter of Deputy Governor Samuel Symonds, who came from Yeldham, Essex. Mrs. Lucy Downing, sister of Gov. Winthrop of Massachusetts, under date of Dec. 12, 1648, wrote to her nephew John Winthrop of Connecticut: "You hear, I believe, our cousin Dorothy Simonds is now won and wedded to Mr. Harrison,[1] the Virginia Minister."

Rev. Dr. Warwick, in a discourse delivered in Dublin, Ireland, April 17, 1862, said, "The history of Dr. Harrison is rather remarkable. He was born in Yorkshire near Hull. While a child his parents removed to America." Perhaps Benjamin Harrison clerk of the Council, in 1634, was his father.

After remaining about two years in, or near Boston, Harrison went to England and never returned to America. Governor Winthrop under date of 8 mo, 20 day, 1648 (O. S.) alludes to the visit in these words: "In the time of our General Court heare arrived from Virginia, one Mr. Haryson, pastor of the Church at Nansemond there, and reported that the church was grown to one hundred and eighteen persons, and many more looking toward it, which had stirred up the Governor there, Sir William Berkeley, to make

---

now Annapolis. In October, 1651, he obtained a grant of land, at the Cliffs of Calvert county. In 1654, he was Secretary of the Province, and in 1657, he united with the Quakers. It is said he went to North Carolina.

[1] On the 21st day, 3d month, 1648 (O. S.) the wife of Edward Harrison, of Virginia, in Boston, gave birth to a son named John. On the 28th day, 8th month, 1649, (O. S.) died Elizabeth, a daughter aged about 7 days, of Thomas Harrison, pastor of the church at Virginia.

persecution against them, and he had banished their elder Mr. Durand and himself (viz. Mr. Haryson) was to depart the country by the third ship, at furthest, which had caused him to come to take advice of the magistrates and elders."

Harrison mentioned how Capt. Sayle of Bermudas and associates had obtained a permit from Parliament to settle on one of the Bahamas, and that under the charter he had liberty of worship, and also an entire separation of church and state, and that Sayle, wished the Virginians to cast in their lot with him. They were advised by Winthrop not to go to the lonely isle of the sea, and to remain if possible where they were.

A public market twice a week was established at Jamestown, in 1649, and the space allotted to it, was from the sandy hollow on the westward, by Peter Knight's store, extending eastward, to the house of Launcelott Elay, and the north side bounded by the Back river.[1] The population of the colony was about fifteen thousand persons, including three hundred negroes. While there were only two hundred horses, and mares, and fifty asses, owned by these

---

[1] Jamestown was first built on the west end of a peninsula of about two thousand acres. In 1611, it had "two rows of houses of framed timber, and some of them two stories and a garret high, and three large store-houses joined together in length." In 1616, as described by Rolfe, it had a population of fifty men under the command of Lt. Sharpe, in the absence of Captain Francis West. In 1619, Governor Yeardley found only the rude houses built in Sir Thomas Gates' time, and a church wholly of timber, fifty feet in length and twenty feet in breadth.

Before 1633, what was called the New Town, was connected by a bridge over the marsh and here resided Stephens, Yeardley and others. It is now under water. The first brick church was begun in 1639, and its foundations are visible, the second brick church whose ruined tower is now visible was built at a later period. The bricks used at Jamestown were made there.

planters, there were over twenty thousand bulls, cows, calves, and five thousand goats, and three thousand sheep. Beef was sold at two and a half pence a pound, and pork at three pence. They had six public breweries while many brewed their beer at home. As yet there was no saw mill for boards, but five water mills, and four wind mills, to grind corn.

Most of the masters of ships like Page and Thomas Stegg, had their horses, servants, and plantations in the colony, and carried to England, timber for masts, and building, as well as tobacco in their vessels. Bricks were also made in abundance, and there is no evidence that it was customary to import bricks for building purposes. During the first week of January, 1649, there were trading on James River, seven vessels from New England, seven from London, two from Bristol, and twelve Hollanders.

Governor Berkeley now lived at Green Spring two miles north of Jamestown, in a house of brick, made in the neighborhood, with a spacious hall way, and six rooms, and had set out an orchard of fifteen hundred trees, consisting of peaches, apricots, quinces and other kinds.

Richard Bennett in 1648, had raised many apples and made twenty butts of cider. Captain Brocas of the Council, a great traveler, had an excellent vineyard, and had made some wine, Richard Kinsman made out of his pear orchard forty or fifty butts of perry. A writer of the period refers to "worthy Captain Mathews, an old planter of above thirty years standing, one of the council, and a most deserving Commonwealth man * * * * He hath a fine house, and all things answerable to it; he sows yearly store of hemp and flax and causes it to be spun; he keeps weavers and hath a tan house, causes leather to be dressed, hath eight shoe-makers in their trade, hath forty negroe servants, brings them up to trade, in his house; he yearly sows abundance of wheat, barley, etc., the wheat he selleth at four shillings the bushel, kills store of beeves, and sells them to victual the ships when they come thither; hath abundance of kine, a brave dairy, swine great store, and poultry: he married the daughter of Sir Thomas Hinton, and in a word keeps a good house, lives bravely, and a true lover of Virginia, he is worthy of much honor."

When, in 1649, news came that Charles the First, his brother's friend, and one whom he had personally known, had been beheaded by order of Parliament, Governor Berkeley was grieved, and indignant, and although Stegg, Bennett, Claiborne, Mathews, and the most enterprising men were his political opponents, he called an Assembly[1]

---

[1] ASSEMBLY OF OCTOBER, 1644.

James City County.

Walter Chiles.	Geo. Read.
Thomas Swan.	Wm. Whittaker.
Wm. Barrett.	John Dunston.

Henrico County.   Wm. Hatcher.

Charles City County.

Capt. Edward Hill.   Cha's Sparrow.

Warwick County.

Capt. Tho's Harwood, Speaker,   John Walker.

Isle of Wight County.

George Hardy.   Robert Pitt.

which met on the 10th of October, and as the Burgesses were his friends, or indifferent whether the King, or House of Commons ruled in England, his sentiments were expressed by them, in a long, and vehement declaration.

But at the very time that Berkeley had action taken in Virginia that would gratify the widow of the King and the Royalists, on October 11, 1649, the Council of State in England, wrote to the Governor that they were informed, by petition of the congregation of Nansemond, that their minister Mr. Harrison, an able man, of unblamable conversation, had been banished the Colony, because he would not conform to the use of the Common Prayer Book, and as he could not be ignorant, that the use of it was prohibited by Parliament, he was directed to allow Mr. Harrison to return to his ministry;" but as has been mentioned he went to England and occupied positions of importance.

Six months before Harrison came to Boston, arrived Sir Edmund Plowden, Kt., who is thus noticed by Winthrop: "Arrived one Sir Edmund Plowden, who had been in Vir-

	Nansemond City Co.
John Carter.	Toby Smith.
	Elizabeth City Co.
Lt. Wm. Worlich.	John Robins.
	Lower Norfolk Co.
Barth. Hoskins.	Thos. Lambert.
	York County.
Capt. Ralph Wormeley.	Rowland Burnham.
	Northumberland Co.
Capt. Fr. Poythers.	Jo. Trussell.

ginia about seven years. He came first with a patent of a County Palatine for Delaware Baye, but wanting a pilot for that place went to Virginia, and then having lost his estate he brought over, and all his people scattered from him, he came hither to return to England for supply, intending to return and plant Delaware, if he could get sufficient strength to dispossess the Swedes," but he never returned.[1]

About the fifteenth day of September, 1649, the "Virginia Merchant," Capt. John Locker, a ship of three hundred tons burden, sailed for Jamestown with many passengers. Among those who engaged passage were Colonel Norwood a relative of Governor Berkeley, Major Francis Morison sympathizers with the King, and Major Stevens[2] who had served under Waller in the Parliament Army when it besieged Exeter, held by Sir John Berkeley, the Governor's

---

[1] In December, 1648, he had published *A Description of the Province of New Albion*. In 1651, he had chambers in London, and on the 29th of July, 1655, he made his will, dated at Waustead, which on the 22d of July, 1659 was proved. He requested to be buried in Lidbury church, in Shropshire, in the chapel of the Plowdens.

[2] Major William Stevens probably for some time remained in Accomac, where Yeardley and others held his political sentiments, and perhaps the same person who in March, 1651, declared his fealty to the "commonwealth of England as it is nowe established without King or House of Lords." He may have been the one who settled near the region, where he was cast away, in 1650, and thus became a citizen of Maryland. In the records of Somerset county, Md., is the following: "Richard Stevens, brother to William Stevens of Somerset County, in ye Province of Maryland, was youngest son of John Stevens of Lebourn in ye Parish of Buckingham in England, died at the house of his brother William aforesaid, ye 22d day of April, 1667, and was buried at his plantation called Rehoboth in ye county and province aforesaid, in America, ye 25th day of April."

In 1679, Col. William Stevens entered a tract of two thousand acres on the shores of the upper part of Assateague Bay near, where, in 1650 the "Virginia Merchant's" passengers landed in distress.

brother. Driven by a storm the ship found itself on the 12th of January, 1650, among the islands of Assateague Bay on the Atlantic coast of Maryland. Upon one of these, Colonel Norwood, Major Morrison, Stephens, Francis Cary and others landed, and after several days, crossed over to the main land and were hospitably treated by the Indians. A white fur trader, Jenkin Price,[1] arrived, and under his guidance, they began their journey to Nathaniel Littleton's plantation, the nearest in Accomac. Toward night of the first day they reached a point opposite Chincoteague Island, and at the close of the second day after twenty-five miles of travel, they came to Price's post on the Littleton plantation. From thence they proceeded to the plantation of Stephen Charlton, who gave them fresh clothing. Lower down in Accomac, now Northampton County, they visited Argall Yeardley, the son of the former Governor, who was born at Jamestown, in 1621, and recently married. Norwood in his Narrative writes: "It fell out very luckily for my better welcome, that he had not long before brought over a wife from Rotterdam that I had known almost from a child. Her father, Custis[2] by name kept kept a victualling house in that

---

[1] In October, 1660, the Assembly gave 5000 pounds of tobacco to Jenkin Price for the preservation of certain persons. Price was now poor and evidently this was a gratuity for his kindness to Norwood, now become Treasurer of Virginia.

[2] John Custis of Rotterdam, according to Meade, was of Irish descent, and was in Northampton county as early as 1640. He had six sons, Thomas of Baltimore, Ireland, Edward of London, Robert of Rotterdam, and John, William, and Joseph, residents of Virginia. The descendants of William are still in Accomac.

His son was a prominent man and High Sheriff of Northampton in 1664, and in 1676, Major General during Bacon's Rebellion. His estate on the eastern shore was called after Lord Arlington. His second wife was a daughter of Col.

town, lived in good repute, and was the general host of our nation there. The Esquire¹ knowing I had the honour to be the Governor's kinsman, and his wife knowing my conversation in Holland, I was received, caress'd more like a domestick, and near relation, than a man in misery, and a stranger. I stay'd there for a passage over the Bay, about ten days welcomed and feasted not only by the Esquire and his wife, but by many neighbours that were not too remote."

About the middle of February, Norwood, in a sloop, crossed the Chesapeake Bay and landed at Esquire Ludlow's²

Edward Scarborough. General John had but one child, a son also named John had several children, one of whom was the John whose tombstone has the following inscription:

"Under this new tombstone lies the body
of the Hon. John Custis Esquire
of the city of Williamsburg
and Parish of Bruton
Formerly of Hungars Parish on the
Eastern Shore
of Virginia, and county of Northampton
Aged 71 years and yet lived but seven years
which was the space of time he kept
A Bachelor's home at Arlington
on the Eastern Shore of Virginia"

On the opposite side is "The inscription put on this tomb was by his own positive orders.
Wm. Cosley, Man., Fenchurch Street
fecit London."

He married in Williamsburgh the daughter of Col. Daniel Parke, and sister of the profligate Col. Daniel Parke, Jr., who was killed when Governor of Leeward Islands. His son Daniel Parke Custis married Martha Dandridge, and the widow Martha Custis became the wife of General George Washington.

¹ Yeardley's father used to send his tobacco to Rotterdam.

² George Ludlow, of Massachusetts notoriety, see page 136.

plantation, near the entrance of York River. Here learning that Captain Wormeley[1], of the Council who lived not a furlong distant, was entertaining some guests who had recently come from England, he crossed the creek and went to the house where he found Sir Thomas Lunsford,[2] Sir Henry Chicheley, Sir Philip Honeywood, and Colonel Hammond. The rest of the winter was passed by Norwood at Green Spring near Jamestown, the plantation of Governor Berkeley. In May he was sent to visit Charles the Second, to solicit for the office of Treasurer of Virginia, then held by William Claiborne, a friend of Parliament, and a brother of his fellow traveler Francis Morison, was placed in command of the Fort at Point Comfort. Norwood found that Charles the Second had left Holland and gone to Scotland, having made a treaty with the Covenanters that he would sustain the Covenant and the church of Scotland.[3]

---

[1] Ralph Wormeley died before 1669, and his widow Agatha, married Sir Henry Chicheley, one of the guests referred to in the text. Wormeley's Creek was well known to the soldiers at the siege of Yorktown in 1781, and also in 1862.

[2] On August 7, 1649, a pass was issued for Sir Thomas Lunsford, wife, and children, to go to Virginia. Some months later, on condition of taking the engagement Sir Henry Chicheley also was permitted to go. Chicheley in later years married Agatha, the widow of his entertainer.

[3] Henry Norwood, in July, 1661, received the appointment for life as captain of Sandown Castle, Kent, and the same year was commissioned as Lt. Colonel of Lord Rutherford's regiment, and deputy governor of Dunkirk. In September, 1663, he came to England and "kissed the King's hand" and began to raise recruits. He is next Colonel of the regiment and at Tangiers, and Capt. Charles Norwood served under him. In a letter dated London Feb. 20, 1665 (O.S.) are these words: "Lord Sandwich goes on Wednesday down to Portsmouth to take shipping for Spain. Henry Norwood goes in the ship with Lord Sandwich, which after the Ambassador's landing, carries him to Tangiers." The

About the time of Norwood's visit in June, 1650, the King at Breda, Holland, appointed a new Council for Virginia, evidently at Berkeley's suggestion, one of whom was Sir W. Davenant, Kt.,[1] whom he also appointed Governor of Maryland, in February, 1649-50, when he was at the Isle of Jersey. The King in Davenant's commission uses this language. "Whereas the Lord Baltimore, Proprietary of the Province of Maryland, in America, doth visibly adhere to the rebells of England, and admit all kinde of schismaticks and sectaries, and other ill-affected persons, into the said plantations of Maryland, so that we have cause to apprehend very great prejudice to our service thereby, and very danger to our plantations in Virginia, who have carried themselves with so much loyalty, and fidelity to the King, our father, of blessed memory." The commission empowered the Governor to see that no danger arose in Maryland "to our loyall plantations in Virginia." Further requiring him "to hold due correspondence with our trusty and well beloved Sir William Berkeley, Knight, our Governor of the said plantations of Virginia, and to comply

---

Prince of Fez presented him with a horse, a camel, and a young lion. In 1667, he was Lt. Governor of Tangiers.

In 1675, he came from Holland to London to confer with Lord Culpepper, and the Agents of the Virginia Colony.

[1] Sir Wm. Davenant, Kt. was Shakspeare's godson, and like his sponsor in baptism, was given to poetry. He never reached the Chesapeake Bay. With the aid of Henrietta Maria, the widow of the beheaded King, he sailed from Normandy, with a company of weavers, and other artisans, but on the voyage was captured and taken to England. Lodged in the Tower of London he there finished his poem, "Gondibert," and at length was released "from durance vile" through the friendly intercession of Secretary John Milton, the great Puritan poet.

with him in all things necessary for our service and the mutual good of both plantations."

Lord Baltimore had been informed of a disposition upon the part of Virginians to take possession of their old trading posts, and in a letter to Governor Stone, dated August 26, 1651, wrote: "We understand that Sir William Barkely hath lately taken upon him, to grant a commission to one Edm'd Scarborough of Accamack, in Virginia, to seat Palmer's Island within our Province."

The Parliament of England in 1650, to protect their commerce, which had suffered from the enterprise of the Dutch, passed the Navigation Act which forbade any goods being carried to the Colonies, except in English vessels, and declared that the Colonies having originated from the authority, wealth, and population of England, they were dependent upon, and subject to the legislation of Parliament. The trade with Holland had been a source of revenue to Virginia, and before the Burgesses in Assembly at Jamestown on March 17th, 1650-1, Governor Berkeley delivered the following violent harangue.

"GENTLEMEN You perceave by the Declaration, that the men of *Westminister* have set out, which I beleeve you have all seene, how they meane to deale with you hereafter, who in the time of their wooing and courting you proposed such hard conditions to be performed on your part & on their owne nothing but a benigne acceptance of your duties to them. Indeed methinks they might have proposed something to us which might have strengthened us to beare those heavy chaines they are making ready for us, though it were but an assurance that we shall eat the bread for which our owne Oxen plow, and with owne sweat we reape, but this assurance (it seems) were a franchise beyond the condition they have *resolv'd on the Question* we ought to be in: For the reason why they talk so *Magisterially* to us, is this, we are forsooth their worships slaves, bought with their money, and by consequence ought not to buy or sell, but with those they shall authorize, with a few trifles, to cozen us of all for which we toile and labour.

"If the whole Current of their reasoning were not as ridiculous, as their actions have been Tyrannicall and bloudy; we might wonder with what browes they could sustaine such impertinent assertions: For if you look into it, the strength of their argument runs onely thus: we have laid violent hands on your Land-Lord, possess'd his Manner house where you used to pay your rents, therefor now tender your respects to the same house you once reverenced: I call my Conscience to witness, I lie not. I cannot in all their Declaration perceave a stronger argument for what they would impose on us, than this which I have now told you: they talke indeed of money laid out on this country in its infancy: I will not say how little, nor how Centuply repaid, but will onely aske, was it theirs? They who in the beginning of this warr were so porre & indigent that the wealth and rapines of three kingdomes & their Churches too, cannot yet make rich, but are faine to seeke out new Territories and impositions to sustaine their Luxury amongst themselves.

"Surely Gentlemen we are more slaves by nature, then their power can make us, if we suffer ourselves to be shaken with these paper bulletts & those on my life are the heaviest they Either can or will send us. 'Tis true, with us, they haue long threatened the Barbados, yet not a ship goes thither but to beg trade, nor will they do to us, if we dare Honourably resist their Imperious Ordinance. Assuredly, Gentlemen, you have heard under what heavy burthens the afflicted *English* Nation now groanes, and calls to heaven for reliefe : how new and formerly unheard of impositions make the wives pray for barrennes, and their husbands deafnes to exclude the cryes of their succourles staruing children : And I am confident you do believe that none would long endure this slavery, if the Sword at their throats Did not compell them to Languish under the misery they hourely suffer. Looke on their sufferings with the eyes of understanding and that will prevent all your teares, but those of Compassion. Consider with what prisons and Axes they have paid those that have served them to the hazard of their Soules : Consider yourselves how happy you are, and have been, how the Gates of Wealth and Honour are shut on no man, and that there is not here an Arbitrary hand, that dares to touch the substance of either poore or rich. But, that which I would haue you chiefly to consider with thankfulness is : That God hath separated you from the guilt of the crying bloud of our Pious Soveraigne of ever blessed memory : But mistake not Gentlemen part of it will yet staine your garments if you willingly submit to those murtherers hands that shed it.

"I tremble to thinke how the oathes they will impose will make those guilty of it, that haue long abhor'd the traiterousnesse of the act: But I confesse having had so frequent testimonies of your courages, I cannot haue a reasonable Suspition of any cowardly falling of from the former resolutions. and haue onely mentioned this last, as a part of my duty and care of you, not of any reall doubts and feares; or if with untryed men we were to argue on this subject, what is it can be hoped for in a change, which we have not already? Is it liberty? The sun looks not on a people more free than we are from all oppression. Is it wealth? Hundreds of examples shew us that Industry & Thrift in a short time may bring us to as high of it as the country and and our Conditions are yet capable of. Is it security to enjoy this wealth when gotten? With out blushing I will speake it, I am confident theare lives not that person can accuse me of attempting the least act against any man's property. Is it peace? The Indians, God be blessed, round about us are subdued: we can only feare the Londoners, who would faine bring us to the same poverty, wherein the Dutch found and relieved us, would take away the liberty of our consciences, and tongues, and our right of giving and selling our goods to whom we please.

"But, Gentlemen, by the Grace of God, we will not so tamely part with our King, and all these blessings we enjoy under him. and if they oppose us, do but follow me, I will either lead you to victory, or loose a life which I cannot more gloriously sacrifice than for my loyalty and your security."

The speech was published with this title:

THE SPEECH
of the HONOURABLE
WILLIAM
BERKELEY
Governour and Capt: Generall of *Virginia*
to the *Burgesses* in the *Grand*
Assembly at *James Towne* on the
17 of *March* 1651½

TOGETHER WITH A
DECLARATION
Of the whole Country, occasioned upon the
Sight of a printed paper from England
Intituled An Act, &c

HAGH
Printed by Samuel Brown, *English*
Bookseller 1651

CHAPTER VII.

UNDER THE COMMONWEALTH OF ENGLAND, A.D., 1652, TO A.D., 1660.

PARLIAMENT COMMISSIONERS APPOINTED. SURRENDER OF NORTHAMPTON PEOPLE. NOTICE OF CAPTAIN STEGG. RICHARD BENNETT, GOVERNOR. THE BENNETT FAMILY. LORD BALTIMORE ACKNOWLEDGES THE COMMONWEALTH. NOTICE OF JOHN HAMMOND AND THOS. WOODWARD. FRANCIS LOVELACE RETURNS TO ENGLAND. SAMUEL DRISIUS, DUTCH CLERGYMAN. FRANCIS YEARDLEY VISITS ROANOKE INDIANS. COL. ED. HILL. WILLIAM BATT. HENRY FLEET. JOHN CARTER. ROGER LUDLOW. THE WITCH MARY LEE. EDWARD DIGGES AND SILK CULTURE. GOVERNOR DIGGES. DEATH OF COUNCILLOR GOOCH. NOTICE OF THE ELDER NATHANIEL BACON. RELIGIOUS CONDITION. INDIANS ATTACKED BY COL. HILL. GOV. DIGGES VISITS LONDON. ASSEMBLY'S LETTER TO CROMWELL. COMPROMISE OF BOUNDARY QUESTION. ARRIVAL OF QUAKERS. RICHARD LEE. HENRY CORBIN. ISAAC ALLERTON. THOMAS GERARD. JOHN WASHINGTON. GOVERNOR SAMUEL MATHEWS. DEBATE ON CONSTITUTIONAL LAW. COUNCILLORS BRIDGER AND MITCHELL. EXPEDITION AGAINST ASSATEAGUE INDIANS. ELECTION OF GOVERNOR BERKELEY. THEODORIC BLAND. COMMISSIONERS FROM NEW AMSTERDAM. SIR HENRY MOODY.

HE Council of State, of the Commonwealth of England, after long deliberation,[1] in 1651, determined to send commissioners, to reduce the plantations of Chesapeake Bay, to due obedience. Instructions

---

[1] As early as December 23, 1649, the Committee of Admiralty summoned to appear before them, Maurice Thompson, Benjamin Worsley, William Penoyer

28

were issued to Capt. Robert Dennis, Mr. Richard Bennett, Mr. Thomas Stegg and Capt. William Claiborne as commissioners. Under the direction of Capt. Dennis they were to proceed with two ships, the "John," and a Guinea frigate of Holland and upon the arrival of all, or any two, in Virginia, they were to assert the power of Parliament, and the Commonwealth of England, and to offer indemnity and issue pardons, with such limitations as they deemed best. Those taking the oath to be true and faithful to the Commonwealth of England, without a King, or House of Lords, were to choose their own Burgesses, who would make all necessary laws for local goverment, not contrary to those of Parliament.

---

and William Allen, to testify what the interest of the Commonwealth required in Virginia, and on the 9th of January, 1649-50, this Committee reported to the Council of State, relative " to the government of Virginia and present juncture of affairs in relation to that plantation" and advised that " Commissioners be nominated by Parliament in whom the government may be immediately placed." It was more than eighteen months after this report, before definite action was taken. On September 23, 1657, Captain Curtis was authorized to act as Commissioner in case of the death of Capt. Dennis. A fleet of armed merchant vessels accompanied the ships of war. On August 15, 1651, Mr. Stegg, to be appointed one of the Commissioners, had liberty to go with the fleet to Virginia, and liberty was given to all going in the fleet, to carry shoes and other goods usually sent thither for trade."

The Virginia fleet arrived reduced by storms, and many men sick, in December, 1651, at Barbadoes. Six hundred men were able to do duty and Sir George Ayscue, taking advantage of their presence, summoned Lord Willonghby to surrender the place, to Parliament. The fleet after remaining seven days, proceeded on its way toward Virginia.

Before the fleet left England, under date of October 2, 1651, the Council of State sent to Richard Bennett in Virginia, some instructions which were not to be opened until after the conutry was reduced to the obedience of the Commonwealth.

Capt. Dennis and Captain Stegg,[1] were lost in the ship "John" in which they sailed, but Captain Curtis arriving

---

[1] Captain Stegg was a prominent Virginian, see p. 135. As early as 1637, he was known as a merchant. On October 5, 1651, just before "John" sailed, he made his will, an abstract of which, by H. F. Waters, is in the *N. E. Hist. Gen. Register*, for April, 1885. In it, he bequeathed to his son Thomas, his whole estate in Virginia, and an interest, in certain vessels; to his daughter Grace, the wife of John Byrd, goldsmith, of London, houses in London; and to his wife Elizabeth, during widowhood, or natural life, his estate after the payment of debts and legacies, but in case of her marriage eight hundred pounds.

His son Thomas, also became an influential man. In 1662, he received a grant of 800 acres in Henrico County and in January, 1663, in Henrico County, 1230 acres including the site of the city of Richmond, and the same year, another 1850 acres in the same county. Upon Heerman's Map drawn in 1670, and published in 1673, the isle at the foot of the Falls of James River, is marked "Stegg's Isle."

The junior Thomas Stegg, made his will March 31, 1670, which was proved on May 15, 1671. His mother had become the wife of Thomas Grendon of London. He left to the children of his sister Grace Byrd, wife of John of London, legacies. His nephew William Byrd, received also a large estate. At the time of making the will William was only eighteen years of age, and he is cautioned "not to be led away by the evil instructions he shall receive from others, but to be governed by the prudent and provident advice of his aunt, the testator's "loving wife."

In 1685, a Thomas Grendon died at sea, and Col. Wm. Byrd in a letter dated June 5th, 1685, wrote: "I am heartily sorry for the death of Coz. Grandon and wish you may secure yourself in England, for the old woman will carry away all here." The latter end of January, 1684-5 his aunt Mrs. Grendon, had married a Mr. Edward Brain who came to Virginia in September, 1684, with thirty servants, and a large amount of goods. Byrd calls Mrs. Grendon, "the old gentlewoman."

About the time that the elder Stegg died, two others connected with the Virginia trade also wrote their wills.

Thomas Fawne about to sail for Virginia, on Dec. 25, 1651, made a will in which he gives to Robert Williams, surgeon of the Virginia trading ship, "Peter," a watch and cornelian ring; to his servant William Martin, passage to Virginia, his freedom there, and a suit of clothes, and he makes John Younge and John Stone his executors.

Robert Nickolson of London, merchant, son of Francis of Ipswich, made his will on November, 10, 1651. He appears to have been religiously disposed, as

with the Guinea frigate, showed the duplicate instructions to Bennett, and Claiborne, who were in Virginia.

At the time that Captain Curtis appeared in the waters of the Chesapeake, Major General Gibbons of New England, who had been commissioned by Lord Baltimore, Admiral of the Province of Maryland, had his pinnace seized by two persons, Wilson and Read, connected with the fleet of Curtis, because the leading men in Maryland were averse to a surrender to the Parliament, as their powers had been derived from the Proprietary of the Province. Gibbons went to England and complained of the treatment received, and asked for damages, but the Council of state reported adversely. They did not think that they could "give the petitioner any relief, because it did not appear, that one penny, of that he lost, came into the hands of the State."

The Commissioners proceeded to execute their commis-

---

he bequeathes ten pounds sterling toward the relief of the English captives in Turkey and forty shillings to Mr. Pickett, minister of Pontibridge, Essex. He was also on the ship " Peter " as he gives to the master of the ship, John Younge, twenty shillings to buy his wife a ring. To Thomas Fawne two pairs of Cordovant gloves and *Leo Afer* [Africanus] a book of History : to John Corbin his waisting coat, stuff coat, Turkey waistcoat, and two pairs of Cordovant gloves; To John Richards two pairs of Cordovant, and Locker's sermons ; to John Stone twenty shilling, two pairs of Cordovants and the rest of the books in the cabin ; " to Capt. Sam. Matthewes of Virginia Esq., one pair of Buckskin gloves, and to Mrs. Matthews his wife two pairs of kid skin gloves ;" to Samuel, his son a pair of buckskin gloves, and to another son a pair of Cordovant. To Mrs. Mary Bernard of Warwick river he gave six pairs of kid gloves, and to each of her daughters three pairs. To Mrs. Veheath Land Vernald, daughter of widow Mary Vernald of Warwick River, he gave a diamond ring, and also a gold ring with the motto " *Idem qui pridem.*"

Cordovan leather so called from Cordova in Spain. Spenser in " Faery Queen " alludes to the " Buskins he wore of costliest cordwaine."

sion,[1] and although Governor Berkeley blustered and talked of resistance, the Commissioners who had the sympathies of some of the best planters, upon arriving at Jamestown, convinced the Burgesses, that resistance would be disastrous to the prosperity of the Colony, and on the 12th of March, 1651-2,[2] it was agreed that they would submit to the Com-

---

[1] Whitelocke in *Memorials of the English Affairs* under date of May 14, 1652, has this : " Letters, that the Inhabitants of Virginia willingly submitted to the Government of the Parliament."

[2] The people of Northampton county, on the eastern shore of the bay, seem to have had the engagement left with them to sign on the 11th of March, and signatures were obtained during the month, as appears from the following on the County Records.

"The Engagm't tendered to ye Inhabitants of Northampton County, Eleaventh of March, 1651 (O. S).

" Wee whose Names are subscribed ; doe hereby Engage and promise to bee true and faithfull to the Commonwealth of England as it is nowe Established without Kinge or House of Lords.

25 of March

Nathan'll Littleton	Argoll Yardley	Rich. Vaughan
Obedience Robins	Wm. Waters	Thos. Johnson
Edm. Scarburgh	Wm. Jones	Dan'll Baker
Edw. Douglas	Thos. Sprigge	Thomas Hlut
Peter Walker	Jno. Dye	Thos. Figby
Wm. Andrews Sen'r	X'ofer Maior	Robert Marryott
Nich. Waddelone	Allex. Harryson	Jno. Parkes
Allex. Addison	Wm. Munds	Wm. Stanley
James Barnabye	Francis Flood	Jno. Ayers
Jno Pannell	Steph. Stringer	Robert Harryson
Sam'll Sone	X'ofer Jarvis	Luke Billington
Jno. Denman	Nich. Scott	Randolfe Hutchinson
James Berry	Anth. Hodgskins	Nich. Granger
Phillip Farrant	Jno. Nuthall	Thos. Truman
Jno. Tilney	Wm. Whittington	Allex. Madoxe
Sampson Robins	Wm. Coake	Henr. Armitradinge
Jno. Ellis	Ben. Cowdrey	Steph. Charlton
Jeffery Minshatt	Levyne Denwood	Jno. Parramore
Georgine Hacke	Robert Andrews	Jno. Robearts

monwealth, "and their subscription be acknowledged a voluntary act, not forced nor constrained by a conquest upon the country." The Commissioners accepted a clause declaring that: "Virginia shall have and enjoy the antient

| Rich. Hamby | Ben. Mathews | X'ofer Dixon |
| Edw. Harrington | Jno. Stringer | |

Triccsimo Die Marty 1651 (O. S.)

Edm. Mathews	Ambrose Dixon	Steph. Horsey
Jno. Custis	Wm. Horose	Jno. Robinson
Jno. Johnson Jun.	Robt. Blake	Symon Bailey
Farmer Jones	Rich. Hill	Jno. Hinman
Jno. Dixon	Jno. Pott	Jno. Coulson
Jno. Taylor	Edw. Marshall	Phill. Mathews
Mathew Stone	Jno. Dolling	Edw. Leene
Tobine Selve	Charles Scarburgh	James Johnson
Rich. Nottingham	Walter Williams	Elial Hartree
Nehemiah Coventon	Wm. Stephens	Charles Ratliffe
Francis Morgan	Jno. Thatcher	Jno. Graye
Wm. Ward	Rich. Smyth	Jno. Willyams
Jno. Johnson, Senr	David Wheatley	Randall Revell
Edw. Southren	Robert Berry	Wm. Smyth
Jno. Merryfin	Wm. Preeninge	Wm. Custis
Dan'll Chadwell	Tho. Butterie	Tho. Miller
Jno. Teeslocke	Jno. James	Robert Baily
Jno. Coulson	Tho. Price	Jno. Whitehead
Jno. Machaell	Rich. Baily	Armstrong Foster
Jno. Cornley	Rich. Hudson	Wm. Andrews Jun'r
Rich. Newell	Rich. Alleyn	Sam'l Calvert
Jno. Lee	Jno. Lewis	Francis Goodman
Phill Merrydayr	Jno. Johnson, Sen'r	Jno. Willyams
Edw. Moore	Wm. Gaskins	Wm. Corner
Jno. Brillyant	Nicholas Jueyre	Rich. Smyth
Jno. Rutter	James Adkinson	Sam'l Robins
Andrew Hendrye	Wm. Gower	Jno. Garnell
Antho. Carpenter	Wm. Boucher	David Kiffyn
Jno. Wise	Jno. Johnson Jr.	Jno Browne
Wm. Taylor	Wm. Jorden	Wm. Moultor
Jno. Waleford	X'ofer Kirke	Wm. Browne
Mick Richett	Thos. Savage	Rich. Kellam

bounds and lymitts granted by the charters of the former Kings, and that we shall seek a new charter from the parliament for that purpose, against any, that have intrencht vpon the rights thereof."

It was further promised that Virginia should have free trade, as the people of England, according to the laws of the Commonwealth, and " be free from all taxes, customes, and impositions whatsoever" and that no forts should be erected without their consent, nor garrisons maintained. That nothing should be done for a year, as to the exclusion of the Book of Common Prayer, and that all who refused the oath, could have a year before removing from the Colony.

Governor Berkeley was permitted to send to the excited King, a messenger, at his own expense, to give an account of the surrender, and that neither he, nor any of his Council for a whole year, should be censured for prayers and kind words about the King in their homes, and quiet social gatherings.

Heretofore, the colonists had been governed by commissioners and instructions from England, but hereafter they were promised freedom in the choice of officers. A Dutch ship had left some goods in the Colony, and cleared for Holland without paying customs due, and it was provided that

Rich. Bruducke	Sam'l Smothergall	Jno. Edwards
Thos. Clarke	Wm. Colebourne	Wm. Mellinger
Thos. Crecro	Alex. Maddoxe	Raph'll Hudson
Sam'l Jones	Sam'l Powell	Rich. Tegger
Hen. White	James Brewee	Samuel Goldfine
X'ofen Calvert	Wm Luddington	

Recordantur vicesino die Augusty Ano. 1652
Teste Edm. Mathews, *Cloc. Cur.*

Governor Berkeley's back salary should be paid by the sale of these goods.

The month after the acknowledgment of the Commonwealth of England, an Assembly duly elected, met at Jamestown, and on April 30th, "after long and serious debate and advice for the settling of the government of Virginia, it was unanimously voted and concluded by the Commissioners appointed by the authority of Parliament, and by all the Burgesses of the several counties and places respectively until the further pleasure of the State be known, that Mr. Richard Bennett Esq., be Governor[1] for the ensuing year, or

---

[1] The Bennett family always had influence in Virginia. The Governor was the nephew of Edward Bennett who had been Deputy Governor of the Merchant Adventurers of England resident at Delft. He was a prominent London merchant. Early in 1621, he visited Delf, and Rotterdam, the tobacco marts. Sir Edwin Sandys, at a meeting of the Virginia Company of London, on April 12, 1621, moved "that in regards Mr. Edward Bennett, a cittizen, had so well deserved of this Company by a treatise wch he made touching the incouvenience that the importacōn of Tobacco out of Spaine had brought into this land; and by his often attendance vpon the Comittees of the Lower howse of Comons about the same, * * * that therefore he might haue the fauor to be admitted a free member of the Company wch mocōn was thought very reasonable, and being putt to the question was generally assented unto and confirmed by the erecōn of hands."

At a meeting of the Company on October 24, 1621, the Deputy mentioned "that the first patent was for a gentleman that had deserved singularly well of the Company before hee was a member thereof. And since his admittance hee had been att a veric great charge for transportinge of people to Virginia, namely Mr. Bennett who now joyns himselfe in this business with Mr. Wiseman and Mr. Ayres, and divers other their associates."

At the time of the Indian uprising in March, 1621–2, more than fifty were killed at what was known as Edward Bennett's plantation, although he never came to America.

In November, 1622, a vessel of twenty tons burden, of which Isaac Madison was Captain and Robert Bennett Master, traded with the Indians around Chesapeake Bay, and in a volume of Virginia manuscript records in the Library of Congress is the following: "Whereas Mr. Robert Bennet of Wariscoyak, Mercht

until the next meeting of the Assembly, with all the just powers and authorities that may belong to the place lawfully. And likewise that Colonel William Clayborne be Secretary of State with all belonging to that office, and is to be next in place to the Governor; next that of the Council of State to be as followeth, Captain John West, Samuel Mathewes, Col. Nathaniel Littleton, Col. Argoll Yeardly, Col. Thomas Pettus, Col. Humphry Higginson, Col. George Ludlow, Col. William Barrett, Capt. Bridges Freeman, Capt. Thomas Harwood, Major William Taylor, Capt. Francis Epps, Col. John Cheesman, and they shall have power to execute, and do equal justice to all the people and inhabitants of this Colony according to such instruction as they have, or shall receive from the Parliament, and according to the known law of England, and the act of Assembly have established."

---

late dec'd is indebted to Mr. William Benet Minister of said plantation the sum of 1533⅓ lbs of tobacco for his salary for two years, this is therefore to require John Chew of James City, Merchant, who hath the management of the business of the s'd Robert Benet to satisfy and pay unto the said William Benet the sum of 1533⅓ lbs.

"James City, March 20, 1623."

Bennet the clergyman arrived at the Bennett or Warosquoyak plantation in 1621, having come in the ship "Sea Flower" and toward the close of 1624, he died. His wife Catherine came in 1622, in the ship "Abigail" and on the 22d of January, 1624–5, was residing at Shirley, a widow, with an infant named William, three weeks old.

On the 25th of January, 1624–5, a muster of Mr. Edward Bennett's servants at Wariscoyak was taken, and the number was twelve, two of whom were negroes.

Richard the nephew, was a Burgess from the Wariscoyak district in 1629, and in 1632, one of the Justices of the monthly Court. In 1624, he was a Councillor. Owing to his Puritan sympathies in 1649, he went to Maryland, but remained a short period, and in 1651, was appointed a Commissioner in behalf of the Commonwealth of England. His subsequent career will be referred to in another chapter.

'This Assembly' declared on the 5th of May that " the right of election of all officers of the Colony appertain to

---

[1] MEMBERS OF ASSEMBLY, CONVENED APRIL 26, 1652.

Henrico County.

Robert Wetherall.
Lt. Col. John Fludd.
Hen. Soane.

Wm. Hatcher

Charles City Co.

Capt. Dan. Mansill.
George Stephens.
William Whittakar.

Isle of Wight Co.

Robert Pitt.
George Hardie.

John George.
John Moore.

Nanzemond Co.

Capt. Thos. Due.

Ed. Major, Speaker.

Lower Norfolk Co.

Cor Lloyd.
Thos. Lambert.

Hen Woodhouse.
Charles Burrowes.

Elizabeth City Co

Peter ———.

John Sheppard.

Warwick River County.

Lt. Col. Sam. Matthews.

Wm. Whitby, Speaker.

York County.

Capt. Francis Morgan.
Henry Lee.

Capt. Austin Warner.

Northampton Co.

Major Obedience Robins.
Edmund Scarbrough.
Thos. Johnson.

William Jones.
Antho. Hoskins.

Northumberland Co.

John Mottram.

George Fletcher.

Gloucester Co.

Hugh Guinne.

Lancaster Co.

Francis Willis.

the Burgesses, the representation of the people," and that the Governor and Council should sit in the same house, and take the same oath as the Burgesses.

Argall Yeardley, and his brother Francis, Richard Lee, Col. Samuel Mathews, and others, of the leading colonists, upheld the acts of Parliament, and after the adjournment of the Assembly, Mathews was sent to obtain a ratification of the articles of agreement with the Commissioners of Plantions. They were read in the House of Commons on the 28th of August, and Lord Baltimore and others objected to the clauses which provided that Parliament should restore to them the region which they had held, before the Province of Maryland had been created. The Committee found that the settlement could not "speedily, be proceeded in." Baltimore, always judicious and politic, where his own interest was concerned, presented among others, the following reasons why Maryland should remain under a separate government. "First. It is much better to keep that government still divided from Virginia (as it has been for these twenty years past), than to unite them, for by that means this Commonwealth will have the more power over both, by making one an instrument, as occasion may require, to keep the other, in its due obedience, to this Commonwealth.

"*Secondly*, In case any defection should happen in either Colony (as lately was in Virginia), the other may be a place of refuge for such as continue faithful to its Commonwealth, as Maryland lately was. Upon that occasion, which it could not have been, in case the government of that place had been at that time united into, or have any dependence on Virginia.

"*Thirdly* It will cause an emulation in both, which of them shall give the better account of their proceedings to the supreme authority of this Commonwealth, on which they both depend, and also which of them shall give better satisfaction to the planters and adventurers of both.

"*Fourthly*, The Lord Baltimore having an estate, and his residence in England, this Commonwealth will have a better assurance of the due obedience of that plantation, and the planters and adventurers thither, of having right done unto them, in case the government thereof have still a dependence upon him, and he upon this Commonwealth (as he had before on the late King), than if the government of that place, at so remote a distance, should be disposed of into other hands, who had little, or nothing here to be responsible for it, and whose interest and residence were wholly there.

"*Fifthly*, By the continuance of his interest in the government, those of this Commonwealth, and the people there, are eased of the charged of a Deputy Governor, which he at his own charge maintains; the inhabitants there being so poor, and so like to be, for many years, as they are not able to contribute anything toward it.

"*Sixthly*, If the Lord Baltimore should, by this Commonwealth, be prejudiced in any of the rights or privileges of his patent, of that Province, it would be a great discouragement to others in foreign plantations, upon any exigency to adhere to the interest of this Commonwealth, because it is notoriously known, that by his express directions, his officers, and the people there, did adhere to the interest of this Commonwealth, when all other English plantations, except New England, declared against the Parliament, and at that time received their friends in time of distress, for which, he was like, divers times, to be deprived of his interest there, by the Colony of Virginia, and others who had commission from the late King's eldest son for that purpose, as appears by a commission granted by him, to Sir Wm. Davenant."

On the 25th of November, 1652, another Assembly convened at Jamestown, and exercised its right to determine the qualifications of its members. John Hammond was expelled because he was well known as "a scandalous person, and a frequent disturber of the peace of the country by libell, and other illegal practices." James Pyland of Isle of Wight county was not permitted to take his seat, because he had circulated a "blasphemous catechise" and was a sympathizer with Thomas Woodward a violent royalist, who had been assayer of the London mint, and was dismissed in 1649, by Bradshaw, President of the Council of State, because of his opposition to Parliament, and who came to Virginia vowing that he would never see England again, until his Majesty's return from exile.[1]

The Assembly[2] transacted but little business as they were

---

[1] Soon after Charles the Second ascended the throne, Woodward was remembered, and he and his son John appointed assay masters of the mint. He remained in Virginia, as when his son John died, in 1665, the wife of John apparently in England, waived all claims and consented to the appointment of a Charles Giffard as assay master.

[2] MEMBERS OF ASSEMBLY NOVEMBER 1652.

Henrico County.   Capt. William Harris.

awaiting intelligence from their agent in London. A new parish was created in Northampton county, formerly Ac-

Charles City Co.

Capt. Hen. Perry.   Capt. Woodliff.
Capt. Dan. Llewellin.   Capt. Chas. Sparrow.
Major Abraham Wood.

James City Co.

—— Wetherell.   Hen. Soane.
Abra. Watson.

Surrey Co.

William Thomas   George Stephens.
William Edwards.

Isle of Wight Co.   Charles Reynolds.

Warwick County

Lt. Col. Matthews.   William Whitby.

Nansemond Co.

Col. Tho. Dew Speaker.   Peter Montague.

Lower Norfolk Co.

Lt. Col. Cor. Lloyd.   Charles Burrows.
Major Thos. Lambert.

Elizabeth City Co.

Peter Ransome.   Theo. Howe.

York County.

Capt. Steph. Gill.   Major X'pher Calthorpe.
William Gonge.

Gloucester Co.

Col Hugh Guinne.   Francis Willis.

Northampton Co.

Lt. Col. Robbins.   Steph. Charlton.

Lancaster Co.

Capt. H'y Fleet.   Wm. Underwood.

comac above Ocquahanock Creek. George Fletcher was granted the privilege for fourteen years, of brewing in wooden vessels. Colonel William Claiborne, and Capt. Henry Fleet, so long identified with Maryland, now one of the Burgesses from Lancaster county, were authorized with their associates "to discover, and enjoy such benefits, and trades for fourteen years, as they shall find out in places where no English have ever been and discovered, nor have had particular trade, and to take up such lands by patents, proving their rights, as they shall think good. Abraham Wood, a representative from Charles City county, was given similar privileges.

Col. Francis Lovelace, who had for his attachment to the King, suffered loss of office and sequestration of property, was in Virginia at the time of the surrender, and received permission from Commissioners Bennett and Claiborne to repair to the late King of the Scots, Charles was called.[1]

The Navigation Act of Parliament, designed to protect English manufacturers and merchants by prohibiting foreigners trading with the colonies, not only inconvenienced the settlers in Virginia, but led them to look upon smuggling, as a necessity. As soon as Dutch vessels ceased to arrive at Jamestown, London traders raised the price of their goods, and ship owners increased the price of transportation. In a short period freight upon tobacco doubled, while the staple only brought one-third what it did before the Navigation Act.

---

[1] Francis Lovelace, upon the accession of Charles the Second to the throne, was made Recorder of Canterbury. He had a son Goldwell and died about 1663. He was probably the Francis who was the son of Richard, Baron Lovelace, and brother of John the second Baron.

VIRGINIA CAROLORUM.

Governor Stuyvesant of New Amsterdam, in May, 1653, sent Commissioners to Governor Bennett to propose a friendly alliance for commercial purposes. The Virginia authorities replied that they were not at liberty to make any arrangements, until they conferred with the Council of State in England.

An Assembly[1] convened on 5th of July, 1653, and Lt. Col. Walter Chiles, a son-in-law of Capt. John Page, was elected

---

[1] ASSEMBLY CONVENED JULY 5, 1653.

James City Co.

Lt. Col. Walter Chiles.   Hen. Soane.
William Whittaker.   Ab Watson.

Surry County.

Capt. W. Batte.   William Edward.

Warwick County.

Lt. Col. Sam. Mathews.   William Whitby Sp.

Charles City Co.

John Bushopp.   Ant'y Wyatt.

Nansemond Co.

Col. Thos. Dew.   Peter Montague.
Lt. Col. Ed. Major.

Lower Norfolk Co.

Col. Francis Yeardley.   Lt. Col. Cor Lloyd.

Gloucester Co.

Abra. Iverson.   Richard Pate.

Isle of Wight Co.

Lt. Col. Rob't Pitt.   Dan. Boucher.
Major Geo. Fowden.

speaker, but as he was agent for a Dutch vessel, which was under seizure, it was not deemed expedient that he should preside, and William Whitby was then chosen. A clergyman had been elected a delegate, but it was voted "that Mr. Robert Bracewell, clerk, be suspended, and is not in a capacity of serving as a Burgess, since it was unpresidential, and may produce bad consequences." Roger Green, also a clergyman of Nansemond, asked permission for himself and others, for a tract of land to those who should first settle near Roanoke river. Secretary Claiborne was also requested to decide whether he would settle at Ramonack on the Pamunky. Edmund Scarborough, the prominent merchant on the Eastern Shore, while he signed the engagement probably chagrined by the effect of the Navigation Act, circulated a scandalous and seditious paper, which led the Assembly to disable him from holding officer, and to appoint

	Northampton Co.
Capt. Thos. Johnson.	Stephen Horsey.
William Mellin.	
	Lancaster Co.
Capt. M. Fantleroy.	William Hackett.
	York County.
X'pher Calthrop.	Wm. Hockway.
Robert Booth.	Capt. F. Morgan.
	Northumberland Co.
Lt. Col. Fletcher.	Walter Broadhurst.
	Henrico Co.
	Capt. Wm. Harris.
	Elizabeth City Co.
John Shepperd.	Tho's. Thornbury.

a committee to visit Northampton county and compose the differences.

The boundaries of Westmoreland county, at this session, were defined as "from the Machoactoke river, where Mr. Cole lives, to the Falls of the great river of Pawtomacke above the Necostines' town."

Thomas Thornbury who 1625, was a servant, was a member from Elizabeth City, had lived for a few years in Maryland, sympathized with Parliament, and was a member of the Maryland Assembly, of 1649, which passed the Act concerning religion.

In November, 1653, the Governor and Council of New Amsterdam having been informed that there was a large quantity of tobacco in Virginia, which for the want of ships could not be exported, and it was proposed that a ship should "make a voyage to Smith's Island[1] on the north cape of the Bay of Virginia, near Haccomaco whereunto is said a sufficient quantity of tobacco lies ready for shipment."

This lonely island, far away from Jamestown, a Dutch vessel could stop at and receive a cargo without molestation.

The authorities at Manhattan, in December, "resolved for the promotion of so laudable an object as the continuation of peace, increase of commerce, and cultivation of correspondence between old friends and co-religionists," to send once more a commissioner to Virginia, and authorized and

---

[1] Smith's Island was named after Sir Thomas Smith the first President of the Virginia Company. Capt. John Smith afterwards claimed that it was named for him.

commanded "the Reverend, and very learned Mr. Samuel Drisius,¹ Minister of the Gospel," to go and inquire of the Governor and Council whether they had heard from England in relation to the proposition which had been made in the early summer. They deputed him to propose, that if they had received no directions, "a provisional continuation of the commerce, and intercourse between the two places," to be terminated at any time after six days notice to merchants and traders to protect them from loss.

During this year, a young fur trader brought to the house of Francis,² a son of the late Governor Yeardley, a chief of a Roanoke tribe, with his brother's assistance Yeardley sent a carpenter, and six laborers, to build the chief a house, and franchise his territory. "They paid for three great rivers and also all such others as they should like of, southerly," and took possession in the name of the Commonwealth of England, receiving as a symbol of surrender, a sod of earth with an arrow shot therein. Subsequently the Roanoke chief, brought a Tuskarora chief, and forty-five of his tribe, to Yeardley's house, and asked that his wife, and son, might be baptized. The Indian child was presented to the minister before the congregation, baptized, and left with Yeardley "to be bred up a Christian."³

---

¹ Drisius died in 1672, respected.

² Francis Yeardley was one of the Maryland Councillors, appointed in 1652, by the Parliament Commissioners. He held some land near Portopaco on the Potomac. but in 1654, left that Province.

³ These facts are from Thurloe, in a letter of Francis Yeardley dated May 8, 1654, written to John Farrar at Little Gidding in Huntingdonshire. It concludes with salutations "to his virtuous country-woman, the worthily to be

At the Assembly[1] which began its sessions on November 20, 1654, Charles Norwood was clerk. The Governor re-

---

honored Mrs. Virginia Farrar." Virginia Farrar had prepared in 1651 a map of Virginia.

John her father was buried Sept. 23, 1657, next to his brother Nicholas. "Virginia, daughter of John Farrar and Bathsheba his wife, Jan. 17, 1687 died."

[1] ASSEMBLY CONVENED NOV. 20, 1654.

Charles City Co.

Col. Ed. Hill, Speaker.	Major Abra. Wood.
Capt. Henry Perry.	Stephen Hamlin.

Elizabeth City County.

William Worlich.	John Sheppard.

Gloucester Co.

Thomas Breman.	Wingfield Webb.

Henrico County.

	Richard Cock.

James City Co.

Thomas Dipnal.	Wm. Whitaker.
Abra. Watson.	H'y Soane.

Isle of Wight Co.

Lt. Col. Pitt.	Francis Hobbs.
Capt. John Moone.	Capt. John Bond.

Lower Norfolk Co.

Barthol. Hoskins.	Lyonell Mason.

Lancaster Co.

John Carter.	James Bagnall.

Northampton Co.

Peter Walker.	Tho's Johnson.
William Waters.	

Nansemond Co.

Col. Tho's. Dew.	Sam. Stoughton.

Northumberland Co.

	John Trussell.

commended Edward Digges,[1] as a member of the Council, the nomination was confirmed, and he took the oath of fidelity. Col. Edward Hill who was elected Speaker, had been charged before the General Court with being a blasphemer and atheist, and Hatcher, a delegate from Henrico County, indignantly declared that "the mouth of this House was a Devil." For his free speech about the Right Worshipful Speaker he was compelled to kneel, and make an humble acknowledgment of his impropriety of speech, and his name appears to have been dropped from the roll. One of the members, from Surrey, was William Batt, a son of

Surrey County.

William Batt.   James Mason.

Warwick Co.

Lt. Col. Sam. Mathews.   William Whitbye.

York County.

Capt. W. Gooch.   John Hayman.
Robert Booth.

Westmoreland County.

John Holland.   Alex. Baynham.

[1] Edward Digges was the son of Sir Dudley, Knight, and his mother was a granddaughter of Sir Thomas Kemp. Sir Dudley was an active public man, but quick tempered. His political opponent at one period was Sir Edwin Sandys. Chamberlain under date of January 17, 1624-5, wrote: "Sir Edwyn Sandys obtained his election for Kent by crying down his rivals, Sir. Nicholas Tufton, and Sir Dudley Digges as papists and royalists." He was active in the impeachment of Duke of Buckingham, with Sir Nathaniel Rich and others. Offending King Charles by his " plain country language," in 1627, he was imprisoned at the Fleet, but after a few weeks, having expressed sorrow for his " unfitting words " was restored to liberty. The King stopped his mouth on November 17, 1630, by granting him the office of Master of the Rolls, in reversion after Sir Julius Cæsar. He died in 1638. A brother of Edward named Dudley, the third son of Sir Dudley, published a treatise on the " *Illegality of subjects taking up arms against their Sovereign,*" which in 1647, was brought to the notice of the Committee of Complaints of Parliament.

Robert Batt, vice Master of University College, Oxford. As early as the 5th of September, 1643, he had entered land on Mobjack Bay, Gloucester county. His sister Catharine, was the wife of Philip Mallory, and a niece Martha, was a wife of Thomas Mallory, the Dean of Chester Cathedral, who refused to pay the ship money tax, and perhaps the Thomas Mallory who in 1660, was a prominent non-conformist London divine. His brothers Thomas and Henry were also residents of the Colony.

In view of some hostile feeling exhibited by the Indians in the region of Rappahannock river, a hundred men from Lancaster county, forty from Northumberland, and thirty from Westmoreland, the frontier counties, were ordered to assemble at the house of Thomas Meade on the Rappahannock, to proceed under John Carter[1] against the Indians, with Capt. Henry Fleet, and David Wheatliff as interpreters.

After this Fleet does not appear in any official capacity. He probably settled near the mouth of the Potomac, known still as Fleet's Point, and accommodated persons, passing from Maryland to Virginia. A deposition has been preserved that shows that one Henry Carline, of Kent county, Maryland, in 1655, stopped at his house with a woman, and that he provided lodgings also for another woman, and a man.

---

[1] Brock supposes that he is the immigrant who arrived May 12, 1611, in the ship "Prosperous," and who had entered before 1625, 40 acres in Charles City, and 100 in Warosquoyake. He was in 1642, a member of the Assembly from Upper Norfolk county. In October, 1660, "Colonel Carter ordered upon his oath to declare the whole truth that passed between him and Colonel Claiborne at the Assembly in 1653 or 1654, concerning an act of non-address to the Right Honorable Sir William Berkeley." His third wife was Sarah, a daughter of Gabriel Ludlow, and on June 10, 1669, he died.

Fleet becoming indignant at Carline's loose behavior, turned him, and the woman who came with him, out of his house, and had them arraigned before the Rappahannock Court. He was fined for keeping the servant woman from her employer, and disowning his wife, and the woman was ordered to receive thirty lashes.[1]

Roger Ludlow[2] who had been ridiculed by Captain Stone,[3] in 1632, as a "Just Ass" left New England, and became in 1654, a resident of Virginia. The western shore of the Potomac about this time began to be occupied by planters.

The deplorable superstition known as witchcraft, manifested itself in Virginia, as in New England. The ship "Charity," John Bosworth, Master, in 1654, left England, for Virginia. The voyage was stormy, and two or three weeks before the vessel entered Chesapeake Bay, the sailors whispered that a witch was on board. Mary Lee a little, and quite aged woman, was the suspected one, and it was demanded of the master that she should be examined, which the captain at first refused to consent to, but as the sailors continued clamorous, after consulting with Henry Corbin, a passenger twenty-five years old, and Robert Chipson, a merchant, he yielded to the demand. Two seamen

---

[1] Hansons "Old Kent," p. 212.

[2] Roger Ludlow was the brother-in-law of Deputy Gov. Endicott fo Massachusetts. In 1630, he settled at Dorchester, and for four years was one of the assistant Governors. In 1635, he went to Connecticut, and for nineteen years was either a magistrate or deputy governor. The inhabitants of Fairfield appointed him, in 1654, to lead an expedition against the Indians, but this was not approved by the Connecticut authorities, and after this he moved to Virginia.

[3] See page 96.

searched her body, and declared they had found witch marks. During the night she was left fastened to the capstan, and the next morning it was reported that the marks "for the most part were shrunk into the body." Corbin was pressed to examine her, and at last, the terrified woman said she was a witch. In opposition to the captain, the crew then hung her, and when life was extinct, tossed her body in the sea.

The relations of trade with New Amsterdam remained unsatisfactory. Edmund Scarborough in the summer of 1655, went to Manhattan and bought some negro slaves for his plantation in Accomac, but he was not permitted to take them thither, until he gave a bond that his vessel would not enter the Delaware River, nor stop, and trade with any of the Dutch plantations.

Edward Digges at Denbigh on the James River, near Mulberry Island, and at Bellfield eight miles from Williamsburg, paid great attention to silk culture, employing two native Armenians, skilled in the business. An interesting letter, written by him in 1654, to John Ferrar the brother of Nicholas, the last deputy of the Virginia Company, has been preserved. Virginia, the daughter of John, and niece of Councillor William of Virginia was also one of his correspondents, and her brother, named John, wove into poor rhyme, the substance of all the letters which she had received from the Colony, extracts from which are interesting as giving the names of the principal persons then engaged in raising silk.

"Sir Henry Chichly that heroick knight
Affirms ther's not an ingenious wight

In Virginia but makes all speed he can
To be ere long a silken, noble man.
And say, Colonel Ludlow certifies
That thence from silk great profit will arise;
Yet, worthy Bernard that stout Colonel
Informs the Lady, the worke most facile
And of rich silken stuffs made wholly there
He hopes that he and others shall soon weare,
So, Major John Westrope ripe smooth silk will be
A gallant designe for that brave country.

* * * * * * * * * *

Mr. George Lobs that prudent old planter
Tells her that worms ne'r'e spun silk
Let's give those gentle women their full dress
Mistress Garrett and Burbage for silk clues
That Colonel's wife needs not far to rove
Her court affords a pleasant mulberry grove,
But noble Diggs carries the bell away
Lass! stint of eggs made so small the essay
His two Armenians from Turkey sent

* * * * * * * * * *

Are now most busy
Lo here, what Mistress Mary Ward hath sent
And to her Lady cousin she presents
The rare bottoms took from her apple trees
That all England may it believe and see;
Her honored kinsman, Esquire Ferrar
To confirm and make the wonder greater
Ten more hath he sent her, which he found
On stately oakes and shrubs which kiss the ground
And Doctour Russell, that learned Physition
Hath with his, made a full addition."

An important principle was asserted by the Assembly in 1655. Every freeman had the privilege of a vote until two years before, when the elective franchise was limited to housekeepers, freeholders, leaseholders, or other tenants, but it was now repealed because it was " hard and unagreeable to reason that any persons shall pay taxes, and have no votes in election." To ensure fair elections it was ordered that the vote should not be by the voice, but by subscription.

About the same time a plan was devised which if effectually carried out might have saved many lives, and civilized the Indians, a plan which is again being urged, in its main features, by philanthropists. It was enacted, that for every eight wolves' heads delivered, by any Indian, to the authorities, the head man of his band should receive a cow " as a step to civilizing them, and making them Christians," and it was also provided, that Indians might bring their children within the white settlements, choose guardians for them, and the Colony would pay for their education. To protect them from heartless speculators, it was ordered that the lands of Indians were inalienable, unless by special permission of the Assembly.

Governor Bennett having gone to England on affairs of the Colony, Edward Digges now thirty-five years of age was chosen as his successor, Claiborne, remaining Secretary. His councillors[1] were chiefly those who had held the posi-

---

[1] COUNCILLORS MARCH 31ST, 1655.

Capt. John West,	Col. Bridges Freeman.
Col. Sam. Mathews.	Col. Edward Hill.
Col. Argall Yeardley.	Col. William Taylor.
Col. Tho's Pettus.	Col. Thomas Dew.
Col. Humphry Higginson.	Lt. Col. Obedience Robins.
Col. George Ludlow.	Lt. Col. Sam. Mathews.
Col. William Bernard.	Capt. Henry Perry.
Capt. William Gooch.	

tion for many years. A son of Col. Mathews, sits with his father. William Gooch, also a new councillor and a young man, died, much lamented, soon after his appointment.[1]

According to adjournment, upon December 1st, 1656, the Assembly convened and Lt. Col. Walker,[2] and Nathaniel Bacon[3] were nominated and confirmed as Councillors, and several new Burgesses admitted to fill vacancies. Henry

---

[1] Upon the Temple plantation, in the suburbs of Yorktown, near the house, where Lord Cornwallis surrendered to Washington, is a tombstone, with this inscription.

"Major William Gooch of this parish
Died October 29, 1655.
Within this tomb, there doth interred lie
No shape, but substance, true nobility.
Itself, though young, in years just twenty-nine,
Yet graced with virtues moral, and divine;
The Church from him did good participate
In counsel rare, fit to adorne a State."

[2] John Walker supposed to be, by Brock, the brother of Joseph Walker, St. Margarets, Westminister. January 29, 1631-2, he entered 1150 acres on Ware River, Mobjack Bay.

[3] Nathaniel Bacon son of Rev. James Bacon, and grandson of Sir James of Friston Hall, Suffolk, knighted in 1604, and buried in February, 1618. The second husband of Councillor Bacon's mother, was Rev. Robert Peck a graduate of Cambridge, rector of Hingham, England, more than 30 years, and for con science sake came to Massachusetts Bay, in 1638, and was for several years pastor of the Congregational church at Hingham, New England, but, in 1641, went back to his church in old England and died its rector, in 1656, during the Cromwellian period.

His daughter Anne Peck, married in New England, Major John Mason, the conqueror of the Pequot Indians, in Connecticut.

Councillor Bacon was baptized August 29, 1620, in St. Mary's parish, Bury St, Edmonds, and in 1647, was residing in France. He arrived in Virginia, about 1650, accompanied by his wife Elizabeth, whose maiden name was Kingswell. Notices of his cousin Nathaniel, also, of the Virginia Council will be found in later chapters of this work.

Randolph was elected clerk in the place of Major Charles Norwood.[1]

The Assembly of 1656, enacted: "For encouragement of the ministers in the country, and that they may be better enabled to attend both publick commands and their private cares; It is ordered, that from henceforth each minister, in his owne person, with six other servants of his family shall be free from publique levies; Allwaies provided they be examined by Mr. Philip Mallory and Mr. John [Roger?] Green and they to certify their abilities to the Governour and Councill, who are to proceed according to their judgment."

It is probable that each congregation was at liberty to worship with, or without, the Prayer Book. Gatford in his treatise "Public Good without Private Interest" dedicated to Cromwell does not give a pleasing account of the religious condition of Virginia at this period. He refers to the majority of the colonists "as these wicked and ungodly wretches heretofore planted there," and while admitting that there are some ministers "religious and laborious" yet there were "not a few, whose wicked and profane lives cause the worship of God not only to be slighted, but to be little less than abhored." Of them he further writes: "The greatest part of them are such as went over thither not out of any desire or design to do God, and that Plantation, much less the poor heathen, thereto adjoining, any service, but out of some by aims and ends of their own,

---

[1] Charles Norwood may have returned to England and be the same Charles who served at Tangiers under Col. Henry Norwood, Henry Randolph had a son William who died before 1660. The father died in 1673.

being indeed such as were ashamed or afraid to live any longer here in this native [England] or at least, such as sought only to get something for themselves." Reference is made to a minister who was accused of a shameless and unnatural act who "was only caused to stand in some public place, for a small time, with a paper in his hat, with his crime written therein. Where on the other side, in the year 1655, other eminent able preachers indeed, were for no crime, unless, for being of a different judgment, in our late unhappy differences, * * * turned out of their employment and livelihood."

An alarm was created by the appearance in 1656, near the Falls of James River, of some strange Indians called Richahecrians, from the western mountains, and Col. Edward Hill, with one hundred men, was sent to confer with them, and avoid if possible blood-shedding. Tottopottomoy with one hundred Pamunkeys also accompanied Hill, and this chief was slain in a fight with the strangers. The conduct of Hill in this campaign was severely censured, the Assembly suspended him from all offices civil and military, and Col. Abraham Wood was appointed to take his place as commander of the regiment of Charles City and Henrico. Gatford writes of this affair: "The Planters did lately, viz. Ano. 1656, (when a numerous people of the Indians more remote from the Colonie, came down to treat with the English about setling of Peace, and withall a liberty of trade with them) most perfidiously and barbarously (after a declaration of their desires and intentions) murther five of their Kings that came in expectation of a better reception, and brought much beaver with them to begin the intercourse of the commerce. This unparallel'd hellish treachery and anti-christian perfidy more to be detested than any heathenish inhumanity, cannot but stink most abominably in the nosethils of as many Indians, as shall be infested with the least sent of it, even to their perpetual abhorring and abandoning of the very sight and name of an English man, till some new generation of a better extract shall be transplanted among them." [1]

In reference to this. Gatford writes. "The Planters have turned some of the Indians out of their places of abode and subsistence, after that the Indians have submitted to the Colony, and to their government, and have taken up their own lands, after the custom, used by the Colony. As they did otherwise also very unchristianly requite the service which one of the Indian kings did them in fighting against other Indians, that were presumed to be enemies to the English, and to draw towards them, to do them mischief. For that, when, the said King desirous to show his fidelity to the English, if not in obedience to some of their commander's orders, did adventure too far with his own Indians, in the pursuit of those other Indians, and thereby lost his life in that action, as some report, though others thought him to be taken alive by the enemies. His wife and children that were by him, at his expiring, recommended to the care of the English * * * * * were so far from receiving the favour and kind usage, merited by their father, that they were wholly neglected, and exposed to shift for themselves.

"And though it be alleged by some, as to the former part of this grievance, that the portion of land which was taken from the said King, before his death, by an English colonel

---

[1] " Public Good_without Private Interest p. 8.

was acknowledged openly in court, yet 'tis generally believed, and by some stoutly asserted, that the said King was affrighted, and threatened into that acknowledgment, by the said Colonel."

Col. Thomas Dew[1] of the Council was empowered, with others, to explore the rivers between Cape Hatteras and Cape Fear. The people of Virginia had grown weary of the attempt to restore their old boundaries. Lord Baltimore, by his adherence to Cromwell[2], had great power with Parlia-

---

[1] Henry Woodhouse when Governor of Bermudas, wrote to London in 1627, that one-third of the settlers were disposed to go to Virginia. Among the prominent planters there were Thomas Dew and Ben. Harrison. They were probably the same persons with these names who a few years after are planters in Virginia.

[2] Cromwell's letters show the conflicting interest. On January 12, 1654-5, he wrote to Governor Bennett of Virginia.

"SIR: Whereas the differences between the Lord Baltimore and the inhabitants of Virginia, concerning the bounds by them respectively claimed, are depending before our council, and yet undetermined; and whereas we are credibly informed, you have notwithstanding gone unto his plantation in Maryland, and countenance some people there in opposing the Lord Baltimore's officers, whereby, and with other forces from Virginia, you have much disturbed that colony, and people, to the engendering of tumults, and much bloodshed there, if not prevented:

"We, therefore, at the request of the Lord Baltimore, and divers other persons of quality here, who are engaged by great adventures in his interest, do, for preventing of disturbances or tumults there, will, and require you, and all others deriving any authority from you, to forbear disturbing the Lord Baltimore, or his officers, or his people in Maryland, and to permit all things to remain as they were before any disturbance or alteration made by you, or by any other, upon pretence of authority from you, till the said differences above mentioned be determined by us here and we give further order herein. We rest your loving friend,

"OLIVER P."

The above letter was written upon, hearing from only one side, in the controversy, but upon further information the Protector wrote.

ment, therefore this Assembly directed that "letters be sent to Colonel Samuel Mathews, and Mr. Bennett, in respect of the differences with Lord Baltimore, concerning our bounds is as far from determination, as at first, that they desist until further orders from this country."

In view of a contemplated visit of Governor Digges, to London, Col. Samuel Mathews was elected as his successor,[1] and it was ordered that Francis Morison, the speaker, should prepare a letter to be taken by Digges for the Protector Cromwell, and his Secretary of State, John Thurloe.

"Whitehall, 26th September, 1655.

"SIRS: It seems to us, by yours of the twenty-ninth of June, and by the relation we received by Colonel Bennett, that some mistake, or scruple hath arisen concerning the sense of our Letters, of the twelfth of January last, as if by our Letters we had intimated that we should have a stop put to the proceedings of those Commissioners who were authorized to settle the Civil Government of Maryland. Which was not at all intended by us; nor so much as proposed to us, by those, who made addresses to us, to obtain our said Letters.

"But our intention (as our Letter doth plainly import) was only to prevent, and forbid any force or violence to be offered by either of the plantations of Virginia or Maryland, from one, to the other, upon the difference concerning their bonds, the said differences being then under the consideration of Ourself and Council here. Which, for your more full satisfaction we have thought fit to signify to you, and rest

"Your loving friend,

"OLIVER P."

The above was addressed "To the Commissioners of Maryland."

[1] Col. Samuel Mathews who was still in England. The Record of this Assembly, mentions; "Edward Digges Esq., at present Governor, to continue and retain during his abode in the country, and in the interim Col Samuel Mathews Governor elect to take place next to him in Council." It was also arranged that after Digges ceased to be Governor, he should be of the Council, and take place after Capt. John West.

The Assembly's letter to Cromwell was as follows :

"*May it please your Highness,*

" We could not find a fitter means to represent the condition of this country to you, than this worthy person Mr. Digges, our late Governor, whose occasions calling him into England we have instructed him with the state of this place as he left it; we shall beseech your Highness to give credit to his relations, which we assure ourselves will be fruitful, having had many experiences of his candor in the time of his government, which he hath managed under your Highness with so much moderation, prudence and justice, that we should be much longer in expressing this truth, but that we fear to have already too much trespassed by interrupting your Highness's most serious thoughts in greater affairs than what can concern your Highness's most humble, most devoted servant. Dated in the Assembly of Virginia, 15th Dec. 1656."

The arrival of Digges in England with his conciliatory disposition, and powerful social influences, did much to settle the long pending controversy, and on the 30th of November, 1657, articles of agreement in the presence of Digges, and others, were signed by Lord Baltimore, and Commissioner Samuel Matthews of Virginia. The paper mentions "that Lord Baltimore, upon a treaty with the said Richard Bennett and Colonel Samuel Mathews, occasioned by the friendly endeavors of Edward Digges Esq'r, about the composure of the said differences." The agreement was to the effect that if those in Maryland would deliver up to Lord Baltimore's Governor and officers, the records of the Province, and the great seal if it could be found, that he would leave all offences that may have arisen to be determined in the way the Protector of England and his Council should direct; that patents should be issued to those who had claimed lands during the difficulties; that all who wished to remove from Maryland should have leave to do so any time within a year; and

"Lastly, the Lord Baltimore doth promise, that he will never give his assent to the repeal of a law established heretofore in Maryland, by his lordship's consent,[1] whereby all persons professing to believe in Jesus Christ, have freedom of conscience there."

The opinions of Cromwell relative to toleration in religion, were in advance of his age.[2] In a letter to Cardinal

---

[1] The law was framed by the Marylanders in 1649, and, in 1650, Lord Baltimore gave his consent thereto.

Thomas Harrison, the Nansemond clergyman, in his letter to Winthrop, rejoiced in the Act, passed by Parliament, in 1647, by which persons were no more compelled to go to parish churches, this is what he called "that golden apple the ordinance of toleration." He was not however, in favor, like Roger Williams, and Patrick Copland, of *unrestricted religious liberty*. He thought that in each community those only should be tolerated who believed in the doctrines of the early creed, and the sacrament of baptism, and the Lord's Supper. He would not tolerate those who denied the divinity of Christ, or the importance of infant baptism. The "Act concerning religion passed by the Maryland Assembly of 1649, with the approbation of the Virginia Puritans, carried out the views of Harrison, and to deny the doctrine of the Trinity made one liable to death and confiscation of goods.

[2] But a few days before he wrote the letter to the Maryland Commissioners, in a speech delivered on September 17th, 1656, at the assembling of Parliament he said: "Our practice since the last Parliament hath been to let all this Nation see that whatever pretentions to Religion would continue quiet, peaceable, they should enjoy conscience and liberty to themselves, and not to make religion a pretence for arms and blood. Truly we have suffered them, and that cheerfully, so to enjoy their own liberties. Whatsoever is contrary and 'not peaceable'

VIRGINIA CAROLORUM. 251

Mazarin, whom he calls a "brother and confederate," he expresses his intention to make "further progress," in his living toward Roman Catholics, and shows that the Cardinal was in sympathy with him against the royal family, then in exile, in France. Alluding to the friend of Charles the Second, Sir John Berkeley, the brother of the Virginia Governor, and the tutor of the Duke of York, he wrote to his Eminency[1] : "I did fear that Berkeley would not have been able to go through and carry on that work; and that either the Duke would have cooled in his suit, or condescended to his brother. * * * * If I am not mistaken in his, the Duke's character, as I received it from your Eminency, that fire which is kindled between them will not ask bellows to blow it, and keep it burning. * * * If this breach be widened a little more, and this difference fomented, with a little caution in respect of the persons to be added to it, I distrust not but that Party which is already forsaken of

---

let the pretence be never so specious, if it tend to combination, to interest, and factions, we shall not care by the grace of God when we meet withal, though never so specious, if they be not quiet.

" And truly I am against all liberty of conscience repugnant to this. If men will profess, be they those under Baptism, be they those of the Independent judgment simply, or of the Presbyterian judgment, in the name of God, encourage them, countenance them, so long as they do plainly continue to be thankful to God, and to make use of the liberty to enjoy their own consciences."

[1] Cromwell, and the Republicans considered it good policy to enlist the Roman Catholic element of England against the royalists. A daughter of Christopher Wandesforde, whose father had been a confidential adviser of the Earl of Strafford, and succeeded him as Deputy of Ireland, mentions a meeting held in her uncle's house, in London, of the Close committee of Parliament to consult about the King's trial, and that Mr. Rushworth kept the key of the room, in which they met, and to which the members privately repaired. One morning he saw several disguised faces enter, " particularly, he knew the Lord Baltimore, * * * and others suspected to be Papists, or fanatics, which strange mixture did much surprize him."

God * * * and noisome to their countrymen, will grow lower in the opinion of all the world."

When the articles of peace were signed by the Virginia and Maryland representatives, a ship was on its way to Chesapeake Bay, and toward the close of December, 1657, landed in Virginia two preachers of the Society of Friends, Josiah Coale, and Thomas Thurston, whose presence created an uproar, and they were treated as disturbers of the peace. It cannot be denied, that some of the people, called "Friends of Truth," during the Cromwellian era, had a "zeal without knowledge," and made themselves ridiculous. That once sturdy soldier, James Nayler, led captive by silly women, and addressed as the "fairest among ten thousand" as he rode through the streets of Bristol, preceded by admirers, strewing the road, with their scarfs, shawls, and handkerchiefs, was of course, laughed at by thoughtless boys, insulted by foul-mouthed men, and pitied by charitable citizens.

William Penn, always calm, and reasonable, in public discourse, mentions that under a wild enthusiasm, one of the gentler sex, in England divested herself of the garments of delicacy, to symbolize the nakedness of the world, where "all is show and counterfeit," but, no one even supposed, that she was not "clothed on with chastity," as much as the woman of the legend, who rode, naked, through the town,

"Godiva, wife to that grim Earl, who ruled
"In Coventry."

The first preachers who entered Virginia, calling upon men to repent, like John the Baptist did in the wilderness, excited serious thought in few minds, but the vigorous opposition of many. As they violated the Colonial Statutes, they were at length thrown in prison, and when released compelled to leave the country. With Thomas Chapman [1] of Virginia who appears to have been a convert, they entered Maryland where they were subject to scourgings, and expelled the Province. Passing northward, they soon were beyond the cabin of any white settler. For food, they depended largely upon the berries, and chestnuts, of the forest, and often were fed by the Susquehannocks, a tribe whose wigwams they found. In a publication printed in London, called "The Deceiver of the Nations discovered, and his Cruelty made manifest more especially his Cruel Works of Darkness laid open, and reproved in Mariland and Virginia," the writer[2] mentions that "the Indians whom they judge to be heathen exceeded in kindness, in courtesies, in love and mercy, unto them, who were strangers."

During the Cromwellian era, there was an increase of population, upon the Virginia side of the Potomac north of York river. From Governor Bennett on November 27, 1654, Giles Brent, who had been Deputy Governor of Maryland, obtained a large grant of land, and Brent's Point is still known. His strong minded sister whose relation to Governor Leonard Calvert had been so peculiar, and intimate, the next year, received a grant from Governor Digges. Among other settlers were Richard Lee,[3] Henry Corbin, Isaac Aller-

---

[1] A Thomas Chapman in 1610, came to Virginia in the ship "Trial" and his wife Ann came in 1617, in the "George." In 1623, a son named Thomas was born, and if living would at this period have been thirty-five years of age.

[2] Francis Howgill, published A.D., 1660.

[3] Upon his father's tombstone, is the following long inscription.

"Here lyeth interred the Body of Sr. Robert Lee Knt., Sonne and heire of Benedict Lee of Huccott, in the county of Bucks, who was second brother to

ton, William Ball, John and Lawrence Washington. Richard Lee, said to have been one of the sons of a poor knight with a large family, was in the Colony, as early as 1642, and in 1647, was a Burgess from York County. He identified himself with the Cromwellian party, and in 1655, was in England. In September, he secured passage to return upon the ship " Anthony," but at Gravesend, his trunk was seized by the searcher of customs, containing two hundred ounces of silver plate, which was afterwards released because of " Colonel Lee being faithful, and useful, to the interest of the commonwealth." Henry Corbin, born in Warwickshire about 1629, in July, 1645, married Alice, daughter of Richard Eltonhead[1] of Eltonhead of Lancashire, England,

---

Sir Robert Lee of Birdsthorn. He was born at Helstrop in the Pr'sh of Drayton Beauchamp, Ao Di'ni, 1545, and married Dame Luce Piggott daughter to Tho's Piggott of Beachampton, in ye county of Bucks, Esq., by whom he had issue VIII sonnes viz: Sir Henry Lee K't a Baronett, Edward, Bennett, Thomas, George, Robert, Richard, and Anthonie, and VI daughters Frances, Elizab., Mary, Margaret, Joyce, and Alice: when he had been married 55 years he dep'ted this life in the faith of Jesus Christ at Statford Langton in ye County of Essex, and was buried at Hardwick Ao. D'ni 1616, Aug. 20, Ætatis 73."

The first wife of Richard Lee, the immigrant, was Elizabeth daughter of William Langdon, of the County of Cornwall, and widow of Nicholas Manyard. It is remarkable that on the tomb-stone of Richard Lee Councillor, son of the first Richard, it should be mentioned that he is of an old and honorable family in Shropshire, without any allusion to the Knight of Essex.

[1] William Eltonhead, a son of Richard of Lancashire, came in 1654, to Maryland as a special messenger from Lord Baltimore, and was shot in the skirmish at Severn river between the partisans of Parliament and Lord Baltimore.

Henry Corbin by his wife Alice, had :

Henry, who died in infancy.

Thomas, who became a London merchant.

Gawin, whose first wife was Catherine, daughter of Ralph Wormely of Middlesex Co., Va.

Letitia, married Richard Lee of Westmoreland Co., Va.

and in 1654, arrived in Virginia. Isaac Allerton[1] settled near Wicomico after 1654, was a graduate of Harvard A.D., 1650, and his mother was a Brewster, the daughter of the celebrated leader of the Puritans who landed, from the "May Flower," at Plymouth Rock, Massachusetts. The families of these men were intimate, and the children intermarried,[2] and in 1670, Allerton, John Lee[3], Henry Corbin, and Thomas Gerard agreed to build a banqueting house, at a point convenient to their residences.

Thomas Gerrard lived not far from Isaac Allerton, at Masthotick Creek, the southern border of Westmoreland county. Like the Brents he had been prominent in the province of Maryland. He was the brother-in-law of Justinian Snow, the first factor of the Maryland province, called by a Jesuit journalist of the period an "obstinate heretic," while Gerard professed to be an adherent of the Church of Rome. He was a physician, and privy councillor in Mary-

---

Alice, married Philip Lightfoot of Middlesex Co., Va.
Winifred, married Le Roy Griffin.
Ann, married William Tayloe of London who settled, and in 1694, died in Virginia.
Frances, married Edmund Jennings of Rippon, Yorkshire, died in London Nov. 22, 1713.

[1] John Davenport, minister of New Haven, on the 27th of 7th month, 1654, in a letter to John Winthrop Jr. Dep. Gov. of Connecticut, referring to Dr. Choyse? writes " He is now upon a voyage for Virginia with Mr. Allerton."

[2] Hancock, son of Richard Lee, married Elizabeth a daughter of Isaac Allerton.

[3] Richard Lee the immigrant, died before September, 1666. In Palmer's Calendar of Virginia State Papers is the following: "Writ issued by Ira Kirkham (Cl'k Sept. 25, 1666), to sheriff of Westmoreland county requiring the arrest of Mr. John Lee, one of the executors of the last will and testament of Col. Ric'd. Lee to appear before Governor and Council on 3d day of next Gen'l Court, in the forenoon, to answer the suit of Edward Lisbro as marrying —— Anne, relict of the said Col. Lee."

land but in 1658, had an unpleasant controversy with a Jesuit missionary, name Fitz Herbert, who threatened to excommunicate him, because he did not bring his wife and children to church, and Fitz Herbert also reported that he had "beaten an Irish servant because she had refused to be a Protestant or go to Prayer with those of his family, that were so."

He was also accused of being intemperate, and opposed to the friends of Lord Baltimore. Upon these last charges, he was tried, deposed from the Council, and declared incapable of holding any office. After this, he removed to Virginia, and was the neighbor of Isaac Allerton, and in 1670, arranged with his neighbors to build a "banqueting house." On Feb. 5, 1672, he made his will, and therein expressed his wish, to buried by the side of his wife, Susanna Snow, in Maryland, and Major Isaac Allerton and John Lee were appointed to settle his estate.

Not far from these, settled John and Lawrence Washington, of whose ancestry nothing is definitely known.[1] In

---

[1] Joseph L. Chester L.LD., D. C. L., the late eminent editor and annotator of *Westminister Abbey Registers* in a letter of Sept. 8, 1877, wrote to me: "In your *Founders of Maryland* is a letter of John Washington. Can you, by any means, obtain for me a fac-simile, or tracing, of his signature? I have lately come upon a Deed, which I have strong reasons to think is his, and if, on a comparison of the two signatures this should prove to be the case, I think my long protracted labors on the Washington history would come to an end." Dr. Chester did not succeed, before his death, in finding in Virginia an autograph of John Washington and having completely destroyed the pedigree as given by Sparks and Irving, nothing positive is known.

General Washington, in a letter to the Earl of Buchan, mentions that his ancestor was a relative of the Fairfaxes of the north of England, to whom Buchan was allied. Henry Fairfax sheriff of Yorkshire and Henry Washington, married sisters Anna and Eleanora Harrison of South Cave, Yorkshire. Henry

1658, John, the ancestor of the illustrious and first president of the United States of America, reached the Chesapeake Bay in a ship owned by Edward Prescott, and the master of which was John Greene. During the voyage from England the crew became excited and declared that one of the passengers, Elizabeth Richardson, was a witch, and when near the Western Islands hung her, and threw her body into the sea. John Washington, as the ship was consigned to Maryland, made complaint to the Provincial Court,[1] and

---

Washington died in 1718, and his widow Eleanora lived in St. Andrew's, Holborn, London. Her eldest son Richard was born at South Cave in 1690, and another child was born there, she had five other children at Doncaster or in London. Perhaps Richard Washington who died in Barbadoes in 1747, was a son of Richard, and grandson of Henry. General Washington corresponded with a Richard Washington of London who may have been the son of the Barbadoes Richard. In the autumn of 1751, George Washington took his sick brother Lawrence, to the Barbadoes From a letter of Theodore Pargiter dated London, Aug. 2, 1654, it is learned that he had a cousin John Washington at Barbadoes. Could this be the John who came to Virginia? See Waters' Gleanings in *N. E. Hist. Gen. Register* October, 1884.

In a footnote on page 137 "*Founders of Maryland*," Munsell, Albany, 1876, Henry, the husband of Eleanor Harrison, by carelessness, is called Richard Washington. And, "it is probable that John Washington" in the same note should read; *It is probable that Richard of Barbadoes*. As it now reads, it is without sense.

[1] Governor Fendall of Maryland on behalf of the Council of Maryland on Oct. 5, 1659, issued the following:

"WHEREAS John Washington of Westmoreland County in Virginia hath made complaynt ag'st Edward Prescott Merch't, Accusing ye s'd Prescott of ffelony, and the Gouernor of this Province alleging how that hee ye s'd Prescott hanged a witch on his ship as hee was outward bound from England hither, the last yeare upon wch complaynt of ye s'd Washington, Gou'r caused ye s'd Edward Prescott to bee arrested, Taking Bond for his appearance at this Provincial Court of 4000 lbs. Tobacco Gyving moreover notice to ye s'd Washington by letter of his proceedings therein (a copie of wch Herewth ye s'd) Washington answers thereto as followeth.

"'Mr. Washington Vpon yor complaynt to me yt Mr. Prescott did in his voyage from England, hither, cause a woman to bee executed for a witch I have

Prescott the owner of the ship was held for trial. Prescott appeared in October, 1659, and declared that as owner of the ship he had protested against the hanging, but that the Captain and sailors would not listen to his remonstrance, and he was discharged. A writer of the period, alludes to such occurrences. His words are : "Another wickedness which some traders thither have practised upon their passengers

caused him to be apprehended uppon suspition of ffelony & I've intend to bind him over to the Provincial Court to answere it, when I doe allso expect you to bee to make good ye charge. Hee will be called upon ye 4th and 5th of October next at ye Court then to be held at Patux't neeare Mr. ffenwick's house where I suppose you will not fayle to bee. Witnesses examined in Virginia will bee of no value here, in this case, for this must be face to face with ye party accused or they stand for nothing. I thought good to acquaynt you with this that you may not come unprovided. This at present Sir, is all from
'"Yor ffriend JOSIAS FENDALL.
" 29th September."'
On the next day, John Washington answered.

"Hon'ble S'r Yors of this 29th instant, this day I received. I am sorry y't my extraordinary occasions will not permitt me to bee at ye next Provincial Court to bee held at Mary Land ye 4th of this next month.

" Because then, God willing, I intend to gett my young sonne baptized. All ye company and Gossips being already invited. Besides, in this short time witnesses cannot bee gott to come over. But if Mr. Prescott bee bound to answer at ye next Provincial Court after this, I shall doe what lyeth in my power to get them over. Sr. I shall desire you for to acquaynt mee whether Mr. Prescott be bound over to ye next Court, and when, ye Court is, that I may have sometime for to provide evidence.
" Yo'r ffriend & Serv't
" JOHN WASHINGTON."
" 30th Sept. 1659."

" To wch complaynt of John Washington the s'd Edward Prescott submitting himselfe to his tryall denyeth not but that there was one Elizabeth Richardson hanged on his ship as he was outward Bound ye last yeare from England and coming for this province, neare unto ye Western Island by his Master & Company (hee having appointed one John Greene for yt voyage Master), though himselfe was both Mercht & owner of ye ship. But further sayth That he wth stood ye proceedings of his s'd Master & Company & protested ag'st them in that business. And that thereupon both ye Master & Company were ready to mutiny."

(scarce ever heard of before, much less practised by any that call themselves Christians) is this, When a storm or tempest hath happened at sea in their passage from hence, thither, or they have otherwise miscarried, through the default of the Master or Pilot of the ship, so that their passage hath been tedious and difficult : Some of those Masters have laide all the blame upon some of their passengers; and not onely accused them for witches, but executed some of them as witches, by their own authority, and without any legal trial and conviction."

John Washington of Westmoreland, in 1661, was a warden of White Chapel in Lancaster county. His brother Lawrence lived a few miles from him, on the banks of the Rappahannock river, Francis Doughty, a brother-in-law of Governor Stone of Maryland, the father-in-law of Hugh O'Neal of Patuxent, formerly, the minister of the English speaking members, of the Reformed Church, at Manhattan, now New York city, was for a time in charge of Settingbourne Parish, and among the records of Essex county, Va., there is the complaint of John Catlett, and Humphrey Boothe, to Governor Berkeley, that he was a non-conformist, and that "he denied the supremacy of the King, contrary to the canons of the church of England" and refused to allow them " to communicate in the blessed ordinance of the Lord's Supper."

William Ball[1] perhaps the person of that name in the Visitation of Cheshire "a soldier under Sir Thomas Fair-

---

[1] He died in 1659, and Brock mentions, that he left two sons, William and Joseph, and a daughter Hannah. Around White Chapel church there is a tombstone over the grave of David Ball ; and of Mary Ann Ball the daughter

fax," came from England in 1650, and settled at the mouth of Corotoman river in Lancaster county, and attended White Chapel church of which John Washington was warden.

Some distance below these planters, at Carter's Creek, on the upper side, and not far from the mouth of York River, in 1648, Lewis Burwell a planter of character entered a large tract of land, and in 1650, obtained a grant of sixteen hundred and fifty acres in Northumberland county. He died in 1656, and was buried at Fairfield on Carter's Creek.

Samuel Mathews having returned from England, as Governor and Captain General attended the Legislative Assembly of March 13th, 1657–8, convened at Jamestown. The former Governor Richard Bennett became a member of the

---

of Rev. John Bertrand. A daughter of Richard Lee of Ditchley was the third wife of James Ball. A Mary Ball married a Washington, whose son, was the "first in war, first in peace, and first in the hearts of his countrymen."

[1] On his tombstone is the following: "To the loving memory of Major Lewis Burwell, of the County of Gloucester in Virginia, gentleman, who descended from the ancient family of the Burwells, of the County of Bedford, and Northampton, in England, who nothing more worthy in his birth, than virtuous in life, exchanged this life for a better on the 19th day of November, in the thirty-third year of his age A.D., 1658."

Meade mentions the following inscriptions at Carter's Creek upon stones marking the resting places of the wives of Lewis Burwell, father and son.

"To the sacred memory of Abigail, the loving and beloved wife of Major Lewis Burwell of the County of Gloucester, Gent, who was descended of the illustrious family of the Bacons, and heiress of Nathaniel Bacon, Esq., President of Virginia, who, not being more honorable in her birth, than virtuous in her life, departed this world, the 12th of November, 1672, aged 36 years, having blessed her husband with four sons and six daughters."

This inscription seems to be to the memory of the wife of Lewis Burwell, Senior.

"The daughter of Robert Higginson. She died November 26th, 1675. She was the wife of Major L. Burwell."

Council.[1] This Assembly is memorable for its discussion of the principles of Republican government, and for the successful assertion that the Burgesses were the representatives of the people, and that in them was vested the power to elect the Governor and Council.

On the first of April, 1658, the Governor announced that the House of Burgesses[2] was dissolved, but the delegates

---

[1] COUNCIL IN MARCH 1658-9.

Richard Bennett.
Col. W. Claiborne. Secretary.
Col. John West.
Col. Wm. Bernard.
Col. Thomas Dew.
Col. Obedience Robins.

Capt. Henry Perry.
Col. George Reade?
Lt. Col. John Walker?
Col. Abra'm Wood.
Col. John Carter.

Mr. W. Horsmanden.
Lt. Col. Anthony Elliot.

[2] BURGESSES MARCH 13, 1657-8.

Henrico County.

Major Wm. Harris.

Charles City Co.

Warham Horsmanden.

Capt. Robert Wynne.

James City Co.

Hen. Soane.
Maj. R'd Webster.

Thos. Loveinge.
Wm. Corker.

Surrey County.

Lt. Col. Thos. Swann.
Wm. Edwards.

Major Wm. Butler.
Capt. Wm. Cawfield.

Upper Norfolk Co.

Lt. Col. Ed. Carter.
Thomas Francis.

Giles Webb.

Lower Norfolk Co.

Col. John Sidney.

Major Leonard Mason.

declared that the step was improper, and asked that he would revoke the order. The Governor and his Council, after deliberation, expressed a willingness to recede, if the House would speedily adjourn, and refer the point in dispute, to the Lord Protector of England, but the House was not satisfied with this answer, and appointed a Committee, consisting of Col. John Carter, Warham Horsmanden, John Sidney, Thomas Swan, Richard Webster, Jeremy Hain, and William Mitchell to consider what were the rights of the House and report thereon. They were of the opinion, after

---

Elizabeth City Co.

Major William.   John Powell.

Warwick County.

John Smith, Speaker.   Thomas Davis.

York County.

Jeremy Haine.   Robert Borne.

Isle of Wight Co.

Major John Bond.   John Brewer.
Thos. Tabernor.   Joseph Bridger.

New Kent County.   William Blacky.

Gloucester Co.

Lt. Col. Anth. Elliot.   Capt. Thos. Ramsey

Rappahannock Co.   Thomas Luceur.

Lancaster Co.   Col. John Carter.

Northumberland Co.

Peter Montague.   John Hanie.
Peter Knight.

Northampton Co.

William Kendall.   Randall Revell.
William Mellinge.   John Willcox.
William Mitchell.

VIRGINIA CAROLORUM.

examining the Constitutions, and present form of government, that the Burgesses were the representatives of the people, and that they could not be dissolved, except by their own consent. After this, the Governor appeared, and acknowledged the supreme power of the House, to elect the Governor and Council. The House then proceeded to the election of Samuel Mathews as Governor, and twelve Councillors. Joseph Bridger an able and useful man, superintended the erection of a brick church five miles south-east from Smithfield. The first brick house in Virginia was erected in 1638, at Jamestown, and this church was built some years afterwards. The son of Joseph Bridger born in 1628, also named Joseph, may have been the member of this Assembly[1] He was paymaster of the troops during the Bacon Rebellion, and a tombstone[2] marks his remains in Smithfield church-yard. William Michell, or Mitchell, a member from Northampton county was not an ornament

---

[1] COUNCILLORS, APRIL, 1658.

John West.	Henry Perry.
Thomas Pettus.	George Reade.
Thomas Hill.	Abraham Wood.
Thomas Dew.	John Carter.
William Bernard.	Warham Horsmanden.
Obedience Robins.	Anthony Ellyott.

[2] "Sacred
To ye Memory of
The Honble Joseph Bridger.
Esqr. Councilr. of State in Virginia
To King Charles ye 2d
Dying April ye 15, A. D., 1686
Aged 58 years Mournfully left
His Wife, 3 sons and 4 daughters."

nor a blessing to the Colony, but an adventurer of ill fame from Maryland. Lord Baltimore had, in 1650, made him a Councillor, but soon deposed him. Leaving his wife in England, he brought over in the ship which he commanded several lewd women, and upon his arrival in the province led a most scandalous life,[1] and scoffed at Christianity.

Randall Revell a Burgess of the same county, followed the trade of a cooper, and had been in 1638, a member of the Maryland Assembly, and at a later period was quite prominent in the affairs of the Eastern Shore. The Assembly in March, 1657-8, resolved that it was expedient to eject all lawyers who were Burgesses, and submitted their decision to the Governor and Council, who replied "The Governor and Council will consent to this proposition so far as it shall be agreeable to Magna Charta.   "WM. CLAIBORNE."

"23 Martii, 1657 [O. S.]

This communication was referred to a Committee who reported: "We have considered Magna Charta, and do not discover any prohibition contained therein," and the position of the Assembly was maintained.

---

[1] Ann, a daughter of Elizabeth Bolton of St. Martin's in the Fields, Middlesex, was hired as a servant, to act as governess, whom he harshly used, and then sold to Francis Brooke, for a wife.

At a court held on June 22, 1652, at St. Mary, Thomas Cole, aged thirty-two years, deposes: "That before coming out of England, he was at Mr. Edmond Plowden's chamber. He asked me 'with whom I lived.' I replied 'Capt. Mitchell.' He persuaded me not to go with him to Virginia, and asked me 'of what religion, he was, and whether I ever seen him go to Church;' I made answer 'I never saw him to Church.' He replied, "that Captain Mitchell being among a company of gentlemen, wondered that the world had been deluded, so many hundred years, with a man and a pigeon,' referring to Christ and the Holy Spirit."

VIRGINIA CAROLORUM. 265

At this period few English ships arrived, and Dutch vessels were prohibited, so that trade was stagnant. Lady Newport, in England, under date of July 14, 1658 wrote: "My daughter Bromley has a son come from Virginia, he has been there almost four years, and there is no profit to be had there, trading is poor."[1]

Among the last official acts of Governor Mathews was the sending a letter[2] dated August 24, 1659, to Governor Fendall of Maryland asking him to co-operate, with an expedition, under Col. Edmund Scarborough, against the Assateague band of Indians, dwelling upon the Eastern Shore near the boundary line of Virginia and Maryland.

Scarborough, then at Occahannock, on the 28th forwarded the letter, which by some delay did not reach the Maryland Governor until the 23d of the next month, and mentioned that it was his intention in ten days to move with three hundred men, and sixty horses, and establish a garrison

---

[1] Sir Richard Newport in October, 1642, was created Baron Newport, his wife was Rachel, sister of Sir Richard Leveson, his daughter Beatrix married Sir Henry Bromley Kt., of Salop, and his son was, probably, the person who had been in Virginia.

[2] "The Concearne of saftie depending on those persons in trust hath directed the Intelligence of our present designes against the Assatage Indians and Confederats, which we haue accomodated with sufficient forces now presumeing the advantage of this opportunity, lying before you reasons politicall will press your Endeavours to assault the Comon Enemy who soe long triumphed in the ruines of Christian bloud, that warr on the Sea Side willbe on our parts prosecuted, and if the Nanticoke and confederats be the Subject of your like Designe, it may, if not vtterly extinguish yet sufficiently Subject the insolencies of those Indians who now despise the English honnour. Vso and improue this from
  "Your humble Servant
   "SAMUEL MATHEWS."
"Aug. 24, 1659.

on the sea-side of the Eastern Shore, and then search for the Indians toward the head of Wicocomoko or Pocomoke river. Governor Fendall replied that he would consult with his Councillors, and on October 9th at Patuxent it was decided to be inexpedient to engage in a war with the Assateagues, the cause of which was not mentioned in the Virginia Governor's letter. The expedition upon the part of the Virginians was not abandoned, as the Assembly at Jamestown in March, 1660, made an appropriation to defray the expenses of the " late war in Accomack."

At an Assembly convened in March 1658-9,[1] was chosen the " Honourable Colonel Samuel Mathews Governour, and

---

[1] BURGESSES MARCH, 1658-9.

Henrico County.

William Hatcher.

Charles City Co.

Col. Ed. Hill, Speaker.

Warham Horsmanden.

James City Co.

Walter Chiles.
Capt. W. Whittacre.

Capt. Tho's Foulke.
Capt. Matt. Edlowe.

Surrey Co.

Capt. George Jordan.
Thomas Warren.

Capt. Wm. Cawfield.

Isle of Wight Co.

Col. Robert Pitt.
Major John Bond.

Capt. English.
James Pyland.

Upper Norfolk Co.

Lt. Col. Ed. Carter.
Capt. Tho's Goodwyn.

Giles Webb.

Lower Norfolk Co.

Col. John Sidney.

Lemuel Mason.

Captain General for two years," and at the expiration of that period it was enacted that the next Governor should be elected from the Councillors, who henceforward should hold office for life unless impeached for misdemeanors. The Council refused to accept the life tenure, and the next session the law was repealed.

A wise law was passed, that if, for any reason, the Governor, or Secretary, should fail to summon an Assembly, that then, the sheriff of James City could issue a call.

During the summer of 1659, it was known in Virginia that Richard Cromwell had given up the office of Protector, and ships which which left England in the beginning of December after a quick voyage of six weeks, anchored in

Warwick County	John Harlowe.
	Elizabeth City Co.
William Batte.	Florentin Paine.
	York County.
Nath. Bacon Esq'r.	Thos. Bushrod.
Major Joseph Croshaw.	Wm. Hay.
New Kent Co.	William Black.
	Lancaster Co.
Col. John Carter.	Henry Corbin.
	Rappahannock Co.
Col. Moore Fantleroy.	John Weyre.
	Gloucester Co.
Capt. Francis Willis.	Capt. Augustine Warner.
	Northampton Co.
John Stringer.	William Jones.
Northumberland County.	Geo. Coleclough.

James River, in January, 1660, with the news "that the Parliament was then sitting," and that General Lambert had gone forth to fight the forces of General Monk. Sir Henry Moody, who was then on a visit to Virginia, sent this intelligence in a letter to any English captain at Manhattan.[1] The Virginians were much excited by the report, as it was evident that another change in the government of England was impending. At this critical period Governor Samuel Mathews suddenly died, and on March 13, 1659-60 [O. S.] an Assembly convened,[2] and the Burgesses declared that

---

[1] Letter of John Davenport, minister of New Haven, to John Winthrop, Jr

[2] ASSEMBLY OF MARCH 1659-60.

COUNCILLORS PRESENT.

Ex. Gov. Richard Bennett.	Col. Obedience Robins.
Col. W. Claiborne, Sec.	Capt. Henry Perry.
Col Wm. Bernard.	Lt. Col. John Walker.
Col. Thos. Pettus.	Col. Abraham Wood.
Col. Francis Morison.	Lt. Col. Edward Carter.
Col. Edward Hill.	Capt. Augustine Warner.
Col. Thomas Dewe.	

BURGESSES.

Henrico Co.

Theodoric Bland, Speaker	Capt. Wm. Farrer.

Charles City Co.

Theodrick Bland.	Charles Sparrow
Capt. Robt. Wynne.	

James City Co.

Henry Soane.	Richard Ford.
Capt. Robt. Ellison.	William Morley.

Surrey Co.

Major Wm. Cawfield.	William Browne.

VIRGINIA CAROLORUM.

there being in England no resident, absolute, and general confessed power," for the present, the "Supreame power of

Isle of Wight Co.

Col. Robert Pitt. Maj. John Bond.
Maj Richard Hill. Nicholas Smith.

Upper Norfolk Co.

Giles Webb. Geo. Catchmaie.
Wm. Denson.

Lower Norfolk Co.

Capt. John Sidney. Lemuel Mason.

Northampton Co.

Col. Edm'd Scarborough. Lt. Col. John Stringer.
Major Wm. Waters.

Warwick Co.

Col. Miles Cary. Major Ed. Griffith.

Elizabeth City Co.

Lt. Col. W. Worlick. Capt. John Powell.

York Co.

X'phen Calthropp. Nathaniel Bacon.
Major Joseph Croshaw. Robert Baldry.

New Kent Co.

Col. Manwaring Hammond. Lt. Col. Robert Abrahall.

Rappahannock Co.

Col. Moore Fantleroy. John Weyre.

Gloucester Co.

Capt. Francis Willis. Capt. Peter Knight.
Capt. Peter Jennings. David Cant.

Lancaster Co.

Col. John Carter. John Curtis.
Henry Corbin.

Northumberland Co. Capt. Peter Ashton.
Westmoreland Co. Capt. Tho's Foulke.

the government," in Virginia was in them, and proceeded to elect one to fill the vacancy caused by the death of Mathews.

It was therefore enacted "that the Honourable Sir William Berkeley bee Governour and Captain Gen'll of Virginia, and that he govern according to the ancient laws of England, and the established laws of this Country, and that all writs issue in the name of the Grand Assembly of Virginia."

To him was given the power to select a Council and Secretary, every two years, but he could not dissolve an Assembly except with the consent of a majority of the Burgesses. "According to the desire" of Governor Berkeley, the Assembly confirmed Col. William Claiborne, Secretary of State. Theodoric Bland,[1] the son-in-law of Bennett, the first Governor under the Commonwealth, was elected Speaker.

The faithful minister, Philip Mallory, was voted two thousand pounds of tobacco for his services, and he and a minister named Lansdale were invited to preach at Jamestown, during the session of the next Assembly.

Good feeling prevailed during the sessions of the Assembly, and republicans and royalists, seemed to be only

---

[1] Theodoric Bland on January 16, 1629-30 was baptized at St. Antholm's London was a merchant in Spain and in the Canary Islands, and in 1654, came to Virginia. His wife was Anne, daughter of Governor Richard Bennett.

In 1676, John Bland of London, his brother, published a memorial with this title *The Humble Remonstrance of John Bland of London, Merchant, on the Behalf of the Inhabitants and Planters in Virginia and Maryland."* The London merchant was prosperous, and did many friendly acts for Virginia. In 1660, a Richard Bland was a commissioner of Elizabeth City County.

Theodoric Bland died in 1671, and was buried within the walls of Westover Church, between the bodies of William Perry and Walter Aston. He left three sons, Theodoric, Richard and John.

interested in promoting the prosperity of Virginia. A resolution of good will was passed, acknowledging the services of the family of Lórd Delaware in these words : " Whereas the many important favours and services rendered the country of Virginia by the noble family of the Wests, predecessors to Mr. John West,[1] the now only survivor, claim at least a gratefull remembrance of their former merrits be still continued to their survivors. It is ordered, that the levies of the said Master West and his family be remitted and he be exempted from payment thereof during life."

In February, it was known at New Amsterdam that the Governor of Virginia was dead, and Governor Stuyvesant

---

"[1] Secretary Brock, of the Virginia Historical Society, contributes the following document signed by John West, to the *New England Historical and Genealogical Register*, January, 1886.

"Oct. 20, 1655. This day Pindabake, the Protector of the young King of Chiskoyak was at my house, intending to have spoken with the Governor, then expected to be heerd but he came not, & therefore hee desyned to leave his mind with mee, Major Will Wiat & divers others, as followith, viz: that Wassahickon the ——— had freely given unto Mr. Edward Wyatt and his heyres, executors, administrators or assigns, all the land from Mr. Hugh Guinn's old marked trees Vttamarke Creeke, including all Pagan——— high Land being freely given, and with the consent of all the rest of the Indians, it was also agreed among them all, that neither the King, nor any other of his Indians should sell, alienate, or dispose of any land belonging unto them, without the consent of Mr. Ed. Wyatt, which was the only business that he had to acquaint the Gov'r therewith in the behalfe of Mr. Ed. Wyat as we heere do testify under our hands this present 29th of October, 1655.

"JOHN WEST."

The witnesses were:

By mark
Pindabake Protector of
   the young King
   Chiskoyake

Willm Benett,
John West Junior,
Toby West,
Wm Godfrey,   ) Sign
John King,   } with
John Talbutt,) mark

and the Council deputed Nicholas Varlett, and Brian Newton to go and express their sorrow, for his "sad and unexpected decease," their wish to renew old friendship, and make a treaty for free commerce. If practicable, they were also desired to enlist soldiers, for service in New Netherlands.

The instructions to the Commissioners were definite and judicious. They were to land at "Kycetan" now Hampton, and "salute Colonel Claborn" who still resided there, and was Secretary of the Colony, "and request his advice, counsel and help, for the greate security of the yacht." After receiving information from Claiborne, they were to present their credentials to the recognized representative of the Colony, and ask for a conference to arrange a preliminary treaty. If consent could be obtained, they were to enlist "some good, resolute men, and among them, as many Scots as possible" in all not more than "twenty-five or thirty."

If they had time, the suggestion was made that they should "cross over to Maryland," and "inquire as secretly as possible whether any preparations against our people in the South river were being made there." They were also instructed in case a treaty was agreed upon with the authorities in Virginia, that it was not final, until revised, and approved by both sides. Should they find upon their arrival, that no Governor had been chosen to fill the vacancy, after remaing eight or ten days, they were to leave, with the understanding, that negotiations would be resumed in the autumn. As Heerman was well acquainted with the English language, they were authorized to obtain his assistance. The Assembly was in session when they arrived, and had elected Berkeley to fill the office of Governor made vacant by the death of Mathews. While for good reasons, the commissioners were not allowed to enlist soldiers to serve under a foreign flag, they were treated courteously and the outline of a treaty settled. In April, they returned to Manhattan, and in June, Sir Henry Moody arrived on the part of Virginia, with credentials signed by the Governor, and Theodore Bland, the Speaker of the Assembly. Four articles were agreed upon, and sent to Governor Berkeley for approval, which however he could not sign for reasons in the following letter, written on August 20, 1660, to Governor Stuyvesant:

"Sir, I have received the letter, you were pleased to send me, by Mr. Mills his vessell, and shall be ever ready to comply with you in all acts of neighbourly friendship and amity. But, truly Sir, you desire me to do that concerning your titles, and claims to land in this northern part of America, which I am in no capacity to do, for I am but a servant of the Assembly, neither do they arrogate any power to themselves, further than the miserable distractions of England force them to. For when God shall be pleased in his mercy to take away and dissipate the unnatural divisions of their native country, they will immediately return to their own professed obedience. What then they should do in matters of contract, donation, or confession of right would have little strength or significance; much more presumptive and impertinent would it be in me to do it without their knowledge or assent. We shall very shortly meet again, and then, if to them you signify your desires, I shall labor all I can, to get you a satisfactory answer."

Sir Henry Moody, Baronet, was the son of Lady Deborah Moody whose maiden name was Dunche. Her grandfather William Dunche, who died May 11, 1579, had two sons, Edward and Walter. Edward was a member of parliament during the reigns of James the First, and also his son Charles.

Walter of Avesbury, Wiltshire, married Deborah daughter of James Pilkinton, first Bishop of Durham under Queen Elizabeth, who was kind to non-conformists. One of the four daughters of Walter, Deborah, married Sir Henry Moody, Baronet[1] of Garsden, Wilts.

About the year 1632, Lady Deborah Moody was left a widow with one son, Sir Henry. After residing some time in London, about A.D., 1639, she sailed for America, and in April, 1640, was a member of the church at Salem, Mass., and in 1641, purchased the farm near Lynn, of John Humpries, whose wife was a daughter of the Earl of Lincoln. Lechford, writes; "Lady Moody lives at Lynn, but is of Salem church. She is a good lady, almost undone by buying Master Humphries farm."

In December, 1642, she was presented for holding that the baptism of infants was no ordinance of God, and the next year she moved to New Amsterdam, for liberty of worship. In March, 1643, in the Massachusetts Records it is mentioned, that the Rev. Mr. Walton "is for Long Island

---

[1] The last wife of Sir John Stafford, was the sister of Sir Henry Moody, Bt. Stafford had been baptized at Geneva January 4, 1555-6, John Calvin standing as sponsor. Stafford's father died in Geneva, May 5, 1557.

shortly there to set down with my Lady Moodie, from under civill and church watch among ye Dutch." For a time she was molested by Indians, but on the 19th of December, 1645, a patent for the town of Gravesend, Long Island, was given unto "Ye honoured Lady Deborah Moody ; Sir Henry Moody, Baronet ;" and others and " to have and enjoye the free libertie of conscience according to the custome and manner of Holland, without molestation or disturbance from any madgistrate, or madgistrates, or any ecclesiastical minister."

In 1655, her house was surrounded by Indians, who were at last driven away by soldiers from New Amsterdam, and about 1659, she died. Her son, Sir Henry Moody may have remained some time in England. After his mother's departure, his father's place at Garsden was sold to a Sir Laurence Washington, chief register, who died in 1643, at the age of sixty-four years. He was as early as 1645, on Long Island.

In September, 1659, a fort belonging to the Dutch, about eighty miles above Manhattan, was for some weeks surrounded by a large body of Indians who destroyed cornfields, and killed settlers. Sir Henry Moody was requested to raise a company, and go to their relief. He marched to the fort, dispersed the Indians, and entering it unfurled the English flag. About this time he disposed of his plantation at Gravesend, Long Island, and this year, made a visit to Virginia.

In October, 1660, the Virginia Assembly ordained: "That Sir Henry Moody bee implored in an embase by the right honourable the Governor, to the Manados, about the affaires of the country shall have elevaen thousand pounds of tobacco out of the levie, this year, as a gratuity for his paines therein."

After this he took lodgings with Daniel Litschoe, an innkeeper of New Amsterdam, whose house according to Gerard, was near the present junction of Wall and Pearl streets, New York City. He appears at this time to have been quite poor, as on the 20th of September, 1661, he left certain books[1] for the payment of his board and lodging.

He returned to Virginia, and died at the house of Colonel Francis Moryson, acting Governor during Berkeley's absence in England. He was the first Baronet who died in Virginia.

While a few of the colonists were educated and able to educate their children in England, the great majority were

---

[1] In N. Y. Col. Doc's, Vol. 4, 8vo, 1851, p. 610, is the following:

"Cathologu containing the names of such books as Sir. Henry Moodie left in security in hands of Daniel Litscho when he went for Virginia.

A latyn Bible in folio.

A written book in folio containing privatt matters of State.

Seventeen severall books of devotional matter.

A dictionaries Latin and English.

Sixteen several latin and Italian bookx of divers matters.

A book in folio containing the voyage of Ferdinand Mendoz.

A book in folio kalleth Sylva Sylvarum.

A book in quarto kalleth, hartas six days worke of the lord and translated in English by Josiah Sylvester.

A book in quarto kalleth the Sume and Substance of the Conference which it please his Excellent Majestie to have with the lords, bishops, &c., at Hampton Court contracteth by William Barlow.

A book in quarto kalleth Ecclesiastica Interpretatio or the Exposition upon the difficult and doubtful passages of the seven Epistles called Catholique, and the Revalation collected by John Mayer.

Eleven several bookx moore of divers subjects.

The verification of his father's knights order given by King James."

not above the grade of laborers, and enjoyed but few of the comforts of life.

Lionel Gatford, B. D., published in 1657, a small treatise entitled "Publick Good without Private Interest." He was friendly to Lord Baltimore, although a Puritan. In a dedicatory epistle to Cromwell, "his Highness, the Lord Protector of England, Scotland and Ireland," he writes, that "poor, neglected, despised Virginia, and the English Colonie there, with the adjacent heathen inhabitants of the same continent, came often and often into his thoughts."

In allusion to the peculiar form of church government in existence, he used this language: "It cannot be expected that either your petitioner, or any other, how zealously affected soever they are to the advancement of God's glory and the propagation of the Gospel of Christ, should leave their preaching, and other ministration here, in their own native Country that so much needs them, though they should be allowed to preach no where but in bonds and fetters, or in caves, and other hiding places (which they fear not, so long as your Highness shall retain the Sovereign power solely in your own hands) and go into Virginia to labour there, in utter impossibilities, or to be thrust out from labouring, when any probabilities of doing good should be offered there, only upon that distast or suggestion of any turbulent or vicious persons that shall complain of them to a Governour as indifferent, and vicious as themselves."

In the treatise among other hindrances to the prosperity of the Colony, are mentioned: "The people that are sent to inhabit in that Colonie, are the most of them the very scum and off scouring of our Nation, vagrants or condemned persons, or such others, as by the looseness and viciousness of their lives have disabled themselves to subsist any longer in this Nation ; and when they come thither either know not how, or will not betake themselves to any sober, industrious course of living. And if they chance to get ought to maintain them in their licentiousness and wickedness fall to practising their old abominable practice there, as much or more than they ever did heer. So that if they come to be members or officers in the said Colonies, whereby they are rendered more conspicuous in their true colours, their idleness, and otherwise evil examples, do not only corrupt and taint others of the same Colonie, but cause the very Heathen to loath both them and the very profession of Christianity for their sakes."

He also lamented "that very many Children and servants sent into that Plantation, that were violently taken away, or cheatingly duckoyed without the consent or knowledge of their Parents or Masters by some præstigious Plagiaries (commonly called Spirits) into some private places, or ships, and there sold to be transported; and then resold there to be servants or slaves to those that will give most for them. A practice proper for Spirits, namely the Spirits of Devils, but to be abhorred and abominated of all men that know either what men are, or whose originally they are, or what their relatives are, either natural, civil, or Christian."

In every country, at its first settlement, will be found hardy adventurers, of obscure birth, and wholly dependent upon their energy, and industry, who rise to positions of prominence, and influence, and it was not remarkable, that the Assemblies in the days of Berkeley, and the Commonwealth, should have contained some of these.

If Abraham Wood, a boy ten years of age, could come to Virginia, and after serving his term as a servant, advance in position, and in 1654, be a Burgess, it is creditable to him, and if in the Assembly of that year should also be John Trussell, who when he was nineteen years of age, in 1622, became a servant in Charles City County, and William Worlich, who came the same year when eighteen years old, and was a servant in Elizabeth City, it only shows what poor immigrant boys like those of the present century who have landed at New York City, may by perseverance, accomplish.

General Monk reached London, early in February, the news of which was received, in Virginia, before the first of May, with the report, that the monarchy would soon be restored. On the 29th of May, Charles the Second entered London amid the acclamations of the people.

CHAPTER VIII.

FROM THE RESTORATION OF CHARLES THE SECOND, TO A.D. 1671.

COLONISTS QUIETLY ACCEPT RESTORATION OF THE KING. INSTRUCTIONS TO GOVERNOR BERKELEY. PHILIP MALLORY, CLERGYMAN, VISITS ENGLAND. BERKELEY IN ENGLAND. FRANCIS MORISON, CHOSEN TEMPORARY GOVERNOR. QUAKERS FINED AND IMPRISONED. OFFICE SEEKERS. ENCROACHMENTS UPON INDIANS. GRANT OF 1662, OF LANDS, TO FAVORITES OF THE KING. PUBLICATION OF "VIRGINIA'S CURE." GOVERNOR BERKELEY'S RETURN. LEGISLATION AGAINST QUAKERS AND BAPTISTS. ATTEMPT TO BUILD UP JAMESTOWN. BIRKENHEAD CONSPIRACY. FUGITIVE SERVANTS. BURGESSES A.D., 1663. PERSECUTION OF QUAKERS. SCARBOROUGH, SURVEYOR GENERAL, CRITICISES QUAKERS. CONFERENCE AS TO CESSATION OF TOBACCO PLANTING. WILLIAM DRUMMOND AND THOMAS WOODWARD. LETTER OF MORISON IN BEHALF OF VIRGINIA. ANNUAL ELECTIONS POSTPONED. NORTHERN INDIANS. CONFERENCE OF 1666, AS TO TOBACCO. BURGESSES IN 1666. SHIPS IN 1667 DESTROYED BY THE DUTCH. COLONISTS DISCONTENTED. SILK PRESENTED TO THE KING. EXPLORATIONS OF LEDERER, AND HENRY BATT. JAIL BIRDS. SUFFRAGE RESTRICTED. BERKELEY'S REPORT OF 1671, TO COMMISSIONERS OF PLANTATIONS.

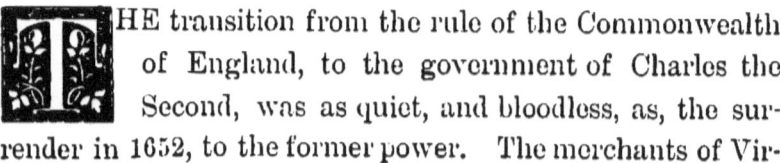THE transition from the rule of the Commonwealth of England, to the government of Charles the Second, was as quiet, and bloodless, as, the surrender in 1652, to the former power. The merchants of Vir-

ginia had little interest in the political disputes of England, and hoped that by the restoration of Charles the Second, they might obtain a repeal of the Navigation Act, which restricted the carrying of tobacco, to vessels owned by Englishmen, and had depressed the commercial interests of the Colony. As the people, by their Burgesses, had freely elected Berkeley, Governor, who had acknowledged,[1] that he was, "but a servant of the Assembly's," and as his brother John was one of the friends and advisers of the King, they believed it to be good policy to cordially accept the changed condition[2] of affairs. The King on the 31st of July, recognized Gov. Berkeley and the Council. The Assembly which convened on the 11th of October, 1660, only transacted absolutely necessary business. The Council and Assembly had been obliged to meet in the houses of Mr. Woodhouse, and of Thomas Hunt, and the Governor was requested "to take into his care the building of a State House," and to make contracts at his pleasure. He was also empowered "to presse tenne men of the ordinarie sort of people, allowing each man two thousand pounds of tobacco, per annum, and to employ them toward the building of a State house," but no work was done. A Committee *ad interim* was appointed, composed of Henry Soane, Speaker, Na-

---

[1] See Chapter VII, Berkeley's letter to New Amsterdam authorities.

[2] Their language in acknowledging the King was not as servile as that of the Massachusetts Colony. Governor Endicott by order of the General Court, of the latter, on Aug. 7, 1661, fulsomely wrote, "Royal Sir: Your just title to the Crown enthronizeth you in our consciences; your graciousness, in our affections; that, inspireth unto duty, this, naturalizeth unto loyalty."

thaniel Bacon, Esq., Col. Miles Cary,[1] Major Nicholas Hill, Capt. Robert Ellyson, Capt. George Jordon,[2] and Mr. Walter Chiles, and until the 23d of March, 1660-1, a recess was taken.

The Council for Foreign Plantations in England directed a letter to Sir William Berkeley, Governor "for the time being" and the Virginia Council, in which, they enjoined that all religious exercises should be according to the profession of the church of England, and that they should encourage learned and orthodox ministers, as it was a shame for a rich and flourishing people to be without a ministry

---

[1] Colonel Miles Cary was a descendant of William Cary, merchant, the Mayor of Bristol in 1546; in 1665, he was one of the Council of Virginia. On March 29, 1666, he was superintending the erection of defences at Point Comfort against the Dutch, and here lost his life. Two of his sons, Miles, and Thomas, were prominent in public affairs and identified themselves with the Quakers. Story, a Quaker preacher, brother of the Dean of Lismore, and Keeper of the Great Seal of the Province of Pennsylvania, and one of the early Mayors of Philadelphia, held in 1690, a Friends' Meeting at Yorktown. Two days after, he writes "Went to Thomas Carey's who had been lately convinced. His wife had been also. His brother Miles, and wife, coming hither to see us were made partakers of the same visitation." Several years later he made another visit and wrote: "Made a visit to Miles Carey, Secretary of the County, who being absent, his wife, a Friend, prevailed with us to stay to supper."

Thomas Cary thought to be the son of the Councillor, married a daughter of Archdale, the Quaker Governor of Carolina, and in 1697, was Receiver General of that Colony.

[2] Jordon is a name found in the earlier records. In the first Assembly of 1619 was Samuel Jordon. Mary Tue, daughter of Hugh Crouch, executrix of Lt. Richard Crouch, in 1622, "assigned 100 acres of land wch lies in Diggs, his Hundred to Samuel Jordon of Charles Hundred, gentleman." Neills' *Virginia Company*, p. 315. In March, 1622, Robert Jordon was slain by the Indians at Berkeley Hundred five miles from Charles City.

Alice the daughter of John Miles, and wife of George Jordon, died January 7, 1650 (O.S.)

proportionate to the population, and such a ministry was necessary to the winning of the souls of those whom they had purchased as slaves."

With this communication was sent the King's Proclamation from Breada, and an Act of Indemnity. The letter was entirely conciliatory, and they were urged to lay aside "animosities begotten by the late distracted and unsettled times, and affectionately unite, so that former differences be buried in oblivion."

The old London Company was reported to be again making an effort for the restoration of their charter, and the Assembly fearing the loss of their liberties, from the Plantation Commissioners, determined to send Sir William Berkeley, at their own expense, to act as their agent, in England and present their wants to the King.

Phillip Mallory, who had "been eminently faithfull in the ministry, and very dilligent in endeavouring the advancement of all those meanes that might conduce to the advancement of religion," was also appointed by the Assembly of March, 1660-1, to undertake to solicit in England, in behalf of their "church affaires."

Berkeley reached London in the summer of 1661, when the Cavaliers were in a frenzy of joy. A formal, political, and hence unlovely, type of Puritanism had succumbed to the noisy, jeering, and pleasure-loving sycophants of the Court. Taverns, brothels, and theaters, had rapidly increased since the Coronation day, and the Virginia Governor was pleased to see the performance on the stage of his tragi-comedy.[1]

---
[1] Pepys on January 19, 1660-1, went to the theatre and saw the "Lost Lady" played, but was not much pleased.

"The Lost Lady" which twenty years before had been entered at Stationers' Hall.

His visit, with his brother, a favorite of the King, and high in power, tended to develop the worse, and restrain his better traits, so that Berkeley before, and Berkeley after the restoration, did not appear the same person.

Francis Moryson,[1] also written Morison, had been chosen Governor during the absence of Berkeley, and the Assembly of March, 1661-2, provided for a revision and modification of the laws of the Colony, and also "sett downe certaine rules to be observed in the government of the church, until God shall please to turne his majesties pious thoughts toward us, and provide a better supply of ministers."

The "whole liturgie" every Sunday was to be "thoroughly read." The word Sunday or Lord's Day is used more frequently than Sabbath in the Acts. The "ornaments" of the church were called "a greate bible, two com-

---

[1] His wife was Cecilia, the sister of Giles Rawlins, who was killed in a duel with one of Lord Dillon's sons, in August, 1662, in St. James Field, Pall Mall. His brother, was Richard who had been in charge of the rude fort at Point Comfort. The latter obtained this appointment through his father's influence with Lord Falkland.

On January 3d, 1648, there was granted to Richard 110 acres in Elizabeth City known as "Fort Field." The widow Winifred Moryson who obtained a grant in 1652, of 400 acres on the south side of Horn Harbor creek was probably the mother. Major Francis Moryson on June 1, 1654, obtained possession of 24 acres near Jamestown, upon which stood the old "Glasse House." In 1621, Capt. William Norton with some Italians were sent by the London Company to establish glass works. Norton died, in 1623, and Sandys, Colonial Treasurer, wrote that the Italians were disorderly, and "Vincenzio had cracked the furnace with a Iron crow-bar." See *Virginia Vetusta*, page 121. The glass factory was not successful and the ground upon which it stood was sold by Governor Harvey to Anthony Coleman, and by successive assignments became the property of Francis Morison.

mon prayer books, a communion cloath and napkin, a pulpit, and cushion."

For the support of the government, a duty of two shillings was imposed upon every hogshead of tobacco shipped to England, and ten shillings upon each hogshead shipped to foreign ports, those ships excepted, belonging to persons residing in the Colony.

Fines were ordered to be imposed upon Quakers, and other non-conformists, holding unlawful assemblies. William Cole of Maryland, a Quaker, soon after visited Virginia, with George Wilson, one of their preachers from England, who violating the law, was imprisoned.[1] A letter written by Wilson, shows that members of the Society of Friends in their plainness of speech, seemed coarse and uncharitable. It was dated "From that dirty dungeon in Jamestown, the 17th of the Third Month, 1662," (O. S.) and is as follows :

"If they who visit not such in prison (as Christ speaks of) shall be punished with everlasting destruction, O what will ye do? Or what will become of you who put us into such nasty, stinking prisons, as this dirty dungeon, where we have not had the benefit to do what nature requireth, nor so much as air, to blow in, at a window, but close made up with brick and lime, so that there is no air to take away the

---

[1] William Robinson, a merchant of London and Quaker preacher, as early as 1658, visited Virginia. In a letter written, at Boston, not long before he, and William Leddra, to the disgrace of the Puritans, was hung, he uses these words :
"I came lately from Virginia, with my brethren Robert Hodgson, Christopher Holden and William Leddra, at which place I was about fourteen months in service, and hard travel, through the Country, for the Seeds Sake. * * * I was in prison in Virginia about six months."

smell our dung and p——[1] who for all their cruelty, I can truly say, 'Father forgive them, for they know not what they do.' But thus saith the Lord unto me 'Tell them that because wilfully they are ignorant, I will strike them with astonishment, and will bring upon them the filth of their detestable things, and in that day they should be glad if they could to eat their own dung and drink their own p——, it shall so odiously stand before them, that it shall be an evil stink in succeeding generations. This you shall eternally witness, for I have spoken with you in the name of the Lord, in whose authority this is to go abroad."

John Grave, also a Quaker, this year wrote a poem which was printed with title "A Song of Sion, written by a Citizen thereof, whose outward habitation is in Virginia; and being sent over to some of his Friends in England, the same is found fitting to be published, for to warn the seed of Evil Doers."

As soon as it was known that negotiations were begun to place Charles the Second on the throne, applicants for places in Virginia preferred their requests. Captain James Neale[2]

---

[1] It is unnecessary to print this word in full, which is now considered vulgar.

[2] Neale was Captain of a Maryland pinnace at an early period. On the 1st of September, 1642, he arrived at Boston with two pinnaces, commissioned by Governor Calvert to buy mares and sheep. While there one of his pinnaces was found to be worm eaten and was abandoned. After the civil war in England commenced, he crossed the ocean, and he and his father fought for the King. In 1660, he returned to Maryland commended by Lord Baltimore, and in 1666, petitions the Assembly for the naturalization of Ann his wife, and children Henrietta Maria, James, Dorothy, and Anthony, born in Spain during his residence there, as a merchant, and when employed there by King and Duke of York "in several emergent affairs." His daughter Henrietta Maria married Richard, the son of Richard Bennett the Puritan, who, for a time, lived near the Severn River, and was subsequently Governor of Virginia.

who had been before the civil war a prominent man in Maryland, and had shed his blood on the royalist side during the Commonwealth period, before the King, left Breda, asked to hold the office of Treasurer of Virginia, but, this was given to Major Henry Norwood, a relative of the Governor. Thomas Ludwell received the Secretaryship which had so long been held by William Claiborne, and in the place of Thomas Lovinge, Edmund Scarborough, became his Majesty's Surveyor General. Philip Honeywood who had been in Virginia, a guest at Ralph Wormeley's returned to England, and in April, 1662, was in command of the garrison, and subsequently Deputy Governor of Portsmouth. Nicholas Downe, the chief cook of his Majesty's kitchen died in Virginia, and Ann his widow petitioned the easy tempered King for an annuity.[1]

In view of the fact that the Colony was threatened with ruin by the excessive planting of a single staple, tobacco, which was sold at so low a rate that "neither merchant, nor planter could well subsist," the Assembly enacted that a quantity of flax seed should be brought from England, and distributed in the several counties, to agents, who were authorized to sell it on time to planters, and a premium of three pounds of tobacco was offered to every one who would spin the flax raised, and weave the yarn into cloth, a

---

[1] Anthony Langston, who had been an ensign in Prince Maurice's Regiment, after fourteen years residence in Virginia, in January, 1662-3, returns to London, and is fond of drinking in the Dog Tavern. In a brawl, he killed a man, was tried, found guilty of manslaughter and sentenced to be burned in the hand. By the effort of friends he was pardoned, and became a captain of the naval service.

yard wide; and for every yard of woolen cloth made of yarn spun in the Colony, a promise of five pounds of tobacco was offered.

A promise of fifty pounds of tobacco was also offered for any sea going vessel built in the country. Henry Soane, Speaker, having died, Captain Robert Wynn took his place. Hon. Nathaniel Bacon[1] having been made one of the Council, Major Edward Griffith was appointed to fill the vacancy in the Committee *ad interim*. The Assembly was not dissolved, but adjourned to meet in March of the next year.

As settlers increased upon the shores of the Potomac, and Rappahannock, collision with the Indians became more frequent, and the Assembly was disposed to protect the savages as far as they could. Captain Giles Brent, Col. Gerard Fowke,[2] Captain George Mason, and Mr. John Lord were censured for the "injuries and affronts done to Wahanganoche," the chief of the "Potowmeck" Indians, and Brent and Folke, for arresting and binding the chief, were heavily fined, and debarred from holding any office civil or military, and Mason, and Ford, were also fined, to a small amount. Col. Moore Fantleroy[3] for his treatment of the Rappannocks

---

[1] See Chapter VII, for a notice of this councillor.

[2] Colonel Gerard Fowke was the son of Roger and Mary Folke of Gunston Hall, Staffordshire, and a Gentleman of the Bed Chamber, in days of Charles the First, and Colonel of Cavalry in battle of Worcester, and now a merchant. He obtained 1400 acres at Paspatany on the Potomac River. Captain George Mason was his cousin and both had been Colonels, in the King's army, during the civil war. Gerard Fowke's daughter Mary, married her cousin, the son of Captain George Mason.—*Dinwiddie Papers*, Vol. I, p. XXIII.

[3] In 1663, Moore Fantleroy in England "an untoward fellow" was suspected of opposition to the King. Perhaps he was a relative of the Virginia immigrant.

was disqualified for holding office, and bound to good behavior.

At this Assembly, it was ordered that Mr. George Harwood, having spoken words "to the dishonour of the right honourable gouernour ffrancis Morrison, esquire," should ask forgiveness upon his knees.

The Virginians now, had occasion to contrast the peaceful government of Governors Bennett, Digges, and Mathews under the Commonwealth of England, with their condition under Charles the Second. The Navigation Act was not repealed, but, more strictly enforced, and court favorites were endeavoring to enrich themselves at the expense of the Colonists, who were indignant, when a communication from the King, dated December 5, 1662, was received, addressed to the Governor, and Council of Virginia, informing them, that he had given away, a large portion of the best land in Virginia, to a few persons, and, in the spring of 1662-3, Francis Moryson went to England, as agent of Virginia to offer remonstrance.

The King informed the Colony that on the 18th of September, 1649, when he was a fugitive, he had given to certain persons all that territory "bound by the rivers Tappahannacke or Rappahannacke, and Quiriough or Patawomacke, and Thaspayoke" which they could not enjoy; and that he had now revoked the grant,[1] and issued a new

---

[1] In July, 1639, owing to the increase of population in Bermudas, the Proprietors of the Island, in London, petitioned for this region "scituate betwixt the two Rivers of Rapahanock, and Patowmack wch by good Informacon your petit'iors finde to be both healthfull and otherwise not yet Inhabited." *Lefroy's Bermudas*, Vol. I, p. 558.

patent to Sir Humphrey Hooke Kt., John Fitz Herbert, Esq., and Robert Vicaredge, merchant, granting them the use and profits of the region, for a certain term of years. In view of rumors of opposition, he wrote in August, 1663, to the Colonial authorities not to place any obstruction in the way of Sir Humphrey Hooke[1] and his associates.

Governor Berkeley was in England from the summer of 1661, to the autumn of 1662, and while there, a small treatise by R. G. was published, entitled *Virginia's Cure or an Advisive Concerning Virginia, Discovering the True Ground of that Church's Unhappiness.* The writer was probably Roger Green, who had been, like Mallory, a respected minister in the Colony. He alludes to his being present at Jamestown in 1656, when the Assembly passed an act for establishing markets, and was sent to England with letters from Governor Morrison in behalf of the interest of the Church, and education. He deplores the want of towns and the evil of living upon isolated plantations, whereby "not only was there a very numerous generation of Christian children born in Virginia unserviceable for any employment of Church or State; but an obstacle was also cast in the way of the conversion of the Heathen."

The Burgesses elected by the people he mentions "were usually such as went over servants thither, and though by time, and industry, they may have attained competent estates, yet by reason of their poor and mean condition, were unskilful in judging of a good estate, either of church or Commonwealth, or by the means of procuring it."

---

[1] Hooke in 1661, was High Sheriff of Gloucestershire, and in 1664, Deputy Lieutenant of Bristol.

The Commissioners of Plantations, in 1662, were frequently seen, by Governor Berkeley, now in England. The proposition to cease planting tobacco in Virginia, for a certain period was discussed by the Board, during the months of May, and June, but was not approved. In July, 1662, Governor Berkeley was ordered to return, and in a communication to the Commissioners, he alludes to the sudden command of the King, to depart for Virginia, and his determination to promote, as far as possible, the culture of silk, flax, and hemp, and the cutting of mast timbers. He further mentions, that hereafter he will see that the laws of the Colony are printed,[1] before they are presented, for the Board's approval. The order to return to Virginia was for a few weeks, suspended, and in August, the Board for Plantations, discussed these questions and decided that the Colony should bear its own expenses. The salary of the Governor was fixed at one thousand pounds sterling, to be raised by a tax of two shillings upon each hogshead of tobacco.

The shipmasters, in the Virginia trade, then in London, objected to the two shilling tobacco tax, and the ten pence castle duty at Point Comfort, because the Colony furnished no proper defence for their ships. On the 26th of August a petition signed by Gov. Berkeley, Sir Henry

---

[1] Soon after, a folio was published in London by Francis Moryson with the title *Laws of Virginia*. To this was prefixed *A Description of Virginia*, which was probably, the same which appeared, in a separate form, of twelve pages, with the title: *A Description and View of Virginia By Sir William Berkeley, the Governour*, London, 1663.

Chicheley, Edward Digges, Richard Lee[1] and others came before the Board, in which it was mentioned that tobacco was now sold at so low a rate, as not to defray the freight charges, and begging that they would order that its planting be restricted. To this, on the 6th of September, again came a remonstrance from the ship-masters and owners.

It was now arranged that Berkeley should leave for Virginia, and on the 12th of September he received his Majesty's instructions. He was to see that the Act of Navigation against which so much had been said, should be strictly respected. The planters were to be encouraged to build towns, and they could not "have a better example, than from their neighbours of New England, who have, in a few years, raised that Colony to breed wealth, reputation, and security." He was also to appoint Commissioners to treat, with those of Maryland, respecting tobacco, and within a month, after his arrival, was to call a General Assembly, and to publish his Majesty's pardon and oblivion to all not attainted of the "horrid murder of our dear Father."

The King and his advisers, do not appear to have approved of a severe policy toward Quakers and other non-conformists. Among other instructions were these: "And because Wee are willing to give all possible encouragement to persons of different persuasion in matters of Religion to transport themselves thither with their stocks; You are not to suffer any man to be molested, or disquieted in the exercise of his Religion, so he be content with a quiet and peace-

---

[1] Richard Lee, now in England, felt that a douceur to Secretary Nicholas would not be unprofitable, and on the 7th of October, 1662, he sent him "ten pieces to buy a little toy, and also some rarities" from Virginia.

able enjoying it, not giving therein offence or scandall to the Government: But Wee oblige you in your own house and family to the profession of the Protestant Religion, according as it is now established in our Kingdome of England, and the recommending it to all others under your government, as farre as it may consist with the peace and quiet of our said Colony.'"

As instructed, in less than a month, after his arrival, at Jamestown, he summoned the Assembly, which had never been dissolved, and on the 23d of December, 1662, it convened, with Capt. Robert Wynne, the speaker.

During the Cromwellian era not only was there a development of the "Society of Friends," but an organization which rejected infant baptism, and particularly the service in the Book of Common Prayer, which asserted, that after the application of water, the child is regenerated with the Holy Spirit. To prevent the spread of the latter class of religionists, the Assembly passed this Act: "Whereas many scismaticall persons out of their averseness to the orthodox, established religion, or out of the new fangled conceits of their owne hereticall inventions, refuse to have their children baptized: *Be it therefore enacted*, that all persons that in contempt of the divine sacrament of baptisme, shall refuse, when they may carry their child to a lawfull minister in that county, to have them baptised shallbe amerced two thousand pounds; halfe to the informer, halfe to the publique." Another act was passed

---

[1] In the *Appendix* will be found a letter of Governor Berkeley to Charles the Second after the Restoration, and also his speeches to the Council and Burgesses in accepting the Governorship of Virginia before the Restoration

intended to check the loose tongues of gossips, in these words: "Whereas oftentimes many babling women often slander and scandalize their neighbours, for which, their poore husbands, are often brought into chargeable and vexatious suites and cast in greate damages ; Bee it enacted * * that in actions of slander occasioned by the wife as aforesaid, after judgment passed shallbe punished by ducking, and if the slander be soe enormous as to be adjudged at a greater damage than five hundred pounds of tobacco, then the woman to suffer a ducking for each five hundred pounds of tobacco adjudged against the husband if he refuses to pay the tobacco."[1]

The absence of any building for the sessions of the legislature and court, more than fifty years after the planting of the Colony, evinced the absence of a proper pride and public spirit, and the King had enjoined upon Berkeley the building up of the capitol. By his energy the legislature ordered that thirty brick houses should be built twenty feet in width, and forty in length, the roof to have a fifteen foot pitch, and to be covered with slate or tile. The bricks were not to be brought from England, as it would have

---

[1] Babbling women were found in all parts of the Colony. The following is from the manuscript record of Northampton County, under date of September 8, 1634: "Upon dew examination it is thought fitt by the board that s'yd Joane Butler shalbe drawen ouer the Rings Creeke [Kings Creek] at the starne of a boate or Canoux * * * also the next Saboth day in the tyme of denyne [divine] seruis, between the first and second lesson, present herselfe before the minister and say after him as followeth:

"I Joane Butler doe acknoweledge to have called Marie Drewe hoare, and thereby I confess I have done her manefest wronge wherefore I desire before this congregatōn that the s'yd Marie Drew will forgiue me, and alsoe that this congregatōn will ioyne [join] in prayer with me, that God may forgiue me."

been as strange as "carrying coals to New Castle," but were to be burned in the neighborhood. The houses were to be regularly placed "in a square or such other forme as the honorable Sir William Berkeley" should deem most appropriate. No more wooden houses were under the act to be built in Jamestown. Each of the seventeen counties was authorized to build and to impress bricklayers, sawyers, carpenters, and other tradesmen. The act however proved unpopular and drove away mechanics. Morison wrote to Earl of Clarendon in 1665 : "Our porre assaye, of building four or five houses, lost us hundreds of people."

Upon the 10th of September, 1663, the Assembly met according to adjournment, and among the Burgesses to fill vacancies was Col. Gerard Fowke formerly of Maryland, now a representative of Westmoreland County, who took the prescribed oath of allegiance and supremacy. Col. William Claiborne, no longer Secretary, and now living in the Pamunky valley, was a delegate from New Kent County.

The indentured white servants, the refuse of the camps of the late civil war, and the alleys of London, with the heathen slaves, from the coast of Africa, were now so numerous as to be a constant source of anxiety to the planters. In Gloucester County there appears at this time to have been a combination for a general uprising, which failed by one Berkenhead, a servant of a planter named Smith, becoming an informer. The legislature felt that the planters had escaped from "a horrid plot" and resolved ''that Berkenhead have his freedom, and five thousand pounds of tobacco given him, in Gloster County, and that his master be satisfied for his time and it was further resolved " that the 13th of September, be annually kept holy, being the day those villains intended to put the plot in execution." Four of the conspirators were tried and executed.[1]

Fugitive white servants began to occasion great trouble. William Drummond complained, in 1662, that the court at Boston, had illegally discharged one of his servants, and the Virginia Assembly retaliated by ordering that "there be seized, to the value of forty pound sterling money, out the estate of some persons, relateing to the said government of Boston, which, is in consideration of wages due for such a servant's time, as was illegally cleared from the said Drummond's employ in New England. William Claiborne, Jr., still living at Kiquotan (Hampton), in August, 1662, arrived at Delaware Bay in search of two escaped servants.

Notwithstanding previous enactments against the Quakers, their traveling preachers persisted in going to out of the way places, without money, and asking for none, yet preaching a gospel of peace, and good will, as far as they understood the teaching of Christ. Their cheerful endurance of hardship, with their plain teaching, attracted the attention and aroused the consciences of rude frontiersmen who, hitherto, had no one to care for their souls, and Quaker meetings multiplied.

---

[1] On April 10, 1665, Secretary Ludwell wrote to Secretary of State in England, that he had "sent the trial of those servants who in September, 1663, conspired to ruin the Government."

In October, 1661, at Bermudas, was discovered a plot of the Irish servants and Negro slaves to rise, cut the throats of their masters, and ruin the country.

VIRGINIA CAROLORUM.

The Assembly,[1] of 1663, determined upon more vigorous measures of repression, and passed the following preamble: "Whereas it is evident of late time, that certaine persons under the names of Quakers, and other names of separation have taken up and maintained sundry dangerous opinions,

---

[1] BURGESSES IN ASSEMBLY SEPTEMBER, 1663.

Henrico Co.
Capt. Wm. Farrar.

Charles City Co.
Capt. Robt. Wynne, Speaker.
Stephen Hamelyn.
Capt. Francis Gray.

James City Co.
Capt. Robt. Ellyson.
Walter Chiles.
Capt. Edw'd Ramsey.

Surrey County.
Capt. Wm. Cockeram.
Thomas Warren.

Isle of Wight Co.
Major Nich. Hill.
Capt. Joseph Bridger.
Dr. Robt. Williamson.

Nansemond Co.
George Wallings.

Lower Norfolk Co.
Major Lemuel Mason.

Elizabeth City Co.
Capt. John Powell.
Col. Leonard Yeo.

Warwick Co.
Major Edw. Griffith.

York County.
Lt. Col. Barber.

New Kent Co.
Col. W. Claiborne.

Gloucester Co.
Capt. Peter Jennings.
Capt. Tho's Walker.

Lancaster Co.
Raleigh Frances.

Rappahannock Co.
Thomas Lucas.
Capt. John Weye.

Northumberland Co.
Wm. Presley.

Westmoreland County.
Col. Gerard Fowke.

and tenets, and whereas the said persons, under pretence of religious worship doe often assemble themselves in greate numbers in several parts of this colony, to the greate endangering its publique peace and safety, and to the terror of the people by maintayning a secrett and strict correspondency among themselves, and in the meantime separating good and loyall subjects from the publique congregations, and usual places of divine service;" it was enacted, after this preamble, that if Separatists, above the age of sixteen years, to the number of five, or more, assembled at any time, and any place, to worship, not according to the laws of England, for the first offence, they were to be fined two hundred pounds of tobacco, for the second offence, five hundred pounds, and for offending the third time should be banished from the colony. If any master of a ship brought into the colony, after the first of July, 1664, a Quaker, except under the laws of England, he should be fined five thousand pounds of tobacco. If any person entertained a Quaker in, or near his house, to preach, he was also liable to a fine of five thousand pounds. In their excessive zeal for the church of England, they expelled John Porter, of Lower Norfolk, because sheriff John Hill, of that county, had represented to the House that he " was loving to the Quakers, and stood well affected towards them, and had been at their meetings, and was so far an ana-baptist as to be against the baptizing of children."

Northampton Co.

Lt. Col. Kendall.　　　　　　　Major Wm. Andrews.

Accomack Co.

Devereux Browne.　　　　　　　Hugh Yeo.[1]

[1] Hugh Yeo cordwainer, was the fourth son of Justinian, of Hartland, Devonshire.

During the autumn of 1663, Mary Tomkins and Alice Ambrose were at the Cliffs in Calvert County, Maryland, and wrote to George Fox, the eminent Quaker preacher: "We have been in Virginia, where we have had a good service for the Lord. Our sufferings have been large * * * we are now about to set sail for Virginia again." Bishop referring to these in "New England Judged" writes: "Mary Tomkins and Alice Ambrose[1] these two servants of the Lord having been at Virginia * * * who had there suffered thirty-two stripes apiece, with a nine corded whip, three knots in each cord, being drawn up to the pillory, in such an uncivil manner, as is not to be rehearsed, with a running knot about their hands, the very first lash of which drew blood, and made it run down in abundance from their breasts."

Lord Baltimore, ever watchful to increase the rentals from his Province, managed to make disturbances in Virginia profitable. Moryson, Governor of Virginia for a brief period, in a letter to the Earl of Clarendon[2] wrote: "I do not complain against so honorable a person as his Lordship, but, admire his prudent management, that never omits to improve the least occasion to his advantage."

Virginia's extremity was always Maryland's opportunity. The law against the Puritans in the former colony in 1648, drove an industrious population to the banks of the Severn River in Maryland, so the law against Separatists, Quakers

---

[1] Alice Ambrose afterwards became the wife of John Gary of West River, Maryland.

[2] Clarendon Papers in *N. Y. Hist. Soc. Col.*, 1869.

and others from the church of England, in 1664, increased the population of Lord Baltimore's province.

In November, 1661, arrangements were made to give lands to certain inhabitants of "Northampton otherwise called Accomack" who wished to remove to the region above Watkin's Point, the north part of the Bay "into which the river Wighco, formerly called Wighcocomico, afterward Pocomoke, then again, at this time, Wighcocomoco."

In February, 1662-3, John Elzey, Randall Revell, and Stephen Horsey were appointed by Governor Charles Calvert, Commissioners for this district. In September, 1663, the Assembly in session at Jamestown ordered Col. Edmund Scarborough, his Majesty's Surveyor General of Virginia, to collect rents, and dues to the Colony of Virginia, of all persons residing below a line, from the "north side of Wicomicoe River, on the Eastern shore, and near unto, and on the south side of the straight limb opposite to Patuxent river."

Scarborough's report to the Governor and Council of Virginia of his proceedings at Anamesseck and Manoakin is stamped all over with the characteristics of a violent and prejudiced partisan.

In company with Col. John Stringer, who had been one the Burgesses of Northampton County, four of the Commission, and forty horsemen, whom he took "for pomp and safety," on Sunday morning, October 11, 1663, he arrived at Anamessecks to repel, as he reports, the contempt threatened "by some Quakers, and a foole in office." He wrote that :

"On Monday morning at ye house of Stephen Horssy an officer of ye Lord Baltimore I began to publish ye commands of ye Assembly, and for y^t ye officer could not read, I often read ye act unto him who made noe reply, but brought a pattent instead of his commission and tould us there was his authority, and y^t hee was put in trust by ye Lord leift. of Maryland, and that he would not be false to his trust."

After some discussion, Scarborough arrested him, because he would not acknowledge the act of the Virginia Assembly and placed the "broad arrow" on his door. "So thus proceeding," he continues, "wee went to ye house of Ambrose Dixon, a Quaker, where a boat and two men belonging to Groome's Shipp, and two running Quakers were, also George Johnson, and Thomas Price inhabitants, and Quakers." They also refusing, he arrested them, for contempt, and placed the "broad arrow" on their doors. He then "marched off to Henry Bostons," who asked a little time for deliberation. Going from thence, to Manoakin, all there acknowledged the Virginia authorities, but Mr. John Elzey, and Capt. William Thorne, officers under Lord Baltimore. In his report he mentions that "at that time one Hollinsworth,[1] merchant of a Northern vessel, came and presented his request for liberty of trade wch I doubted was some plott of ye Quakers." His portraiture of the Quakers was vivid, but not flattering. "Stephen Horssy, ye ignorant yet insolent officer, a cooper by profes-

---

[1] William Hollinsworth of Salem, Mass., had been licensed by the Province of Maryland to trade with the Indians.

sion, who lived long in ye lower parts of Accomack,[1] once elected a burgess by ye comon crowd, and thrown out by ye assembly for a fractious and tumultuous person, a man repugnant to all gov'mt, of all sects, yet professed by none, constant in nothing, but opposing church govm't, his children at great ages, yet uncristened. That left ye lower parts to head rebellion at Anamessecks."

"George Johnson, ye proteus of heresy who hath been often wandering in this county, where, he is notorious for shiffting schismatical pranks, at length pitched at Anamessecks where hee hath bin this yeare and made a plantation,' etc.

"Thomas Price,[2] a creeping Quaker, by trade a leather dresser, whose conscience would not serve to dwell amongst the wicked, and therefore retired to Anamessecks, where he hears much, and says nothing els but y^t hee would not obey gov'm't for w'ch he also stands arrested."

"Ambrose Dixon, a caulker by profession, that lived long in ye lower parts was often, in question, for his quaking profession, removed to Anamessecks there to act what hee could not be here permitted, is a prater of nonsence. * * * A receiver of many Quakers, his house ye place of their report."

"Henry Boston, an unmanerly fellow y^t stands condemned on o^r records for slighting and condemning ye laws of y^t county, a rebell to gover'nt and disobedient to author-

---

[1] He signed the engagement to the Commonwealth of England, in March, 1651-2.

[2] A signer in March, 1651-2.

ity, for w'ch he received a late reward w'th a rattan, hath not subscribed, hid himself, and so escaped arrest. These are all, except two or three loose fellows, y' follow the Quakers for scrapps, whom a good whip is fittest to reform."

Governor Calvert, incensed at Scarborough's proceedings, visited Governor Berkeley at Jamestown, who disclaimed the acts of his Surveyor General, and in the spring of 1664, did order Scarborough, and the surveyors Catlett and Lawrence, with Capt. Joseph Bridger, Capt. Robert Ellyson, and Mr. Bulmer Mitford to go to Manoakin, and on the 10th of May confer with commissioners upon the part of Maryland, and if possible adjust the boundary dispute.[1]

---

[1] In 1666, the region in dispute became a portion of Somerset County, Maryland, named after Lord Baltimore's sister Lady Mary Somerset. The first County Judges were Stephen Horsey, William Stevens, William Thorne, James Jones, John Worden, Henry Boston, George Johnson, and John White. Horsey was the first sheriff of the County; he and Johnson, and Boston, were the Quakers from Accomac. William Stevens was instrumental in bringing a number of Presbyterians to Somerset County. George Fox, in 1673, preached at his house to the Quakers. He lived near Rehoboth in the valley of the Pocomoke River. Bowen in "*Days of Makemie*" gives the following from the Somerset Records: "Richard Stevens, brother William Stevens of Somerset county ye Province of Maryland was youngest son to John Stevens of Lebourn in ye Parish of Buckingham in England, died at the house of his brother William aforesaid, ye 22d day of April, 1667, and was buried at his plantation called Rehoboth, in ye county and province aforesaid, in America, ye 25th day of April, 1667."

Over the remains of Judge Stevens is a slab with this inscription:

> "Here lyeth the body of William
> Stevens Esq, who departed this
> Life, the 23 of December 1687.
> Aged 57 years, he was 22 years
> Judge of this County Court one of
> His Lordships Councill, and one of ye
> Deputy Lieutenants of this
> Province of Maryland
> VIVIT POST FUNERA VIRTUS."

In April, 1663, Governor Berkeley wrote to the Governor of Maryland : "I and the Councell here haue considered of the means of Redresse [relative to the excessive planting of tobacco] and authorize the Gentlemen of the Councell Co^{ll} Richard Lee, Co^{ll} Robert Smith, Co^{ll} John Carter & Mr. Henry Corbin, our Commis^{rs} to communicate our Results to yo^u & appoynted the eleuenth day of May next to be the time & the County Court house of Northumberland County the place of Conference."* * * * * * *

"This worthy Gentleman Mr. Richard Bennett[1] at the ininstance of mee & the Councell hath taken upon him, the trouble of deliuering this to yo^u by whome if yor returne yor acceptance & that the urgency of yor affayres might permitt us the honour to see yourself at the Conference, both I and Mr. Secretary unless hindered by the interposall of some unexpected and pressing occasion, would come to wayte uppon yo^u at the time & place appoynted."

On the 8th of May upon the part of Maryland, Philip Calvert, Secretary Henry Sewall, Mr. Henry Coursey and Mr. Edward Lloyd were appointed Commissioners to confer with those of Virginia. The meeting took place on the

---

[1] Richard Bennett, son of Governor Bennett of Virginia, after the Puritans settled on the banks of the Severn was identified with Maryland and the reference I think is to him rather than his father. Richard Bennett, Gent, in 1663, was one of the Burgesses from Baltimore County, in the Maryland Assembly, and in 1665, a Commissioner of Kent County. His wife was Henrietta Maria Neale, the eldest daughter of Capt. James Neale. Bennett was drowned and left a son Richard. His widow afterwards married Philemon, a son of Edward Lloyd, one of the Puritans who came from Virginia to Maryland.

Richard Bennett, the grandson of Governor Bennett, married Elizabeth Rousboy.

12th of May, at Major Isaac Allerton's at Wiccocomoco, a tributary of the Potomac.

The conference was harmonious, and the Maryland Commissioners agreed that it should be proposed to their respective Assemblies, that no tobacco should be planted in either colony, in 1664, after the 20th of June. The Maryland Assembly however, refused to ratify the agreement. The agents of Virginia in England, Sir Henry Chicheley, John Jeffreys, Edward Digges, and Francis Moryson urged the Privy Council on November 16, 1664, to issue an order restricting the raising of tobacco. In their communications it was estimated that the population of Virginia was forty thousand and that English manufactures were imported to the value of £200.000 sterling, while they raised only about 50.000 hogshead of tobacco, which sold at £3 sterling per hogshead, would leave them £50.000 in debt to English creditors. Three days after Lord Baltimore opposed the proposition. He was not in favor of restricting the planters in Maryland. If in Virginia "any live in a poor manner" he thought it was "not from the low price of tobacco, but from their own sloth, ill husbandry, and purposely spending their cropps in Brandewine, and other liquors, it being evident and known that such as are industrious were not destitute." After the discussion it was not considered expedient to take any action upon the subject.

After Francis Yeardley left Maryland, and explored the Roanoke region, Englishmen began to settle in North Carolina, and immigration was accelerated by the oppressive laws against Quakers existing in Virginia and Maryland. William Durand, Secretary of Maryland during the Cromwellian era in 1657, began to attend Friends' meeting near Annapolis, and as his name does not appear after this in the records of the Province, it is supposed, that he went to Carolina and that the place marked *Durands*, on the Roanoke, Heerman's map of 1673, indicates his plantation.[1] John Porter of Virginia was "loving to the Quakers," and John Porter prominent in Carolina in the beginning of the eighteenth century, was the son of a Quaker.

While Governor Berkeley was in England, a company was formed, of which he and his brother were members, who in 1663, obtained a grant of Carolina.[2] To turn the

---

[1] George Durand conspicuous in the early days of Carolina was probably his son. William Hawley, a brother of Jerome, who in 1650, with William Durand and others signed the Declaration of Maryland Protestants, as early as 1639, had appeared in Virginia as "Governor of Carolina" and land was granted by the Virginia legislature that it might be colonized by one hundred persons from Virginia, freemen, being single and disengaged of debt."—Bancroft's *Hist. U. States*, Edition of 1876, Vol. I, p. 485.

[2] The charter set forth, in the usual language, that the proprietors, "excited by a laudable and pious zeal for the propagation of the Gospel have begged a certain country, in the parts of America, not yet cultivated and planted" etc., and saving the allegiance due the King, they were invested with as ample privileges, within their palatinate, as any Bishop of Durham enjoyed within his diocese.

Of all the proprietary grants, the charter of Maryland was the only one which contained a clause, requiring all churches and chapels to be erected in accordance with the church of England.

A. D. 1621, NOVA SCOTIA — Mentions "desire for the propagation of the Christian Religion," and gives Proprietor patronage of churches and chapels.

A. D., 1628, AVALON — Mentions " desire to propagate Christianity," gives privileges of a Bishop of Durham and patronage of churches.

A. D. 1627, BARBADOES — Mentions "laudable and pious design of propagating the Christian religion," and gives privileges of Bishop of Durham etc.

A. D. 1629, CAROLANA — Mentions "laudable zeal for the propagation of the Christian faith" with privileges of Bishop of Durham, etc.

flow of immigration now toward Maryland, in another direction, the proprietors granted to the settlers complete liberty of conscience, and it was left to Governor Berkeley to visit the country, and also select the first Governor. William Drummond, a Scotchman of ability who had been in Virginia for several years, was appointed Governor of Albemarle, and on January 7th, 1664–5, his instructions were forwarded by the proprietors. Another chapter will note his subsequent career. The first surveyor of the proprietors was Thomas Woodward of York river, formerly of London.

After Moryson had been two years in England as the accredited agent of Virginia, Governor Berkeley on April 12, 1665, wrote to the Secretary of State, afterwards created Lord Arlington, that he was not begging for himself, " knowing that no seasonable showers or dews can recover a withered root," but he asked, that Col. Francis Moryson who, as well as his father, had fought for the King, might remain two years longer as agent, with a salary of £200 derived from the tax on tobacco.

In July a great alarm was created by the rumor that the Dutch Admiral De Ruyter was approaching, with a hostile fleet, and the Governor commanded the colonels and cap-

---

A. D. 1632, MARYLAND — Mentions "laudable and pious zeal for extending the Christian religion' gives privileges of Bishop of Durham, but adds that all places of worship are " to be dedicated and consecrated according to the ecclesiastical laws of our kingdom of England."

Thomas Thorougood, in 1650, in an essay published, giving probabilities that the American Indians were Jews, remarks : "In the Charter of Maryland the pious zeal for the propagation of the Gospel is first mentioned * * * and there is a special provision against the prejudice or diminution of God's holy and truly Christian religion, and the allegiance due to the King's Majesty, his heirs and successors."

tains of the several counties to be ready with their men to cover the ships in harbor with small shot, if necessary. He wrote to England that he thought he could procure fifteen hundred horsemen, and two thousand foot soldiers, but was in need of great guns for the fort which was in process of erection.

A letter of the Virginia agent was addressed to Clarendon, Lord High Chancellor of England at this time, which he called

"AN HUMBLE ADDRESSE IN THE BEHALFE OF VIRGINIA.

"May it Please yo' Lor^d :

"The only Shipp that is likely to goe this yeare being wth in a few days ready to Sayle, occasions this Speedy and most humble Addresse to yo' Lor'.

"The narrative delivered to yo' Lor^p att Salisbury sett forth the Two maine parts of my instruccons from Virginia, To represent Marylands dissent from them in the State for planting. To gett Bristoll Patent for Rapahanock revoakd, I shall not trouble y^{or} Lo^p wth particulars in either.

"ffor the first, The comon calamitie hath a little raysed the price of our comoditie wch perhapps will supply his Lo^{hp} wth better Arguments than formerly to oppose vs, Soe that I shall lett that rest as it doth, wholy to decline it, I dare not vntill further Order from the Countrie.

"ffor the Bristoll Patent Since I vnderstood that it was y^{or} Lo^{pps} oppinion, That it would appeare hard to oppose a new Graunt to those hono^{bl} Persons concern'd in the Old, therefore I shall only p'sent the same necessary restrictions of my former Narrative, and most humbly leave it to y^or Lo^pp: determination.

"ffirst, That there might bee noe alteration in point of Government altogether in consistant wth the peace of the rest of the Countrie. Secondly, That the Rights of the p'sent Possesso's may.be p'served, their Rents not raysed, nor new ffines imposed, or their Tenures altered. Thirdly, That there may bee time perfixed for peopling of the Places soe granted or in case of ffaylure, Liberty to others to take vpp the Lands. My Lord, this is a Law as old as the first planting the Countrie, and a most wholsome one, for otherwise perticuler men would keepe great tracts of Land in their hands, in hope of getting a great rate for it, and neither people the Places themselves, nor lett others that would doe it, If the time seemes too short that the Law injoynes, I shall most humbly leave it to y^or Lo^pp to inlarge it, only desiring y^t his M^a pleasure may be consulted wth before the grant passes.

"But now Lord, the maine busines of this Paper is to p'sent some generall Propositions to make the neighbourhood of Maryland less p'judiciall to vs. If they shall appeare (vpon yor Lo^pp view) Reasonable, then most humbly to desire y^o^u Lo^bp to Signifie soe much by yor Letter to the Countrie wch will both infinitely satisfie them, and cleere yor Represento^r from neglect in their service.

"My Lord, this will appeare att first Sight a Proposition rather of envy ag^t Maryland, than of Advantage to Virginia, But if yor Lo^pp pleases to looke into the Reasons yo^u will finde yo' Represento' in this Labours to p'serve, from a necessary Ruine the poor Countrie that hath intrusted him.

"All taxes (my Lord) wth vs are by Pole, not Acre, the losse of the poorest man as great to Virginia as the richest, all paying equall Soe that if any comand comes from hence, that requires men or money to effect it, his Lo^pp Countrie, lyes ready att the Doore, to invite them, wth as good land free from all Incombrances. By this meanes, wee yearely Loose considerable numbers of People, and by it have fewer hands to Act any thing for our Advantage, or for the Advance of his Maties Service, and fewer Purses to pay for it.

"My Lord this is no Ayric notion of mine wch I should not have p'sumed to offer to soe great a minister of State as y^or Lo^pp Vnlesse I could demonstrate the truth, by the Sadd effects of it.

"His Maties instructions by Sr William Berkeley, though they did not positively enjoyne the building of a Towne, yet they soe recommended it to vs, that wee must have Showne a supine negligence if we had not att least indeavord it, Our poore Assay of building ffower or ffive houses lost vs hundreds of people wch I hope will wipe off that odium that is throwne vpon the Governm't, That wee vse our people worse than Maryland, and therefore they Leave vs, and flye to them. But the true reason (my Lord) is, That wee are ready vpon all comands to expresse our zeale to his Maties Service to the vttermost of our abilitie.

"I shall trouble yor Lo^pp wth an other Demonstration of the reasonableness of this Proposition. This Parliament made a

Law, That noe Sectary or Quaker shall bee transported to Virginia or New England, Wee were extreamely joyfull of it, hopeing wee should have beene securd from those disturbances, That those people make where they come, But, my Lord it was soe farr from working the good effect we hope for, and I am confident the Parliament intended, that it hath proved most infinitely ruinous to vs, ffor his Lo^{pp} taking his Maryland for part of neither, and soe not concerned in the Law, grants a Tolleration to all Sorts of Sects, wch by their neighbourhood (a River only severing vs) Infect our People, and by that drawes them from vs, or spreads their Venome amongst vs, Thus (my Lord) by not bringing both Countries vnder One Standard, we cannot have benefitt of any Act of Grace, though made never soe much to our Advantage.

"My Lord, I aime not, by this, to bring Maryland Subordinate to Virginia. But I desire they may bee both Soe, to the King and Councell, nor doe I att all intend any thing, in this, a complaint ag^t soe hono^{ble} a Person as his Lo^{pp} but rather Admire his prudent management. That never Omitts to improve the least occasion to his Advantage, I know (my Lord) it is his Lo^{pp} interest to gett People to him, as it is ours, to fix them with vs, for it is an vndoubted truth, That the Riches of all Plantations chiefly consist in the well Peopling of them, ffor had wee Mexico and Peru vnder ground, and wanted People to bring it above Ground wee should for all that, remaine as poore and indigent as though Planted on Bagshott Heath, the barrenest place I know.

"Peace and Warr is vndoubtedly (my Lord) his Maties Prerogative in all his Dominions. If Virginia and Maryland have not the Same ffriends and Enemies wch allwayes they have not, it must of necessitie bee a Consequence, That att one time or other wee shall fight English and Indians, ag^t Indians and English, Soe that the reasonableness of this Proposition appeares in every p'ticular can be imagined.

"But (my Lord) after all I shall humbly follow that part of my Instructions to Acquiesse in yor Lo^pps decision (for there the Countrie hath laid it) I would I had as well performed the other part of soe fully Stateing their miserable Condition, That they might receave redresse for it.

"Having expressed this zeale to his Maties Servis and the Countries Good, I should bee loth to bee soe partiall to my selfe as not to remove the least Obstruction that any Interest of mine can bee to either, I therefore (my Lord) most humbly p'sent you wth my Commission, desireing of yor Lo^pp That when there is a ffort built, for it hath been a Castle only in the Ayre this 30 yeares, yo^u Lo^pp will be pleased that my nephew Charles Morrison may have the comand, a Youth every way (if my neereness to him doth not make me misstake) capeable of the Place, my Lord of ffawkland gott it for his ffather, the only compensation any of vs had, for the Lievtenantship of the Ordinance purchased by my ffather, and settled vpon my elder Brother, by the composition wth Sr Edward Villers for Master, and disposed of by his Matie to Sr William Heydon wth a promise to conferre vpon my Brother a place of equal Valleu, But (my Lord) I intend not to Capitulate but most freely render it vpp, leaving both my Selfe, and nephew to yo' Lo^{pp'} Goodness and ever remaining

"y^o Lo^{pp} most humble and Dutyfull Servant
"and Creature
"Francis Moryson."

It was the policy of Berkeley not to encourage elections for Burgesses, so that, the Assembly of 1664, was only an adjournment of that of the previous year, and this was prorogued to October 10th, 1665, when a stringent law relative to Indians, was passed. It enacted, that if any Englishman was murdered by any Indian, that the nearest Indian town should be answerable for it with their lives or liberties. The Indians were also deprived of the power of choosing their own chief or werowance, and ordered to receive as their chief commander an Indian appointed by the Governor. All white inhabitants going to courts or churches, were ordered to bear arms to prevent the Indians making "some desperate attempt upon them."

The incursion of the Seneca and other Northern Indians had created quite a panic, and Governor Berkeley did not feel very kindly toward them. He wrote in 1665: "To my honored friend Major General Smythe."

"Sir: I wrote my first letter to you in haste, the minute after I read yours, but since I have collected myself, I think it necessary to destroy all these Northerne Indians, for they must needs be conscious of the coming of the other Indians. If you the Council were willing, and the Council of War be of this opinion, it may be done, and that without expense. For the women and children will defray all expense. Let me hear from you, and what you think of it, and if the first impulse do not deceive me, and lead me too much, I think this resolution to be of absolute necessity. If your young men will not undertake it alone, there will be enough, from these parts, who will undertake it, for their share of the booty."[1]

About the same time John Catlett, Thomas Goodriche, Jno. Weire, and Humphrey Boothe, Justices of Rappahannock County Court, wrote to Berkeley:

"Hon'ble Sir: Upon serious consideration of the honorable Governor's letter, and your honorable desire of our opinion of them, we are, by many circumstances, and 'tis our joynt opinion that the execrable murders are and have been committed by a combination of Northern Indians above, as their complices. We doubt not, by the assistance of Almighty God, and by the strength of our Northerne parts, we can utterly destroye and eradicate them, without further pay, and encouragement, than the spoyles of our enemies."

At the Assembly's session in October, 1666, it was decided that the law was too full of severity, which held the neighboring Indian town, responsible for a murder by any Indian, without any proof of their being involved therein, and it was modified, and enacted that all Indians coming within certain bounds, after being duly notified, might be killed by any Englishman.

Until after the days of Cromwell, the acting of plays was considered injurious to the commonwealth, and in the

---

[1] This letter copied from Essex County Records appeared July 16, 1877, in *Richmond Despatch*.

daily prayer, appointed for the plantation of Virginia, and published in A. D., 1612, is the following petition: "Let Sanballat & Tobias, Papists & Players and such other Amonits & Horonits the scum & dregs of the earth, let the mocke such as helpe to build vp the wals of Jerusalem, and they that be filthy let them filthy still." It is not therefore surprising that on November 16th, 1665, John Fawsett, the King's attorney for Accomack, should have presented Cornelius Wilkinson, Philip Howard and William Darby "for acting a play, by them, called "ye Bare and ye Cubb, on ye 27th of August last past." The court ordered that the accused "appeare ye next Court in those habili- m'ts that they then acted in, and give a draught of such verses, or other speeches & passages wch were then acted by them." The evidence against them was not con- clusive, for in the records of the court held January, 1655-6, is the following " Whereas Edward Martin was this Day examined, concerning his informacon given to Mr. ffawsett his ma^{ties} Attorney for Accomack County about a play called "ye bare and ye Cubb, whereby severall persons were brought to Court, and charges thereon arise, and ye Court finding the said p'sons not guilty of fault, suspended the payment of Court charges, and forasmuch as it appeareth upon ye oath of ye said Mr. ffawsett that upon ye s'd Edward Martin's informa^{c}on, the Charge and trouble of that suit did accrew, It's therefore ordered that ye said Edward Martin pay all ye Charges in ye suit and ex's."

The spring of the year 1666, found few vessels in the waters of Virginia or Maryland seeking tobacco, while every planter and merchant had more than they desired. To prevent utter ruin,[1] it was determined that there should be another conference of Commissioners at Jamestown, from Maryland, Virginia, and Albermarle or Carolina. They assembled on the 12th of July, and Virginia was represented by Thomas Ludwell, Jr., Colonial Secretary, Major General Robert Smith, Major General Richard Bennett, Esq., of the Council, and by Capt. Daniel Parke[2], Capt. Joseph Bridger,

---

[1] Berkeley, versed in the language of the courtier, wrote on May 1, 1666, to the Secretary of State, that the colonists are compelled to "live after the simplicity of the past age, indeed, unless the danger of our country gave our fears, tongues and language, we should shortly forget all sounds that did not concern the business of our farms. As we are further out from danger, so we appear nearer to Heaven with our prayers that His Sacred Majesty's enemies may either drink the sea or lick the dust."

[2] Col. Daniel Parke was from Surrey, England, and was one of the first vestrymen of the Williamsburg parish. His son Daniel, whose wife was the daughter of Philip Ludwell, was a violent and licentious man. Under Governor Andros, he was Collector and Naval officer for the Lower James River District. By invitation, the wife of the distinguished clergyman Blair, Commissary of the Bishop of London, sat in the pew of Lady Berkeley, now the wife of Ludwell, and one day Parke, an enemy of her husband, mad or drunk, went to church, and pulled her out of his mother-in-law's pew. As he was faithless to his marriage vows, he hated the minister Eburne because he had preached against the violators of the Seventh commandment. Leaving two daughters in Virginia, owing to his offences, he fled to England, purchased an estate in Hampshire, managed to obtain a seat in Parliament, from which he was soon expelled for bribery. Again a fugitive, he joined the army in Holland, as a volunteer, and became an aide-de-camp of Marlborough, and through his interest in 1706, became Governor of Antegoa, where his corrupt public acts, and gross private life incurred the hatred of the inhabitants, and on the 7th of December, 1710, he was killed by a mob. While on the field, Marlborough wrote to his wife, under date of August 13, 1704: "The bearer, my aid-de-camp, Colonel Parke, will give her [the Queen] an account of what has passed."

Col. Parke's portrait by Sir Godfrey Kneller, represented him with the Queen's picture in miniature, suspended from his neck by a red ribbon, a despatch in his right hand, and the battle field in the back ground.

His daughter Lucy became the wife of Col. Wm. Byrd, and Fanny married John Custis of Accomac, the descendant of the Rotterdam Inn-keeper. His son Daniel Parke Custis married Martha Dandridge, who when the widow Custis, married the venerated George Washington.

Capt. Peter Jennings, and Mr. Tho's Ballard, gent. of the Burgesses. Upon the part of Maryland were present Philip Calvert, Henry Coursey and Robert Slye, and the commissioners from Carolina were William Drummond Governor of Albemarle, and the Surveyor General Thomas Woodward, the devoted royalist who had been assayer of the London Mint. It was agreed that it would be beneficial to trade to suspend the planting of tobacco from the first of February, 1666-7, for one year.

The next day the Governor and Councillors Robert Smith, Richard Bennett,[1] Thos Stegg, Henry Corbyn and Theodoric Bland, wrote to England as to the action of the Council, and mentioned that they had more tobacco in store than would be carried away in three years.

On the 18th of July, Secretary Ludwell, in a letter to the Secretary of State, in England, bolstered up the waning reputation of the Governor, by describing him, "as pious and examplary, prudent and just in peace, diligent and valiant in war."

Governor Berkeley on the 23d of October, again called the old Assembly[2] elected several years before, to meet. The

---

[1] Under the military organization of the Colony, Smith, and Bennett, were two of the three Major Generals; Stegg was the son of Capt. Thomas Stegg, lost at sea, see p. 219, and Bland was the son-in law of Bennett.

[2] ASSEMBLY CONVENED OCTOBER, 1666.

Capt Robert Wynne, Speaker.

Henrico County.   Capt. William Ferrar.

Charles City Co.

Mr. Speaker.   Capt. Tho's Southcoat.

next day he addressed the following to the Chancellor of Maryland, and also to the Governor of Carolina:

York Co.

Lt. Col. Wm. Barber.   Capt. Dan'l Parke.

New Kent Co.

Col. Wm. Clayborne.   Capt. Wm. Berkeley.

James Co.

Capt. Edward Ramsey.   Mr. Thomas Ballard.
James City.   Mr. Theo. Hone.

Surrey Co.

Capt. Laur. Baker.   Mr. Tho's Warren.

Isle of Wight Co.

Adjt. Gen. Bridger.   Rob't Williamson.
Major Nich. Hill.

Nansemond Co.

Col. John Blake.   Capt. John Leare.

Lower Norfolk Co.

Capt. Adam Thorougood   Capt. Wm. Cowen

Elizabeth City Co.

Capt. Leonard Yeo.   Capt. John Powell.

Gloucester Co.

Adj't Gen. Jennings.   Major Thomas Walker
Lancaster Co.   Raleigh Traverse.

Rappahannock Co.

Capt. John Weye.   Mr. Thomas Lucas.
Stafford Co.   Col. Henry Mees.

Westmoreland Co.

Col. Nich. Spencer.   Col. John Washington.
Northumberland Co   Mr. William Presley.

Northampton Co.

Lt. Col. Kendall.   Capt. John Savage.

Accommack Co.

Col. Ed. Scarborough   Mr. Hugh Yeo.

"Most Honoured Sir : I must once more beg your pardon for importuning you to send us your declaration of the governour, and councels assent, to a cessation, for indeed not only our assembly, and courts, but all our commerce have their dependence on the assurance of that our former results receive no interruption by the alteration of our opinion, and its the voice of all, that a cessation will make some few merchants venture their goods to us, in these dangerous times, which, otherwise, they will keep by them, and then in what a miserable condition will these poor colonies be; for however we are at a greater distance from danger, we shall be the first that for want of necessarys shall feel the pressure of a terrible war. The last ship, that came to us, informs us that the scales yet hung formidably ballanced, and that few will venture to us, but on hopes of great gaines. This with many other considerations make us desire you to hasten this messenger, with your answer, which we are confident will satisfie all our hopes and wishes.

"Your most humble servant
"Jamestown, the assembly
"setting 8 ber. 24th, 1666.   "William Berkeley."

In this dearth of manufactured goods, the Assembly passed the following, intimating that want of industry was a partial cause of suffering. "Whereas the present obstruction of trade, and the nakedness of the country doe sufficiently evidence the necessity of providing supply of our wants by improveing all means of raysing, and promoteing manufactures amonge ourselves, and the governours honour haveing by apparent demonstrations manifested that our poverty and necessity proceeds more from want of industry, than defect of ability, since that five women or children of 12 or 13 yeares of age, may with much ease provide suffitient cloathing, for thirty persons, if they would betake themselves to spinning which cannot be objected against, if weavers and loomes, were once provided; for the better effecting whereof" it was enacted that within two years, each county should set up a loom, and provide a weaver at the charge of the county. Berkeley at this period, made a vigorous effort to raise flax upon his plantation, but the crop failed.

At the request of the colonists, the English guard ship "Elizabeth" of forty-six guns, Capt. Lightfoot, was sent to the mouth of the James River, to protect merchant vessels from Dutch war ships. Early in June, 1667, the "Prince William" with two or three other Hollanders, attacked the merchant shipping in Chesapeake Bay near Point Comfort, and Conway, captain of one of these ships fought them for six hours, but was obliged to surrender. The enemy then sailed up the James River, and found the captain of the "Elizabeth" absent, with his mistress, at a wedding. After firing one gun, the "Elizabeth" surrendered, and was burned. Having destroyed seven merchant ships, and captured thirteen more, the enemy sailed away[1] leaving the people in consternation.

Berkeley now found his position most embarrassing. Secretary Ludwell wrote to Lord John, his brother, that his condition was very sad. The court party at home was ready

---

[1] On the 24th of August Capt. White, in the English frigate "Oxford" gave chase to three Holland war vessels and defeated. The Dutch Admiral was killed, and said to have been the officer who burned the "Elizabeth." *Col. State Papers*, 1667.

to reduce the colony, to a proprietary government; the people of the Colony were restless, because, the Council composed of a few wealthy monopolists and their relatives[1], had virtually abolished the election for burgesses and thus created discontent, and the Governor in his perplexity determined to solicit his recall. A letter signed by all the Council requested that he might be continued in office. Letters however reached England with much censure of the Governor's passion, weakness, and infirmities of age, and complaint of the great sway of the Council.

To the miseries caused by war with Holland, was added another affliction. During the month of August, there had been constant and violent rains, and on the 27th of the month, a dreadful hurricane in a few hours destroyed almost the entire crop of corn and tobacco, and blew down the frail houses of a large portion of the inhabitants.

The Assembly convened the next month, and "whereas by the violence of the late storme, many barnes have been blowne downe, and the corne therein endangered by the

---

[1] For years, Virginia was controlled by a few rich tobacco merchants and planters, whose families had intermarried. Governor Spotswood in a letter to the Commissioners of trade dated March 9, 1713 (*See Spotswood Letters*, Vol. I, p. 60), uses these words: "The greater part of the present Council are related to the family of the Burwells. And as there are sundry other gentlemen of the same family whose qualifications may entitle them to be of the Council, if they also should be admitted upon the said private recommendation as Mr. Berkeley hath been, the whole Council in a short time would be of one kindred. As it is now, if Mr. Bassett and Mr. Berkeley should take their places, there will be no less than seven, so near related that they will go off the bench whenever a cause of the Burwells comes to be tried."

In the Records of Northampton County, Va., it is mentioned that in 1640 William Burwell transported Lewis Burwell, George Burwell and Elizabeth Burwell.

raine, many fences overthrowne, and the corne within devoured by cattle and hogs," it was enacted, that no grain, for a year, should be exported.

The late invasion of the Dutch convinced the Assembly that a Fort at Point Comfort, would not protect their shipping, and they resolved to erect forts on the James, Nansemond, and York Rivers, at Corotoman on the Rappahannock, and at Yeocomico on the Potomac. Captain Silas Taylor[1] who had been in Virginia applied to the authorities in England to be appointed engineer in charge of the defences of the Colony.

In 1668, the people of Virginia were much encouraged, by peace declared between England and Holland, and trade began to revive. To revive an interest in the colony, and prove that some thing beside tobacco could be produced, a present of silk, that had been delayed by the Dutch war, was forwarded to the King, with the following letters.

"To the King's Most Sacred Majestie
  "The Governor, Councell and Burgesses of his
    "Majesties Collony of Virginia.

"In all humility doe pray that your Majestie will be pleased graciously to accept their present of three hundred pounds of silke, being the first fruites of their labours in

---

[1] Taylor was at this time in charge of the military stores at Harwich, he had served under a distinguished military engineer on the continent. Oldenberg, Secretary of the Royal Society, who wrote to Governor Winthrop: "How happy would it be if there were an union of all our English Colonies for free communication with martial assistance;" in a letter dated August 5, 1663, writes about "Capt. Silas Taylor, also an ingenious and knowing person who is now going for Virginia, for his private occasions." Pepys, in his Diary, speaks of taking a drink with Taylor in the Sun Tavern, King street, London, and on July 1, 1668, goes to the chapel at White Hall to listen to an anthem composed by Taylor.

that kind, which they humbly hope your Majestie will be the more inclined to doe, in regard it is a Royall commodity and that your favorable recepcōn of it will be a very great incouragement to us to make a greater progresse in that worke. And allthough it be a truth that our want of that skill which other countryes, longer conversant in and better acquainted with the makeing of that comodity have is a very great retardment to our making better and greater quantityes of it, yet we hope that your Majestie upon this small experiment of our industry will be graciously pleased hereafter to grant us your favourable assistance by commanding men better skilled in that and other staple comoditycs, for which this country is very proper, to come and reside amongst us, that in some short tyme we may (to the honor of your Majestie and the advantage of our nation in generall and ourselves in perticular) introduce silke, flax, hempe, and potash amongst us, and noe longer depend wholly upon tobacco, to the ruine of the colony, and decay of your Majesties customs. This we most humbly hope from your Princely goodnesse, and may God for ever and for ever blesse your Majestie with all happyness.

"Your Majesties most humbly and faithful and obedient subjects and servants.

"WILLIAM BERKELEY,
"in the name of the Councell.
"Virginia   "THO. LUDWELL, *Secretary.*
"22 July, 1668, ROBERT WYNNE, *Speaker.*

"May it please your Sacred Majestie
"Now that the peace has given us some security that our first fruites of silke may come safe to your Majestie, we

have with al humble acknowledgments of your Majesties gracious protection of us sent it to your Majestio. The present is smal of itselfe, but the hopes and consequences of this exelent commodity may be hereafter of an inestimable benefit to your Majesties kingdomes. It is not ful three score yeares since France began to make silke, yet this amongst others is one cause of the immense wealth of France. This country, both for the clymate and fruitfulnesse of it, is more proportioned suddenly to produce this admirable commodity than France can be ; but for this flax and hempe we want some able skilful men to instruct us.

"With your Majesties gracious permission I wil lay my selfe at your Majesties feet this yeare, and wil beg leave to goe into France to procure skilful men for al thes, great workes. The great God of heaven protect your Majestie and keepe you safe from al your ennimies of what nature soever they are, this for ever shal pray.

"Your Sacred Majestie most
"humble, most obedient
"Virginia   "subject and servant
"July 22, 1668.   WILL. BERKELEY."

The King returned this acknowledgment "To our Trusty and Welbeloved Sir William Berkeley Knt, Our Governour of our Colony of Virginia, to be communicated to ye Councill of that Our Colony."

"Trusty and welbeloved, wee greet you well. Wee have received wth much content ye dutifull respects of that Our Colony in ye present, lately made us by you, & ye Councell there of ye first product of ye new Manufacture of Silke, w^{ch}, as a mark of Our Princely acceptation of yo' dutyes & of y' particular encouragement, Wee resolve to give to yo' industry in ye prosecution and improvem't of that or any other usefull Manufacture, Wee have commanded to be wrought up for ye use of Our owne person, and herein Wee have thought good to give you this knowledge from Our owne Royall hand, and to assure of Our more especiall care & protection in all occasions that may concern that our ancient Colony and Plantation, whose laudable industry, raysed in good part & improved by y^d sobriety of ye government we esteem much & are desirous by this & any other seasonable expression of Our favour, as farre as in us lies, to encourage. And soe Wee bid you Farewell. Given at Our Court at Whitehall, the 25 day of November, in ye 20th year of our Reigne 1668.

To encourage the manufacture of silk, the Assembly of October, 1669, renewed the former premium of fifty pounds of tobacco for each pound of wound silk.

As the expense of sending Burgesses to the Assembly which did nothing more than carry out the orders of the Governor and Council, a county frequently sent but one Burgess, it was enacted "that after this present session each county shall be enjoined to return two burgesses for the better service of the publique."

While the Indians, when provoked, were dangerous, yet an estimate, made at this time, shows they were not numerous.

County.	Bands.	Bowmen.
Nanzemond	Nanzemonds	45
Surrey	Powchyicks	30
"	Weyenoakes	15

County	Tribe	Number
Charles City County	Menheyricks	50
" "	Nottoways	90
" "	Appamattux	50
Henrico County	Manachees	30
" "	Powhites	10
New Kent County	Pamunckies	50
" "	Chickahominies	60
" "	Mattapanies	20
" "	Rapahanocks	30
" "	Totas-Chees	40
Gloucester County.	Chiskoyackes	15
Rappahannock County	Portobaccoes	60
" "	Nanzcattico } Mattehatique }	50
Northumberland County	Wickacomico	70
Westmoreland County.	Appomatux	10
	Total	725

John Lederer an intelligent German, in 1669 made an exploration from the head waters of York River, toward the mountains, and on the 20th of May, 1670, began a second tour, with Major Harris, twenty white men, and five Indians. They started from the Falls of James River, and on the twenty-second of the month reached the Indian village, Monakin. From thence proceeding westward, on the 3d of June they came to the south branch of the James River, computed to be one hundred miles from the Monakin village. For some reason, from this point the Englishmen retraced their steps, but Lederer with a Susquehanna Indian pushed on in a south-westerly direction, and on the 9th arrived at Sapon, an Indian town upon a branch of the Shawan

[Chowan]. Proceeding fifty miles south by west, he found a strong Indian village on an island in Roanoke River, and there found some Rickohockans, on a visit, who were afterwards killed in a quarrel with their entertainers. On the 19th of June, he was at Watery, and going westward he came to Sara, and on the 26th of June reached the Lake of Ushery. Here he rested for two days, and then began his return and on the 14th of July was at the seat of the Chief of the Tuskioras [Tuscaroras] and on the 18th arrived at the white settlements on the Apomatuck River.

Not considering that he had been fairly treated by the Virginia authorities he went over to Maryland, and in April, 1671, petitioned for naturalization. The Secretary of that Province, Sir William Talbot, found him a modest and ingenious person and his journal written in Latin, he translated and published.[1]

Major General Wood received a commission to send out an expedition beyond the mountains the year after Lederer returned, and on Friday, September 1, 1671, Thomas Batts,[2]

---

[1] "The discoveries of John Lederer, from Virginia to the west of Carolina. Translated out of Latin, by Sir William Talbot. London, S. Heyrick, 1672." 3 pl., 27 pp., 1 map, sm. 4to.

[2] Robert Batt, grandson of Henry of Okewell near Bristoll, was fellow and vicar-master of University College, Oxford. By his wife Mary, daughter of John Parry, he had several children, among others:

1. John Batt, Captain and Justice of the Peace who married Martha, daughter of Thomas Mallory, Dean of Chester who had John, drowned at sea coming from Virginia with his father. William living in Virginia 1667; Thomas in Virginia 1667; Henry in Virginia 1667; Martha in Virginia 1667.

2. Catherine daughter of Robert, sister Capt. John, J. P., married Philip Mallory. *N. E. Hist. Gen. Reg.*, April, 1885.

William Batt, perhaps brother of Capt. John, in 1643, entered 220 acres, on Mobjack Bay, and in 1649, 182 acres at Pacolacke, Chipoke Creek, James City

moving in a mountainous region. Mohetan country was reached on the 16th, and the next day they found the falls of a river, like those of the James, probably the Kanawha. From this point, they began the return journey, and on the 21st arrived at the village of the Hanohaskies, to find that Thomas Wood had died and was buried. On Sunday morning, the first of October, they reached Fort Henry, now the site of Petersburg.

On the 20th of April 1670, a communication from the inhabitants of York, Gloucester, and Middlesex counties was read to the Council, representing their apprehensions that the peace of the Colony was "endangered by the great numbers of fellows, and other desperate villaines, sent hither from the several prisons in England." The Council after considering the paper, ordered "that it shall not be permitted to any person trading hither to bring in, and land any jaile birds, or such others, who for notorious offences have deserved to dye in England, from and after the twentyeth day of January next. * * * And we Thomas Wood, Robert Falland, Jack Nesan, once a servant of General Wood, Perecute an Apomatuck chief, with five horses proceeded westward from the Apomatuck town, and on the 4th came to a town of Sapong. The next day they reached a village of Hanohaskies, where Thomas Wood remained on account of sickness, and on the 9th slept at the Talera Indian village. On the 12th they were by the side of the Roanoke River, and on the 14th, they were slowly

---

County. Thomas and Henry Batt entered 5878 acres on August 29, 1668, on the south side of James River, the valley of the Appamattock.

William Batt, in April 1670, entered 700 acres in Charles City County.

have been the more induced to make this order, by the horror yet remaineing amongst us, of the barbarous designe of those villaines, in September, 1663, who attempted, at once, the subversion of our religion, lawes, libertyes, rights, and proprietyes, the sad effect of which desperate conspiracy we had undoubtedly felt, had not God of his infinite mercy prevented it, by a tymely and wonderfull discovery of the same; nor hath it been a small motive to us to hinder and prohibit the importation of such dangerous and scandalous people,[1] since thereby we apparently lose our reputation, whilst we are believed to be a place only fitt to receive such base and lewd persons."

Gradually the forms of popular government, long in use, were obliterated, and the power lodged with an oligarchy. The Assembly, the creature of the Governor and Council, in October, 1670, passed the following: "Whereas the usuall way of chuseing burgesses by the votes of all persons who haveing served their tyme are ffreemen of this country who

---

[1] On March 28, 1667, the following convicts were sent from Newgate to Virginia, William Payne, Edward Evans, John Ward, Tho's Harwood, Robert Allen, William Allen, Jonas Sonier, Dorothy Bywater, Nicholas Danse, John English, George Windrewe, William Alexander, Mathew Cotter, William Kellam, Isaac Oliver, John Coughtland, John Smith, Mathew Jones.

Luttrell, in his Diary, under November, 1692, wrote "That a ship lay in Leith, going for Virginia, on board which, the magistrates had ordered 50 lewd women out of the house of correction, and 30 other who walked the streets after 10 at night."

Jonathan Boucher, the learned colonial clergyman and the tutor of General Washington's stepson John Parke Custis, in his autobiography, has the following: "Mr. Washington was the second of five sons; of parents distinguished neither for their rank nor their fortune. * * * George who like most people, thereabouts, at that time, had no other education than reading, writing, and accounts, which he was taught by a convict servant, whom his father bought for a school-master."

haveing little interest in the country doe oftner make tumults at the election to the disturbance of his Majesties peace, than by their discretions in their votes provide for the conservasion thereof, by makeing choyce of persons fitly qualifyed for the discharge of soe great a trust. And whereas the lawes of England grant a voyce in such election, only to such as by their estates real or personall have interest enough to tye them to the endeavour of the publique good ; *It is hereby enacted* that none but ffreeholders and house keepers who only are answerable to the publique, for the levies, shall hereafter have a voice in the election of any burgesses in this country, and that the election shall be at the court house."[1]

The Commissioners of Plantations in 1670, sent over certain queries to Governor Berkeley, which in 1671, he answered, as follows:

1. What councils, assemblies, and courts of judicature are within your government and of what nature or kind ?

---

[1] The Assembly of 1722-3, made a further restriction of suffrage. It was then enacted that " no free negro, mulatto, or Indian whatsoever shall have any vote at the election of burgesses, or any other election whatsoever." As required, the statutes of this session were sent to England to be approved by the Commissioners of Trade and Plantations. Their attorney was Richard West, son-in-law of the distinguished Bishop Burnet, and brother-in-law of Governor Burnet of New York. He did not approve of the law, and wrote "I cannot see why one freeman should be used worse than another, merely on account of his complexion. * * * * * It cannot be right to strip all free persons of a black complexion from those rights which are so justly valuable to any freeman." His opinion was rejected. West, on Dec. 3, 1726, died Lord Chancellor of Ireland, and was buried in Dublin.

George Mason of Gunston Hall, in the Virginia Declaration of Rights of June, 1776, re-incorporated the idea of the suffrage law of 1656, that it was "something hard and unagreeable to reason, that any persons shall pay taxes, and have no votes in election."

Answer. There is a Governor, and sixteen counsellors, who have from his sacred majestie a commission of *Oyer and Terminer*, who judge and determine all causes that are above fifteen pounds sterling; for that is under, there are particular courts in every county, which are twenty in number.

2. What courts of judicature are within your government relating to the admiralty?

Answer. In twenty-eight yeares there has never been one prize brought into the country; so that there is no need for a particular court for that concern.

3. Where the legislative and executive powers of your government are seated?

Answer. In the governor, councel, and assembly, and officers substituted by them.

4. What statute laws and ordinances are now made and in force?

Answer. The secretary of this country every year sends to the lord chancellor, or one of the principal secretaries, what laws are yearly made; which for the most part concern only our own private exigincies for contrary to the laws of England we never did, nor dare make any, only this, that no sale of land is good and legal, unless, within three months after the conveyance it be recorded in the general court or county courts.

5. What number of horse and foot are within your government, and whether they be trained bands or standing forces?

Answer. All our freeman are bound to be trained every month in their particular counties, which we suppose, and do not much mistake in the calculation, are near eight thousand horse; there are more, but it is too chargeable for poor people as we are, to exercise them.

6. What castles and fforts are within your government, and how situated, as also what stores and provisions they are furnished withall?

Answer. There are five fforts in the county, two in James River, and one in the three other rivers, of York, Rappahannock and Potomek; but God knows we have neither skill or ability to maintain them; for there is not, nor as far as my enquiry can reach, ever was one ingenier in the country, so that we are at continual charge to repair unskilfull and inartificial buildings of that nature. There is not above thirty great and serviceable guns; this we yearly supply with powder and shot as far as our utmost abilities will permit us.

7. What number of privateers do frequent your coasts and neighbouring seas; what their burthens are; the number of their men, and guns, and the names of their commanders?

Answer. None to our knowledge since the late Dutch war.

8. What is the strength of your bordering neighbours, be they Indians or others, by sea, and land; what correspondence do you keep with your neighbours?

Answer. We have no Europeans seated nearer to us than St. Christophers or Mexico that we know of, except some few ffrench, that are beyond New England. The Indians, our neighbours are absolutely subjected, so that there is no fear of them. As for correspondence, we have none with any European strangers; nor is there a possibility to have it with our own nation further than our traflick concerns.

9. What arms, ammunition, and stores did you find upon the place, or have been sent you since, upon his majestye's account; when received; how employed; what quantity of them is remaining, and where?

Answer. When I came into the country, I found only one ruinated ffort, with eight great guns, most unserviceable, and all dismounted, but four, situated in a most unhealthy place and where if an Enemy knew the soundings, he could keep out of the danger of the best guns in Europe. His Majesty, in the time of the Dutch warr, sent us thirty great guns, most of which were lost, in the ship that brought them. Before, or since this, we never had one great or small gun sent us, since my coming hither; nor I believe in twenty years before. All that have been sent by his sacred majesty, are still in the country, with a few more we lately bought.

10. What monies have been paid as appointed to be paid by his majesty, or levied within your government for and towards the buying of armes, or making or maintaining any ffortifications or castles, and how have the said monies been expended?

Answer. Besides those guns I mentioned, we never had any monies of his majesty towards the buying of ammunition or building of fforts. What monies can be spared out of the publick revenue, we yearly lay out in ammunition.

11. What are the boundaries and contents of the land within your government?

Answer. As for the boundaries of our land, it was once great, ten degrees of latitude, but now it has pleased his majesty to confine us to halfe a degree, [on the Atlantic coast ?] Knowingly, I speak this. Pray God, it may be for his majesty's service, but I much fear the contrary.

12. What commodities are there of the production, growth and manufacture, of your plantation; and particularly, what materials are there already growing, or may be produced, for shipping, in the same ?

Answer. Commodities of the growth of our country, we never had any, but tobacco, which in this yet is considerable, that it yields his majesty a great sense, but of late we have begun to make silk, and so many mulberry trees are planted, and planting, that if we had skilful men from Naples or Sicily to teach us the act of making it perfectly, in less than half an age, we should make as much silk in one year, as England did yearly expend three score years since; but now we hear it is grown to a greater excess, and more common and vulgar usage. Now for shipping, we have admirable masts, and very good oaks; but for iron ore I dare not say there is sufficient to keep one iron mill going for seven years.

13. Whether salt-petre is, or may be produced within your plantation, and if so, at what rate may it be delivered in England?

Answer. Salt-petre we know of none, in the country.

14. What rivers, harbours, or roads are there in or about your plantation, and government, and what depth and soundings are they ?

Answer. Rivers we have four, as I named before, all able safely, and severally, to bear and harbour a thousand ships of the greatest burthen.

15. What number of planters, servants, and slaves; and how many parishes are there in your plantation?

Answer. We suppose, and I am very sure we do not much miscount, that there is in Virginia above forty thousand persons, men, women and children, and of which, the reare two thousand black slaves, six thousand christian servants, for a short time, the rest are born in the country, or have come into settle and rent, in bettering their condition in a growing country.

16. What number of English, Scot, or Irish have, for these seven years last past, come yearly to plant and inhabite within your government; as also what blacks or slaves have been brought in within the said time?

Answer. Yearly, we suppose there comes in, of servants about fifteen hundred, of which, most are English, few Scotch and fewer Irish, and not above two or three ships of negroes, in seven years.

17. What number of people have yearly died, within your plantation, and government, for these seven last years past, both whites and blacks?

Answer. All new plantations are, for an age or two, unhealthy, till they are thoroughly cleared of wood; but unless we had a particular register office for the denoting of all that died, I cannot give a particular answer to this query, only this I can say, that there is not oft unseasoned hands (as we term them) that die now, whereas heretofore not one of five escaped the first year.

18. What number of ships do trade yearly to and from your plantation, and of what burthen are they?

Answer. English ships, near eighty come out of England and Ireland, every year, for tobacco; few New England ketches; but of our own we never yet had more than two, at one time, and those not more than twenty ton burthen.

19. What obstructions do you find to the improvement of the trade and navigation of the plantations within your government?

Answer. Mighty and destructive, by that severe act of parliament which excludes us the having any commerce, with any nation in Europe, but our own, so that we cannot add to our plantation any commodity that grows out of it, as olive trees, cotton, or vines. Besides this we cannot procure any skilfull men, for our new hopeful commodity, silk; for it is not lawfull for us to carry a pipe stave, or a barrel of corn to any place in Europe, out of the King's dominions. If this were for his majesty's service, or the good of his subjects we should not repine, whatever our sufferings are for it; but on my soul it is the contrary for both. And this is the cause why no small or great vessels are built here; for we are most obedient to all laws, whilst the New England men break through, and men trade to any place that their interests bind them.

20. What advantages or improvements do you observe that may be gained to your trade and navigation?

Answer. None unless we had liberty to transpose our pipe staves, timber, and corn, to other places besides the King's dominions.

21. What rates and duties are charged and payable upon any goods exported out of your plantation, whether of your own growth or manufacture, or otherwise, as also upon goods imported?

Answer. No goods either exported or imported pay any; the least duties, here, only two shillings the hogshead; on tobacco exported, which is to defray all public charges; and this year we could not get an account of more than fifteen thousand hogshead; out of which, the Kings allows me a thousand [pounds sterling] yearly, with which I must maintain the part of my place, and one hundred intervening charges, that cannot be put to public account. And I can knowingly affirm that there is no government after years settlement, but has thrice as much allowed him. But I am supported by my hopes, that his gracious majesty will one day consider me.

22. What revenues doe or may arise to his majesty within your government, and of what nature is it; by whom is the same collected, and how answered and accounted to his majesty?

Answer. There is a revenue arising to his majesty, but out of the quit rents; and of this he hath given away to a deserving servant, Col. Henry Norwood.

23. What course is taken about the instructing the people, within your government, in the christian religion; and what provision is there made for the paying of your ministry?

Answer. The same course that is taken in England, out of towns, every man according to his ability, instructing his children. We have fforty eight parishes, and our ministers are well paid, and by my consent should be better if they would pray oftener, and preach less.

But of all other commodities, as this, the worst are sent us, and we had few that we could boast of, since the persecution in Cromwell's tiranny drove divers worthy men hither. But I thank God, there are no free schools, nor printing, and I hope we shall not have, these hundred years; for learning has brought disobedience, and heresy, and sects into the world, and printing has divulged them, and libels against the best government. God keep us from both."

CHAPTER IX.

AFFAIRS FROM A.D., 1672 TO A.D., 1685.

GOVERNOR BERKELEY'S IRRITABILITY. HIS MARRIAGE. SECOND ATTACK AT P'T COMFORT BY THE DUTCH. GODWYN, THE CLERGYMAN, CRITICISES THE COLONY. NATHANIEL BACON, THE YOUNGER. INDIAN TROUBLES. RASHNESS OF MASON AND WASHINGTON. BACON'S REBELLION. BERKELEY'S REMONSTRANCE. BACON'S CONFESSION. SUBSEQUENT TROUBLES. EXECUTION OF INSURGENTS. ARRIVAL OF TROOPS. DEPUTY GOVERNORS JEFFREYS AND CHICHELEY. GOVERNORS CULPEPPER AND HOWARD.

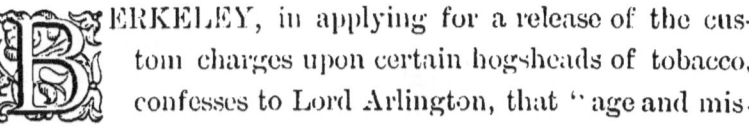ERKELEY, in applying for a release of the custom charges upon certain hogsheads of tobacco, confesses to Lord Arlington, that "age and misfortune have withered his desires, as well as his hopes. Though ambition commonly leaves sober, old age; covetousness does not." In the desire for gain, it is probable, as his enemies charged, that he favored contractors, and monopolists and thus produced a wide spread discontent.

Edmundson, a Quaker preacher, whose zeal was not without knowledge, and a companion of the celebrated, "mellow voiced," George Fox, visited Virginia in 1672, and in his journal, has described an interview with the Governor, on his journey from Carolina. He writes: "As I returned, it was laid upon me, to visit the Governor Sir William Barclay [Berkeley] and to speak with him about Friends sufferings. I went about six miles out of my way to speak with him, accompanied by William Garrett[1], an honest and ancient Friend. I told the Governor, that I came from Ireland, where his brother[2] was Lord Lieutenant, who was kind to our Friends; and if he had any service for me, to his brother, I would willingly do it; and as his brother was kind to our Friends in Ireland, I hoped he would be so to our Friends in Virginia.

"He was very peevish and brittle, and I could fasten nothing on him, with all the soft arguments I could use * * * The next day, was the men's meeting at William Wrights' house,[3] the justice [Taverner] went to the meeting, about eight or nine miles, and several other persons came to the meeting, particularly Richard Bennett, alias Major General Bennett. Justice Taverners wife came to me, and told me, that the Major General, and others, were below, staying to speak with me; so I went down to them. They were courteous, and said, they only stayed to see me, and acknowl-

---

[1] William Garrett, bricklayer, was one of the first immigrants arriving in 1607, at Jamestown. In April, 1620, there was present at a meeting of the Virginia Company in London, a William Jarratt (Garrett ?) described as an inhabitant of Virginia, for thirteen years.

Another William Garrett aged about 17, came in the ship "George," in 1619, as one of the servants of Abraham Piersey.

[2] Lord Berkeley of Stratton was one of the sons of Sir Maurice of Bruton, was knighted in 1638, and in 1640, a member of Parliament, in 1642, Commissary General under Hopton, in 1654, was present at the baptism of Henrietta Maria infant of the King. Fled with King Charles and resided in Paris. From 1652 to 1655, served under Turenne the great French officer. He was created by Charles the Second Baron Berkeley of Stratton May 19, 1652, and in 1659, was made Lord President of Connaught. In 1668, he brought Twickenham Park, and in 1670, was made Lord Lieutenant of Ireland.

[3] A William Wright was under sheriff of James City County.

edge what I had spoken, in the meeting, was truth. I told them the reason of our Friends, drawing apart from them, was to lay down a method to provide for our poor widows and fatherless children. * * * * The Major General replied, he was glad to hear there was such care and order among us. He further said, he was a man of great estate, and many of our Friends, poor men; therefore he desired to contribute with them. He likewise asked me "How I was treated by the Governor?" I told him 'he was brittle and peevish, and I could get nothing fastened on him' He asked me 'If the Governor called me dog, rogue, etc.' I said 'No.' 'Then,' said he, 'You took him in his best humor, those being his usual terms, when he is angry, for he is an enemy to every appearance of good.' They were tender and loving, and we parted so, the Major General desiring to see me at his house, which I was willing to do and accordingly went." Bennett did not live long after this, for Edmundson writes: "He was a solid, wise man, receiving the truth, and died in the same, leaving two Friends, executors."

About this time the gossips of the Colony were busy with their tongues. The old Governor frequently did things which occasioned surprise, but astonishment was never greater, than when it was announced, that Berkeley, now more than three score years of age, had married Frances[1] the

---

[1] At a meeting of the General Court on April 20, 1670, the petition of Mrs. Frances Stephens relict of Capt. Samuel was read, asking that she might be immediately possessed of the lands and personal estate at Boldrux, Warwick County, where John Hill then lived, and the next day the will of her husband was recorded.

The prominent men of Virginia were inclined to widows. Governor Harvey married in his declining years the widow of Councillor Richard Stephens. The

vigorous and energetic widow of Samuel Stephens. After Drummond's term as Governor of Albemarle expired, Samuel Stephens of Warwick County, in October, 1667, was chosen to succeed him, and died about two years after, leaving his widow a good estate.

Difficulties again occurring between England and Holland, eight ships of war bearing the flag of the latter, in July, 1673, appeared off Point Comfort, and for four hours fought two English men-of-war, took eight merchant vessels and sunk five. A sloop containing Capt. James Carteret the weak and dissipated son of Sir George, and his young bride was suffered to be run ashore. One of the captured vessels, was a schooner from New York, and a passenger, Samuel Hopkins, informed the Dutch Admiral, that New York was not well protected, and the fleet then proceeded thither, and took the town.

About the time that Philip Mallory, the respected clergyman, went to England, Assembly of 1660-1, asked, that the King would request the Universities of Oxford, and Cambridge, to send over competent ministers. Morgan Godwyn, also written Godwin[1] who belonged to a family of theo-

---

widow of Governor Seth Sothel, of Carolina, whose maiden name was Ann Willis of Ipswich, Massachusetts, took for her fourth husband Col. John Lear of Virginia. Sir Henry Chicheley married the widow Agatha Wormeley. Richard Lawrence, the insurgent, married a prosperous widow who kept a tavern at Jamestown. No explanation has been found of the following, in a letter of Sir John Berkeley written at Paris, as early as Sept. 20, 165-, to Edward Hyde, afterwards Earl of Clarendon : " Will. Berkeley is married in Virginia. His sister Jane is coming to France."

[1] His great-grandfather was Thomas Godwin, chaplain in ordinary to Queen Elizabeth and advanced to the Bishopric of Bath and Wells.
His grandfather was Francis Godwin, born A. D., 1561, educated at Christ church, Oxford, and made by King James, Bishop of Hereford.
His father, Morgan, died in 1645, and was Archdeacon of Shropshire

logians, on March 16th, 1664 5, received the degree of A. B., from Oxford, and came to Virginia, and took charge of Marston parish, which adjoined Middle Plantation, now Williamsburg.

In a letter to Berkeley he admits that the Governor had : " As a tender father, nourished and preserved Virginia in her infancy, and nonage. But as our Blessed Lord once said to the young man in the Gospel, ' Yet lackest thou one thing,' so may we, and I fear too truly, say of Virginia that there is one thing, the propagation and establishing of religion in her, is wanting." In another passage he declares "The Ministers are most miserably handled by their Plebeian Juntos, the Vesteries ; to whom the hiring (that is the usual word there) and admission of ministers is solely left. And there being no law obliging them to any more than procure a lay reader (to be obtained at a very moderate rate), they either resolve to have none at all, or reduce them to their own terms; that is to use them how they please, pay them what they list, and to discard them whensoever they have a mind to it. And this is the recompense of their leaving their hopes in England (far more considerable to the merest curate, then what can possibly be apprehended there)" together with their friends and relatives, and their native soil to venture their lives into those parts, amongst strangers and enemies to their profession, who look upon them as a burden; as being with their families (when they have any) to be supported out of their labour." Apologetically he continues : " I would not be thought to reflect herein upon your Excellency, who have always professed great tenderness for churchmen. For alas ! these things are kept from your ears; nor dare the Ministers had they opportunity, acquaint you with them, for fear of being used worse. And there being no superior clergyman, neither in Council, nor in any place of authority, for them to address their complaints to, and by this means have their grievances brought to your Excellencies knowledge, they are left without remedy."

In another place he declared; "Two-thirds of the preachers are made up of leaden lay priests of the vestries' ordination, and are both the shame and grief of the rightly ordained clergy there." He soon left Virginia, and for a time was in the West Indies.[1]

Moryson, agent for Virginia, in England, wrote to the colonial authorities "We have lately received, from the most worthy Bishop of Winchester, to whom the country hath great obligation, for assisting us, powerfully, in all our negociations, a virulent libel against all the plantations, and Virginia, in particular, a copy of which we send you, and think it necessary that an answer of it be directed from you, to the Archbishop of Canterbury, and Bishops of Winchester, in vindication of your government. It is written by Godwin who sometime served in Maston [Marston] Parish, and copy of it hath been given to all the bishops of England. We have since seen the fellow, and demanded his hand to it which he refuseth, and in your further orders shall proceed against the inconsiderable wretch."

---

[1] In January 1667-8, Col. Dodman obtained judgment against Morgan for 1000 lbs. of tobacco, and in April, 1670, upon Godwyn's petition, Major George Mason, Sheriff of Stafford County was ordered by the General Court to arrest Dodman. Upon investigation, the claim was adjudged illegal and Dodman expressed sorrow, and delivered up Godwyn's books which he had seized.

Godwyn had counted the cost of presenting his views to the Bishops and could not be deterred by a storm of words, and in 1680, he published in London a pamphlet[1] called, "The Negroes and Indians Advocate suing for their admission into the church, or a persuasive to the instructing and baptizing the Negroe's and Indians in our Plantations; showing that as the compliance therewith can prejudice no man's just interest, so the willful and neglectful opposing of it is no less a manifest apostacy from the Christian faith, with a Brief Account of Religion in Virginia."

In this treatise, he contended that negroes whether slaves or freemen, had an equal right with other men to the exercise and privileges of Christianity, and alludes to planters who ridiculed his position, and declared that although the black slave bore the resemblance, had not the qualities of a man, of which "atheism and irreligion were the parents, and sloth and avarice, the foster nurses," wrote Godwyn.

He was not silenced by vindicative planters, and five years later was permitted to preach in Westminister Abbey on the inhumanity of slave-holding, taking for a text the 34th verse of the 2d chapter of Jeremiah: "In thy skirts is found the blood of the souls of the poor innocents, I have not found it by secret search, but upon all these."

The discourse was printed with the title of "Trade preferred before Religion, and Christ made to give place to Mammon, represented in a sermon relating to Plantations."

Nathaniel Bacon, Junior, arrived in Virginia, about the year 1674, when thirty years old, where his father's cousin,

---
[1] In 1681 a supplement was printed.

also named Nathaniel Bacon, was a respected planter, and member of the Governor's Council. The young man was the son of Thomas Bacon of Freestone Hall, Suffolk, an ancient seat, and his mother was the daughter of Sir Robert Brooke, Kt. He was entered on November 22, 1664, as a student at Grays Inn, London, and subsequently was permitted to travel. Upon his return he was gay, extravagant and headstrong, and with the disapprobation of friends of the bride, married Elizabeth, the eldest daughter of Sir Edward, and sister of Sir John Duke of Benhill Lodge, near Saxmonham, Suffolk. His father as a measure of prudence furnished him with a stock of goods which cost eighteen hundred pounds sterling, and with his wife now twenty-four years old, he settled at Curles, on the banks of the James River.

In the early summer of 1675, the Doegs, a tribe of the Potomac River, charged a planter, named Mathews, with unfair dealings, and retaliated by stealing his swine. The Indians were pursued, and some killed. Then Robert Henn, a herdsman was found wounded, at the door of his cabin, in Stafford County, Virginia, who lived long enough to say, that his assailants were savages. A party in July, under Col. George Mason, and Capt. Brent, crossed the Potomac, in pursuit and divided their forces. The horsemen, under Brent, found a wigwam of Doegs, surrounded it, and killed the chief and ten others as they came out. Col. Mason found an encampment also near by, and with those on foot, killed fourteen, when a chief ran up, and told him that they were friendly Susquehannas, and that the murder which had incensed the whites was committed by a band of wandering Senecas.

After this, great excitement prevailed upon the Maryland, as well as the Virginia shore of the Potomac, and a joint movement against the Indians was arranged. The Virginians were under Col. John Washington, Col. George Mason and Major Isaac Allerton; and the Marylanders, were commanded by Major Thomas Trueman. The latter reached a fort of the Susquehannas, on Sunday morning, September 25th, 1675, and was informed that the marauding Senecas had done the injury to the settlers, but, they had left four days before, and were probably near the head of the Patapsco River. The next morning there was a junction of the Marylanders and Virginians, and the officers of the latter were Col. John Washington, Col. George Mason, and Major Allerton. About six of the principal Indians came out of their earth fort, and showed by their certificates and medals that they held friendly relations with the people of Maryland, but Col. Washington said "Why keep them any longer? Let us knock them on the head."

The rash suggestion was adopted, and the fort in marshy ground, surrounded with limbs of trees, was besieged. The outraged savages held out, for six weeks, and then upon a moonlight night, stole away. The indignity heaped upon them was quickly revenged, and ten white people were speedily killed for each chief that had been murdered. The authorities of Maryland were shocked at what they termed the "barbarous and inhuman" act of Major Trueman and his associates, and he was impeached by the Assembly, and debarred from holding office, while all possible reparation was made to the Indians. Virginia was requested to censure the act of Col. Washington, and others, and it is said that Governor Berkeley was willing, but no steps were taken by the Council and Burgesses. Passing round the rude stockades erected at the heads of the principal rivers, the Indians commenced the work of retaliation, and from the Falls of the Potomac, to the Falls of the James, stealthily crept, scalping the isolated planter, and mutilating the bodies of helpless women, and babes, and among others who fell, was the overseer of the younger Nathaniel Bacon.

For the protection of frontiersmen, the Assembly which convened, in March, 1676, declared war against those savages, who had lately committed murders, and robberies, and arrangements were made for the raising of five hundred men, in the older, and more secure counties, to be paid by the Colony, and stationed at points, liable to attacks from the savages. Eighty-four men, under Captain Peter Knight were to be in a place of defence, near the plantation of John Mathews, on the Potomac River, in Stafford County; one hundred and eleven, under Major Lawrence Smith, near the Falls of Rappahannock River; fifty-two, under Col. William Claiborne, Jr., on Mattaponi River; sixty one, under Major George Lyddall near Mahixon, on Pamunky River; fifty-five, under Lt. Col. Edward Ramsey at Falls of James River; thirty-eight, under Major Peter Jones, near the Falls of the Appomattox at Major General Wood's or Fleet's; forty, under Captain Roger Potter upon the Black Water near the house of Richard Atkins in the County of Surrey; forty, under Capt. Edward Wiggins at the head of Nansemond; and a fort in Accomac, between John Reddings, and the Pocomoke River.

The persons appointed to press men, and horses, were Col. St. Leger Codd, and Major Thomas Brereton of Northumberland, Col. William Bull, and Col. John Carter of Lancaster, Col. Christopher Wormeley, and Major John Burnham, of Middlesex, Col. Francis Willis, and Col. Philip Ludwell of Gloucester, Col. Robert Abrahall, and Col. John West, of New Kent, Col. Nathaniel Bacon, Esq., and Major John Page, of York, Lt. Col. Edward Ramsey, Major William White, and Capt. Hubert Farrell of James City County, Col. Pritchard, Lt. Col. Cole, and Major Thomas Cary, of Warwick, Lt. Col. Charles Morrison, and Capt. Anthony Armested of Elizabeth City County, Lt. Col. Edward Hill, and Capt. Nicholas Wyatt, of Charles City County, Col. Thomas Swann, and Lt. Col. George Jordan, of Surrey, Col. Joseph Bridger, Col. John George, and Major James Powell, of Isle of Wight, Col. Thomas Godwin, Lt. Col. John Lear, and Major Thomas Millner of Nanzemond, Col. Lemuel Mason, and Major Francis Sawyer of Lower Norfolk.

The following commissioners were appointed to use Indian scouts, receive hostages, and reward Indians for services rendered ; Col. William Farrer (Ferrar), and Lt. Col. Francis Epes, of Henrico, Col. Nicholas Spencer, and Lt. Col. John Washington, of Westmoreland, Col. William Traverse, and Capt. Thomas Hawkins, of Rappahannock, Col. George Mason, and Mr. James Austin, of Stafford County.

Roaming Indian traders had been accustomed to sell powder, shot, and guns, to the Indians, at extravagant prices, and to break up this dangerous custom, it was enacted, that if any person, ten days after the close of the session of the Assembly, should be found selling directly, or indirectly, powder, or fire arms; after conviction, should be put to death, without benefits of clergy, and forfeit his estate. The County Courts were authorized to nominate, in each county, not more than five persons to supply, with necessary goods, the peaceable Indians, but none of the late traders could be appointed.

Nathaniel Bacon, junior, as a merchant had been engaged in the Indian trade, having nearly completed a new trading post, was greatly disappointed, when he found, that he could not obtain a license to traffic with the savages.

Others were chagrined because they received neither appointments as officers of the forces to operate against the Indians, nor profits from the erection of the several stockades. Throughout the Colony, moreover, there was a good deal of discontent because the Governor gave the offices, and contracts, to a few favorites, and Bacon determined to lead this element, and intimidate the Governor. As one of the council, he told his neighbors, that he would pursue the Indians, without any expense to the public, and thus rallied them to his support. He then applied for a commission to lead a force against the Indians, but Berkeley did not grant it, but ordered the military officers, of each county, to appoint officers necessary to suppress Indian hostilties.

In the hope of composing difficulties, the Governor, on the 3d of May, 1676, with an escort of three hundred men proceeded to visit the upper part of the York and James Rivers, and found that Bacon had gone with a force of two hundred persons to the great village of the Ockinagees on an island, in a river, two hundred miles southward, and there while the Indians were friendly in disposition, provoked a quarrel in which the Indians lost fifty, and he, eleven men.[1]

Governor Berkeley became convinced that there was wide spread discontent among the people, who, for a long time had been deprived of the privilege of electing Burgesses for an Assembly. Those not free holders, or house holders, while subject to taxation, were not, as formerly, permitted to vote. For the first time, in fourteen years, he now gave notice of an election for Burgesses, to a new Assembly.

At the same time, he issued this declaration, to be read in every county.

"The Declaracon and Remonstrance of Sr William Berkeley his most sacred Maties Govern^r & Capt Gen^{ll} of Virginia.

"Sheweth, That about the year 1660, Coll Mathews the then Govern^r dyed, and then in consideracon of the seruice I had don the Country, in defending them from, and destroying great numbers of the Indians, without the loss of three men in all the time that warr lasted, and in contemplacon of the equall and vncorrupt Justice I had dis-

---

[1] In the catalogue of Thorpe Manuscripts, 1834, sold in London, are the following titles.

"Mrs. Bacon to her sister concerning a murder committed by the Indians, May, 1676."

"The Virginians plea for opposing the Indians without the Governor's order humbly offered as a test of their utmost intentions to vindicate them from all misapprehensions of disloyalty and disobedience."

"Gen. N. Bacon's description of the fight between the English and Indians, May, 1676."

tributed to all men, Not onely the Assembly,¹ but the vnanimous votes of all the Country concurred to make me Govern' in a time, when if the Rebells in England had prevailed, I had certainly dyed for accepting itt, 'twas

---

¹ The following address of Governor Berkeley in view of his election, after the death of Governor Mathews, shows his true position.

"Mr. Speaker, wee have all had great and pressing feares of offending a Supreame power which neither by present possession is soe, nor yet has a publiquely confessed politique capacity to be a Supreme power. I alsoe Mr. Speaker have my pressing feares too, and am seriously afraid to offend him, who by all Englishmen is confessed to be in a naturall, politique capacity of being a Supreame power. I have bin once already outed by a Supreame power. I doe therefore in the presence of God and you make this safe protest alone, and for us all, that if any Supreme settled power appeares I will imediately lay down my commission, but will live most submissively obedient to any power God shall set over me, as the experience of eight years have shewed I have down. When this is recorded and you are still in the same mind, I am ready most thankfully and acknowledgingly to serve you, in which alsoe I shall desire to secure the concurrence of the Council."

His speech to the Council, March 19, 1659-60, concluded in these words:

"I will passionately speak this last truth, I doe give thanks to God; I doe give thanks to you, and pray that this admirable Harmony of consents which you have shown to be in you all may be ominous and exemplary to our nation, that peace may at last return to our long afflicted, miserable distracted country, and let every one say Amen."

In his address to the Speaker and his honored friends, the Burgesses, dated "From my house" the same day, he said, after referring to Charles the First, having first commissioned him as Governor, "Immediately after his Royal Sonne (whom I beseech God soe to bless that he might exceed his admired Father in wisdom, pietie and justice) resigning his judgment to his Father's choice, sent me a comition to governe here under him, which I exercised with all faithfulness and humilitie to his command." He then mentions the arrival of the Parliament ship after the battle of Worcester, with a small force which "finding me defenceless" a change "was quietly affected."

After the surrender to Parliament he wrote on May 14, 1652, to Charles, in exile, and besought "pardon for giving up the Colony of Virginia to the rebels," and spoke of Colonel Lovelace the bearer of the note, who had been in Virginia since A. D., 1650, and would give fuller information.

Two days after the address to the Councillors, the following was prepared:

Gent. an vnfortunate Love, shewed to me, for to shew myselfe greatfull for this, I was willing to accept this Government againe, when by my gracious Kings favour[1] I might have had other places much more profitable and

" Wo doe unanimously concur in the Election of Sr. William Berkeley to be the present Governour of this Colony.
March 21th, 1659.

Richard Bennett   Edward Hill
William Bernard   Thomas Dewe
John Walker   Edward Carter
George Reade   Thomas Swann
Thomas Pettus   Augustine Warner."
Tho: Claiborne

[1] Charles the Second after the Restoration, upon July 31, 1660, renewed his commission as Governor, and Berkeley under date of March 18, 1660-1, wrote :

" May it please your Majestie I have received a Commission from your Sacred Matie to be Governour of this your Maties Colony of Virginia, and at your Maties fleet in a dutifull thankfullness to your Majestie that you yett think me worthy of your Royall Commands. It is true, may it please your most Sacred Majestie that in a fervent desire to doe your Majestie all the service I could with possibility arrive to, I did something which if misrepresented to your Majestie may cause you to think me guilty of a weakness I should ever abhor myself for. But it was noe more, may it please your Majestie, than to leape over the fold to save your Matie's flock, when your Majesties enemies of that fold had barred up the lawfull entrance into itt, and enclosed the Wolves of Seisme, and rebellion ready to devour all within it.

" Nor did I adventure in this without the advice and impulsion of your Majesties best subjects in these parts (wch I believe more timely inspired with the same spirit your Majesties other subjects after were) threatened me with the omission of that duty which I owed to your Majestie if I neglected my utmost endeavours of preserving all your Majesties then perishing Loyall subjects in this Country ; I have a thousand witnesses of this beside the Awful Reverence I ever had of your Sacred Majestie which would never suffer me to support myselfe by an untruth, who would rather begg your Majesties pardon for my endeavours to doe your Majestie Service than justifye myselfe in the wrong interpreting the best way to it. But this relation I only make your Majestie which before God is my witness (as farr as I am able to know my own heart) I always in all conditions had more feare of your Majesties frownes than the Swords or Tortures of your enemies.

less toylesome than this hath beene. Since that time yt I returned into the Country I call the great God, Judge of all things in heaven and earth, to witness, that I doe not know of any thing relateive to this Country, wherein I have acted vnjustly, corruptly, or negligently, in distributeing equall Justice to all men, & takeing all possible care to preserve their proprietys, & defend them from their barbarous enimies.

" But for all this, p'happs I have erred in things I know not of, if I have I am soe conscious of humane frailty, & my own defects, yt I will not onely acknowledge them, but repent of, and amend them, and not like the Rebell Bacon p'sist in an error, onely because I have committed itt, and

---

" God of Heaven turn these years of affliction your Majestie has suffered for, and by your Subjects to ages of happiness : Soe forever prayes
" Your Majestie most Humble
" most Dutifull, Loyall & obedient
" Subject, Servant, Creature
" March 18, 1660. " WILLIAM BERKELEY.
From your Majestie
" Colony of Virginia.

An erroneous statement has been made that Berkeley invited Charles to Virginia. Clarendon in his *History of the Rebellion* mentions not that Governor Berkeley really invited the King to Virginia, " but *almost* inviting him hither, as to a place that wanted nothing. And the truth is, whilst the Parliament had nothing else to do, the plantation in a short time was more improved in people and stock than it had been from the beginning, to that time, and had reduced the Indian to a very good neighbourhood. But, alas, they were so far from being in a condition to defend themselves, all their industry having been employed in making the best advantage of their particular plantations without assigning time or men, to provide for the public service, or building forts, or any places of retreat, that there no sooner appeared two or three ships from the Parliament, than all thoughts of resistance were laid aside. Sir William Berkeley the Governor, was suffered to remain there as a private man, upon his own plantation, which was a better subsistence, than he could have found any where else."

tells me in diverse of his letters that itt is not for his honour to confess a fault, but I am of opinion y' itt is onely for divells to be incorrigable, & men of principles like ye worst of divells, and these, he hath, if truth be reported to me, of diverse of his expressions of Atheisme, tending to take away all Religion and Laws.

"And now I will state the Question betwixt me as a Govern^r and Mr. Bacon, and say that if any enemies should invade England, any Councell^r, Justice of peace, or other inferiour officer might raise what forces they could to protect his Maties subjects. But I say againe, if after the Kings knowledge of this inuasion, any, the greatest peere of England, should raise forces ag^t the Kings p'hibiçon this would be now, & euer was in all ages & Naçons accompted treason. Nay I will goe further, that though this peere was truly zealous for the preseruaçon of his King & subjects, and had better and greater abillitys than all the rest of his fellow subjects, to doe his King and Country seruice, yett if the King (though by false informaçon) should suspect the contrary, itt were treason in this Noble peere to p'ced after the King's prohibiçon, and for the truth of this I appeale to all the laws of England, and the Laws and constitutions of all other Naçons in the world. And yett further, itt is declared by this P'liament that the takeing vp Armes for the King & P'liament is treason, for the event shewed that whatever the pretence was to seduce ignorant & evill affected people, yett the end was ruinous to both King & people, as this will be, if not prevented, I doe therefore againe declair that Bacon, proceeding ag^t all Laws of all Nations modern & ancient is Rebell to his sacred Ma^{ty} and this County, nor will I insist vpon the sweareing of men to live and dye togeather, which is treason by the very words of the Law.

" Now, my friends, I have lived 34 yeares amongst you, as vncorrupt and diligent as ever Govern' was, Bacon is a man of two years amongst you, his p'son and qualities vnknowne to most of you & to all men else, by any vertuous action y' ever I heard of, And that very action which he boasts of, was sickly & fooleishly, & as I am informed treacherously carried to the dishonour of the English Nacon yett in itt, he lost more men, than I did in three years Warr, and by ye grace of God will putt myselfe to the same dangers & troubles againe when I have brought Bacon to acknowledge the Laws are above him, and I doubt not but, by God's assistance, to have better success than Bacon hath had, the reason of my hopes are, that I will take Councell of wiser men then myselfe, but Mr. Bacon hath none about him, but the lowest of the people.

" Yett, I must further enlarge, that I cannot without your helpe, doe any thinge in this but dye in defence of my King, his laws. & subjects, which I will cheerefully doe, though alone I doe itt, and considering my poore fortunes, I can not leave my poore Wife, and friends a better legacy, than by dyeing for my King & you: for his sacred Ma^{ty} will easeily distinguish betweene Mr. Bacons actions & myne, and Kings have long Armes, either to reward or punish.

" Now after all this, if Mr. Bacon can shew one president or example where such actings in any Nacon what ever, was approved of, I will mediate with the King, and you, for a p'don, and excuce for him. but I can shew him an hundred examples where brave & great men have beene putt to death for gaineing Victorys ag^t ye comand of their Superiors.

"Lastly my most assured ffriends I would have preserued those Indians that I knew were howerly att our mercy, to have been our spyes and intelligence, to finde out our bloody enemies, but as soone as I had the least intelligence that they alsoe were trecherous enimies, I gave out Commissions to destroy y^m all as all the Commissions themselves will speak itt.

"To conclude, I have don what was possible both to friend and enimy, have granted Mr. Bacon three pardons, which he hath scornefully reiected, suppoaseing stronger to subuert, then I and you to maineteyne the Laws, by which onely, and Gods assisting grace and mercy, all men must hope for peace and safety. I will add noe more things much more is still remaineing to Justifie me & condemne Mr. Bacon, but to desier that this declaracon may be read in every County Co^{rt} in the Country, and that a Court be presently called to doe itt, before the Assembly meet. That your approbacon or dissattisfaction of this declaracon may be knowne to all ye Country, and the Kings Councell, to whose most revered Judgments itt is submitted, Giuen ye XXIXth day of May, a happy day, in the XXVIIIth yeare of his most sacred Maties Reigne, Charles the second, who God grant long & prosperously to reigne, and lett all his good subiects say Amen."

At the election for Burgesses in Henrico County, the sheriff attempted to read the above declaration, the court being in session, when Bacon violently took it from him, and by intimidation was elected a Burgess. In a sloop with fifty followers he went to Jamestown to sit in the Assembly which was to convene, on the 5th of June. He reached the place at night, and in the darkness visted his confederates Drummond, and Lawrence, and before sunrise returned to his vessel. His arrival having been made known, he was pursued by Captain Gardiner of the "Adam and Eve," to Sandy Point, and was there arrested by Sheriff Hone. When he was brought before the Governor, Berkeley said "Mr. Bacon have you forgotten to be a gentleman?" The reply was "No," then said the Governor, "I will place you on parol."

Four days after the Assembly convened, on the 9th of June, the Governor stood up and said : "If there be joy in the presence of the angels over a sinner that repenteth, there is joy now: call Mr. Bacon," then, Bacon upon his knees, offered this confession "I Nath. Bacon, Jr., of Henrico County in Virginia, doe hereby most readily, freely and most humbly acknowledge that I am and have been guilty of diverse late unlawfull, mutinous, and rebellious practices, contrary to my duty to his most sacred majesties gouvernour, and this country, by beating up of drums, raiseing of men in armes, marching with them into severall parts of this his most sacred majesties colony, not only without order, and commission, but contrary to the express orders and commands of the Rt. Hon. Sir William Berkeley, Kn't his majesties most worthy governour, and captain general of Virginia. And I doe further acknowledge that the said honourable govornour hath been very favourable to me, by his severall reiterated gracious offers of pardon, thereby to reclaime me from the persecution [prosecution?] of those my unjust proceedings (whose noble and generous mercy and clemency I can never sufficiently acknowledge) and for the re-settlement of this whole country in peace and quietnesse. And I doe hereby upon my knees most humbly begg of Almighty God, and of his majesties said governour, that upon this my most harty and unfeigned acknowledgment of my said miscarriages, and unwarrantable practices, he will please to grant me his gracious pardon and indemnity humbly desireing also the honourable councell of state, by whose goodnesse I am alsoe much obleiged, and the honourable burgesses of the present grand Assembly to interceed and mediate with his honour to grant me such pardon.

"And I doe hereby promise, upon the word and faith of a Christian, and of a gentleman, that upon such pardon granted me, as I shall ever acknowledge soe great a favour, soe I will alwaies bear true faith and allegiance to his most sacred majestie, and demeane myself dutifully, faithfully, and peaceably to the government, and the laws of this country; and am most ready, and willing to enter into bond of two thousand pound stirling, and for security thereof bind my whole estate, in Virginia, to the country, for my good and quiet behaviour. for one whole yeare from this date, and doe promise and obleige myself to continue my said duty and allegiance at all times afterward. In testimony of this my free and harty recognition, I have hereunto subscribed my name, this 9th day of June, 1676.
NATH. BACON."

"Wee of his majesties councell of state of Virginia doe hereby desire, according to Mr. Bacon's request, the right honourable, the govenour to grant the said Mr. Bacon his pardon. Dated the 9th of June, 1676."

Phill. Ludwell	Nath'l Bacon
James Bray	Thos. Beale
Wm. Cole	Tho. Ballard
Ra. Wormeley	Jo. Bridger
Hen. Chicheley."	

The day after his confession, the Assembly declared war against the Indians, and a force of a thousand men were authorized to be raised, one-eighth to be cavalry. Indians taken in war were to be divided among the conquering party as slaves for life. The fort in Henrico County under Col. Edward Ramsey, in New Kent County. under Col. W. Claiborne, Jr., and in Rappahannock under Major Lawrence Smith were abandoned, and the soldiers placed upon the frontier. "Nathaniell Bacon, jun'r Esq., gen'll and commander in chiefe of the force raised," was so designated, in the Act. After promising, Berkeley, with characteristic obstinacy, refused to sign the commission. Bacon, as hot-headed as the Governor, asked to be excused from the council table, alleging that he wished to go home to visit his sick wife.

Not many days after, on the 21st of June, the bold Bacon marched into town, with four hundred footmen, and one hundred and twenty horsemen. Surrounding the house, in which, the Governor, Council, and Burgesses were assembled, he demanded a commission, as general. By the earnest entreaty of the Council, and Assembly, it was reluctantly signed the next day, and issued by the Governor. "Out of a hearty and pious desire to put an end to all suites, and controversies," all treasons and misdemeanors, committed between the first of March, and the twenty-fourth day of June, were "put in utter oblivion," and then, the Assembly was dissolved. Bacon and Berkeley, were as antagonistic as before. The Governor left Jamestown, and went to Gloucester County, and again proclaimed the General a rebel, and that his commission having been given under threats, was of no validity.[1]

Bacon with six hundred foot, and seven hundred horsemen, and provisions for two months, on the 29th of July, arrived at the Middle Plantation, now Williamsburgh, seven miles from Jamestown, and informed that the Governor was in Gloucester County raising forces against him, having taken possession of the forts of James and York Rivers, issued the following on the next day, called

"THE DECLARACON YE PEOPLE."

"1st. For haveing vpon specious pretences of publique works raised great vnust taxes vpon the Comonality for ye advancement of private favorites & other sinister ends, but noe visible effects in any measure adequate. For not haveing dureing this long time of his gou'men^t in any measure advanced this hopefull Colony either by fortificaͭons, Townes, or Trade.

"2. For haveing abused & rendered contemptable the Magistrates of Justice, by advanceing to places of Judicature scandalous and Ignorant favourites.

---

[1] The King's Commissioners reported that: " The Gloucester petition was the unhappy accident that made the Indian war recoil into a civil war."

"3. For haveing wronged his Maties prerogative & interest by assumeing Monopoly of ye Beaver trade, & for haveing in y^t uniust gaine betrayed, & sold his Maties Country & ye lives of his loyall subiects to the barbarous heathen.

"4. For haveing protected, favoured, & Imboldned the Indians ag^t his Maties loyall subiects, never contriveing, requireing, or appointing any due or prop', meanes of sattisfaçon for theire many Inuasions, robberies, & murthers committed vpon us.

"5. For haveing when the Army of English was just vpon ye track of those Indians, who now in all places burne, spoyle, murther, & when we might with ease have distroyed y^m who were then in open hostillity, for them haveing expressly countermanded & sent back our Army, by passing his word for ye peaceable demeanour of ye said Indians, who immediately p'secuted their evill intencons, comitting horrid murthers & robberies in all places, being p'tected by ye said ingagem^t & word past, of him ye said Sr Wm Berkeley, haveing ruined & laid desolate a greate part of his Maties Country, and have now drawne y^m seules into such obscure & remote places, & are by theire success soe imboldned & confirmed, by theire confederacy soe strengthned y^t ye cryes of blood are in all places, and the terror and constirnaçon of ye people soe greate, are now become, not onely a difficult, but a very formidable enimy, who might att first with ease haue beene distroyed.

"6. And lately when vpon ye loud out cryes of blood ye Assembly had with all care raised & formed an Army for the preventing of further mischiefe & safeguard of this his Maties Colony.

"7. For haveing with onely y'e privacy of some few favourites, w'th out acquainting the people, onely by the alteraçon of a figure, forged a Commission, by we know not what hand, not onely without, but even ag't the consent of y'e people, for the raiseing & effecting civil warr & distruçon, which being happily & without blood shed prevented, for haveing the second time attempted y'e same, thereby calling downe our forces from the defence of y'e fronteeres & most weekely expoased places.

"8. For the prevencon of civill mischiefe & ruin amongst ourselves, whilst y'e barbarous enimy in all places did invade, murther & spoyle vs, his ma'ties most faithfull subiects.

"Of this & the aforesaid Articles we accuse S'r William Berkeley as guilty of each & eu'ry one of the same, and as one who hath traiterously attempted, violated & iniured his Ma'ties interest here, by a losse of a greate parte of this his Colony & many of his faithfull, loyall subiects, by him betrayed & in a barbarous & shamefull manner expoased to the Incursions & murther of y'e heathen. And we doe further declare these y'e ensueing p'sons in this list, to haue beene his wicked & pernicious councell'rs Confederates, aiders, and assisters ag't y'e Comonality in these our Civill comotions.

S'r Henry Chichley   Nich. Spencer
L't Coll Christop'r Wormeley[1]   Joseph Bridger
Philip Ludwell[2]   W'm Claiborne Jr[3]

---
[1] Capt. Christopher Wormeley in November, 1671, married the relict of Justinian Alymer, late minister of Jamestown.
[2] Succeeded Thomas Ludwell as Secretary.
[3] Secretary Claiborne married Jane Butler of London and had three sons. The eldest William Claiborne, Jr., of Romancock on the Pamunky. Thomas killed by the Indians, and Leonard who went to the West Indies.

Robt Beverley
Ri: Lee
Tho: Ballard
Wm. Cole
Richd Whitacre

Tho. Hawkins
Wm Sherwood
Jo{n} Page, Clerke[1]
Jo{l} Cluffe, Clerke[2]

John West : Hubert Farrell : Tho. Reade : Matt. Kempe.

" And we doe further demand yt ye said Sr Wm. Berkeley, with all ye p'sons in this list be forthwith delivered vp or surrender ym selves within fower days after the notice hereof. Or otherwise we declare as followeth,

" That in whatsoever place, house, or ship, any of ye said p'sons shall reside, be hidd, or p'tected, we declaire ye owners, Masters, or Inhabitants of ye said places to be confederates & trayters to ye people, & the estates of ym is alsoe of all ye aforesaid p'sons to be confiscated, & this we the Comons of Virginia doe declare, desiering a firm vnion amongst our selues that we may joyntly & with one accord defend ourselves agt the comon Enimy, & lett not ye faults of ye guilty be ye reproach of ye inocent, or ye faults or

---

William Jr., had a son William, and two daughters, **Ursula** and **Mary.** Ursula married William Gooch.

Thomas Story, Recorder of Philadelphia, and a friend of William Penn, visited a member of the Society of Friends, one Edward Thomas at Bangor House on the 21st day of 11th month (O. S.) 1698, accompanied, he writes in his journal, by "Captain William Clayborne grandson of Colonel Clayborn who subdued the emperor of the Indians of those parts, and his people between the Mattapony and Pamunkie."

In March, 1699, he went to the house of William Clayborne at Pamunky Neck, and held a meeting at Ramoncock, at which was present Captain Clayborne, Major Palmer and Doctor Walker.

[1] John Paige, in 1680, had charge of the churches in Elizabeth County.

[2] In 1680, John Clough or Cluffe was rector of Southwark, Surry County.

crimes of y^r oppress^rs deuide & sep'ate vs who have suffered by their oppressions.

"These therefore in his ma^ties name to comand you forth with to seize ye p'sons above mentioned as Trayters to ye King & Country, & them to bring to Middle plantaton, & there to secure y^m vntill further order, and in case of opposition, if you want any further assistance you are forthwith to demand itt in ye name of ye people in all ye Counties of Virg^a.

"NATH. BACON,
"Gen^ll by Consent of ye people."

On the first day of August a detachment of three hundred men under Giles Bland,[1] a nephew of Theodoric Bland was sent to James River, and captured a ship commanded by a Captain Larimore, and on the eighth of the month, Bacon took Sir Henry Chicheley prisoner, and sent him to Mehick-

---

[1] John Bland, the London merchant, in June, 1658, wrote to the Admiralty that he had "a plantation in Virginia, but servants being very scarce there, he went to Chelsea College to see if any prisoners there had lived slaves and servants in the Indies, would go to Virginia; two mulattoes offered to go rather than remain eternally in prison."

He was the father of Giles who had been suspended from the Collectorship of Customs in Virginia, by Governor Berkeley. The manuscript Records of the General Court in possession of the Virginia Historical Society show that there was great enmity between Secretary Thomas Ludwell, and Giles Bland. The latter before the 18th of November, 1674, had called the Secretary abusive names, and " the said Bland taking one of his [Ludwell's] gloves, without his knowledge or consent, did ignominiously, presumptuously, and unworthily nayl the same up at the State House doore, with a most false and scandalous Libel, which contained these words, That, the owner of that glove was a son of a whore, mechanic fellow, puppy, and a coward."

Thomas Ludwell went to England to counteract the influence of some letters which Bland had written. At a meeting of the General Court in Jamestown upon October 7, 1675, the Governor mentioned that Bland was suspended from office.

son Fort, on the Pamunky River, and seized the plantations of Thomas Ludwell, Col. Parks, Maj. Gen. Smith; and of the Governor, at Green Spring.

The sympathy with Bacon must have been widely extended, or the Governor would not have retired to Accomack on the eastern shore of the Chesapeake Bay. Giles Bland and Captain Carver, were sent with Larimore's ship of sixteen guns, a barge of four guns, and a sloop, with a force of two hundred and fifty men to watch Berkeley, and Bacon after issuing a call for an Assembly to convene on the 4th of September, began to march against the Indians. Larimore who was a prisoner, in his own ship, privately sent a note to Berkeley, that with a small force the insurgents could be captured.

Philip Ludwell volunteered to lead an expedition, and with twenty-six men went out in some small boats and, without difficulty the vessels were disarmed, Bland and Carver brought ashore, and the latter quickly hung. The Governor now returned to the western shore with five ships and ten sloops and a large force, and anchoring near Jamestown, on the 7th of September, demanded its surrender, offering pardon to all except Drummond, and Lawrence,[1] the advisers, and friends of Bacon. Lawrence and others fled, and the next day Berkeley entered. Bacon informed of this, marched toward the place, and soon commanded its approaches. Jamestown, was then described as a small peninsula with the main river on the south, encompassed

---

[1] Richard Lawrence, son of George, of Stapleton, Dorsetshire, when eighteen years of age, in 1636, entered Magdalene Hall, Oxford, but did not graduate. He was probably, the same person as the insurgent, who was known as having been an Oxford student.

on the north, from the east point, with a deep creek flowing in a semi-circle to the west within ten paces of the river, and by a neck, joined to the mainland. The peninsula was about two miles from east to west, and about a mile from north to south. The town was about the middle close to the river, extending east and west three-fourths of a mile, and containing a church of brick, and some sixteen or eighteen houses, not all inhabited. Drummond and Lawrence lived in two of the best. In the settlement there were only about twelve families, and most of these, quaintly wrote a chronicler of the day, "getting their liveings, by keeping of ordnaries, at extraordnary rates."

After Bacon planted his cannon, Berkeley became alarmed, evacuated, and by night with his ships descended the river, while the forces of Bacon[1] entered and burned the

---

[1] John Verney, in London, on December 7, 1676, wrote to Sir Richard Verney "Yesterday came news that Mr. Bacon had taken and burnt Jamestown, in Virginia, and made Sir Thomas [Henry] Chicheley, prisoner, clapping him in chains, but keeping him alive to exchange for Mr. Bland, and that Gov. Sir Wm. Berkeley had again fled." Seventh *Royal Historical Commission Report*. Clayton, the parson of Jamestown, in 1684, describes it as situated on a peninsula, connected with the main land, by a neck twenty or thirty yards wide, which at certain tides was overflowed. A swamp ran diagonally through the peninsula, owned by one Sherwood. Clayton wrote of "Jamestown Island which is much of an oval figure. A swamp runs diagonal-wise over the island whereby is lost at least 150 acres of land, which could be meadow * * * I have talked several times thereof, to Mr. Sherwood the owner of the swamp, yet nothing is essayed in order thereto."

In the Jamestown churchyard, was a stone with this inscription, when the writer was there in May, 1886.

"Here Lyeth William Sherwood that was Born in the parish of White Chappel near London. A Great Sinner Waiting for a Joyfull Resurrection." At the beginning of the swamp was a half moon brick wall for defence. This was built after 1673, for on May 17th of this year, complaint was made to the General Court that Drummond and Howe who had agreed to build a fort, had

church[1] and dwellings of the town. Lawrence set fire to his own house, and directed the other incendiaries.

Bacon then marched to the Governor's plantation, at Green Spring, where he rested for two or three days, and then proceeded to Gloucester County, and made his headquarters, at the plantation of Colonel Warner. Here he became sick and on the first of October, died at the house of Mr. Pate.[2] After this In-

---

brought the bricks and then the work had ceased. There was also near it a deserted tetragon earth-work.

[1] The church now in ruins, Bishop Meade in his *Old Parishes of Virginia* thinks was not erected, until after 1676, and his reasons for this opinion are good.

It must not be forgotten that there were no brick buildings before A.D., 1640, in Jamestown. Governor Harvey in a letter, alludes to the brick house erected by his Secretary, Richard Kemp, "the fairest ever known in this country for substance and uniformity." At this time Harvey mentions that contributions had been made for the first brick church. Near the present ruined church, there can be seen, the ruins of another brick church 28 × 56 feet in dimensions, with a tower 18 ft. square. This is the remnant of the church that the insurgents burned.

After the burning, the parish was served by the John Gough who died January 15th, 1683–4, and his successor a parson of Jamestown, was John Clayton, a correspondent of Rober Boyle the philosopher and philanthropist. The building whose tower is still seen by the traveler, must have been erected between 1677, and 1684.

[2] Richard Pate, Dec. 12, 1650, entered 1141 acres, on north side of York river, died in 1657, and letters of administration were issued to his nephew John Pate. Bacon probably died at John Pate's house. Oldmixon often inaccurate, mentions that he died at the house of Dr Green.

A pamphlet appears to have been published in London, in 1677, relative to the rebellion, with the title " Strange News from Virginia being a relation of all the occurrences in that Country since the death of Nathaniel Bacon, with an account of thirteen persons tried and executed for their rebellion there." A writer in London " Notes and Queries " 2 Ser., Vol. XI, p. 200, mentions that is chiefly extracts from a letter of Sir John Berry, the commander of the troops sent out. This however may be the pamphlet of eight pages, whose real title page is: " Strange News from Virginia ; Being a full and true Account of the Life and

gram¹ assumed command, Major Robert Beverley a friend of Berkeley, captured a Colonel Hansford born in Virginia, carried him to Accomack, where he was brought before a court martial and quickly suspended from the gallows. Beverley returning to the western shore, seized Major Cheeseman, and Captain Wilford who was the second son of a poor knight, who had been killed while fighting for King Charles. The former died in prison, while his wife was insulted by the coarse words of the Governor. The latter was "a small man with a great heart" who had for some years been an Indian interpreter. Captain Farlow, whose niece was the wife of Cheeseman, a good scholar, and liked by his neighbors, was executed about the same time.

Death of Nathaniel Bacon, Esq., who was the only cause and Original of all the late troubles in that Country. With a full relation of all the Accidents which have happened in the late War there between the Christians, and Indians. London, published for William Harris, 1677."

The writer of the pamphlet, published by Harris, makes the following remarks on Bacon's death: " It is reported, by some, that this Mr. Bacon was a very hard drinker, and that he dyed by imbibing or taking in too much brandy. But I am informed by those who are Persons of undoubted reputation, and had the happiness to see the same letter which gave his Majesty an account of his death, that there was no such thing therein mentioned; he was certainly a person indeed with great natural parts, which, notwithstanding his juvenile extravagances he had endued with many elaborate acquisitions, and by help of learning and study knew how to manage them, to a Miracle, it being the general vogue of all that knew him that he usually spoke as much sense, in a few words, and declared that sense as opportunely * * * * * * wherefore as I am myself a lover of Ingenuity, though an abhorrer of disturbance, or Rebellion, I think fit, since Providence was pleased to let him dye a Natural death in his Bed, not to asperse him, with saying, that he killed himself, with drinking." Bacon's only daughter, Mary, married Hugh Chamberlain, physician to Queen Anne.

¹ Probably William Ingram of New Kent to whom on April 5, 1671, there was a grant of 2500 acres at the head of Pamunkey River. John Hansford who died in 1671, left two sons, John and William.

17

After Bacon's death, and these executions, Berkeley left Accomack, and came to the mouth of York river, when a ship commanded by Capt. Grantham, arrived from England. Capt. Christopher Evelin had arrived in England, with the startling intelligence, that there was an insurrection.[1] The King immediately ordered troops to be raised for the support of the Governor. As recruiting officers with men beating drums, for men, to enlist for the Virginia campaign, marched up and down the streets of London, there was much discussion among the merchants, whether this first sending of troops to the Colony, was a wise step. In September, Sir. John Berry, Herbert Jeffreys, and Francis Moryson, once Governor, were appointed Commissioners, to proceed to Virginia, to examine, and report on the condition of the Colony, and at the same time, a royal pardon was sent out, for all except Bacon. Governor Berkeley having sent over his resignation on the ground of his age, and bodily weakness, Jeffreys, on the 11th of November, was also commissioned as his successor.

Sir John Werden, secretary of Duke of York; on the 30th of November, 1676, wrote from St. James, to Governor Andros of New York, enclosing an order " from his Ma^{ty} to forbidd yor admitting any of the accomplices of Bacon, the chiefe of the seditious in Virginia, into yor governm'nt, a caution wch I presume you needed not, but ye order from the King will by shewing His Ma^{ns} displesure agst y^m, obviate all such plausible pretences as they may have scattered about to

---

[1] In the proceedings of the General Court at James City on April 5, 1671, there is notice of a suit of William Drummond and Capt. Christopher Evelin against the estate of John Currer.

debauch the fidelity or attract the pitty of the neighbour colonyes.

"Att the same time, I may tell you besides, that Sr John Berry is already gone with the Bristol frigate, and a ketch; that the forces desyned to reduce those people unto their due obedience are now well embarked and in the Downes wayteing for the first opportunity of fayre wind to sett sayle: I wish them good successe y^r being a matter of noe small importance to His Ma^{ts} service."

Capt. Thomas Grantham, who had passed the winter of 1672-3, in Virginia, sailed from England, with the ship "Concord" carrying thirty-two guns, and by the first of January, 1677, was at the mouth of York River, with the news that soldiers were coming. The presence of a ship of war, under a kind, firm, and prudent commander, acted like oil upon troubled waters, and the authority of the King's Governor, began to be recognized. Grantham soon after his arrival, went to Portopatank, and near Mr. Pate's house held a conference with the insurgent leaders, and showed the folly of a small band holding out in opposition to the strength of England and concluded his address in these words. "Have you not heard what numerous forces are coming from England to suppress your tumoultuous proceedings? * * * Hearken therefore to the tenders of peace, before it is too late; consult, like men of sense, your own felicity; and quietly lay down your arms."

Governor Berkeley could not resist the influence of such a peace-maker, and as the result of moderation many took an oath renouncing the rebellion.[1]

---

[1] The oath was in these words "I —— do willingly and heartily declare that I know, and in my conscience, believe *Richard Lawrence*, and many others

Before the disturbances were quieted Captain Hubert Farrell, accompanied by Councillor Bacon, the relative of the deceased insurgent, and Colonel Ludwell, went with an armed party, to dislodge Major Thomas Whaly, in possession of Councillor Bacon's house. In the attack upon the house, Farrell was killed, and his men fled.

Grantham arriving at West Point, at the junction of the Pamunky with the York River, had a most satisfactory talk with the insurgents there, and they sailed down with him, to Tindall's Point, to give in their submission to Governor Berkeley who was still at this place

Dummond and Lawrence, at this time, remained with a small force at a brick house, in New Kent County, on the south side of York River, two miles from West Point.

The ships with the troops and commissioners, of which they had been informed, by Captain Grantham, on the 29th of January, 1676-7, entered the Chesapeake Bay. Berkeley came to Kiquotan now Hampton, and went on board the ship "Bristol" to confer with the Commissioners, and gave them a list of those then executed.[1] An Assembly was

---

with him, to be in open rebellion against the King's most Sacred Majesty, and against the Right Honourable the Governor of Virginia, and the good establish'd laws and peace of this Colony of Virginia. Which rebellion I do from my heart abhor and detest and do therefore most willingly, freely, and from my heart, swear my full allegiance to the King's most Excellent Majesty ; and that I will with my life and whole estate, serve and obey the Right Honourable, the Governor and obey all such magistrates and officers as he shall from time to time appoint over me; and with them, or any of them, use my utmost endeavour to my life's end, to take, seize, kill, and destroy all such persons whatsoever as either now are, or hereafter shall be in such rebellion as is recited. This oath I do most heartily, freely and willingly take, in the presence of Almighty God. So help me God."

[1] The immoral and immodest Aphra Behn wrote a play which was published with the title:

called to meet on the 20th of February at Green Spring, the Governor's home. While the King had ordered a general amnesty to all, except Bacon, the Governor in opposition to the wish of the Commissioners, executed in all, twenty-three persons. At a court martial held on board Capt. John Martin's ship, in York River on January 11th, Thomas Hall was condemned to be hung, and the next day Thomas Young, Henry Page and James Wilson.

William Drummond, in Chickahominy swamp, was captured and when brought before Berkeley, he was stripped, the ring torn from his finger, and treated in a barbarous manner. Although he had not borne arms, nor held any office under Bacon, he was arraigned on the 20th of January, before a court martial which met at the house of Col. James Bray, condemned at one o'clock and hung at Middle Plantation, three hours after his sentence was passed.

"The Widdow Ranter, or The History of Bacon in Virginia, A Tragi-comedy. Acted by their Majesties Servants"

In it two friends at Jamestown thus converse

"*Hazard.* This unexpected happiness o'erjoys! Who could have imagined to have found thee in Virginia!

"*Friend.* My uncle's dying here, left me a considerable plantation. * * * * but pr'ythee what drew thee to this part of the new world?

"*Hazard.* Why, faith, ill company, and the common vice of the town, gaming. * * * * I had rather starve abroad, than live pitied, and despised at home.

"*Friend.* Would he [the new Governor] were landed, we hear he is a noble gentleman.

"*Hazard.* He has all the qualities of a gentleman, besides he is nobly born.

"*Friend.* This country wants nothing but to be peopled with a well born race, to make it one of the best colonies in the world * * * * but we are ruled by a Council, some of which have been, perhaps, transported criminals, who, having now acquired great estates, are now become Your Honour and Rt. Worshipful, and possess all places."

On the 24th of the month, another court martial was held at Green Spring, and sentence of death passed upon James Crewes, William Cookson, John Digby, William Rookings, William West, and John Turner. The last two made their escape.

After the legislative Assembly convened, civil courts were resumed and prisoners were tried by a jury of freeholders and house-keepers. A court was held on the 8th of March, when the King's Commissioners sat on the bench, and Giles Bland[1] and Robert Jones were found guilty of treason, and condemned to death, the next day Anthony Arnold, Richard Turner and Robert Stoakes were sentenced to be hung and the third day John Isles and Richard Pomfroy.

On the 16th of March, John Whitson, and William Scarborough were found guilty, and sentenced to die.

The Assembly, "because mercy is acceptable to God" enacted that Col. Thomas Goodrich[2] and Thomas Gordon, a

---

[1] Giles Bland, nephew of Theodoric, had been opposed to the Berkeley clique for some time. He was arraigned before the General Court, Nov. 21, 1674, at Jamestown, for calling Thomas Ludwell Secretary of the Colony, "a puppy, a pitiful fellow, and son of a whore," as has been mentioned in another foot note.

The father of Giles Bland according to O'Hart was the John Bland of London of whom Pepys wrote in his Diary of June 12, 1680 "Mr. John Bland Merchant was buryed in ye chancil in St. Olave's Church, Hart Street."

Giles married Frances Proby and left a son Giles whose wife was Mary Brown. Giles the grandson was born in 1703, and in 1756, died childless.

[2] Among the manuscripts of Leed Castle, County Kent, England, there is a letter from F. Berkeley dated Aug. 9, 1677, in which the writer says he sends a narrative compiled from the memoirs of Robert Holden, Langston, Gutteridge, [Goodrich] and others. He wrote perhaps to Governor Berkeley as the letter has no address, that as soon as the addressee's back was turned the "Lieut Governor said he would lay £100 that the addressee would not be permitted to see

church of England minister, on bended knees, with ropes about their necks, should appear before Rappahannock court and acknowledge their rebellious acts, the former also to pay a fine, and the latter never to perform ministerial function in the Colony. Several others were ordered to endure similar disgrace. Joseph Ingram, Gregory Walklett, and George Milner, who were insurgent officers when West Point was surrendered were declared incapable of any office other than that of constable, and road surveyor, yet Milner had used his influence to quell the insurrection.[1]

Richard Lawrence, and Major Thomas Whaly, expecting neither justice, nor mercy, from the implacable Governor,

---

the King, but would be sent to the Tower.— Appendix, 6th *Report Royal Historical Commission.*

Reference is made to Col. Thomas Goodrich, John Langston, and Robert Holden. The last became a prominent citizen in Carolina, and in 1679, was commissioned to explore to " or beyond the Apalatian mountains."

[1] " On January 7, 1676-7, Milner sent this note to Capt. Grantham.

" Sir: You have undertaken a work that will speak your everlasting fame and glory; the consolidating our sad differences, preventing the sword and famine, with other horrors, that gaping, were ready to swallow up this miserable country. The service you will do herein to the Almighty, to our dread Sovereign, the Governor, and the Country, will make you honourably spoken of throughout the World I have only to add, that since now, as I hope it will appear by the whole series of my actions, my life, and fortune are both shipp'd off with the Governor and his friends; if therefore I may be thought worthy to advise, I shall leave to your serious consideration; that if you think good the Honourable Governor be persuaded to proceed by the same method his Majesty did, at his restoration, by a Declaration from Bredagh. Such a one here from his Honour, would abundantly settle the minds of hundreds, that are at present amnms'd [amazed] and at a full stand. All I add is that Mercy and Indemnity were over yet a greater friend to Peace, than Severity, tho' Justice were on the same side. I beseech you to dispatch the bearer, back, lest I am forc'd to come single, and then render myself incapable of doing that service to the Honourable Governor, which is designed by

" Your faithful servant,
" Geo. Milner."

left the Colony, and many of the common people, panic stricken went to Carolina, Maryland, and other places[1] to find a home.

Among the Harleian MSS., in the British Museum is the following list of Berkeley, which has been published in the Force *Historical Tracts*.

"A List of those that have been executed for ye late Rebellion.

1. One Johnson a stirer of the people to sedition, but no fighter. [John Johnson.]

2. One Barlow, one of Cromwell's soldiers very active in this rebellion and taken with forty men coming to surprise me in Accomack. [George Farloe ?]

3. One Carver a valiant man, and stout seaman, taken miraculously, who came with Bland, with equal com'n, and 200 men, to take me, and some other gentlemen that assisted me, with the help of 200 soldiers, miraculously delivered into my hand. [William Carver.]

4. One Wilford an Interpreter that frightened the Queen of Pamunkey from ye lands she had granted her by the Assembly, a month after peace was concluded with her. [Thomas Wilford.]

5. One Hartford a valiant stout man and most resolved rebel. [Thomas Hansford ?]

---

[1] In the Boston Town Records, under date of July 29, 1678, is this entry: " William Mason, brick-layer, Charles Cleate dancing-master, Clasen Wheeler his seru't fiddler, of Virginia, all at John Smith's butcher, and p. George Joy, said to be in the rebellion of Nathaniel Bakon there."

AT YORK WHILST I LAY THERE.

1. One Young, commissionated by General Moncke long before he declared for yᵉ King. [Thomas Young.]

2. One Page, a carpenter, formerly my servant, but for his violence used against the Royal Party, made a colonel. [Henry Page.]

3. One Harris, shot to death a valiant, loyalist prisoner.

4. One Hall, a Clerk of a County but more useful to the Rebels than 40 army men, that dyed very penitent, confessing his rebellion against his King and his ingratitude to me. [Thomas Hall of New Kent County.]

ATT MIDDLE PLANTATION.

One Drummond a Scotchman that we all suppose was the originall cause of the whole rebellion, with a common Frenchman [John Baptista] that had been very bloody.

CONDEMNED AT MY HOUSE.

1. One Col'l Crewe, Bacon's parasyte that continually went about yᵉ country extolling Mr. Bacon's actions (justifying his rebellion). [James Crewes.]

2. One Cookson taken in rebellion. [Wm. Cookson].

3. One Danby from a servant made a captain. [John Digby?]

[Signed] "WILLIAM BERKELEY."

James Wilson, formerly a servant, condemned the same day, as Page, does not appear on the list. Thomas Young, was the son of Capt. Thos. Young, who in 1634, explored the Delaware River. Scull in *The Evelyns in America*, gives the following from the Public Record office, London.

"An Account of the Estate of Thomas Younge who was taken prisoner, he being an Officer in the Rebellion was condemned by a Court Martiall, and hanged in York County in January last. This being taken upon the oath of Mary, his relict, who hath given bond for the same: Imprimis, a Plantation with a good dwelling house, a very good tobacco house, and an Indifferent good Orchard, their seat being 400 acres of land in James City County."

George Evelin was his cousin, who was formerly commander of Kent Island in Chesapeake Bay. Evelin in 1649, bought of Thomas Grandon, land in James City County which the next year he gave to his son Mountjoy. Gov. Berkeley on June 20, 1651, granted 600 acres in James City County to Mountjoy. On the 29th of November, 1653, he married Dorothy, the daughter of Col. Obedience Robins of the Eastern Shore of Chesapeake Bay, and after his death, she became the wife of William Andrews Jr., Andrews in the proceedings of the General Court, in April, 1670, appears as the guardian of George, the son of Mountjoy Evelin[1].

The Commissioners one of whom, Jeffreys, held the Commission as Governor, remonstrated with Berkeley upon his harsh and impolitic course, and had no intercourse with

---

[1] The following extracts from the Register of St. Peter's Church, Cornhill, London, published by the Harleian Society, show the relation of the Youngs and Evelins.

"1579, August 16, Sonday: Christneng of Thomas Yonnge sonne of Gregory Young grocer, the child was born the 10th daye, being Monday."

"1590, October 19, Monday: Wedding of Robert Eueling sonne of George Eueling, And Susan Young daughter of Mr. Gregory Young, grocer."

"1592, Christninge of George Eueling sonne of Robert Eueling, Armerer, the child was borne the 31th of January being Monday."

him except in their official capacity. On one occasion he sent them from his house,[1] in his own carriage, but with the common hangman acting as postillion. During the month of April, Berkeley sailed for England and Commissioner Jeffreys became Governor. In his first proclamation he mentioned that his commission was dated November 11th, 1676, and then uses the following language relative to the King, who "hath upon ye humble representation of the Rt. Hon. Sir William Berkeley, his great age and bodily weakness in respect whereof he held himselfe unable to perform and execute the duty of his place & office, and therefore did most humbly & earnestly beseech his gracious Matie for leaue to returne: His Majesty declared that s'd William Berkeley should speedily return into England, whither hee is now gone." A few weeks after his arrival in England, on the 13th of July, Berkeley died.[2] The remaining Commissioners, Sir John Berry and Francis Moryson, also during the summer, returned to England, and their reports created an unfavorable impression of the late Governor.

The Governor's brother, Lord Berkeley, met Sir John Berry in the Council Chamber and "with an angry voice and a Berklean look, told him that he and Moryson[3] had

---

[1] Berkeley's mansion was a plain brick building containing a hall, six rooms, and a garret. The bricks were were not brought from England, as has been been mentioned, but were made on the spot. Green Spring is two miles north of James River, and five from Jamestown.

[2] He was buried in Twickenham in England.

[3] Governor Berkeley's wife was severe in her remarks upon Moryson, and was a woman who had a vigorous tongue. In a letter of Moryson in 1677, to Philip Ludwell; who, in 1680, became her husband, he writes " Mr. Secretary Coventry says he will vindicate me to all the world, that neither before my going, nor after my return have I offere I any thing to the King and Lords but with a respect

murdered his brother." The Lord Chancellor after the report of the Commissioners said that "he knew not whether it was lawful to wish a person alive, otherwise he would wish Sir William Berkeley so, to see what could be answered to such barbarity." Upon October 22, 1677, in an order of the King for the relief of the widow, it was declared that Drummond "had been sentenced and put to death contrary to the laws of the Kingdom."

Thomas Ludwell, who had been Secretary of the Colony, under Berkeley, for more than fifteen years, died soon after the Governor. In Bruton[1] church yard, Williamsburg, he was buried, and the stone which marks his resting has this inscription:

"Under this marble lyeth the body of Thomas Ludwell, Esquire, Secretary of Va., who was born at Bruton, in the county of Somerset, in the kingdom of England, and departed this life in the year 1678. And near this, lye the bodies of Richard Kemp, Esquire, his predecessor in the Secretary's office, and Sir Thomas Lunsford,[2] Knight.

ful tenderness to Sir Wm. Berkeley, nor have I ever spoken of his Lady but with a courtesy that belongs to her sex, though she was pleased to tell Madam Jeffries she wondered I would be so impertinent as to go to Virginia where I was so hated the people would tear me to pieces. Pray remember my service to her, and tell her ladyship she was very uncharitable [that] she would not forwarn me of the danger I went to, but I did not mind it, for I had no gun shot off, nor bonfires made for joy of my going away.'

[1] Bruton parish named after Bruton, Somerset, England, where was the family seat of the Berkeleys.

[2] Sir Thomas Pelham and Thomas Lunsford Senior, were neighbors in Sussex and near kindred. On the 26th of June, 1632, while Pelham was hunting, his dog went into Lunsford's grounds and was shot, which led to ill-feeling. In August, 1633, as Pelham was returning from church in his coach, with his wife and others, Thomas Lunsford Junior, with an associate stepped out from a copse with swords and pistols, to attack Pelham.

In memory of whom this marble is placed, by order of Philip Ludwell, Esq., nephew of the said Thomas Ludwell in the year 1727."

It was a surprise to the Virginians, in 1669, to learn, that the lands between the Potomac and Rappahannock, had been given to a royal favorite, Lord Culpepper, but sur-

---

Lunsford was arrested, tried and imprisoned, and fined £5,000, but in October, 1631, escaped, by bribing his keeper. His father was in the Fleet four years, and in 1637 Dr. Alexander Leighton certified that he had grown so weak, that he ought to be permitted to go to his own house in London. This Leighton was the physician and preacher, father of Archbishop Leighton, and also prisoner, having lost both his ears and been branded and imprisoned for writing a seditious pamphlet against the King. Lunsford died on the 4th of November, of that year. Three of his sons were Colonels on the Royalist side during the civil war.

1. Henry born A.D., 1611, was killed July 25, 1643, at the siege of Bristol.
2. Herbert was knighted July 6, 1644, and survived the war.
3. Thomas was knighted Dec. 28, 1641, and made Lieutenant of the tower of London. The citizens were indignant at the appointment of one who had been outlawed and was notorious as a profligate. The House of Commons declared him unfit for the office, and the apprentices of London became so unruly in consequence of it, the King was forced to take from him the the keys of the Tower.

On the 27th of December while walking through Westminister Hall with twenty or thirty of his friends and meeting a band of apprentices, he and his companions drew their swords, and wounded twenty or thirty of them and denounced them as "roundheads," because it was their fashion to cut the hair round.

Secretary Windebank, writing from Oxford, May 22, 1644, tells Col. Ashburnham. "Att London they apprehend us very weeke, but I assure you Sir Tho. Lunsford this day came from army and saith there are about 10,000 horses and foote, of as likely men as he ever sawe in his life."

He was married, in 1640, to Katerina, daughter of Henry Nevill of Co Berks, and she was his second wife. By her he had a daughter Elizabeth, born in 1642, who in 1667, married a Daniel Norton of Co. Berks; Philippa who died young; and Maria born in the Tower of London, who in November, 1665, married Thomas Collyer, a brewer of Shoe Lane, London.

A pedigree of Lunsford in the British Museum, mentions that he "sould all, and went into Virginia, where he married his third wife."

prise was turned to indignation when, in 1673, the profligate and improvident King gave to this covetous lord, and associates, "all the dominion of land and water called Virginia," for a period of thirty-one years.

The Assembly which convened in September, 1674, "deeply sencible of the many and grievous pressures dayly growing" "thought fitt that a humble supplication be made to his sacred Majestie," "That he would be gratiously pleased to revoke the said grants, to the said Lord."

On the 21st of September, Governor Berkeley wrote to Lord Arlington informing him that Col. Francis Moryson, Secretary Thomas Ludwell, and Major General Robert Smith, had been appointed agents for Virginia, in England.

The agents opened their negotiations by asking that Virginia might be allowed to purchase the land between the Potomac and Rappahannock which had already been given to Lord Culpepper and associates; that the people of the Colony should rely directly upon the Crown for protection, free from the intervention of any Proprietary; that as before, the Governor and Council should reside in Virginia; that there be no departure from the custom, of the Assembly levying all taxes upon the people; that all laws made by the Assembly be operative, unless within two years, the King expressed his disapproval.

On the 19th of November, 1675, the Commissioners for Foreign Plantations, presented to the King and Privy Council a report recommending in substance what the representatives of Virginia wished, and the King ordered a charter to be prepared in conformity therewith. Culpepper and his friends offered some objections, especially to the proviso that the colonists should not be taxed except by their own Assembly, to which the agents replied that it "contains that which we conceive to be the right of Virginians, as well as all other Englishmen, which is not to be taxed but by their consent, expressed by their representatives."

Before the charter was signed by the King the startling intelligence of the wide spread insurrection under Bacon was received, and negotiations were suspended.

Before the insurrection, three of the solid, sober men, who for years had been acknowledged leaders, died, Governor Bennett,[1] and Digges,[2] and Secretary Claiborne. Bennett died a Puritan, apparently, in sympathy with the Society of Friends. Digges, cautious, and moderate in his views, was honored by his neighbors. Before the late civil war, upon a tombstone, at Bellville, on York River, eight miles from Williamsburg, could be seen the following:

"To the memory of Edward Diggs, Esq., sonne of Sir Dudley Diggs of Chilham in Kent, Knight and Baronett,

---

[1] The General Court at Jamestown on Nov. 3, 1672, requested Major General Richard Bennett, to see that the sheriff of Lower Norfolk take into custody William Carver of Elizabeth River who had stabbed and killed a man. The last mention of him is on November 18, 1674, in the court proceedings.

[2] A fragment of the Records of the General Court of Virginia under date of June 15, 1675, has the following: "A probate of ye last will and testament of Edw'd Diggs Esq., dec'd is Granted Mrs. Eliz'h Digges ye Relict & Executrix, for that ye Court are of opinion yt was all of Edw'd Diggs Esq., his owne writing and being proved by ye Oath of Capt. Wm. Diggs one of ye witnesses to ye said Will.

William Digges married a daughter of Henry Sewell or Sewall of Patuxent Maryland. Her mother after her father's death in 1661, became the wife of Charles, the third Lord Baltimore. Col. Digges, was a prominent citizen in Maryland, at the accession of William and Mary to the throne of England.

Master of the Rolls in the reigne of Charles the 1st, who departed this life the 15th of March, 1675, in the 55th year of his age, one of his Majesty's Councill for this his Colony of Virginia. A gentleman of most considerable parts and ingenuity, and the only introducer and promoter of the silk manufactures in this Colonie, and in every thing else a pattern worthy of all pious imitation. He had issue six sonnes, and seven daughters, by the body of Elizabeth his wife, who of her conjugal affection hath dedicated to him, this memorial." His father was a Knight but not a Baronet, as the inscription mentions.

Col. Claiborne, in the Assembly of 1666, was a Burgess from New Kent County. How long he lived after this period has not been ascertained. John Clayton[1] the parson of James City, who in 1682, came to Virginia, alludes to

---

[1] Clayton in a letter to the Royal Society wrote; "I was told a pleasant story of an old gentleman, Col. Cleyborn, as I remember, was his name, the same that sent the rattlesnakes to the Royal Society, some years since. He had the odd fancy of keeping some of these snakes always in barrels, in the house, and one time an Indian pretending to charm them, so as to take them, by the neck, in his hand, without biting of him, the old gentleman caused a rattlesnake to be brought forth; the Indian began his charm with a little wand, whisking it round and round the rattlesnake's head, bringing it by degrees nigher and nigher, and at length flung the switch away, and whisked his hand about in like manner, bringing his hand still higher and higher, by taking less circles, when the old gentleman hit the snake with his crutch and the snake snapped the Indian by the hand, and bit him very sharply betwixt the fingers, which put the charm to an end, and he roared out, but stretched his arm out as high as he could, calling for a string wherewith he tied his arm as hard as possibly he could and clapped a hot burning coal thereon, and singed it stoutly, whereby he was cured."

Capt. William Claiborne a descendant, was living in 1699. Story, the Quaker preacher, in his journal, mentions, that on the 10th of the second month [O. S,] he visited the Chickahominy village, reduced to eleven wigwams, on Pamunkey neck, and then, went one mile, to the house of the grandson of Secretary Claiborne.

him, as one who had given some rattlesnakes to the Royal Society, an aged man who had carried a crutch, and then dead.

Jeffreys, during his brief term of office proved a judicious and conciliatory Governor. The Assembly of October, 1677, William Traverse, speaker, met at the house of Capt. Otho Thorpe, in Middle Plantation, and as some persons were disposed to call others, "traitors, rebels, rogues, or such like," retarding " the former estate of love and friendship desired by all good people," it was enacted that all, using opprobrious epithets, should be fined. Arrangements were also made for the establishing of marts or fairs whither friendly Indians would come and trade. The King had issued instructions, which arrived early in 1677, requiring the Assembly to meet once in two years, and except for good cause not to sit more than fourteen days, and that the members be elected "only by free-holders as being more agreeable to the custom of England." Thomas Ludwell, Secretary, and Daniel Parke were both in England as Council agents, at the time of the calling of the Assembly by Governor Jeffreys, and were directed not to dispose of any more money of the Virginia Colonists, without the King's order in Council.

In May, 1677, a conference was held with the representatives of the Indian tribes, and a peace concluded. The Indians agreed to acknowledge the King, by an annual tribute of three arrows, and some beaver skins, and in return, no Indian was to be imprisoned, except by a legal warrant, their reservations of land were to be inalienable, and they were to be permitted to catch fish, and oysters, within the ceded territory.

Among the chiefs present were two women, one known as the Queen of Pamunkey, a relative of Powhatan and Opecancanough. She wore a turban, made by a three inch plait, of black and white wampum, and her robe was of deerskins with the hair on the outside, ornamented with a twisted fringe six inches deep from the shoulder to the feet. From the earliest days of the Colony prominent white men had found temporary alliances with Indian women. Sir Thomas Dale sent Hamor,[1] to Powhatan, "to procure a daughter of his, reputed to be his delight, and darling" "to be his nearest companion, wife, and bed-fellow."[2] The Queen of Pamunkey at the time of the treaty, had by her side, a son, twenty years of age, whose father, was reputed to be an English colonel.

Upon the 30th of December, 1678, Jeffreys died, and Sir Henry Chicheley, Deputy Governor, a sober, kind, moderate man, who when a widower had married Agatha, the widow of Ralph Wormeley, and had lived in Virginia, for more than a quarter of a century, became the acting Governor, which met the approval of the King. During his term of office, on the 25th of April, 1679, an Assembly convened, at James City, and elected Mathew Kemp, speaker.

For the defence of the country from the incursion of savages, it was enacted that a garrison or store-house should

---

[1] *Virginia Company of London*, pp. 92, 93.

[2] This custom is not entirely discontinued. In *Forty years among the Sioux* by Rev. S. R. Riggs, LL.D., his wife writes July 31, 1837, from the vicinity of Fort Snelling, Minnesota: "Until my location here I was not aware that it was so exceedingly common, for officers in the army to have two wives, or more, but one, of course, legally so. For instance, at the Fort, before the removal of the last troops, there were but two officers who were not known to have an Indian woman, if not half Indian children."

be erected at the heads of the four principal rivers, and Major Isaac Allerton, grandson of Brewster of Plymouth Rock, Col. St. Leger Codd,[1] and Col. George Mason were designated to superintend the building of a house sixty feet in length, and twenty-two in breadth, and a magazine ten feet square at Neapsico, near Occoquan, on the Potomac river.

Upon condition that Capt. William Byrd would settle two hundred and fifty persons on both sides of the James river within the space of a mile, there was granted to him, "beginning on the south side of James river, one mile and a half below the Falls, and so continuing five miles up the river, in a straight line, and backwards, one mile in the woods; and on the north side of the said river beginning a half mile before the Falls, and thence continuing five miles up the river; and two miles backward into the woods."

On the 31st of July, Col. William Kendall, and Col. Southey Littleton of the Eastern Shore arrived in New York,[2] with credentials from Governor Chicheley, to confer

---

[1] Codd afterwards resided in Maryland.

[2] Col. Kendall was in the Assemblies of 1659, 1663 and 1666, one of the Burgesses from Northampton.

Col. Southey Littleton, was the son of Nathaniel Littleton, and Ann his wife, who was a daughter of Lewis and Elizabeth Southey early settlers at Jamestown. The father of Southey had a plantation at Nandua Creek which the son inherited. The father died in 1654, and the mother in 1656. At the time of her death she resided at Magothy Bay, Northampton County. In her will she requests the non-conformist brother-in-law of Governor Stone, "Mr. Francis Doughty, Minister and preacher of ye word in this parish, to Councell my children, not only in the management of their estates, and ciuill behavior in ye World. But bee a meanes to instruct them in the feare of God & seruice of the Allmighty and Creator, and in ye true faith in Jesus Christ, into whose hands I committ in common, all our soules when it pleaseth him to take them from vs out of this sinfull life to wch desire I say Amen and Amen."

with Governor Andros, on Indian affairs, and it was arranged to hold a council, at Albany, in the autumn with the Onondagas and other bands of Iroquois.[1]

Her eldest child Edward was made the executor. Her daughter Esther, in 1662, had married John the second son of Col. Obedience Robins.

The younger son Southey, whose plantation was at Nandua, was born in 1645, and a record of the Robins family mentions, that he died in New York City probably at the time of his visit as a Commissioner from Virginia. He left children : 1. Nathaniel who married Susanna Waters. 2 Bowman who died before A.D., 1700. 3. Southey who married Mary, daughter of Thomas and Susan Upshur Brower. 4. Esther married Col. William Whittington 5. Sarah married John Dennis of Somerset Co., Md. 6. Elizabeth married Richard Waters of Somerset, Md. 7. Gertrude who married a Mr. Harmanson.

[1] In Palmer's Calendar of Virginia Papers is the following account of the conference.

"The Onondagas answer upon the Propositions of Col. Wm. Kendall Agent for ye Country of Virginia.

"Names of Sachems — Carrackkondre — Otrienachce — Canisicktoe and 5 souldiers.

"BRETHREN OF VIRGINIA.

" 1st. We are come here in the Prefixed Housse, where we are used to make Propositions, and have understood that wch is by you Represented. All our Indians (meaning their souldiers) have been destracted, or without their senses, in committing of this act against the Christians in Virginia, for itt is done without our order, and against our will. They have been like a child, who having an ax in itts hand, is not sensible, what itt doth with itt, and cannot discern between good and Evil. Its made known to us by you, the dammage that our people have done in Virginia in plundering your houses. We doe Confesse itt, but do say again, as above, that they have done very wickedly. We have likewise understood that when our young Indians come near any Christians, must lay down their arms, as a token of friendship. It is likewise told us, that if any of our People shall goe to warr towards your parts, against any Indians, not in friendship with you, that they shall forbear to come near your Plantacons, all which we absolute undertake, and do thank you that you have Propounded ye same.

" We have Likeways understood that by the Informacon, his honr, ye govr here, hath given you, you haue forgiven that, which is past, for which we do thank you hertily. You are People of understanding, butt we are Brutish, Blinde, and without understanding as we have said above ; and we are thankful and glad that you Imputed and Communicate some knowledge to us, and if our young Indians come amongst you, be friendly to ym, for they goe against their Enemys the Downaganhoes, doe present a Belt of zewant 20 deep.

In May, 1680, there appeared in Virginia as Governor, the capable, but corrupt, and pleasure loving, Thomas Lord Culpepper,[1] who with Lord Arlington, and others, had

---

"2d. We thank them of Virginia & commend and praise their understanding that they show such favour to the Oneydes, our children, and Include them in such a friendship. Doe give 8 faddom zewant.

"3d. When our Young Indians goe out a fighting against their enemies, lett them be well used, and do not look so narrowly upon a Little Indian corn or Tobacco, but let us live like friends. As for ye burning of your houses, it is unknown to us, but the Plundering of some goods, and ye killing of a Beast, wee do not deny; as for killing of horses, we have no hand in; but ye Oneydes have, and Pointed to some of them then Present have shot foure.

"And when wee come for Indian Corn or any Provision doe not lett our guns and armes be taken from us, seeing it was the beginning of these last troubles. We doe thank you for your Tobacco and Rum, doe give 7 faddom ze'n't."

[1] Lord John Culpepper father of the Governor was a devoted friend of Charles the First. In 1640, he was an able member of Parliament, and spoke against monopolies as follows: "I have one grievance to offer you but this one compriseth many. It is a nest of wasps, a swam of vermine which have over crept the land, I mean the monopolies. These like the frogs of Egypt have gotten possession of our dwellings, we have scarce a room free from them They sup in our cup, they dip in our dish, they sit by our fire. We find them in the dye vat, wash bowl, and powdering tub, etc., etc."

He was subsequently Master of the Rolls and one of the Privy Council, and on October 21st, 1664, he was created Baron Thoresway of Lincoln. During the civil war he was a trusted counsellor of the King, and after Charles was beheaded, he was confided in by the widow Henrietta Maria, and his son. A letter of the widow to him has been published in the Appendix to 6th Report of Royal Historical Commission. It is dated Paris, April 23, [1665, and begins "My Lord Culpepper, I have seen by several letters which you have written to Lord Jermyn that you think it would be for the benefit of the King, my son, that there should be a better understanding than heretofore, between him and me, than there is This causes me to write this letter to inform you that there is no fault on my side, but that I have been unfortunate enough that the King has not put in me the confidence which I deserved at his hands, both as his mother, and as a person who has not, and has never shown herself as having any other interest than his." The letter is long and signed "Your very good friend."

In 1660, the first Baron Thorseway died, and his son Thomas Culpepper, by his second wife, became the second Baron. The latter alleged that he had lost ten

obtained the grant of Virginia, and for several years had been a member of the Board for Plantations. He was instructed to see that voters were restricted to freeholders and householders, that legislative assemblies were summoned by the special direction of the crown, and that laws were not to originate with them, but to be prepared by the Governor and Council, and transmitted to the crown, and when approved be presented to the Burgesses to accept or reject.

To him was given the "full power and authoritie to suspend any member of the Councell if you see just cause; and our will and pleasure is, that every member of our Councell suspended by you, shall be uncapable during such suspension of serving as member of the General Assembly."

Soon after his arrival, an Assembly was summoned, which convened on the 8th of June, at Jamestown. Thomas Ballard was chosen speaker, and the clerk, was Robert Beverley. The first Act passed had been prepared in England, and was a free and general pardon to all, who had participated in the Bacon Rebellion, but the estate of the late Nathaniel Bacon, Junior, was declared to be forfeited

---

thousand pounds sterling in consequence of his loyalty, and in July, 1661, was appointed by the King, Governor of the Isle of Wight, with power to appoint a deputy. With Secretary Bennett, afterwards Lord Arlington he was intimate, and on the 4th of January, 1662-3, he sent him a mire as a Christmas present, and an acknowledgment of obligation. Toward non-conformists he was severe. He sent Priscilla Moseley a Quakeress to prison, who died while in confinement. He seized two strangers called "Desperate canters" and put them in jail, and with grim humor gave them the Koran in English, to read, and one of his friends wrote "If they should turn Turks, it would be a great blow to the whole sect."

By his arbitrary measures, the inhabitants of the Isle of Wight learned to dislike him, and in 1666, presented a petition to the King, stating their grievances.

to the King, and also the estates of Giles Bland, Anthony Arnold, Richard Turney, Richard Pomfrey, John Isles, Robert Stoakes, John Whiston, and William Scarborough, all of whom had been executed for treason, and also that of Richard Lawrence, "who fyred James City and is since fled," while Joseph Ingram, Gregory Walklett, Thomas Whaley, and John Forth, were disqualified holding any public office.

On the 10th of August, entrusting affairs to the Lieutenant Governor, Sir Henry Chicheley, he sailed by way of Boston, for England, taking with him the servants and soldiers, that he brought to the Colony, and all his plate and furniture.

On the twenty-second of August, before daylight, the ship in which he embarked, owned by Capt. Jarvis, and named the "Betty" in compliment to his wife who was the widow of the insurgent, ran aground. At daylight, he was taken ashore, with two of his men, and walking through the woods reached Sandwich, about sixty miles from Boston, where horses and a guide were obtained, and on the twenty-fourth, he reached the latter place, and the next day was tendered a banquet, and escorted to the hall, by the eight military companies of the town. Capt. Jarvis did not arrive with his ship until the first week in October. On the 17th of October, Governor Andros of New York came to consult Culpepper, but found that he had sailed two days before.[2]

---

[1] Letter of Culpepper, *Va. Hist. Reg.*, 1850.

[2] Hull's Diary.

To his sister Culpepper wrote, from Boston : "My Lady Berkeley is married to Mr. [Philip] Ludwell,[1] and thinkes no more of our world. I shall now marry Cate[2] as soone as I can, and then shall reckon myselfe to be a freeman without clogge or charge."

In December, Culpepper reached England. Bacon's widow, now the wife of Captain Jarvis, with her husband, brought suit in 1681, to obtain a portion of the estate of Sir Edward Duke, her father. In his will he wrote that she was to have a legacy of £2000, "but if she marry Bacon, void." The case was decided against her and the Lord Chancellor spoke of "such an example of presumptuous disobedience highly meriting such a punishment, she being only prohibited to marry with one man, by name; and nothing in

---

[1] Philip Ludwell, and his brother, Secretary Thomas Ludwell were grandsons of Philip Cottington of Godmanster, Surrey. Their mother's uncle was Francis, Lord Cottington, and she was the daughter of James Cottington. Thomas Ludwell died in Virginia, but Philip went to England after having been Governor of Carolina, and died near Stratford. His son Philip was a prominent citizen of Virginia.

[2] His only daughter Catherine, married Thomas the 5th Lord Fairfax, and their son, through his mother obtained Leeds Castle in Kent, England, and five millions of acres in northern Virginia. The first Fairfax, who came to America to reside, was Colonel William, a widower, who settled in Salem, Massachussetts, where he married Deborah the daughter of Francis Clarke. He had been Collector of Customs, and in 1733, was Justice of the Peace. In 1734, in June, he left Massachusetts, and went to Virginia as the agent of Lord Fairfax, and built Belvoir, near Mount Vernon, a very modest residence, yet at the time one of the best in Virginia. It was of brick, and two stories in height. Upon the first floor, were four rooms, and a hall, and on the second floor, were five rooms. The sixth Lord Fairfax died in 1781, a bachelor, and was buried at Winchester, Virginia. His brother Robert, in England, was the seventh Lord, who died childless, and then Bryan the son of Col. William and wife Deborah rector of Fairfax parish, Va., became the eighth Lord. The eleventh Lord now living, is John Fairfax MD., residing in Maryland, near Washington, D.C.

the whole fair Garden of Eden would serve her turn, but this forbidden fruit." ·

The Assembly of June passed a law that no tobacco should be shipped before the 20th of March, 1681, and that it must be from certain designated landings, but when the time arrived ship captains and merchants found that no warehouses, had been prepared at these places, to shelter the tobacco, and no inns for themselves, and they suffered loss and inconvenience, and trade was depressed.

Lord Baltimore on the 19th of July, 1681, in a letter to the Earl of Anglesea, refers to the then condition of Virginia, and the sympathy of its Secretary, with Fendall, formerly Governor of Maryland. He writes: "This Fendall has a great influence on, and interest in, most of the rascalls in North part of Virginia, where he was for some time, when he was forced to absent himselfe from Maryland, and at that time I gave notice to Sir Henry Chicheley to sett eyes over him, the same notice I gave to Coll. Nicholas Spencer, Secretary of Virginia, but I feare the latter, either through want of resolution, or loyalty, did not prevent (what he might) the seditious practices of this Rebell, and I may the more boldly affirm this, since formerly, and but few days afore my apprehending this fellow, he had openly entertained and cherisht this Rascall in his house, which give me cause to be confident that he has encouraged Fendall in his designes against Mary Land forgetting or (as I suppose) not considering that a defection in my government, may raise another Bacon in Virginia, the people there being as ripe and readdy for another Rebellion as ever they were, and I know not but one, of the two, I've caused to be apprehended, might have served their own turne. My Lord, if his Maj^tie please not to send in some Loyall active person to command under Sir Henry Chicheley (who is now super annated) very speedily, the government of Virginia will be in danger, I pray God, Secretary Spencer be owner of so much loyalty, as to deserve the trust and dignity now conferred on him, had I the honor to be one houre with your Lordshipp I could give your Lordshipp satisfaction in some things, relating to His Maj^ties service, which I dare not committ to paper in this juncture. I therefor humbly begg your Lordshipps' pardon for breaking in upon you, with this fresh trouble, afore I've expiated the rudenesse of my former address."

An Assembly met in April, 1682, which after much debate, adjourned, without providing any remedy, for the excessive production of tobacco. Early in May a number of persons banded together, and after destroying their own tobacco plants, went to the plantations of their neighbors, and cut up their plantings. Acting Governor Chicheley took immediate steps to check these riotous proceedings. Philemon Lloyd, one of the Council of Maryland, who had married the widow of Richard Bennett, Jr., while in Albany, attending a Indian conference, in a letter dated June 25, 1682, refers to the disorders, in these words : "The tumultuous rabble have destroyed my tobacco in four counties, computed to be eight or ten thousand h'heads and persists notwithstanding ten or twelve have been slain and many taken prisoners, yet there was hope y^t that they would be fully suppressed in some short time, for y^t the Gov^t had very timely, secured all armes. The news you heard of Sr Henry Chicheleys house being burnt is too trew, but my Lord [Baltimore] informs me it was not by them, but by accident, whereby S'r Henry had a very great losse, saving no part of his goods."

A little while after this Chicheley, infirm from age but respected by all, for his probity, and mildness died. His widow Agatha, in the autumn of 1683, visited England, under the protection of her husband's friend, and neighbor, Major General Robert Smith. During this summer a Captain John Williams, who had seized a two mast vessel in Cuba, landed at and visited the Custis plantation, and neighborhood in Accomac, and frightened the planters by the piratical bearing of his crew, then sailed into Maryland waters and attempted to seize the proprietor, Lord Baltimore. The reckless crew proceeded to Connecticut and Rhode Island, and were seized by the authorities of the latter, and two were sent to Governor Chicheley for trial.

When the news of the riotous proceedings relative to tobacco planting reached England, Culpepper was ordered to return to his post as Governor, and was directed to take notice of his Majesty's resentment of a seditious declaration made by the Assembly of Virginia during the government of Jeffreys, whereby they asserted " that his Majesty's commissioners having called for and forced from the Clerk of the Assembly, all the original journals of the Assembly which power they supposed his Majesty would not grant them, for that, they find not the same to have been practiced by any of the Kings of England, and did therefore take the same to be a violation of their privileges, desiring with all satisfaction to be given them, that they might be assured no such violation of the privileges should be offered for the future."

While the King was ready to pardon the Burgesses for their resolution, he directed Culpepper to express his disapproval thereof, and have it erased from the record, and also have a resolution passed at the next Assembly declaring the right of his Majesty and officers at their pleasure, to call for public records and journals.

He was also instructed " to administer the oath of allegiance and supremacy to the members and officers of the Council and Assembly, all judges, and justices, and all other persons, that hold any office in the said Colony by virtue of any patent under our great seal of England, or the public seal of Virginia, and to permit a liberty of conscience to all other persons, except Papist, so they be contented with a quiet peaceable enjoyment of it, not giving offence, or scandal to the government."

Soon after his arrival, he stopped execution against John Pleasants, a quiet and peaceable Quaker, indicted in Henrico County, under the statute, which imposed a fine of twenty pounds for not going to church, and attending a conventicle. The tobacco riotors were tried, three were hanged, and one pardoned, on condition, that he would render service to the public, by building a bridge.

Culpepper was unpopular and charged with buying up piasters, a silver coin of Spain, equivalent to eight reals, at the rate of five shillings each, and then, by proclamation, declaring the " piece of eight " a legal tender to the amount of six shillings. When the soldiers of Sir John Berry's regiment were paid for their services, they received the "piece of eight" at six shillings, and thus the Governor enriched himself.[1]

---
[1] Oldmixon.

Without permission, he again returned to England, on the ground that it was necessary to report in person to the crown, but, the plea was not admitted, and he was deprived of office.

The Council[1] under date of May 4, 1683, in a communication to the authorities, in England, wrote : " That whereas his Majesty had granted all the quit rents of the southern part of this Colony, to the Lords Arlington and Culpepper, for a certain term of years, that his Majesty would be pleased to give those noble lords something in lieu, and appropriate the quit-rents and all escheat to the use of the government."

An arrangement was length concluded by which Culpepper abandoned all claims, except to a portion of the Northern Neck, and for the remainder, received an annual pension for twenty years, of six hundred pounds.

Francis. Lord Howard of Effingham, in August, 1683, was appointed Governor, but it was not, until the following February, that he reached Virginia. Among other instructions, he was directed to see, that no person used a printing press.[2] After a conference with the Council on the 21st of February, it was determined to call the Assembly to meet on the 16th of April. While it was in session Major Robert Beverley was tried before the General Court for being a ring leader in creating the disturbances in connection with the

---

[1] Councillors at this time were Robert Smith, Jos. Bridger, Phil. Ludwell, Jno. Page, Wm Byrd, Nich. Spencer, Nath. Bacon, Wm. Cole, Rich. Lee, son of the first councillor Richard Lee.

[2] On Feb. 21st, 1682-3, "John Buckner called before Lord Culpepper, and his Council, for printing the laws of 1680, without his Excellency's licence ; and he and the printer ordered to enter into Bond, in £100, not to print any thing hereafter, until his Majesty's pleasure shall be known."

illegal cutting of tobacco plants, and for other misdemeanors. On the 11th of May, 1682, he had been arrested under a warrant from Governor Chicheley, and placed on board the ship "Duke of York," John Purvis, commander, and on Saturday evening the 13th, he demanded as a free born subject of England, to be informed as to the charge upon which he had been committed. On the last day of this month, he was transferred to the ship "Concord," Capt. William Jeffreys, and in the middle of June, he was placed on board of a sloop belonging to Colonel Custis, to be taken to the Eastern shore to be delivered to the sheriff of Northampton County. He escaped from the sloop, but was again seized at his house in Middlesex, and brought before the Governor and Council at Jamestown. In September he petitioned by his attorney William Fitzhugh for a *habeas corpus* to be directed to the sheriff of Northampton, which was denied, as Lord Culpepper was expected. On January 10th, 1682-3 he was charged with having refused as clerk to deliver copies of the journal of the House of Burgesses, of 1682, to the Lt. Governor and Council without the leave of his masters, the members of the Assembly. In May, 1684, he was found guilty of high misdemeanors, and was pardoned, having presented the following, on bended knees, to the Governor, and Council, sitting as a Court.

"To his Excellencie ffrancis Lord Howard Baron of Effingham, his Majesties Lieut. and Governor General of Virginia, and to the honorable Councell of State.

"Robert Beverley most humbly presenting, sheweth,

"That the true sence of his misfortunate offenses hath brought him to that degree of compunction, that hee is

under an unexpresible sorrow for the same which is much
augmented, by the consideration that hee should soe incon-
siderately forfeited that esteem for the government, that he
had with the often hazard of his life endeavored to purchase,
and which had been gratiously laid upon him beyond his
deserts, the weight of which consideration is enough to
smite him into an abysse of dispair ; but that, the hope
hee hath, that hee shall not miss that mercy which is most
obviously inherent, and an inseparable concomitant in your
lordshipps noble breast, and those of the honorable his
majesties councell of state, here not only buoys him up, and
withholds him from perishing in that gulph, but also gives
him confidence most humbly to address himselfe to your
excellency and the honorable court to looke upon him with
an indulgent eye, lying at the foot of your justice, and
most humbly imploring your mercy; this my Lord, is the
only way he hath to approach your Lordship by the free
confession of his offences, and true repentance his heart is
filled with, not without almost an assured hope, that it will
meet with a benigne reception in your lordships merceful
heart, because the Kings of Kings and Lords of Lords is well
pleased that the prayers, tears, and true repentance of every
sinner should reach his blessed throne, even to the expi-
ation of their sins, and re-establishment in grace.

"Your lordship hath been gratiously pleased to assign
councell for this your sorrowful petitioner to make his defence in law; but he is resolved not to make use of any
meanes, either to vindicate himself, or to exterminate his
crimes, but most humbly to throw himselfe upon the mercy
of your lordship and the court, which if your lordship shall
be pleased to extend towards him all the days of his life, shall

be spent in the study to expiate his guilt, and truly and faithfully to serve his most gratious sovereign in a ready and most willing obedience to your lordships and the councell's commands with the last drop of his blood, and shall most heartily pray for a long and happy reigne to his most excellent majestie, and health, honor, and prosperity for your lordshipp, and the councell.

"May 3, 1684. "ROBERT BEVERLEY."

While the Assembly was in session Lord Howard received a visit from Charles, Lord Baltimore, on his return from Maryland to England, and Col. Philip Ludwell[1] now the husband of Lady Berkeley, came back from his visit to London. During the month of June a letter writer mentioned that Governor Howard was going to New York in the "Quaker ketch" to pass the warm season, and that the merchants Kennon and Pleasants had received "thirty-four negroes, seven or eight tuns of rum, and sugar, and dry goods for sale." During the summer Lady Berkeley was very ill, and after this little mention of her is found in the chronicles of the period.[2]

Among the older families, there was much talk, in January, 1684-5, concerning the unexpected marriage of the widow Grendon, the sister of the second Thomas Stegge,

---

[1] R. R. in Va. Hist. Register, Vol 1, p. 60, mentions that Ludwell was a widower, with two daughters and a son, when he married the widow of Governor Berkeley. The usual statement is that he had a son and daughter by the widow Berkeley.

[2] Nicholas Bacon the elder, and for a time acting governor, in his will made in March, 1691-2 (O. S.) left her his riding horse, and ten pounds sterling. In May 1886, the writer found at Jamestown, a portion of the stone, which was placed over her grave, and all of the inscription left was "Lady Frances Berkeley."

and aunt of Capt. William Byrd, founder of Richmond, "to one Mr. Edward Brain," writes her nephew, "a stranger to all, here, but pretends to be worth money, if not, the old woman may thank herself."

During this year a party of fifty roaming Seneca Indians from New York were met within a few miles of Westover. Trade in negroes was rapidly increasing, while Governor Berkeley reported in 1671, not more than two thousand black slaves, the number now was doubled.[1]

Howard of Effingham had not been long in office, when Charles the Second, was taken sick. The King after receiving the Sacrament, from a priest of the Church of Rome, with one of his mistresses weeping, by his bed-side, and with thoughts of another, whispering "Do not let poor Nelly, starve," in February, 1685, died.[2]

---

[1] Governor Spotswood in 1712, estimated negroes and other servants, *above sixteen years of age* as more than 12,000 and Governor Dinwiddie in 1756, estimated the entire negro population at 120,156 nearly as many as the whites, which was supposed to be 173,316.

[2] Green's *History of England*.

APPENDIX

ADDITIONAL NOTES.

PAGE 13.

The tobacco trade, as early as 1621, was a source of revenue to James the First, King of England, as will be seen from the following correspondence of Lionel Cranfield, the Lord Treasurer, with Marquis of Buckingham.

"Chelsey July 21, 1621. The King's rent of £15,500 for tobacco, is in danger to be lost, or at best, to decline much, and all the money spent about the plantations of Virginia and Burmothes will be lost, if there be not some present course taken to restrain the planting of tobacco, here in England."

"December 4, 1621.

" I have agreed with the farmers of tobacco for this year, for £8000, and have told them to bring in but three score thousand weight, and have left the Virginia, and Bour moothes, free to bring in without restraint, and his Majesty to have the benefit of the impost. * * * * This is £2000 more than could be gotten by the Lords at Hampton Court * * * * * The Virginia and Burmoothes Company have no reason to complain, there being no restraint, but they left to free trade."

PAGE 20.

Capt. John Martin, councillor. At a meeting of the Virginia Company of London, held on February 3, 1622-3; "Sr John Brooke moued the Court in the behalfe of Capt. John Martin, that they would please accordinge to my Lord of South'tons promise, to graunt him a Patent with as ample priuileges as hath bin graunted to his L'p, or any other ancient Aduenturer, and that his shares of land menconed in his former Patent, or shall become due for transportacon of p'sons at his charge may be laide out in Martin Brandon, wch request the Court agreed unto hauinge alwaies offered as much unto him.

" But whereas Captaine Martin moued that he might haue therewith those Swamps and boggs as lay neare thereabout, wch for keepinge of his Swyne

The Court made him Aunsweare that he must be contented to take his due proporcon of land together, as it shall fall out in that place of Martin Brandon of wch as he saith, he was formerly possessed."

PAGE 22.

"THE COPPIE OF ABRAHAM PEIRSEY HIS WILL.

P. R. O.
Colonial
Papers.
Vol VIII
no. 5. 1.

In the name of God Amen, I Abraham Peirsey of Peirsey's hundred Esquire, being sicke in bodie but in perfect memory thankes be to the Everlasting God I doe by these presents ordeyne constitute and make this my last will and testament. First, I bequeath my soule unto my heavenly Father my Creator hopinge and surelie trustinge that by the meritts of his sonne Jesus Christ that all my sinns are wholelie and cleerlie washed away by the deer blood of my Saviour Christ Jesus, and that after this life I shall sett in glory with his Angells and for my corporall bodie I bequeath that to the earth from whence it came to be decentlie buryed with out any pompe or vayne glorie in the garden plott where my new frame doth stand.

Secondlie, I ordayne and appointe my deare and well beloved wife Francis Peirsey to be my absolute and sole executrix and also I doe earnestlie entreate my welbeloved frends Mr. Grevill Pooly Mynister and Mr. Richard Kingsmill of James Citty Island gentelmen to be my overseers in Virginia and to bee as helpetull and aydinge unto my executrix in all things to the uttermost of theire power which she shall stand in need of your helpes.

Thirdlie, I would have all my debtes both in Virginia and England to be paid as shall appeare by bond bill or by other good proofe in the lawe which I will sett downe in a scedull what debts in tobaccoes I owe & what is oweinge me. And further I ordeyne and appoynt my deare and welbeloved friend Mr. Delionell Russell of London Merchant to be another of my overseers for all businesses whatsoever doth concerne my executrix in England for the debts in England you shall receave from me a scedull thereof.

Fourthlie, I ordeyne and appoynt my executrix to make sayle of all my land housinge and other buildings whatsoever now doth or hereafter shall belonge to the aforesaid Abraham Peirsey either by purchase or by patent for men which I the said Abraham Peirsey have transported upon my owne charge and also so much land as is due to me for divers servaunts which hath beene transported by me Abraham Peirsey sence my goeinge for England which was in the begininge of March 1620, of which servants I have not taken upp one foote of land for the men theire will appere how many there be for the women about eight. Also I will and ordeyne my executrix to make sayle of all the estate I the said Abraham hath in Virginia as namelie Servanuts cattle Hoggs corne tobacco and all other kinde of goods moveables or housell stuffe or chattels whatsoever which did nowe or at any tyme belonge to me Abraham Peirsey and that my executrix shall within two monthes after my decease deliver up to the Governor and counsell a true Inventorie in upon her oath of all my estate soe left as aforesaid and then my executrix shall imeadiatelie goe about with the helpe of the overseers aforesaid make saile of all the estate as aforesaid to the profitt it can be sould for. And beinge soe don I bequeathe as a legacye my debt being paid unto my sister Judath Smitheson in England twenty pounds sterlinge in money unto my brother John Peirsey twenty pounds sterlinge in money yf he be liveinge further I doe bequeath unto my two overseers Mr. Poly Mynister and Mr. Kingsmill unto each of them for their paynes the sum of three hundred pounds of the best tobacco which maketh six hundred pounds of the best tobacco to be paid unto them by my executrix when all my estate shall be brought into tobacco or money or both or else within eighteene mounthes after my death Also I bequeath as a legacie unto my deere friend in England Mr. Delionell Russell merchant the some of thirty pounds sterlinge to be paid him by my executrix within the space of two years for his paynes which he is to take in the behalfe of my executrix and my childrens estate which I should dispose unto them notwithstandinge he is to have factoridge for all busines cominge to his hands.

Also I bequeath unto Nathaniell West sonne unto my deare beloved wife Francis Peirsey the some of Twenty pounds sterlinge money when he shall attayne the age of twenty-one yeares and not afore. Further I bequeath unto my dearelie beloved wife beinge my sole executrix my debts and legacies paid one-third part and one-twelfth part out of my estate aforesaid the other one-third part one-sixth part and one twelfth part of my estate remayninge I bequeath it to Elizabeth Peirsey and Mary Peirsey my daughters equally to be devised betwixt them within one yeare and a halfe after my decease to be consigned to Mr. Russell merchant as aforesaid in the best merchauntable tobacco for the use of my two children as aforesaid or else my executrix to make the said some good as aforesaid in the best tobacco out of her owne estate and that my two daughters aforesaid shall have sufficient diett lodgeinge washinge and apparell unto theire portions aforesaid be paid over unto Mr. Russell and they shipped carefully for England and to Mr. Russell the charges to goe out of their porcons and if either of my foresaid daughters doth marry without the consent of theire Mother in lawe and the consent of Mr. Delionell Russell both had togeather if it be possible to be had then for such account the other sister shall enjoy halfe the porcon soe not offending for better preferment but and if they both shall soe offend in that kinde then my will is that they shall have but halfe of the porcons before resited and the other to goe to my brother John Peirsey, yf any of my daughters should die before they attayne to be married my will is that the one should be heire to the other my will is that my children should remayne in the custody of my deare friend Mr. Russell till they be married and that theire porcons to be put forth to good men upon securitie for theire mayntenaunce. Thus not doubtinge that my deare wife Francis Peirsey my full and absolute executrix and my two overseers before mentioned will doe theire best endeavours for accomplishinge this my last will and testament written under my owne hand this first day of March 1626 [26-7, O. S.] and hereunto have fixed my seale and subscribed my name the day and yeare above written.

ABRAHAM PEIRSEY,
Seale.

Witnesses hereunto
Grenville Pooly
Cleric.
Vera copia
Ben Harryson
Ck Con.

PAGE 39.

Jabez Whitacre of the Council of 1626, was probably the brother of Alexander, the devoted clergyman at Henrico who about the year 1617, was drowned. The second wife of William Whitacre or Whitaker the head of Saint John's College, Cambridge, and father of Alexander, soon after husband's death, gave birth to a son, who was christened Jabez. See *Athenæ Cantabrigienses*, Cambridge, 1861.

PAGE 69.

The ministers of the lower parish of the Accomac County were first Francis Bolton. The next of whom we have any account is William Cotton, whose mother lived in Bunbury, Cheshire, England. He was a brother-in-law of William Stone the first Protestant Governor of Maryland. He had great trouble in collecting his tythes, and in proceedings instituted in court in 1634, for the recovery of them, is the following: "John Waltham aged 24, Randall Reuell 21 yeares & John Ford 25 yeares therabouts, sworne and examined say that they heard Henry Charlton say that if had had Mr. Cotton without the Church yeard he would have kict him ouer the Pallysados calling of him, black cotted raskoll. Upon the Complaynt of Mr. Cotton ag'st the s'yd Charleton, and the depositions aboue expressed it is ordered that the s'yd Charleton shall for the s'yd offence byuld a pare of stocks, and sitt in them three senerall Sabouth days in the time of Dyuine Seruis, and there aske Mr. Cotton forgiuencss."

The same yeare a babbling woman, see page 294, was dragged in King's Creek behind a canoe, and then obliged to go to Mr. Cotton's church, and confess her sin. There was no formal organization of a vestry in Accomac until 1635, and in September a parsonage was ordered to be erected, of wood, 40 feet wide and 18 feet deep, and 9 feet to the valley, with a chimney at each end, and upon each side a room, one for a study, and the other for a "buttery."

Cotton died in 1640, and his successor was John Rozier. One of the colonists in his will calls him his "dear and respected friend," and John Holloway a physician bequeaths to him a folio Greek Testament. Nathaniel Eaton the first Principal of Harvard, when he fled from Cambridge, Massachusetts, came to

APPENDIX. 407

Accomac, and for a time assisted Rozier in ministerial duties. Thomas Palmer succeeded Rozier, and John Armourier was the next minister of the parish, and he was followed as early as 1651, by Thomas Higby who married the widow of John Wilkins, vestryman. Before 1655, Higby died, and Francis Doughty, a brother-in-law of Governor Stone and non-conformist, is called in 1656, in the will of Ann, the widow of Col. Nathaniel Littleton, "Minister and Preacher of ye word, in this parish" now in Northampton County. On June 8, 1657, Doughty issued the following: "To all xtian people to whome this present wrightinge shall come.

"Knowe yce that whereas there is a marriage to bee had and solemnized between me ffrancis Doughty of Northampton County in Virginia & Ann Eaton of ye same County, and yt the s'd ffrancis Doughty may by virtue of marriage haue or expect to haue a right or interest " in her estate, "do disowne and discharge all right, to her estate, and to her children."

It is thought that the widow was the second wife of Nathaniel Eaton whom he had deserted, when he went to England.

When Governor Berkeley fled to Accomac, another non-conformist was preacher in the lower parish, as the following correspondence indicates

"Whereas Mr. Daniel Richardson o'r late minister, for want of orders, was found not orthodox, and therefore hired him from yeare to yeare (to supply the place of Minister so farr as the Lawes of England and this Countrey could make him capable) until wee could supply ourselves with an able, orthodox divine. And forasmuch as Mr. Isaac Key did present whom wee find very able and worthy wee of the Vestry & subscribers hereof doe certifye unto yor Honor that at a vestry the 8th day of May last past did discharge the said Richardson from his said ministry as may fully appear by an order of the said Vestry there made, And have since made choice of the said Mr. Isaac Key for o'r minister who hath accepted, and most willingly promised to serve, Wherefore wee hereby request yor Honor's confirmacon by Inducting him into this o'r parish as minister, And yor supplycants shall ever pray.

JOHN STRINGER
WILLIAM KENDALL
WILLIAM WATERS.
JOHN ROBINS
JAMES PIGOT "

"To which, Governor Berkeley, assents, in these words: This worthy learned Gent. Mr. Key is soe well knowne to me, that I am most certaine you will be happy in haueinge soe deseruing a person to officiate to you & aduise and comfort you in all yor spirituall wants and necessityes, and I doe require that he bee immediately Inducted

Nov. 18, 1676.   WILLIAM BERKELEY."

Richardson was living in 1680, in Somerset County, Maryland.

APPENDIX.

PAGE 71.

Chene Boise or Cheney Boys was probably a relative of Capt. Isaac Bargrave, the first person with Captain Ward, in 1618, to establish a private plantation in Virginia. Doctor Bargrave, Dean of Canterbury, was the brother of Isaac and the successor of John Boys in the Deanery who had married his sister. In the first Legislative Assembly of Virginia, in 1619, was a John Boys, and Cheney was no doubt a member of the same family. In Hotten's "Muster of 1625," Chene Boise is recorded as Chyna Boyse, living at Charles City, and then 26 years of age, and as having arrived in May, 1617, in the "George."

PAGE 79.

Reference is not to Gusman the Spanish Spy, as mentioned on page 79, but to the hero of the Spanish romance by Mateo Alemon of Seville, called Guzman de Alfarache the Rogue.

It was translated into English, by James Mabbe, a graduate of Oxford, Secretary to Sir John Digby afterwards Earl of Bristol, when on an embassy to Spain. The following entries are in the Registers of Stationers' Hall. Under date of February 28, 1620-1, was entered. "A booke called the first part of the life of Gusman of Alfarach written in Spain by Matthew Aleman, and translated into English by J. M: provided it is not to be printed unless translation be allowed."

Under date of August 21, 1622, was entered "A booke called The Second part of the life of Gusman de Alfarach by Matthew Aleman" Ben Jonson in some verses upon the translation writes.

> "For tho' Spaine gave him his first care and vogue
> He would be called hereafter, the English Rogue."

The hero of the romance begins his career as a scullion in Madrid, then became an errand boy, steals and hides himself in Toledo, when he acts the gentleman, then returns to Madrid and cheats his creditors.

PAGE 81.

Gov. Winthrop of Massachusetts was informed on April 30, 1631, by his son in London, that a contract had been made with Capt. Claiborne then in that city to bring grain to Boston, and he mentions that "the ship that bringeth it wch is the "Africa," whereof, Capt. Cleyborne is commander.

In the proceedings of Accomac Court, under date of May 4, 1635, appears the following: "Were you Richard Thompson with Capt. Wm. Clayborne in the ship called the "Affrica" at the post of Susquehanna in the Bay of Chesapioque about September in the year 1631?"

Thompson then 23 years of age, replied that he was not in the ship, but in a boat, at the post, "a littell before the fall of the leaffe" and did see Capt. Claborne trading with the Indians

APPENDIX.

PAGE 82.

Daniel, brother of Sir Vincent Gookin, was married in 1609, to Mary, daughter of Richard Bird. His son Daniel was born in 1612, and about 1639, he was married a second time, to Mary Dolling of St. Sepulchre's Parish, London, aged about 21 years. After her death he married Hannah, who was a widow Savage, and daughter of Edward Tyng of Massachusetts. Upon February 1, 1630, Daniel Gookin, Junior, conveys to Thomas Addison, late servant of Daniel his father, 150 acres above Newport News, at the place called " Marie's Mount "

PAGE 90.

Charles Harmar also written Harmer, by following the careless transcription of Hotten, appears in this volume as Harman was the son of John Harmar, Warden of Winchester. He was an enterprising planter at Magothy Bay of the Eastern Shore, and a prominent man. When only twenty-four years of age, he came, in 1622, in the ship " Furtherance," to Virginia. His brother John, born at Chursdon, Gloucestershire, was a graduate of Magdalene College, Oxford, and a distinguished scholar and clergyman, having translated into Greek and Latin the Westminster Catechism. In 1653, he delivered an address at Oxford, to Oliver Cromwell, and by the influence of Richard Cromwell, in 1659, was chosen Greek professor, but lost the professorship, after the return of Charles the Second.

Charles Harmar in 1635, entered land because of the transportation of eight negroes, and the following white servants: Evan Jones, Thomas Cole, James Courtney, Lazarus Manning, Thomas Davis, Richard Wyett, John Symons, Richard Newton, Elizabeth Burnett, Rebecca Slaughter, Mary Chest. He died before A. D. 1644, as 150 acres were granted on the 17th of September of this year to Eliza, daughter and heir to said Charles Harmar, and on May 1, 1654, this land was assigned by Thomas Harmar the son of Dr. John the Greek professor, who calls himself the heir of Eliza Harmar, to Nathaniel Littleton.

In the Northampton County Records the widow of Charles Harmar is said to have married a Captain Littleton.

Obedience Robins, born A. D. 1601, was with Charles Harmar, a member in 1632, of the first County Court of Accomac, and was a brother of Richard of Northamptonshire, and of Edward a merchant in Accomac. His name and associations seem to indicate that he was of Puritan affinities. His wife was the widow of Edward Waters, one of the two ship-wrecked persons, who in 1610, refused to leave the Bermudas, with Sir Thomas Gates and Sir Geo. Somers, being pleased with the island. In 1618, the ship "Diana" arrived at the Bermudas and among the passengers was Grace O'Neil then a girl sixteen years old. She became the wife of Waters and they then removed to Elizabeth City, now Hampton, Virginia, where their first child, William was born, who became an active citizen of Northampton County. Before A.D., 1628, Edward Waters died, and his widow married Obedience Robins. In February, 1633, William Cotton, minister of the parish, complained to the Accomac Court, that Robins had refused to issue warrants for the minister's tithes.

Edward Robins, merchant in Accomac and brother of Obedience died in July, 1641, and his daughter Rachel married Richard Beard, and Elizabeth became the wife of William Burgess. After William Stone of Northampton became its first Protestant Governor, Beard and Burgess removed to Maryland. Beard made the first map of Annapolis and belonged to the people "in scorn called Quakers," and Burgess was in sympathy with Cromwellians at least, for a period. Jane the wife of George Puddington a member of the Maryland Assembly, from Ann Arundel County, in 1650, was a sister-in-law of Obedience Robins. Mountjoy Evelin, the second son of George formerly of Kent Island, Maryland, married in 1653, Dorothy the third child of Obedience and Grace Robins.

Thomas Higby the then minister, was complained of by Obedience Robins because he had abused him. Probably Robins, had as in 1633, been negligent as to the minister's tithes, he died in 1662, but his widow Grace lived twenty years longer.

PAGE 97.

William Cotton, minister, on October 25, 1634, complained to Accomac Court, that the administrator of Capt. John Stone, deceased, had not paid tithes.

PAGE 121.

Among the Records of Northampton County, Va., is the following order from Claiborne.

"The Marylanders have taken my pinnace the Long Tayle with her company and some others of my men trading in other places; Philip Taylor go to Patow. meeks and Patuxent. Given at Kent, eleventh of May, 1635."

In subsequent years Jane, the widow of Philip Taylor, married William Eltonhead of Maryland. Taylor, in 1635, was 24 years of age.

PAGE 128.

Francis Pott, and his nephew John, in 1647, had a plantation at Magothy Bay, and in 1654, a Francis Pott was sheriff of Northampton County.

PAGE 135.

Rawl MS., A. 271 fo. 30.

A COPPY OF DR. COXE'S TITLE HE CLAIMES IN NORFFOLK COUNTY.

This indenture made the 22d Jany Anno Dom: 1637, and in ye 13th year of or Sou'r: Lord Charles by ye Grace of God King of England, Scotland ffrance & Ireland Defender of ye faith, &c., Between Sr. John Harvey Knt. Gou'r for ye time being of the Colony of Virginia with ye Consent of ye Councel of State of ye same, on ye one part, and the Rt. Honble Henry Lord Matravers of ye other part WITNESSETH that whereas it hath pleased the King's most excellent majtie by his royal letters bearing date ye 11th day of April in ye 13th year of his Majts reign to authorize & comand me ye sd Sr. John Harvey wth ye sd Counce to assign & sell unto ye sd Henry Lord Matravers & his heires for euer a competent tract of Land in ye Southern part of ye Colony to beare a name of a County & be called ye County of Norfolk upon such conditions for ye time & manner of planting it as shall be found requisit for ye General good of ye Colony, and wth such powers and priviledges as may be fitt for a person of his quality, Reseruing to his majtie his heires & successors ye yearly rent 20s. to be paid by ye sd Lord Matravers & his heires for ye said County.

Now KNOW yee that ye sd Sr. John Harvey Knt. Govr. & Capt. Gentt of Virginia wth the Consent of ye sd Councel of State By virtue of his majt's said royal Letters to me & ye sd Councel directed, and in Consideration of ye undertaking of the said Henry Lord Matravers to transport at his own Costs and charges & to settle & plant diuers Inhabitants in ye Colony for ye advancemt. & General good of ye Plantation Haue Granted allotted assigned & confirmed ye said Henry Lord Matravers & his heires for euer a certaine Territory & Tract of Land situate Lying & being on the southern side of James River in the Branch of ye sd River hereafter to be called Matravers River, towards the head of ye sd Nanzinum ats Matravers River being bounded from that part of Nanzimum River ats Matravers River where it diuides it self into Branches one degree in Longitude on either side of ye River and in Latitude to ye height of 35 Degrees Northerly Latitude by ye name and appellation of ye County of Norfolk. And further I ye said Sr. John Harvey Knt. wth the consent of ye sd Councel do grant & agree to and wth ye sd Henry Lord Matravers & his heires that when he or they haue planted & peopled ye aboue menconed tract of Land hereby to him & his heirs assigned & appointed that then it shall be lawfull for him ye sd Lord Matravers or his heires to make choice of & to enter into & haue as much more Land in Virginia as is herein contained. With ye same & ye like priviledges to be had & chosen in such place & places where no English shall be then settled or Inhabitted or haue made choice of & the same granted to them either by Patent or order of Court to haue and to hold ye aboue menconed Tract of Land according to ye Limits & bounds thereof as also all & singular the Lands to be chosen as aforesaid with their & euery of their appurtces with all mines, as well Royal mines of Gold & silver as other Mines & Minerals woods fiishings ffowlings waters Rivers & all other profits comodities & hereditamts whatsoeuer wth in ye prcincts of ye aforesd Territory or tract of Land as to the aforesd Lands to be chosen unto ye sd Henry Lord Matravers & his heirs for euer. In as large & ample manner any Grants haue hereto fore been made to any adventurers or undertakers whatsoeuer, either by ye Late treasurer & Company or at at any time since To be held of o'r sd Sou'r Lord the King his heirs & Successors as of his mannor of East Greenwich in free & comon Soccage by fealty, and not in Capite nor by Knts seruice. Yielding & paying unto our said Sou'r Lord ye King his heires and Successers for euer

APPENDIX.

one-fifth part of ye said ore ye Mines of Gold & Silver which shall be found within ye limits of ye sd Tract of Land & County of Norfolk and ye Lands to be chosen and taken up as aforesd And likewise yielding & paying unto or sd Sou'r Lord the King his heires & Successrs for ye sd County of Norfolk the yearly Rent of 20. shill at ye feast of St. Michael ye Archangel unto ye hands of his Majts Treasurer of Virginia to begin after ye expiration of ye first seuen yeares after ye date hereof and further it shall be lawfull to & for ye sd Henry Lord Matravers or his heires his or their tenants & seruants & such as he or they shall contract with or send or Imploy for ye sd County to go and return trade & traffick wth ye Natives or otherwise within ye Limitts of ye Colony Also to Import & transport their goods & merchandizes at their will and pleasures paying only such duties to ye Kings Majts heires & Successrs as ye sd late treasurer & Company did, or ought to haue paid (vizt.) five pounds per cent for all imported Goods & five pounds per cent: for all Exported Goods wth out any other taxes imposicons, burdens or Restraints upon them to be Imposed otherwise than by ye Grant or Consent by Grand Assembly of ye General Colony of Virginia & for ye publick necessary seruice thereof And It is further granted & agreed that ye persons to be transported shall not be taken away nor comanded either by ye Gov'r for ye time being of Virginia or any other Authority there, from the business & employmt of ye sd Henry Lord Matrauers or his heires & others contracted with & employed as aforesd upon any pretence whatsoeuer (necessary defence of ye Country, Preseruation of ye peace suppressing tumults ariseing wthin ye Land & tryals in matters of Justice in Criminal Cases of life & death, or in civil Laws by appeal only excepted) And ye sd Sr Jno Harvey with the Consent of ye Councel aforesd do further agree to & with ye sd Henry Lord Matravers & his heires that It shall be Lawfull to & for ye sd Henry Lord Matravers & his heires to make & Ordaine such Officers & Comanders, Also to name & fframe such Orders Ordinauces & constitutions from time to time for ye Rule & Govormnt. Ordering & directing of all persons to be transported & settled within ye sd County so that ye sd Orders Ordinauces & constitutions be not repugnant to ye Laws of England or to the particular Laws of the Colony as to such Orders and Instructions as shall be from time to time directed from ye King Majistie or from ye Lords of his Majts most Honble privy Councel to the Govern'r & Councel in Virginia (ordinary appeals to ye Court at James City held by the Governs and Councel only Excepted) and the sd Lord Matravers for him & his heires doth Coven't & agree so & wth ye sd Govr & Councel that he or they shall & will with in ye time or terme of seuen yeares from ye date hereof plant & secure with a sufficient strength of people the said County of Norfolk herein by these presents Granted And further that ye sd Henry Lord Matravers or his heires shall from time to time dureing the said seven yeares make or cause to be made a true Certificate to the Gouernour & Councel in Virginia for the time being of euery person transported and Landed in Virginia or shipped for Virginia and dying before arrival to be entered by his Majts Secretary in Virginia in the

Court Rolls kept at James City. In witness whereof I the said Sr. John Harvey Knight, Govern'r haue to the one part of these present Indentures sett his hand and the seal of the Colony and to the other part thereof the said Henry Lord Matravers hath sett to his hand and seal.

PAGE 136.

George Ludlow on February 20, 1642-3 gave a deed for a house to Argall Yeardley, and Nathaniel Eaton the minister, and formerly of Harvard College, Cambridge, Mass., was one of the witnesses, see Northampton County Records.

Roger Ludlow who came to Virginia in 1654, was a brother of George, and there was another brother Gabriel, whose children were in England. George Ludlow of York County, and parish, became a member of the Council in Virginia in 1642, and in 1655, not long before his death was a member of that body.

In his will, he gives legacies to the children of Roger, his brother, namely, Jonathan, Joseph, Roger, Anne, Mary and Sarah. The codicil to his will was dated October 23, 1655, and the children are called minors. Jonathan was at that time in Dublin, Ireland, where resided Nathaniel Brewster, a minister, one of the first graduates of Harvard, whose wife was a Sarah Ludlow, probably the sister of George and Roger. Sarah Ludlow supposed to have been the daughter of Roger, was the last wife of John Carter of Virginia, and her son Robert, born in 1661, was the large slave holder known as King Carter.

Colonel Daniel Park, Jr., married a Miss Ludlow of Green Spring. Col. George Ludlow in his will, an abstract of which is given by H. F. Waters in *N. E. Hist. Gen. Register* for July, 1886, bequeaths to George, the son of Col. William Bernard, his great silver tankard with his arms on it, and to George, son of Capt. Richard Webster, of Jamestown, a silver tankard that had been brought in 1655, by Mr. Bowler. At the time the will was made, there was living at his house in York Parish, a Rebecca Hurst in the capacity of housekeeper or privileged servant, whom his nephew Thomas, son of Gabriel, proposed to marry, and it is provided that if he carries out his intention, all bequeathed to him shall go to Jonathan, son of George.

PAGE 142.

Before going to Maryland Capt. William Hawley as early as A.D. 1644, lived in Northampton County, Virginia.

PAGE 144.

Until the year 1635, there had been no formal organization of a church vestry in Accomac County. William Cotton whose mother, Joane, resided at Bunbury in Cheshire, England, was then, minister, and after his death, in 1640, John Rozier, became the preacher, and was a respectable person. Rozier employed Nathaniel Eaton as an assistant, and owing to a difference between them,

Nathaniel Littleton, Obedience Robins, John Neale, and John Gookin were appointed arbitrators, and they on March 23, 1642-3, decided that Rozier should pay six hundred pounds of tobacco to Eaton ; and that the next year the vestry should pay him that amount. Eaton left in 1646, and that there is record of a suit brought in January, 1646-7, against the estate of Nathaniel Eaton, Clerk, that is clericus, clergyman. See *Note to Page* 69.

PAGE 149.

Abstract of George Donne's Essay " *Virginia Reviewed* " among the Harleian Manuscripts 7021, fol. 289, in the British Museum.

It begins " Most sacred and most gracious Sir : The Benefitts they are greate. The blessings wherewith yor People have beene fedd since yor possession of yor inheritance ye Crowne are to all Nations an Admiartion (admiration) with an Envy. Peace and plenty setled in the trueth of Religion, flourishing by the Establishment of an Empire." After a few more fulsome sentences, several pages are devoted to " a search into antiquities for succession of their names who first by land, and afterwards by Sea attended as well their labours, by conquering, as their diligence by opening unknowne Countries."

The essay then gives four reasons for the discovery of new countries, and the foundation of colonies, namely " Enlargement of the Church, employment of shipps, maintenance of artificers & mariners, & increase of treasure to King and Kingdom."

Twenty-one reasons are then given why Virginia " hath undergone a disreputed fame." There is then considered the danger of surprisal by the Spaniards and the defence of the colony. Next the duties of Governors of Colonies are pointed out, and the proper kind of immigrants described. In this connection follows the criticism upon New England which appears on pages 148, 149 of this volume. Maryland is then praised for its fertility and Lord Baltimore commended for " siding with our endeavors in Virginia."

The author in concluding the essay " his first presumption & very likely his last " writes :

" Concerning one chief poynt why I onely undergoe a censure by Entrance on the buisiness of Virginia after soe manie interested in it, since the first Plantation, why I alone should seeme to bee wise, whilse others more instructed keep silence, I pleaded by way of answere, as did one, long since, in Salust. Those things they heard, or read, I p'sonally have seene, and done what they have learned by Information, I have tryed by action, and experience, beinge soe much the more capable of what I p'sent as deeds and proofs are before words and intimations * * * * * I have submitted these few papers to yor Majesty (as free from Affectation, as full of Affection.)

" The Memory of yor gracious, excellent, singular favours to my father in his life, and unto his end, requires the best of my services, if I deserve the honor of being acknowledged his sonne, or the greater, of living under yor scepter. The bounty of your Grace to myself during my imprisonment in Spaine, freely granted. * * * * In all duty, endeavors to bee knowne amongst yor most Faithfull, yor Majesties

Most humble subject
GEORGE DONNE."

PAGE 151.

Perhaps a relative of Christopher Wormeley; one Ralph Wormeley, about 1644, married the widow of Luke Stebbins, merchant, upon the Eastern Shore of Chesapeake Bay.

PAGE 152.

On the 20th of January, 1644-5, dame Elizabeth Harvey asked the Court to substitute Richard Kemp and Captain William Peirce as trustees in place of Capt. Samuel Mathews, Capt. D. Gookin, George Ludlow and Capt. Thomas Bernard, former trustees, under a feoffment, made by the said dame Elizabeth for the use of Samuel Stevens gent., her son by a former marriage.

PAGE 181.

After Chapter 6th was printed there were found in the Northampton County Records, two letters from William Webb of London, dated July 20, 1642, one letter directed "to my worthy friend Mr. Thomas Copley at his plantation in Maryland;" the other, "To his Noble Reverend Mr. Andrew White, Esq., att Maryland." These letters mention that Sir Edmund Plowden was about to sail for America. These letters have been printed in the Pennsylvania Historical Society Magazine.

An account appears in the Records with the following items.

"Sir Edmund Plowden.

Dr. to Edw: Mathews

1643. ffor takinge flower Depositions att the Soxochar, aff, and cop. attested under my hand wch Sir Edm. Plowden p'tended to carry for England, the busines a description of New Albion	lb. tob. 150
ffor searching several Books att yt office in Jamestowne, and transcribinge Cop. of manuscripts here described, to have to testifye to his friends in England,	150."

In October, 1640, Plowden was still in prison for contempt of Court, in refusing to pay his wife's alimony. It was not long after his release when he went to America.

APPENDIX.

PAGE 187.

Captain Robert Moryson in a deposition, upon record in Northampton County, mentions that during the year, 1644, his ship left Smith's Island for England by way of Dublin, Ireland, and that Captain "Clayborne" and his wife, and Capt. Philip Taylor were passengers.

PAGE 194.

Lt. Thomas Rolfe, Campbell mentions upon the authority of Richard Randolph, as having married a Miss Poythers who had an only daughter Jane, which was also the name of John Rolfe's last white wife. Jane married Robert Bolling upon whose tombstone in Prince George County was this inscription: "Here lyeth interred in the hope of a joyful resurrection the body of Robert Bolling, the son of John & Mary Bolling of All Hallows, Barkin Parish, Tower Street, London. He was born on the 26th day of December in the year 1646, and came to Virginia October 2, 1660, and departed this life the 17th day of July 1709, aged 62 yeares, six months, and twenty-one days."

PAGE 195.

Capt. Roger Marshall had lived in Northampton County, and Ann the wife of Col. Nathaniel Littleton had stood as god-mother at the christening of his eldest son.

PAGE 201.

William Stone, Governor of Maryland, was in 1633, a resident of Accomac County, as the whole Eastern Shore was then called, whose commissioners were William Claiborne, Obedience Robins, William Stone, William Burdett, John Wilkins, and William Andrews.

In September, 1635, he was a vestryman, and at a meeting when his brother-in-law the minister William Cotton, was allowed a parsonage which was to be 18 × 40 ft. with a chimney at each end, and annexed to that chimney a room, "one for a study" the other for a "buttery." In 1640, he held land "between Mattawomex and Hungar's Creek." On the 27th of October, 1640, he was a witness to an agreement as were also Nathaniel Littleton, and Nathaniel Eaton the minister of unsavory reputation. In 1646, he was sheriff of Northampton County, and his under sheriff was Thomas Hatton, without doubt, the same who in 1648, with his wife and two sons Robert and Thomas went to Maryland. Job Chandler, a brother of Samuel a merchant of London, was at this time in Northampton, and afterwards was a Maryland councillor. Francis Doughty the nonconformist minister was the Governor's brother-in-law. Verlinda, daughter of William Cotton the minister and his wife Anna, married Thomas Burdett, who settled in Charles County, Maryland, in 1658, she was a widow residing at Nanjemie where Governor Stone, also lived. Verlinda her aunt, was the Governor's wife. In 1653, the Governor sold his house, at Hungar's Creek, Virginia to Capt. William Whittington. Joane, the mother of the clergyman Cotton, lived at Bunbury, Cheshire, England.

APPENDIX. 417

PAGE 207.

Major Philip Stevens was given by the Council of State of England, by an order, dated August 10, 1650, "£50, as a reward for his sufferings in Virginia." While William Stevens was an officer under Waller, there is no evidence that he came to Virginia, as assumed on page 207. Philip was probably the person who, with Norwood, was ship-wrecked.

There was however a William Stevens in Accomac before 1642, who came out as the servant of John Seavern, surgeon and is called a carpenter. He is probably the same person as William of Pingoteague who died in 1663, and whose son was also named William. The widow of the elder William was named Ann and she married a Wilson, the wife of the son William was named Priscilla. The Col. William Stevens who went to Maryland may have been a different person.

PAGE 209.

A John Custis, in 1657, married the widow of Peter Walker.

PAGE 210.

Sir Thomas Lunsford's wife was Catherine, daughter of Sir Henry Neville, Kt. and his wife Elizabeth the child of Sir John Smith of Osterhanger, Kent. The General Court at James City, October 12, 1670, refer to Lunsford as deceased, and three daughters in England, and "Katherine" in Virginia.

PAGE 210.

Major Henry Norwood was imprisoned in the Tower, London, in January, 1654–5, and owing to his poverty, on Sept. 23, 1657, 10 shillings a week were allowed to him. Burton in his "Diary" under date of March 16th, 1658–9 writes: "Major Norwood is at liberty by virtue of an order of his Highness and his Council * * * Mr. Norwood not to come to England, without leave."

After the accession of Charles the Second, he was one of the officers of the forces which reduced the Dutch at Manhattan, and in 1665, he returned to England and Governor Nicoll of New York recommended him as his successor, because he was a person, "whose temperament would be acceptable both to the soldiers and the country."

Richard Fox who arrived at Jamestown in the winter of 1650, with Norwood, seems to have gone back with him to England, as on June 22d, the Council of State ordered that "Richard Fox be discharged from prison on condition that he leaves town in four days, and to be of good behaviour."

PAGE 211.

Aubrey in "in Bodleian Letters" referring to Davenant's residence in France has this language: "Here he layed an ingeniose designe to carry a considerable number of artificers (chiefly weavers) from hence to Virginia, and by Mary the Queen mothers meanes he got favour from the King of France, to goe into the prisons, and pick, and choose, and when the poor damned wretches knew what the designe was they cryed *uno ore* 'Tont Tisseran.' We are all weavers. Well [he took] 36 as I remember, and shipped the , and as he was on his voyage towards Virginia, he and his Tisseran, were all taken by the ships, then, belonging to the Parliament."

His commission came into the hands of the Puritan minister formerly of Virginia, and upon November 10, 1652, the Council of State directed " Thomas Harrison, minister of St. Dunstan's in the East, London, to bring to Council, the commission lately granted by Charles Stuart to William Davenant, to have command in some English plantation, in America."

PAGE 212.

Edmund Scarborough was one of the early merchants of Accomac and Northampton Counties. In 1651, he sent a vessel into the Delaware River to trade with the Indians, which was stopped at Fort Nassau nearly opposite Philadelphia, by the Dutch commander Andreas Hudde. He was a royalist in his sympathies, and a friend of Gov. Berkeley. The following is among the Northampton Records:

"Collonell Littleton

" I pray (vpon sight hereof) deliuer vnto Mr. Edmund Scarbrugh Towe [two] of yor best Ewe Lambe wch I have giuen him, for his Daughters Tabitha & Matilda, charge ye same to Accott, fr

"yor Llovinge frend

" April 10, 1652.   WILLIAM BERKELEY."

Col. Obedience Robins, in February, 1653, entered the following protest against an outrageous proceeding of Scarborough. " Capt. John Jacob a High Germayne of Frankendall in the palatiate, who in ye yeare 1651, engaged to ye State of England & embarked himselfe theire in a London or New England shipp whereof Capt. Rich: Thurston was comandr & with a good quantitye of English goods came into New England, and thence with Mr. Cuttin vnto Severne [now Annapolis] & returned to New England with John Bennett vnto Boston, in New England, and by unfailable testimony imployed vnto Virginia by Mr. Samll Mauericke, Mr. Robert Knight & Mr. Nathll Gardner three principal mrchants liuinge in Boston in New England came vnto mee, and complayned that beinge in a New England vessell belonginge vnto ye aboue Mr. Rob't Knight, at Nominy in patomack Riuer att Anker, in a small creeke, aground there, came a vessell called ye Hobby horse belonging vnto & sett forth by Left Coll. Edm. Scarburgh wth eight armed men ; & in his absence did seize his vessel as they s'd for the State of England.

" Towe [two] of his men being Aboard And hee about half a Howre after, came on board, and finding these five men armed, hee demanded their intent, they answered they seized the vessell & goods for ye State of England, wherevpon hee asked them if they had a comission soe to doe, they replyed he should see it, then he s'd that not only his vessel but his Body alsoe was readdy to doe ye State seruice, but afterwarde Hee tould them, that if they came to take any vessell without a commission they were pirate, wherevpon they grew to hard words & one of them presente I a pistol att him, and as hee presented itt, afterward confessed had not his mayster Mark Magge stept between them, he had shott him, hee seeing a pistoll cockt att him stept into ye cabbin & fetched out a gunn & towe of ye men took hold of ye gun, until ye ten named Rich. Wayman strucke him ouer ye head with ye butt end of his gun & very sore wounded him, the other wth his pistoll cockt ready to fyre vpon him. And soe viollently carryed away his vessell & disposed of most of his goodes, at their pleasure. And when he had desiered them to lett ye goods alone, they tould him, hee had a knock vpon one side of his head already & if hee would not be quiett they would knock his brayne out, or ye other side. Hee therefore desired mee to go with him & p'test against their proceedinges; his s'd vessell being brought into or Harbour, and the stearue of the ship 'Speadwell' of Bristoll, Capt. peter Wraxall being commander thereof, who had giuen a coppie of his commission from ye Admiralty of England vnto Left. Coll. Edm. Scarburgh By wch power hee sett forth his Hobby Horse on the 26th daye of this instant moneth. I went aboard ye aforesaid ship 'Speedwell.' And in the name of the Keepers of the Libertye of England, by authority of Parlim't did require of Mr. Dauis Maysters Mate of ye shipp the s'd vessell & goods to be deliuered vnto mee, ye Capt. John Jacob, and hee ye s'd Mr. Dauis replyed, ansorde that hee had orders from Capt. Wraxall not to deliuer her vnto any person or persons whatsoever, and vntil he had further orders he would not deliuer."

In the investigation which took place, Mark Magge the Master of the Hobby Horse deposed that he came down from Ockahannock and found the New England vessel by the Mills, and that after they were anchored by the "Bristol ship," came aboard Argall Yeardley, Obedience Robins, Capt. John Stringer, and Mr. Lamberton, and as they were leaving the chirurgeon abused the master, and said "that he had a horse at home, and thought to bring, but he was afraid they would have made him a Colonel, Major, or Justice of the Peace" and that he further declared, "that most all of them here were Rogues or whores, or vagabonds, or theives, or beggars, and many other scandalous names."

Col. Scarborough in consequence of this and other actions, for a time left the country. He died in 1671, and left a widow Mary, and son Charles. His sons-in-law were John West, and Devereux Browne. The administrators of his estate were Col. Kendall, Capt. John Custis, William Custis, and Major William Anderson.

PAGES 226, 256.

Austine or Augustine Warner of the Assembly of 1652, whose eldest son was born October 20, 1643, was named also Augustine, and in 1658, was enrolled a pupil of the Merchant Tailors' School, London.

Milred Warner his sister, married Lawrence, son of John Washington the immigrant. Mildred Washington was left a widow, with three children, John, Augustine, and Mildred. She afterwards married George Gale, and was buried in January 1700-1, at St. Nicholas Church, White Haven, Cumberland, England. Mildred's son Augustine, was the father of George Washington, the first President of the Republic.

PAGE 233.

Roger Green was alive in 1671, and designated in the records of the General Court, as "preacher." On the 23d of November, 1671, the Court ordered the vestry of the parish of James City, to pay to Green, 12,000lb of tobacco, for the accommodation of Mr. Samuel Jones, minister of the parish. See p. 244.

PAGE 235.

The Reverend and learned Samuel Drisius preached perhaps during this visit as Commissioner from Manhattan. In May 1654, in a deposition, Sarah the wife of John Hunman, incidentally mentions that, "the last Sabbath Mr. Drisius preached here [Northampton County] this deponent, her husband and daughter went to Richard Jacobs."

PAGE 231.

Thomas Mallory, Dean of Chester, was not the same person as Thomas Mallory, the London minister at a later date. The Dean was the son of Sir William Mallory, of Stewdley, Yorkshire, and after being in Mobberley for a number of years, he went to Chester and at the age of 78, in April, 1644, died, and was buried in the Cathedral.

PAGE 245.

Samuel Butler the author of "Hudibras" was alive at the time of the Indian troubles, and fond of far-fetched allusions, thus refers to the Indian chief Tottopottomoy.

"Our brethren of New England use
Choice malefactors to excuse,
And hang the guiltless in their stead
Of whom the churches have less need
As lately 't happened: in a town
There lived a cobler, and but one,
That out of doctrine could not use,
And mend men's lives as well as shoes,
This precious brother having slain
In times of peace, an Indian,
Not out of malice, but mere zeal
Because he was infidel
The mighty Tottippottimoy
Sent to our elders an envoy
Complaining sorely of the breach."

APPENDIX. 421

Page 254.

William Eltonhead, of Maryland, the brother-in-law of Henry Corbyn, may have been the same person who married Jane, the widow of Philip Taylor, a Burgess of Northampton County in 163-, and a former associate of Claiborne.

Page 255.

Hancock, son of Richard Lee, who married the granddaughter of William Brewster, the leader of the Puritan Colony at Plymouth Rock, was in 1677, one of the Commissioners of Northampton County, and was in the county in 1682, in 1688 he was a resident of Northumberland County and built the place called Ditchley.

Page 256.

See page 226.

Page 275.

On May 6, 1650, a pass was issued " for Sir Henry Moodie and Francis Lovelace, with six servants, to Long Island, they subscribing the engagement."

Page 287.

Anthony Langston prepared a letter on the condition of Virginia, and especially the need of Iron works, which is among the Egerton MSS. of the British Museum.

Page 290.

Among the Egerton MSS. is also preserved the Remonstrance of Virginia, dated March 28, 1663, and signed by Berkeley, Francis Moryson, Thomas Ludwell, Sec. Richard Lee, Nathaniel Bacon, Ab: Wood, John Carter, Edward Carter, Theodore Bland, Thomas Stegge, and Henry Corbyn, protesting against the grant of lands to certain Lords.

Page 293.

The letters of Governor Berkeley to the Virginia Assembly in 1659-60, and to Charles the Second after the Restoration are in footnote of Chapter Nine, on pages 352, 353.

A.

Abbe, Thomas, 23.
Abbot, Archbishop, describes George
  Calvert, 63.
  Maurice, Va. Commissioner, 12.
Abdy, Anthony, Va. Commissioner, 12.
Abraham, an Indian dies in London, 29.
Abrahall, Lt. Col. Robert, burgess, 269,
  349.
Accomac County, 177, 181.
  called Northampton, 169.
  first parsonage in, 406, 416.
  early ministers of 406, 407.
  church censures, 406.
  play actors, 315.
Addams, Ann, servant, 19.
Addison Alexander, 221.
  Thomas, 184, 409.
Adkinson, James, 221.
Africa, Claiborne's ship at Susquehanna,
  408.
Albemarle, Commissioners, 317.
Alciat, the poet, 46.
Aleman, Matthew, Spanish novelist, 408.
Alford, Richard, servant, 18.
Alfrach, the Rogue, a Spanish romance,
  79, 408
Allen, William, of London, 217.
  burgess, 72.
  servant, 23.
Allerton, Isaac, son-in-law of Puritan
  Brewster, 167, 255.
  Junior, 157; settles in Virginia,
  255; pursues Indians, 317, 387;
  daughter marries Hancock Lee, 421.

Alleyn, Richard, 221.
Ambrose, Alice, Quakeress, 299.
Anacostan Indians, 92.
Anderson, Major William, administrator
  of Edmund Scarborough's estate,
  419.
Andrews, William of Accomac, 221, 298,
  416.
  Junior, 221.
Angelo, negro slave, 35.
Anamessex, settlement, 300.
Anthonie, a servant, 20.
Antony, a negro, 40.
Appleton, Richard, 40.
Appomattox, region, 171, 192.
  Fort, 194.
Apsley, London merchant, 103.
Argall, Governor Samuel, 12, 19, 22,
  34; at Cadiz, 36, death of, 37.
  Ann, daughter of, 37.
Arlington, Lord Henry, 192, 307, 382,
  390.
  in Accomac, 208, 209.
Armenian silk workers in Va., 240.
Armested, Capt. Anthony, 349.
Armitadringe, Henry. 221.
Armourier, John, clergyman, 407.
Arnold, Anthony, sentenced to die,
  374.
Arundel Marbles, 135.
  Ann, servant, 16.
  John, a Justice, 90.
  Richard, servant, 16.
  Thomas, Earl of Surrey, 102, 134.
Assateague, Bay, 208.
  Indians, expedition against, 265.

424 INDEX.

Assembly of Virginia, claims supreme power, *pro tem*, 269.
  A. D., 1629, 71.
  1629-30, 77.
  1631-32, 88.
  1635, 118.
  1637-8, 138.
  1639-40, 145, 158.
  1642, 157.
  1644, 184.
  1645, 189.
  1645-6, 191.
  1646, 193.
  1647, 198.
  1649, 205.
  1650-51, 212.
  1652, April, 224.
  1652, November, 229.
  1653, 232.
  1654, 236.
  1655, 241.
  1656, 243.
  1657-58, 260.
  1658-59, 266.
  1659-60, 268.
  1660, October, 281.
  1662, 293.
  1663, 295.
  1664, 313.
  1665, 313.
  1666, 317.
  1667, 321.
  1668, 322.
  1669, 329.
  1670, 329.
  1676, 348, 360.
  1676-77, 373.
  1677, 385.
  1679, 386.
  1680, 390.
  1682, 398.
  1683, 397.
Ashmore, William, killed, 121.
Ashton, Capt. Peter, burgess, 269.
  (Aston) Walter, burgess, 90, 167, 171, 270.
Atkins, Richard, 348.
Ayers, John, 221.
Aylmer, Justinian, clergyman at Jamestown, 363.

B.

Babbling woman ducked, 406.
Bacon, Ann, daughter of the rebel, 369.
  Elizabeth, wife of the rebel, 243, 346, 351; her second marriage, 391; law-suit of, 392.
  Francis, Lord Verulam, letter from Capt. John Smith, 83.
  James, clergyman, 243.
  Nathaniel, son of James, his baptism 243; early life, 243; stepfather a Puritan minister in New England, 243; mention of, 260; 267, 269, 282, 288, 348, 360, 372, 397, 400.
  Nathaniel, son of Thomas, early life, 346; attacks Indians, 350, 351; suppresses Gov. Berkeley's declaration, 357; sails to Jamestown, 357; asks for pardon, 358; elected general, 360; proclaimed a rebel, 361; his appeal to the people, 361-363; captures Sir Henry Chicheley, 365; his death, 368; mention of 369; his widow, 391.
Bagwell, James, burgess, 193, 236.
  Thomas, burgess, 72.
Bailife, George, servant, 17.
Baily, Richard, 221,
  Robert, 221.
  Symon, 221.
Baker, Alexander, metallurgist, 105.
  Daniel, 221.
  Lawrence, burgess, 318.
  William, servant, 18.
Baldry, Robert, burgess, 269.
Baldwin, John, servant, 17.
Baley, Temperance, 42.
Ball, William, burgess, 193, 349; family of, 259.
Ballard, Thomas, burgess, 317, 318, 360, 363, 370.
Baltimore, The Lords, see *Calvert*.
Bamford, John, servant, 23.
Banks, Sir John, Kt., 85.
Bankus, Christopher, servant, 18.
Banqueting House, 255
Baptists, legislation against, 293.
Baptista, John, insurgent, 377.
Barber, Gabriel, London merchant, 85.
  Lt. Col., burgess, 297, 318.
Barebones, Praise God, 192.

INDEX. 425

Bargrave, Doctor, Dean Canterbury, 408.
   Isaac, 408.
Barker, Capt. John, 128.
   William, burgess, 190.
Barnabye, James, 221.
Barnett, Theophilus, servant, 16.
Barrett, William, burgess, 186, 193, 205, 225.
Basse, Capt. Nathaniel, burgess, 73, councillor, 78, 88; deputed to invite New Englanders to Delaware Bay, 91; founder of Isle of Wight plantation, 133.
Bateman, Robert, 13.
Bates, John, servant, 23.
Batt, Catherine, 238, 327.
   John, 238, 327.
   Henry, 327, 328.
   Martha, 327.
   Michael, 71.
   Robert, of Oxford, 238, 327.
   Thomas, 327, 328.
   William, burgess, 232, 237.
Baugh, John, burgess, 186.
Bayley, Arthur, burgess, 167.
Baynham, Alexander, burgess, 237.
Beale, Thomas, councillor, 360.
Beard, Richard, Quaker, 410.
Beaumont, Giles, 30.
Behn, Aphra, play writer, 373.
Bell, Robert, London merchant, 13.
Bellingham, Herbert, 86.
   Richard, 86.
Bellson, John, 121.
Benge, William, 18.
Bennett, Edward, London merchant, 113, 224.
   Philip, burgess, 166, 186, 190.
   Richard, Governor, 73, 157, 166, 184, 186, 187, 193, 201, 218, 224, 225, 242, 249, 268, 316, 340, 353, 383.
   Richard, Jr., 304, 394.
   Robert, 224, 225.
   William, minister, 225.
Bentley, William, burgess, 94.
Beriston, Theophilus, servant, 16.
Berkeley, Sir Charles, Kt., 155.
   Lady Frances, 379, 392; her tombstone, 400.
   Lord George, 75.
   John of Stratton, 155, 207, 251, 281, 320, 340, 379.
   Maurice, 155.

Berkeley, Richard, 19.
   William, burgess, 318.
   Governor, ancestry of, 154, 155; arrival in Virginia, 154; first councillors, 155-157; entertains Captain De Vries, 178; visits England, 179, 188; captures Opechankano, 193; opposes Nansemond Puritans, 202; grief at the execution of Charles the First, 205; speech against Navigation Act, 212; surrenders to parliament, 221; elected Governor, 270, 273; speeches to burgesses and council of Virginia, 352; letter to Gov. Stuyvesant, 273; recognized as Governor, by Charles the Second, 281; his apology to the King, 353; his stage play enacted, 283; visit from Governor Calvert, 303; letters of, 307, 308, 313, 316, 319; despondent, 321; on silk culture, 324; his replies to Commissioner of Plantations, 330-338; his covetousness, 339; described by Quaker preacher, 340; marriage of, 341; visit to upper James River, 350; calls an Assembly, 351; address to the colonists, 351-357; referred to in Clarendon's History, 351; his course during Bacon's rebellion, 360, 361, 366, 368; resigns his office, 370; rudeness of, 379; his house described, 379; wife of, 379; death of, 379.
Berkenhead, a servant, discloses a conspiracy, 296.
Bermudas, trade with, 28; toleration at, 197.
Bernard, Mary, bequest to, 220.
   George, bequest to, 220.
   Thomas, burgess, 158, 184, 185, 186, 190.
   William, councillor, 186, 193, 198, 241, 242, 261, 268, 353-4.
Bernardo, the Italian, 18.
Bernardoe, Philip, 31.
Berry, James, 221.
   Robert, 221.
   Sir John, brings troops, 369, 370; censured by Berkeley of Stratton, 379.
Betts, Capt. Leonard, 127.

54

426 INDEX.

Bevercott, Samuel, of Scrooby, 99.
Beverley, Major Robert, 364, 369, 390, 397, 398.
Bew, Robert, 41.
Billington, Luke, 221.
Bishop, John, burgess, 185, 232.
  Henry, visits England, 192; Postmaster General, 192; notice of, 192.
Black, William, burgess, 262, 267.
Blackman, Capt. Jeremy, 128.
Blackwood, Susan, servant, 39.
Blake, Col. John, burgess, 318.
  Robert, 221.
Bland, Giles, 365, 374; abusive of Secretary Ludwell, 374; executed, 374; family of, 374.
  John of London, 270, 365, 374.
  Richard, 270.
  Theodoric, 268, 270, 273.
Blaney, Edward, councillor, 38; widow of, 40.
Bohune, Doctor, slain, 59.
Boise (Boys), Ann, 264.
  Cheney, burgess, 71, 408.
  John, Dean of Canterbury, 408.
  John, burgess, 408.
Bolling, Robert, his tomb-stone, 416.
Bolton, Francis, clergyman, 69, 406.
Bond, John, burgess, 236, 262, 266, 269.
Bonde, Martin, 113.
Bones, fossil discovered, 131.
Booth, Henry, servant, 18.
  Humphrey, 259, 314.
  Robert, burgess, 233, 237.
Borne, Robert, burgess, 262.
Boston, privateer at, 179; ministers of, denounce Capt. Stegg, 180.
  Henry, Quaker, 301, 303.
Boswell, Sir William, 75.
Bosworth, Capt. John, 239.
Boucher, Daniel, burgess, 232.
  Jonathan, clergyman, 329.
  William, 221.
Boundary, dispute, 247, 248, 249.
Boyle, Richard of London, 253.
Bracewell, Robert, clergyman, 233.
Brain, Edward, 219, 401.
Branch, John, burgess, 236.
Bray, Col. James, 360, 373.
Brennan, Thomas, burgess, 236.
Brent, Giles, 177, 236, 253, 288, 346.
  Margaret, 183.
Brereton, Major Thomas, 343.

Brewce, James, 221.
Brewster, Jonathan, 97.
  Nathaniel, minister, 413.
  Richard, burgess, 72.
  William, of Plymouth, 24, 86, 167.
Brick house, first at Jamestown, 263.
  houses ordered, 294, 295, 300.
  made in Virginia, 204, 294.
Bridger, Col. Joseph, 262, 263, 297, 303, 318, 349, 360.
Bridges, Thomas, servant, 22.
Briggs, Henry, mathematician, 104.
Brillyant, John, 221.
Broadhurst, Walter, burgess, 233.
Broadshaw, Richard, servant, 23.
Brocas, William, councillor, 117, 134, 156, 184, 193, 198, 204.
Brock, R. A. Sec., Va., Hist. Society, 57.
Bromley, George, 13.
  Sir Henry, 265.
  Sir Thomas, 22.
  Francis, 264.
  Virginia merchant, 264.
Brooke, Sir John, Kt., 85, 403.
  Sir Robert, Kt., 346.
Brooks, Thomas, servant, 23.
Browne, Devereux, 297.
  John, 221.
  Henry, councillor, 118, 133, 156, 184, 86, 193, 198.
  Susan Upshur, 388.
  Thomas, 388.
  William, burgess, 268.
Browne's Maryland, error in, 65.
Brownell, Capt. Isaac, 127.
Browning, John, burgess, 70, 74.
Brudricke, Richard, 223.
Bruton Parish, 380.
Buckam, Capt. Richard, 127.
Bucke, Richard, clergyman, 69; children of, 137.
Buckingham, Duke of, 21, 62, 63; letters to, 403.
Buckner, John, printer, fined, 397.
Burbage, Thomas, merchant, 136, 241.
Burgess, William, 410.
Burnham, Major John, 349.
  Rowland, burgess, 184, 189, 206. 1
Burroughs, Charles, burgess, 226, 236.
  Christopher, burgess, 186, 189.
Burwell, Abigail, 260.
  Elizabeth, 321.
  George, 321.
  Lewis, 260, 321.

INDEX. 427

Bushell, William, 57.
Bushrod, Thomas, burgess, 267.
Butler, Joane, ducked for slander, 291.
  Nathaniel, letters of, 28-30.
  William, burgess, 158, 261.
Butterfield, John, servant, 18.
Butterie, Thomas, 221.
Button, Capt. William, 93, 91, 113.
Byrd, Grace, wife of John, 219.
  John, London goldsmith, 135, 219.
  William, 135, 219, 387, 398, 401.

C.

Cæsar, Sir Julius, 11, 20.
Calthorp (Caulthrop) Christopher, burgess, 184, 186, 189, 230, 232, 269.
Calvert, Ann, daughter of George, 62.
  George, 1st Lord Baltimore, 11; early life of 61; Secretary of State, 62; brilliant courtier, 62; friend of Spanish ambassador, 62; loses favor with Buckingham, 63; created Baron of Baltimore, 63; visits New Foundland, 63; letter to Wentworth, 63; goes to Virginia, 64; refuses the required oath, 65; his first wife, 67.
  Cecil, 2d Lord Baltimore, arrival of his colony, 98; aided by Governor Harvey, 100; requests aid of Windebank, 128; desires settlers from New England, 173; wishes to be Governor of Virginia, 173; reference to, 188; invites Edward Gibbons of Boston to be Admiral, 198; complains of Gov. Berkeley, 212; adheres to Parliament, 227; pledge to sustain Act on Religion, 250; an adroit politician, 299, 311; opposes the restriction of tobacco planting, 305.
  Charles, 3d Lord Baltimore, his wife, 383; calls Virginians rascals, 393; censures Gov. Fendall, 393.
  Leonard, Gov. of M'd, 98; authorized to collect taxes in Va., 175; visits England, 179; writes to Gov. Berkeley, 183; flees to Va., 187.
  Philip, 68, 317.

Calvin, John, sponsor at Geneva, 274.
Campbell, James, 12.
Campion, Capt. Clement, 128.
Can iayack, Indian village, 75.
Cant, David, burgess, 269.
Canterbury, Archbishop, of, 102.
Capps, William, planter, 14, 47, 55, 64.
Carleton, Henry, placed in the stocks, 406.
Carline, Henry of Maryland, 238.
Carolana, Heath's charter of, 75.
Carpenter, Anthony, 221.
Carter, Col. Edward, 261, 266, 268, 353.
  Col. John, 168, 206, 236, 238, 261, 263, 267, 269, 304, 349.
  Rosanna, servant, 17.
Carteret, Capt. James taken by Dutch, 342.
  Sir George, 342.
Carver, Captain William, hung, 366, 376.
Cartwright, Abraham, 12.
Cary, Francis, shipwrecked, 208.
  Miles, councillor, 269, 282.
  Miles, Junior, Quaker, 282.
  Thomas, Quaker, 282
  William, 282.
Catchmaie, George, burgess, 269.
Catlett, John, 259, 303, 314.
Cattle from Ireland, 81.
  in A.D., 1649, 203.
Cawfield, Capt. William, burgess, 261, 266, 268.
Ceeley, Thomas, burgess, 73.
Census of A D., 1634-5, 114.
Chadwell, Daniel, 221.
Chamberlain, Hugh, son-in-law of rebel Bacon, 369.
Chambers, Alice, servant, 22.
  James, servant, 17.
  Thomas, servant, 23.
Champion, Pascoe, 40.
Chandler, Job, 416.
  John, burgess, 190, 198.
  Samuel, London merchant, 416.
Charles the First, proclamation of, 10.
  Second, his reply to Va. Assembly, 161; conciliatory, 282, 292; gives away lands, 289; acknowledges receipt of silk, 324; censures the Assembly, 396; death of, 401.
Chapman, Nicholas, 21.
  Thomas, Quaker, 253.

Chappell, Capt. John, 127.
Charlton, Stephen, burgess, 186, 199 208, 221, 230.
Charter of Avalon, as to Christianity, 306.
  Barbadoes, as to Christianity, 306.
  Carolana, as to Christianity, 305.
  Maryland restrictive, 307.
  Nova Scotia, 306.
Cheskiake plantation, 73, 142, 171.
Cheesman, Captain, burgess, 168, 225.
  Major, dies in prison, 367.
Chester, Dr. J. L. Chester, on Washington ancestry, 256.
Chesterfield, Countess of, 192.
Chew, John, merchant, 69, 73, 136; burgess, 168, 184, 225.
Chicheley, Agatha, 386, 395.
  Sir Henry, arrival of, 210; marries widow Wormeley, 210; mention of, 240, 292, 305, 360; captured by Bacon, 365; Deputy Governor, 386, 391, 394; infirm with age, 394; death of, 395.
Chichester, Lord Arthur, 11.
Children for Virginia, 47, 77; kidnapped, 278.
Chiles, Walter, burgess, 158, 167, 171, 189, 193, 205, 232, 266, 282, 297.
Chipson, Robert, 239.
Chiskoyake, Indian chief, 271.
Christison, Quaker preacher, 121.
Church of England, rites ordered, 282.
Claiborne, Leonard, 43, 363.
  Thomas, 43, 363.
  William, Secretary, 24; notice of, 43, 363; councillor, 37, 78, 88, 184, 186; witness to a will, 48; defeats Indians, 75; takes grain to Boston, 80; trades with Potomac Indians, 91; with the Susquehannas, 408; asks advice of Va. council, 100; at P't Comfort, 106; his trading vessel captured, 120; letter to Sir John Coke, 121; arrives from Kent Island, 125; treasurer of Va., 157, 187, 188; Parliament commissioner, 217; Secretary of State, 225, 231, 233; Secretary under Gov. Digges, 242; under Gov. Mathews, 261, 264; under Gov. Berkeley, 268, 270, 272; visits Dublin, 416; burgess from New Kent, 268, 270,

Claiborne, continued
  272; old age, 384; wife mentioned, 416.
  William, Junior, 296, 348, 363; children of, 364.
  William, grandson of Secretary, 364; attends Quaker meeting, 364, 384.
Claiborne's Island, 121.
Clarendon's notice of Gov. Berkeley, 354.
Clarke, John, mate of May Flower, 30, 31.
  Thomas, 221.
Clayton, John, clergyman, describes Jamestown, 367; alludes to Claiborne, 384.
Claxton, John, servant, 17.
Cleate, Charles, dancing master, 376.
Clement, Elizabeth, 19.
  Jeremy, 19.
  John, 123.
Cloberry, William, London merchant, 56.
Close, Phettiplace, burgess, 73.
Clough, John, clergyman, 364.
Coake, William, 221.
Cock, Richard, burgess, 236.
  William, burgess, 193.
Cocker, Richard, burgess, 185.
Cockeran, William, burgess, 873.
Codd, Col. St. Leger, 348, 297.
Coke, Sir John, K't, 85, 102, 121.
Cole, Josiah, Quaker, 252.
  Thomas of Maryland, 264.
  William, councillor, 74, 349, 360, 364, 398.
  William, Quaker preacher, 285.
Colebourne, William, 2243.
Coleclough, George, burgess, 267.
Coles, Ann, servant, 201.
Collowe, Stephen, 49.
Comes, John, 18.
Comon, Nicholas, 17.
Common Prayer Book prohibited, 206.
Conaway, Aaron, servant, 21.
Concubinage with Indian woman, 386.
Convicts sent to Virginia, 328, 329.
Conway, Captain, fights the Dutch, 320 Maurice, describes old tombstone, Sir Edward 11.
Cooke, Christopher, servant, 21.
Cookson, William, 374, 377.
Cooper, Thomas, 21.

Cooper, Walter, 21.
Copland, Patrick, clergyman, 31, 195, interest in Va., 195, 196; at Bermudas, 196; erects a free school, 197; becomes a non-conformist, 197; goes to Isle of Eleuthera, 197; letter to Gov. Winthrop, 197.
Corbin, John, bequest to, 221.
  Henry, notice of, 239, 254; burgess, 267, 269, 304.
Cordovant gloves, 221.
Corker, John, burgess, 186.
  William, burgess, 261.
Cornley, John, 222.
Cornwallis, Caroline, 99.
  Lord at Yorktown, 99.
  Sir Charles, 99.
  Sir John, 99.
  Sir Thomas, 99.
  Sir William, 99.
  Thomas of Maryland, 99, 106, 121, 141, 177.
  Thomas, clergyman, 99.
  William, clergyman, 99.
Corotoman river, 260
Coryat, the traveler, 83.
Cottington, James, 392,
  Philip, 392.
Cotton, Ann, wife of William, 417.
  Joane, mother of Wm., 406, 414.
  Verlinda, 417.
  William, minister, 406, 410, 414.
Coulson, John, 221.
Couper, Walter, servant, 15.
Coursey, Henry, 304, 317.
Coventon, Nehemiah, 222.
Coventry, Thomas, Lord, 102.
Cowdrey, Ben., 221.
Cowen, Capt. William, burgess, 318
Coxe, Dr. Daniel, claim to Norfolk Co., 411
Cradack, Matthew, 136.
Cranfield, Lord Treasurer, on tobacco revenue, 403.
Crecro, Thomas, 221.
Crew, Randall, burgess, 168, 185, 190, 194, 199.
Crewes, James, sentenced to die, 374, 397
Cripps, Zachary, justice, 94.
Crocker, Henry, 40.
Cromwell, Oliver on boundary dispute, 247, 248, 249; views as to toleration, 250; letter to Cardinal Mazarin, 251.

Cromwell, Richard, 267.
Crosse, Thomas, 40.
Croshaw, Joseph, burgess, 267, 269.
Crouch, Hugh, 282.
  Richard, 282.
Curtis, Captain, Parliament commissioner, 218, 220, 221.
  John, burgess, 269.
Custis, Daniel Parke, 209, 316.
  Edward, 208.
  John, 208, 221.
  John, Junior, 209.
  Joseph, 208.
  Martha, 209.
  Thomas, 208.
  William, 208, 221, 417.
Culpepper, Lord John, his speech in Parliament, 389; letter to, from Henrietta Maria, widow of Charles the First, 389; created Baron Thorseway, 389.
  Lord Thomas, Second Baron of Thorseway, 381; grant of land to, 382; arrival in Virginia, 389; notice of, 389; visits Boston, 391; letter to his sister, 392; returns to Virginia, 395; his instructions, 396; unpopular, 396, Catherine, daughter of Thomas, marries Thomas, 5th Lord Fairfax, 392.

D.

Dacker, William, burgess, 158.
Dalby, William, servant, 22.
Dale, Sir Thomas, 29, 30, 386.
Danby, Earl of, 85.
Dancy, John, servant, 17.
Dandridge, Martha, 209, 316.
Davenant, Sir William, Kt. and poet, appointed Gov. of Maryland, 211, 417, 418.
Davenport, John, Puritan minister, 201, 255.
Davies, Capt. James, 30.
  John, servant, 19.
Davis, Jane, servant, 14.
  Sir John, Kt., 85
  Thomas, burgess, 262.
  William, burgess, 167, 198.

INDEX.

Davison, Christopher, Secretary of Va., 24, 25, 87.
    Frances, 25.
    Walter, 24.
    William, Kt. and Ambassador, 87.
Dawson, George, servant, 23.
    William, 21.
Day, John, servant, 17.
Death, Richard, burgess, 168, 185.
Delaware, Henry, Fourth Lord, 56.
    Thomas, Third Lord, 56, 85, 102, 118, 144.
    River, Falls of, 106.
Denman, John, 221.
Dennis, John of Somerset, M'd., 388
    Robert, Parliament commissioner, 218.
    lost at sea, 219.
Denson, William, burgess, 269.
Denwood, Levin, 221.
De Ruyter, Dutch Admiral, 307.
Desmond, Earl of, 80.
Deverill, Geo., servant, 16.
De Vries, Dutch captain, 83, 93, 94, 127, 177, 178.
Dew, Thomas, burgess, 158, 226, 230, 232, 236, 242, 247, 261, 263, 268, 353.
Dichfield, Edward, 13.
Digby, Sir Kenelon, Kt., 85.
    John, sentenced to death, 374, 377.
Digges, Sir Dudley, Kt., 85, 237, 383.
    Edward, 237; attention to silk culture, 249; Gov. of Va., 242, 248, 249, 292, 305; death of, 303.
    Elizabeth, 303.
    William, 303.
Dipnall, Thomas, burgess, 236.
Dixon, Ambrose, Quaker, 221, 301.
    Christopher, 221.
    John, 222.
Doctors' fees excessive, 191.
Dodman, Colonel, 344.
Doe, Theodore, burgess, 73.
Doeg, Indians attacked by John Washington and others, 346, 347.
Doleman, Thomas, servant, 19.
Dolling, John, 221.
Donne, George, councillor and muster master, 132, 133, 146, 148, 149; his essay on Virginia, 414.
    John, D D., father of George, 132.
Dorset, Earl of, 56, 85, 102.
Doughty, Francis, non-conformist minister, 259, 387; proposes marriage 407.

Douglas, Edward, burgess, 185, 194, 221.
Douglass, Captain, 127.
Downe, Nicholas, of the King's kitchen, 287.
Downes, George, justice, 90.
    Richard, 196.
Downeman, John, burgess, 74.
Downing, Lucy, sister of Gov. Winthrop, 203.
Drayton's ode to George Sandys, 45.
Drisius, Samuel of Manhattan, 235; preaches in Virginia, 420.
Drummond, complains of Boston Court, 296; Gov. of Albemarle, 307, 342; tobacco commissioner, 317; at Jamestown, 358; mention of, 371, 372; executed, 373, 377, 380.
Duffill, Thomas, 121.
Duke, Elizabeth, wife of rebel Bacon, 346, 391, 392.
    Sir Edward, Kt., 346, 392.
    Sir John, Kt., 346.
Dunche, Deborah, wife of Sir H'y Moody, 274.
    Edward, M.P., 274.
    Walter, 274.
    William 274.
Dunn, Thomas, servant, 16.
Dunston, John, burgess, 205.
Dunton, Captain John, 87.
Durand, George, of Carolina, 306.
    William, Secretary of M'd., 201, 306.
Dutch attack at P't Comfort, 320, 342.
    New York, 242.
Dye, John, 221.

E.

Eaton, Ann, Widow, 407.
    Nathaniel, disgraced principal of Harvard College, 143, 144, 406, 413, 414.
Edlowe, Matthew, burgess, 71, 266.
Edmonds, Sir Thomas, Knight, 102.
Edmunds, Robert, servant, 18.
Edmundson, Quaker preacher, visits Gov. Berkeley, 339.
Edwards, John, 17, 221.
    Richard, 13.
    Sir Thomas, 11.
    William, burgess, 230, 232, 261.

INDEX. 431

Elective franchise, 242; restriction of, 330.
Elfrith, Capt. Daniel, 34.
Elliott, Anthony, burgess, 198, 262.
Ellis, John, 221.
Ellyson, (Ellison) Robert, burgess, 268, 282, 297, 303.
Eltonhead, Alice, 254.
   Jane, 410.
   Richard, 254.
   William, 254, 421.
Elzey, John, Maryland commissioner, 300, 301.
Endicott, Dep. Gov. of Mass., 230.
English, William, burgess, 90, 116, 266.
Epes (Epps) Francis, burgess, 90, 190, 225, 349.
Errors typographical, noted, 194, 257.
Essex, Earl of, 35, 36.
Evans, John, 18.
   Thomas, 40.
Evelin, (Evelyn) Capt. Christopher, 369.
   George, commander at Kent Island, 152; his christening, 378.
   Mountjoy, son of George, 158, 378, 410.
   Robert, Senior, 378.
   Robert, Junior, 101, 105; at Falls of Delaware River, 106; councillor, 132; Surveyor General, 132, 153; his book, 153, 180; in Maryland, 180, 181.
Evelinton Manor, 152.
Eyres, Nicholas, servant, 17.
   Robert, burgess, 194.

F.

Fairchild, James, servant, 15.
Fairfax, Bryan, 8th Lord, 392.
   Catherine, wife of 5th Lord, 392.
   Frances, wife of Col. William, 392.
   John, 11th Lord, 392.
   Robert, 7th Lord, 392.
   Thomas, 6th Lord, 392.
   William, collector at Salem, Mass., 392; councillor in Va., 392; residence of described, 392.
Falland, Robert, explorer, 328.
Fallows, Thomas, burgess, 158.
Fanshaw, Thomas, 12.
Fantleroy (Fauntleroy), Moore, burgess, 185, 186, 198, 233, 267, 269, 288.

Farlow, Captain, executed, 369, 376.
Farnebough, John, 134.
Farrant, Philip, 221.
Farrell, Capt. Herbert, 349, 364, killed, 372.
Fawcett, Thomas, burgess, 73
Fawdowne, Mr., burgess, 193.
Fausett, John, attorney, 315.
Fell, Planter, shipwrecked, 54.
Fellgate, Capt. Robert, burgess, 72.
Fendall, Gov. of Md., 257, 265, 393.
Ferrar (Farrar), John, 85.
   John, Junior, 285, 240.
   Nicholas, 14, 25, 41, 85, 240.
   Virginia, 236, 240.
   William, councillor, 38, 42, 116, 240, 268, 297, 317, 349.
Figby (Higby?), Thomas, 221.
Filmer, Henry, burgess, 167.
Finch, Jane, 13.
   Hen., councillor, 78.
   Sir Thomas, 13.
Fisher, Philip, Jesuit, 187, 200, 201.
Fitz Herbert, Jesuit, 256.
Fitz Hugh, William, 398.
Flax culture, 287, 320.
Fleet, Henry, Captain, 52, 53, 87, 88, 91, 92, 187, 189, 230, 231, 238.
Fletcher, George, burgess, 226, 231.
Flint, Thomas, burgess, 73, 90, 167, 199.
Fludd (Flood), John, burgess, 167, 189, 226.
Francis, 221.
   Nathaniel, 41.
Ford, John, of Acconmc, 406.
   Richard, burgess, 268.
Fort Charles, James River Falls, 189.
   Henry, Appomattox, 189, 194, 328.
   James, Chickahominy, 187, 194.
   Royal, Pamunkey, 187, 191.
Forts, desired, 312, 322.
Foster, Armstrong, 221.
Fowlke, Thomas, burgess, 266, 269.
Fowden, George, burgess, 232.
Fowke, Col. Gerard, burgess, 288, 295, 297.
Fowler, Francis, 18, 232.
Fox, George, Quaker preacher 297, 299.
Francis, Thomas, burgess, 261.
   Raleigh, burgess, 297.
Franklin, Ferd., burgess, 158.
Freeman, Bridges, councillor, 198, 225, 242.

INDEX.

Freeman, Ralph, 12.
Freethorne, Richard, servant, 58.
Free trade, petition for, 137.
Friends, Society of, see *Quakers*.
Fruits, cultivated in A. D., 1649, 204.

G.

Gale, George, marries widow of Lawrence Washington, 420.
Gambling, prevalence of, 94, 178.
Gardiner, Captain, 358.
Gardner, Nathaniel, 418.
Garnell (Garnett ?), John, 221.
Garrett (Jarret), William, 23, 340.
Gaskins, William, 221.
Gaston, Sir Francis, 11.
Gates, Sir Thomas, 171.
Gatford, Lionel, his treatise, 244, 277, 278
George, John, burgess, 199, 226, 349.
Gerrard, Thomas, physician of Md., 255, intemperate, 256, will of 256.
Gibbons, Capt. Edward of Boston, trades in Va., 180, 172, 180, 198; Admiral of Md., 173, 220; his ship captured, 220.
Gibbs, Francis, 19.
  Thomas, 12, 50, 85.
Giles, Jonathan, servant, 14.
Gill, Stephen, burgess, 230.
Glass works, 284.
Godwin (Godwyn), Francis, Bishop of Hereford, 342.
  Morgan, Senior, 342.
  Morgan, Junior, clergyman in Va., 342, 343; writings of 343, 344, 345; suit against, 344.
  Thomas, Bishop of Bath, 342.
Goldfine, Samuel, 223.
Goldsmith, Arthur, servant, 22.
Gondomar, Spanish Ambassador, 62.
Gooch, William, councillor, 237, 242; tomb of, 243.
Good Friday, massacre, 179.
Goodman, Francis, 221.
Goodrich, Col. Thomas, 314; fined, 375.
Goodwyn (Godwin) Thomas, burgess, 266, 349.
Gookin, Daniel, Senior, 31, 81, 82, 83, 409.
  Daniel, Junior, 82, 134, 166, 183, 184, 409.

Gookin, John of Nansemond, 134, 414.
  John of Ripple Court, 81.
  Sarah, 134.
  Sir Vincent, Kt., 81, 409.
Gordon, Thomas, rebellious clergyman, 375.
Gorges, Sir Ferdinand, 11.
Gossips, law concerning, 294.
Gotherson, Major Daniel, 155.
Gouge, William, burgess, 230.
Gough, John, clergyman, 368.
  Matthew, burgess, 167.
  Nathaniel, burgess, 158.
Gower, William, 221.
Grandon (Grendon), Thomas, 152, 219.
  widow, 219, 400.
Granger, Nicholas, 221.
Grant, Capt. John, 128.
Grantham, Capt. Thomas, bearer of dispatches, 370, 371; conference with insurgents, 372.
Grave, John, Quaker, his song, 280.
Graves, Robert, servant, 23.
  Thomas of Mass., goes to Va., 144.
  Justice, 90.
Gray, Francis, burgess, 297.
Graye, John, 221
Green, Roger, clergyman, 233, 234, 290, 420.
Greene, John, shipmaster, 257.
Green Spring, Governor Berkeley's house at, 204.
Gregory, Richard, servant, 16.
Griffith, Edward, burgess, 269, 288, 297.
Guinne, Hugh, burgess, 226, 230, 297.
Gundry, John, 133.
Gusman (Guzman), Spanish Spy, 79, 408.
  of Alfarache, a Spanish Romance, 79, 408.
Guy, Capt. Arthur, buys negroes, 59.
  Robert, servant, 16.

H.

Hacke, Georgine, 221.
Hacker, John, 41.
Hackett, William, burgess, 233.
Haine, Jeremy, burgess, 262.
Hall, Susan, servant, 16.
  Susanna, 48.

Hall, Thomas, 16; at Delaware River, 126; at Manhattan, 127.
Thomas, insurgent, 373, 377.
Thomasine, 71.
Hamby, Richard, 221.
Hamlin, Stephen, burgess, 236, 297.
Hamor, Elizabeth, 19.
Ralph, 19, 38, 43, 69
Hammond, Colonel, 210.
Francis, 157.
Joane, 157.
John, burgess, expelled, 229.
Lawrence, 157.
Mainwaring, burgess, 157, 269.
Margaret, 157.
Hancock, Richard, 121.
Handford, Sir Humphrey, 12.
Hanie, John, burgess, 262.
Hanolaskie Indians, 328.
Hansford, Colonel, executed, 369, 376.
John, 369.
John, Junior, 369.
William, 369.
Hardy (Hardie), George, burgess, 158, 185, 186, 189, 205, 226.
Harlowe, John, burgess, 267.
Harmar (Harman), Charles of Accomac, 90, 91, 92; burgess, 93, 120, 409.
Eliza, daughter of Charles, 409.
John, Warden of Winchester, 409.
John, Oxford professor, 409.
Thomas, 409.
Harmer, Ambrose, burgess, 137, 186, 187, 193.
Harris, Capt. Thomas, burgess, 267.
William, burgess, 229, 233, 261.
an insurgent, 377.
Harrison, Benjamin, Clerk of Council, 146, 157, 202, 406.
Edward, wife died in Boston, 202.
Elizabeth, 202.
John, 202.
Thomas, clergyman, 195, 197, 200; marries in Massachusetts, 206; his views of toleration in Maryland's Act of Religion, 250; minister in London, 418; in possession of commission to the poet Davenant, 418.
Harryson, Alexander, 221.
Robert, 221.
Hartree, Elial, 22.
Harvard, John, 112, 143.

Harvey, Elizabeth, widow of Richard Stephens, 152, 341
Gov. John, 36, 38, 51, 77; arrival of, 92; friend to Lord Baltimore, 100; dispute with Va. Council, 115-118; mention of, 120, 123, 128, 133, 143, 152; marriage of, 152, 341.
Mary, 112.
Sir Sebastian, 21, 112.
Harwood, George, 289.
Thomas, burgess, 73, 123, 158, 186, 205, 225.
Hatch, Thomas, servant, 16.
Hatchey, William, burgess, 185, 205, 226, 257, 266.
Hatton, Robert, 416.
Thomas, 416.
Hawes, Michael, 12.
Hawkins, Capt. Thomas, 349 364.
Hawley, Gabriel, 132, 153, 173.
Henry, 131, 142.
James, 142.
Jerome, 131, 138, 141, 142, 174.
William, 131, 142, 306, 414.
Hawte, Jane, 13.
Sir William, 13.
Hay William, burgess, 267.
Hayman, John, burgess, 237.
Heath, Sir Robert, 11, 75, 45.
Heerman, Augustine, 272; map of, 193, 206.
Helder, Edmund, physician, tombstone of, 91.
Hely, John, 42.
Hendrye, Andrew, 221.
Henn, Robert, 346.
Heyrick, John, burgess, 185, 186.
Hickes, Sir Baptist, 11.
Higby, Thomas, Accomac clergyman, 407, 410.
Higginson, Humphrey, councillor, 157, 184, 186, 225, 212.
Robert, 260.
Hill, Edward, Speaker of Assembly, 53, 158, 185, 186, 190, 198, 205, 236, 242, 245, 268, 349, 353.
John, burgess, 158, 166, 298.
Nicholas, burgess, 282, 297, 318.
Richard, burgess, 221, 269.
Thomas, councillor, 263.
Hinman, John, 221.

Hinton, Sir Thomas, Kt., councillor, 21, 111, 112, 126, 205.
William, son of Thomas, 111.
Hobbs, Francis, burgess, 236.
Hobson, John, councillor, 133, 156.
Hobby Horse, name of vessel of Scarborough, 418.
Hockway, William, burgess, 233,
Hodden (Hodin), John, burgess, 167, 185.
Hodges, Capt. John, 136.
Hodgskins (Hoskins), Anthony, burgess, 221, 226.
Hodgson, Robert, Quaker, 285.
Hoe, Rice, burgess, 171, 186, 190, 193.
Hogben, Joseph, 155.
Hogg, Capt. John, 128.
Holden, Christopher, Quaker, 285.
Holland, John, burgess, 237.
Hollinsworth, William, from New England, 301.
Holloway, John, surgeon, 406.
Holmes, George, visits Delaware River, 126, 127.
Holt, Randall, 40.
Hone, Theodore, burgess, 318, 358.
Honeywood, Sir Philip, 210.
Philip, 210.
Hook, Capt. Francis, 114, 125, 134, 138.
Sir Humphrey, Kt., 291.
Hopson, Thomas, servant, 22.
Horsey, Stephen, burgess, 221, 233, 300;
Quaker, 303.
Horsmanden, Warham, burgess, 261, 263, 266.
Hoskins, Bartholomew, burgess, 206, 236.
Howard, Lord Francis, Gov. of Va., 397, 400.
John, servant, 20.
Philip, supposed play-actor, 315.
Howe, Theodore, burgess, 230.
Hubberstead, Edward, servant, 23.
Hudibras, satirical poem, 421.
Hudson, Leonard, carpenter, 196.
Raphael, 221.
Richard, 221.
Hudson's River of Chesapeake Bay, 121.
Hull, George, servant, 14.
Jeffrey, 19.
Peter, 185.
William, 71.

Hunt, Thomas, 281.
Hurd, Edward, 57.
Hurricane, very severe, 321.
Hutchinson, Randolph, 221.
Robert, burgess, 167, 184, 186, 198.
William, 90.

I.

Idiot, first in Virginia, 136.
Immigration agents in London, 108.
Indian Queen of Pamunkey, 386.
traders forbidden to sell fire arms, 349.
Indians, die in London, 29; attack pinnace of Pountis, 52; kill Spelman, 58; murder a clergyman, 74; attack settlers,, 93; kill Capt. John Stone, 97; massacre on Good Friday, 179; dispersed, 191; plan to civilize, 242; expedition against, 245; injustice to, 246; incursions of, 313; legislation as to, 313, 314, 348; census of, 325; conference with tribes, 377.
Ingle, Captain Richard, charges against, 176, 177; befriended by Thomas Cornwallis, 177; attacks Saint Mary, 187.
Ingram, Joseph, sentenced to death, 375.
William, 369.
Ireland, cattle brought from, 81, 82.
Italian glass workers, 284.
Iverson, Abraham, burgess, 232.

J.

Jackman, Solomon, servant, 23.
Jackson, John, 58.
Walter, servant, 23.
Jacob, Capt. John, his vessel seized in Potomac River, 418, 419.
Jail-birds, fear of, 328.
James, Edward, 12.
the King, 62, 63.
John, 221.
Thomas, Puritan minister, 167.
Jamestown, 68, 203, 366, 367; brick church, when built, 144, 203, 368; fort at, 367.
Jansen, Peter, 183.
Jarvis, Capt., marries the widow Bacon, 391.

INDEX. 435

Jarvis, Christopher, 221.
Jefferson, Thomas, his report, 33.
Jeffreys, John, 305.
   Herbert, Governor, 370; first proclamation of, 379; calls an Assembly, 385; confers with Indians, 385; death of, 386; his wife, 380
   William, Captain, 398.
Jennings, Edmund, 255.
   Peter, burgess, 269, 297, 318.
Jermayne, Philip, 12.
Johnson, Capt. Cornelius, 82, 83.
   George of M'd, schismatic, 301, 302.
   James, 221.
   John, 70, 221.
   John, Jr., 222.
   Joseph, burgess, 158, 171.
   Robert, London grocer, 12. 91.
   Thomas, burgess, 190, 191, 221, 226, 233, 236.
Jones, Anthony, servant, 16.
   Arthur, burgess, 168.
   Farmer, 221.
   Henry, servant, 21.
   Nathan, servant, 23.
   Major, 348.
   Peter, 23
   Robert, insurgent, 374.
   Samuel, clergyman, 420
   Thomas, Capt. of May Flower, 31, 32, 33.
Jordan (Jordon), Cecilia, 41.
   Margaret, 42.
   Robert, 282.
   Samuel, 41, 282.
   Thomas, burgess, 73, 90.
   George, burgess, 181, 193, 198, 266, 282, 349.
Jorden, William, 221.
Justices for A.D. 1631-32, 90.

K.

Kellam, Richard, 222.
Kemp, Richard, Secretary, 114, 118, 119, 120, 141, 142, 144, 145, 150, 155; acting Governor, 179, 184, 186, 193, 198; monument to, 380.
   Matthew, burgess, 364, 386.
Kendall, Governor of Bermudas, 34.
   William, burgess, 262, 298, 318, 387, 388, 407, 419.

Kent Island, 81, 100.
Key, Isaac, clergyman, 407.
   Thomas, life of, 70.
Killin, David, 221.
Killigrew, Sir Robert, 11, 85
Kingsley, William, 22.
Kingsmill, Richard, 49, 72, 79, 404, 405.
Kingston, Thomas, burgess, 73.
Kingswell, Edward, 97.
Kinsman, Richard, his pear orchard, 204.
Kirke, Christopher, 221.
Knight, Mordecai, 19.
   Robert, Boston merchant, 418.
   Peter, 203.
Knowles, John, minister from New England, 166.

L.

L'Amy, Hugh, 76.
Lacton, Henry, 18.
Lakes, toward the Western Sea, 104, 105.
Lambard, Capt. Richard, 127.
Lambert, Thomas, burgess, 206, 262, 230.
Land laws of Virginia, 56.
Langston, Anthony, visits London, 287; urges the erection of iron-works, 421.
   John, 375.
Lansdale, a preacher, 270.
Lapworth, Michael, 26.
Larimore, Captain, captured by Bacon, 366.
Latham, John, 62
Lathrop, John, 23.
Lawerenson, Peter, 183.
Lawrie, Capt. Christopher, 88, 133.
Lawrence, Richard, 303; associate of Bacon, 358; notice of, 366, 368; burns his own house, 368; declared a rebel, 371, 372; escapes 375.
Lawson, Alice, 18.
   Christopher, 18.
Lawyers troublesome, 191, 264
Layden, Katherine, 23.
Lea, Thomas, 23.
Leare, John, Colonel, 318, 349.
Leate, Nicholas, 13.
Lederer, John, explorer, 326, 327.

Leddra, William, Quaker, 285.
Lee, Ann, wife of Richard, 255.
  Benedict, 253.
  Christopher, 221.
  Elizabeth, 253.
  Hancock, commissioner of Northampton, 421; removes to Northumberland, 421; marries granddaughter of Puritan Brewster, 255, 421.
  John, 255.
  Mary, hung as a witch, 239.
  Richard, Senior, burgess, 198; notice of, 253; faithful to Parliament; 292; tobacco commissioners, 304.
  Richard, Junior, 260, 364, 398.
  Sir Henry, Kt., 254.
  Sir Robert, Kt., 253.
Leighton, Dr. Alexander, 381.
Leister, Thomas, 40.
Lewd women sent to Virginia, 329.
Lewes, Roger, 23.
Lewis, John, 221.
Ley, Chief Justice, 23.
Licques, Peter de, 76.
Lidcott, Robert, 114.
  Sir John, 114.
Lightfoot, Capt., surrenders to Dutch, 320.
Littleton, Ann, widow of Nathaniel, 387, 407, 416.
  Edward, 387.
  Nathaniel, councillor, 156, 225, 387; plantation in Accomac, 208; acknowledges Parliament, 221; mention of 407, 413, 418.
  Southey, 387.
Liquors, sale of restricted, 185; price of, 185, 196.
Lisbro, Edward, 255.
Liturgy, enjoined, 284.
Llewellin (Luellin) Daniel, burgess, 167, 185, 193, 230.
Lloyd, Cornelius, burgess, 168, 185, 189, 199, 226, 232.
  Edward, 186, 194, 304.
  Philemon, 304, 394.
Lobs, George, old planter, 241.
Lobbolly, food, 58.
Locker, Capt. John, 207.
Logsward, John, 57.
London Mint, assay master goes to Va., 229.

Longe, Elias, servant, 18.
  Jane, servant, 18.
Long Island granted to Plowden, 181.
Lopham, James, 134.
Loveing, Thomas, burgess, 184, 193 261, 287.
Lovelace, Col. Francis, 231, 352, 421.
Lucar (Lucas), Thomas, burgess, 262, 297, 318.
Luddington, William, burgess, 194, 223.
Ludlow, Anne, daughter of Roger, 413.
  Gabriel, brother of Roger, 413.
  George, brother of Roger, 413; councillor, 136, 137, 157, 184, 186, 193, 198, 209, 225, 241, 242; his will, 413.
  Mary, daughter of Roger, 413.
  Jonathan, son of Roger, 413.
  Joseph, son of Roger, 413.
  Roger, brother of George, 96, 239, 413.
  Roger, son of Roger, 413.
  Sarah, supposed sister of George, 413.
  Sarah, daughter of Roger, 413.
  Thomas, nephew of George, 413.
Ludwell, Philip, Senior, 349; councillor, 360, 363; captures insurgents 366; notice of, 392; marries Lady Frances Berkeley, 392.
  Philip, Junior, 381, 392.
  Thomas, Secretary, 282, 296, 317; flatters Gov. Berkeley, 317; attacked by Bland, 365; visits England, 365, 380, 385; monument to, 380.
Lunsford, Catherine, 381, 417.
  Elizabeth, 381.
  Herbert, 381.
  Henry, 381.
  Katerina, 381.
  Thomas, Senior, 380; in the Fleet prison, 381; death of, 381.
  Thomas, Kt., pass for Va., 210; waylays Pelham, 380; imprisoned, 381; knighted, 381, L't of Tower of London, 381; his family, 381, 417; monument to, 380.
Lusan, William, 21.
Lyddall, Major George, 348.

INDEX. 437

M.

Mabbe, James, translator of Gusman of Alfarache, 408.
Machaell, John, 222.
Macock, Sarah, 18.
Madison, Capt. Isaac, councillor, 21, 38.
  Mary, 23.
Madox, Alexander, 221, 223.
Magge, Mark, Master of the boat Hobby Horse, 419.
Major, Christopher, 221.
  Edward, 190, 194, 226, 232.
Mallory, Catherine, 238.
  Philip, clergyman, 238, 244, 270, 283.
  Thomas, Dean of Chester, 238, 327, 420.
  London non-conformist, 420.
  William, K't, 420.
Maltravers, *alias* Nanzemund River, 135.
  Lord Henry, 135; grant of Norfolk County, 411.
Manchester, Henry, Earl of, 102.
Manhattan, commission from, 234.
Manoakin in Maryland, 303.
Mansell, Capt. Dan., burgess, 226.
  Robert, servant, 42.
Mansfield, David, servant, 17.
Marryott, Robert, 221.
Marsh, Margaret, 201.
  Thomas, 201.
Marshall, Capt. Roger, 195; son christened, 419.
  Edward, 221.
Martian, Nicholas, burgess, 93.
Martin, Brandon, 403.
  Captain, 116
  Edward of Accomac, 315.
  John, councillor, 20, 26, 50; London Company concerning, 403.
Martyne, John, Mayor of Plymouth, 123.
Maryland, charter restricted, 307.
  colonists arrive, 98
  first settlers chiefly Protestants, 99.
  dissents as to restriction of tobacco culture, 308.
Mary's Mount, Massachusetts, 113.
  Virginia, 113, 409.
Mason, George, censured, 288, sheriff, 344, 346, 349, 387.

Mason, James, burgess, 237.
  Leonard, burgess, 261.
  Lyonell, burgess, 236.
  Lemuel, burgess, 266, 269, 297, 349.
  William, bricklayer, 376.
Massachusetts, adulation of Charles the Second, 287.
Matheman, John, servant, 14.
Mather, Cotton, 184.
Matthews, Edward, 221, 223.
  John, 348.
  Philip, 221.
  Robert, 21.
  Samuel, councillor, 20, 21, 38, 78, 88, 90, 225, 242; expedition against Indians, 80; builds a fort, 94; described by Gov. Harvey, 101; his plantation, 112, 205; dispute with the Governor, 116, 128, 131; colony agent, 227; chosen Governor, 248, 260, 266; concerning Assateague Indians, 265; death of, 268.
  Samuel, Junior, bequest to, 220; burgess, 226, 230, 232, 237, 242.
Matrum, John, burgess, 190.
May, Sir Humphrey, 11.
May Flower, the ship, 30.
Meade, Thomas, 238.
Meares, Thomas, burgess, 186, 194, 199.
Mede, Joseph, the clergyman, refers to Capt. Henry Fleet, 53; his notice of Lord Baltimore, 67; refers to Indians, 74.
Mees, Col. Henry, burgess, 318.
Mellinge, William, burgess, 223, 233, 262.
Menefie, George, councillor, 68, 72; his house, 112; dispute with Gov. Harvey, 116, 117, 119, 131, 134; obtains a minister for Cheskiak, 142; councillor under Berkeley, 156, 184, 187; brings negroes from England, 187.
Merryday, Philip, 221.
Merryfin, John, 221.
Mildmay, Sir Henry, 11.
Miles, Alice, 282.
  George, 282.
Miller, Thomas, 221.
Mills, in A. D. 1649, 204.
Milner, George, 375.
  Thomas, 349.

438 INDEX.

Ministers, supported by colonists, 77; criticism of, 244.
Minshall, Jeffrey, 222.
Mitchell, William, burgess, 262; notice of, 263, 264.
Mitford, Bulmer, 303.
Mole, George, 13.
Molton, Thomas, servant, 18.
Monakin, Indian village, 326.
Monk, General, in London, 279.
Montague, Peter, servant, 21.
    burgess, 230, 232, 262.
    Sir Charles, 11.
Moody, Lady Deborah, 127; sketch of, 276.
    Sir Henry, Kt., 127; pass for, 421; visits Virginia, 268; his father's place in England, sold to Sir Lawrence Washington, 275; notice of, 275, 276.
Moone, Capt. John, burgess, 236.
Moore, Edward, 221.
    John, burgess, 226.
Morer, Richard, 13.
Morgan, Francis, burgess, 198, 221, 226, 233.
    Capt. Richard, 127.
Morison (Moryson), Charles, 312, 349.
    Cecilia, 284.
    Francis, 138; shipwrecked, 207 in charge of Fort P't Comfort, 210; speaker of Assembly, 248; acting Governor, 284; mention of, 289, 290, 307; letters to Lord Clarendon, 308; censures Godwyn, the clergyman, 344; his report on Bacon's rebellion, 370, 379.
    Sir Richard, 416.
    Robert, 416.
Morley, William, burgess, 268.
Morris, John, servant, 40.
    Mary, servant, 40.
Mosely, Priscilla, Quakeress, 390.
Mottram, John, burgess, 226.
Moulton, William, 221.
Moyses, Theodore, burgess, 73.
Mund, William, 221.
Munday, Robert, 40.
Mynne, Ann, wife of George, Lord Baltimore, 67.

N.

Nansemond non-conformists, 202, 206.
Nasawattocks Creek, 171.
Navigation Act, Berkeley's speech against, 212-216; effect of, 231; effort to appeal, 281; enforced, 292.
Neale, Ann, 286.
    Anthony, 286.
    Dorothy, 286.
    James, 286, 287.
    John of Accomac, 414.
    Henrietta Maria, 286, 304.
    Walter, 87, 132; applies for office in Va., 132.
Neale's (Nele's), bark, 143, 286.
Negroe slaves, 15, 33, 34, 35, 58, 59, 187, 401.
Neile, Archbishop of Yorke, 122.
Nesan, Jack, explorer, 328.
Newce, Thomas, 81.
    Sir William, Marshall of Va., 81.
Newce's Town, Ireland, 81.
Newell, Richard, 221.
New England ministers visit Va., 165, 172.
    sharply criticized by Donne, 149.
Newport, Lady, 265.
    Sir Richard, 265.
Nickolson, Francis, 219.
    Robert, will of, 219.
Non-conformists, law relating to, 199.
Norfolk County, why named, 135, 411.
    Upper parishes of, 169.
Northampton County parishes, 169; submits to parliament, 221; upper parish formed, 231.
Norton, Capt. William, 284.
Norwood, Col. Henry, wrecked on Maryland coast, 207; at Littleton's plantation, 208; visits Argall Yeardley 208; relation of Gov. Berkeley, 209; visits Wormeley, 210; returns to England and visits Charles the Second, 210; imprisoned, 417; at Tangiers, 210; at the surrender of Manhattan, 417; treasurer of Virginia, 337.
    Major Charles, clerk of Assembly, 244.
Nottingham, Richard, 221.
Nuthall, John, 221.

O.

Oath of allegiance and supremacy, usage as to, 64, 65, 78.
Okley, Robert, servant, 23.
Onondaga Indians reply to Va. commissioners, 388.
O'Neal, Daniel, Post Master General, 192.
Hugh, of Patuxent, Md., 259.
O'Neil, Grace, 410.
Opechankano, Indian Chief, 187, 189, 193.
Orchard, Capt. Richard, 127.
Osborne, Thomas, burgess, 71, 90.
Ottowell, Thomas, servant, 41.
Overbury, Sir Thomas, 114.
Owin, Benjamin, servant, 15.

P.

Pacific Ocean, route sought to, 104.
Page, Capt. John, 232, 349, 397.
    clergyman, 364.
    Henry, carpenter, executed, 373, 377.
    Robert, 111.
Pagett (Paggit), Anthony servant, 23; burgess, 72.
    Lord William, 11.
Paine, Florentine, burgess, 267.
Pale built from James to York River, 74.
Pallavacino, Edward, 13.
Palmer, Edward, projector of University and School of Art, for Va., 27, 114.
    Thomas, 72, 90.
    Thomas, clergyman in Accomac, 407.
    William, 13.
Palmer's Island, 27, 81, 114, 212.
Pamunkey, Queen of, 386; her son, 386.
Panton, Anthony, Rector of Chespiak, 142, 143, 144, 150.
Pargiter, Theodore, of London, 257.
Parke, Daniel, councillor, 209, 316, 318, 385.
    Junior, 209; unprincipled, 316; aid to Marlborough, 316; killed by a mob, 316.

Parke, Fanny, wife of John Custis, 316.
    Lucy, wife of Col. William Byrd, 316.
Parnell, William, servant, 16.
Parramore, John, 221.
    Mr., 25.
Pate, John, 368.
    Richard, burgess, 232, 368.
Pawlett, Thomas, burgess, 90, 156.
Peach orchard, first in Va., 112.
Peake, Robert, servant, 16.
Peasley, William, brother-in-law of 2d Lord Baltimore, 62.
Peck, Ann, 243.
    Robert, clergyman, 243.
Pedro, John, a negroe servant, 15.
Peirce (Piers, Pearce, Pierce), Capt. William, 19, 35; his house, 59, 68; councillor, 88, 128, 131, 157, 184, 186.
    Jane, daughter of William, relict of Capt. John Rolfe, 19, 59.
Peirsey (Piersey, Persey), Abraham, 22; councillor, 38, 43, 48; marries widow of Nathaniel West, 49; will of, 49, 403, 404.
    Elizabeth, 405.
    Frances, 405.
    Mary, 405.
Pelham, Herbert, brother-in-law of Gov. West, 86.
    Junior, 86.
Pembroke, Earl of, 114, 134.
Penn, Robert, servant, 22.
    William, philanthropist, 252.
Penoyer, William, 217.
Pepys Samuel, notices Gov. Berkeley's stage play, 283.
Pequod Indians, 96, 97.
Percevall, Samuel, 37.
Percy, George, Dep. Governor, alludes to false statments, 84.
Perecute, Indian Chief, 328.
Perkyns, William, London merchant, 13.
Perry, Capt. Henry, burgess, 230, 236, 242, 261, 263, 268.
    Lt. William, 72, 270.
Pettus, (Pettys), Thomas, councillor, 157, 186, 193, 198, 225, 242, 263, 268, 353.
Pidgeon, Elizabeth, 157.
    William, 157.
Pigot, James, 407.

440 INDEX.

Pilkington, Margaret, servant, 18.
William, servant, 18.
Pilkinton, James, Bishop of Durham, 275.
Pindabake, an Indian, 271.
Pirates, Irish proposal to transport, 36.
Pitt, Robert, burgess, 205, 226, 232, 236, 266, 269.
Play-actors in Accomac, 315.
Pleasants, John, Quaker, 396, 400.
Plowden, Sir Edmund, Kt., notice of, 180, 183; in Fleet Prison, 181; deserted by servants, 182; visits Boston, 206; death and will, 207; his chambers in London, 264; bill for preparation of New Albion, a book, 415.
Pocahontas, in London, 29; marriage of her companion, 29.
Poconoke River, conflict in, 120.
Point Comfort, fort at, 137, 312; London ships at, 178; Dutch attack, 320.
Pollington, John, burgess, 46.
Pomfroy, Richard, insurgent, 374.
Poole, Daniel, Frenchman, 17.
Henry, burgess, 198.
Pooley, Greville, preacher, 41, 49, 74, 404, 405.
Popham, Francis, 21.
John, 21.
Popleton William, burgess, 172.
Population, increase of, 89, 93, 114, 130, 203.
Poquoson River, 113.
Pory, John, Secretary of Colony, 16, 17, 25, 33, 67.
Porter, John, friendly to Quakers, 298, 306.
Peter, 40.
Pott, Doctor John, councillor, 38, 78; physician to Colony, 39; Governor, 69, 71; bequest to, 71; described by Sandys, 79; trial and pardon of, 79, 86.
John, Junior, 221, 410.
Elizabeth, 39, 70, 80.
Francis, 114, 116, 123, 128, 410.
Porter, Capt. Roger, 348.
Pountis, John, his pinnace attacked by Indians, 52.
Powell, Captain, 33, 131.
James, 349.

Powell, John, burgess, 262, 269, 297, 318.
Samuel, 12, 23.
Thomas, 19.
William, burgess, 40, 41.
Powhatan, Indian Chief, 29, 52.
Poythers, Francis, burgess, 185, 186, 189, 198, 206.
Preen, Capt. John, 46.
Preeninge, William, 221.
Prescott, Capt. Edward, complaint against, 257.
Presley, William, burgess, 199, 297, 318.
Preston, Roger, servant, 42.
Price, Arthur, burgess, 186, 189.
Jenkyn of Pangoteague, assists shipwrecked persons, 208; gratuity to, 208.
Thomas, a Quaker, 302.
Walter, burgess, 72.
Prince, Edward, burgess, 186, 190.
Governor at Delaware River, 181.
Pritchard, Thomas, 40.
Privy council uphold Gov. Harvey, 126.
Protestant Religion enjoined, 293.
Puddlington, George, 410.
Jane, 410.
Purify, (Purifrie, Purfury), Thomas, councillor, 88, 90, 117, 133.
Puritans, 24, 30; criticism of, 148, 149; removed from Va., 201.

Q.

Quakers, punished, 285, 289; laws against, 293, 297; censured by Scarborough, 301.
Queen of Pamunkey Indians, 386.

R.

Rabnet, Maryland colonist, 126.
Ramsey, Capt. Edward, burgess, 297, 318, 348, 360.
Capt. Thomas, burgess, 262.
Randolph, Henry, clerk of Assembly, death of, 244.
William, death of, 244.
Ransome, Peter, burgess, 230.
Rappahannock Indians, 187.
Ratliffe, Elkinton, 19.

INDEX. 441

Ratliffe, Charles, 221.
Ravis, Bishop of Loudon, 137.
Rawlins, Cecilia, 284.
  Giles, 284.
Reade, George, 142; burgess, 205, 261, 263, 353.
  Robert, 142.
  Thomas, 364.
Redding, John, 348.
Redhead, Christopher, servant, 18.
Religious liberty, views of Roger Williams and others, 250.
Revell, Randall, burgess, 221, 262, 264, 406
Reynolds, Charles, burgess, 230.
Rich, Sir Nathaniel, 12,
  Robert, 31.
Richett, Mick, 221.
Richaheerian Indians, alarm settlers, 245; village, 327.
Rickahock, see *Fort Royal*.
Ricroft, Capt. James, 127.
Rideoute, Antoine, 75.
Ridley, Peter, burgess, 189, 198.
Roanoke River, explored, 327.
Roberts, John, 221.
Robins, Dorothy, 410.
  Edward, 410.
  Elizabeth, 410.
  Grace, 409.
  John, lost at sea, 158.
    Junior, 193, 206.
    son of Obedience, 407.
  Obedience, 9', 158, 185, 221, 226; burgess, 230; councillor, 226, 263, 388; protests against seizure of New England vessel, 418; family of, 409.
  Rachel, 410.
  Richard, 409.
  Sampson, 221.
  Samuel, 221.
Robinson, John, Puritan pastor at Leyden, 30.
  searcher at Gravesend, 105
  of Northampton Co., 221.
  Matthew, 40.
  William, Quaker, 285.
Roe, Sir Thomas, Kt., 85.
Rogers, George, 41.
  John, burgess, 186.
Rolfe, Capt. John, his widow, 19, 59, 194; his daughter Elizabeth, 194; his son Thomas, 194; his granddaughter, 194.

Rolfe, Lt. Thomas, notice of, 416.
Rookings, William, sentenced to death, 374.
Roper, Clement, servant, 23.
Rossingham, Edmund, nephew of Gov. Yeardley, 50, 51.
Rotterdam, ship at Jamestown, 177.
Rowinge, Henry, servant, 23.
Rowlston, a burgess, 74.
Rozier, John, preaches in Accomac, 406, 413.
Russell, Dellionell, London merchant, 404, 405.
  John, 41.
    physician, 241.
Rutter, John, 221.

S.

Sabbath, a Sunday Legislation, 89.
Sadler, Rowland, burgess, 167.
Salisbury, Earl of, letter to, 83.
Salter, Elizabeth, 18.
Saltonstall, Merriall, 86.
  Richard, 86.
  Sir Richard, Kt., 84.
  Sir Samuel, Kt., 84.
  Wye, 84.
Sancé, Baron de, 75.
Sanders, Alexander, servant, 16.
  Henry, servant, 20.
Sands (Sandys), David, minister, 21.
Sandys, Archbishop, 159.
  George, colonial treasurer, 17, 18, 45, 61, 65; writings of, 44, 45, 158; agent for Va., 159; ancestor of, 159.
  Margaret, 13, 14.
  Samuel, 13, 14.
Saracen's Head Inn, London, 85.
Sassacus, Indian chief, 97.
Savage, Thomas, 221.
  John, burgess, 318.
Savin, Robert, burgess, 73.
Sawell, Thomas, servant, 23.
Sawier, William, servant, 41.
Sawyer, Major Francis, 349
Sayle, Gov. William, visits Va. Puritans, 197, 203.
Seneca Indians near Westover, 401.
Scarborough (Scarburg), Charles, 221, 419.
  Edmund, merchant, burgess, 168, 186, 190, 199, 221, 220, 269, 318; buys slaves at Manhattan, 240;

56

Scarborough, Edmund, continued:
    Surveyor General, 287, visits Auamessex, 300, report of 301; expedition against Assateagues, 265; sends vessel to Delaware River, 418; his men seize a New England vessel, 418; death of, 419; executors of, 419.
    Matilda, 418.
    Tabitha, 418.
    Mary, widow of Edmund, 419.
    Charles, son of Edmund, 419.
School, bequest for a, 71, 112, 113.
    building begun at Charles City, 196.
Scott, Dorothea, memoir of, 155.
    Nicholas, 221.
    a physician and surgeon, 105.
Scull, G. D., memoir of Dorothea Scott, 155.
Seaverne, John, surgeon, 417.
Seawell, Henry, 134.
Seeley (Ceeley), Thomas, justice, 90.
Selve, Tobine, 221.
Sergeant, Richard, servant, 22.
Servants, agencies for white, 108.
    of Edward Blaney, 41.
    Ralph Hamor, 19.
    Isaac Madison, 23.
    John Martin, 20.
    Samuel Mathews, 21.
    John Pott, 39.
    Roger Smith, 18.
    William Tucker, 40.
    Francis West, 15.
    Francis Wyatt, 14.
    Gov. Yeardley, 16, 17.
    Indenture, 57.
    Sufferings, 58.
    Insurrection, 295.
    elevation of, 279, 290.
Severence, Capt. John, 128.
Sewall, Henry of Maryland, 304, 383.
Seward, John, burgess, 189.
Sharpe, Peter, Quaker physician, 121.
    Samuel, burgess, 46, 55, 71.
Sharpless, Edward, ears cut off, 25, 26.
Shaw, Annis, servant, 22.
Sheaperd, Robert, servant, 17, 41; burgess, 193, 198.
Shelley, John, servant, 41.
Shepherd, John, burgess, 184, 226, 233, 236.
Sherwood, William, 364; tomb of, 637.

Ship-building encouraged, 288.
Sibsie (Sibsey, Sypsey), John, wrecked in Barnstable Bay, 54; councillor, 132.
Sidney (Sydney), John, burgess, 185, 199, 261, 266, 269.
Silk presented to Charles the Second, 322-325.
Slaves, negro, 33, 34, 35, 58, 59.
Smith, Arthur, burgess, 186.
    Capt. John, quarrels with Francis West, 52, 83; notice of, 84, 85.
    John, burgess, 262.
    John of Nibley, 18.
    Nicholas, burgess, 269.
    Osmond, servant,
    Robert, 304; letter from Berkeley, 313.
    Roger, councillor, 18, 38, 43, 68.
    Toby, burgess, 167, 206.
    Sir Thomas of London, 9, 11; Va. Indians die at his house, 29.
Smith's Island, why so named, 234.
Smithson, Judith, 405.
Smothergall, Samuel, 223.
Smyth, John, burgess, 72.
    Richard, 22.
    William, 221.
Snow, Justinian, 255.
Somerset, Lady Mary, 303.
Sone (Soane), Henry, burgess, 226, 230, 232, 236, 261, 268 281; death of, 288.
    Samuel, 221.
Southampton, Earl of, 9, 20.
Southcoat, Capt. Thomas, burgess, 317.
Southerne, John, 71.
Southren, Edward, 221.
Southey, Ann, 387.
    Elizabeth, 387.
    Lewis, 387.
Sparks, John, servant, 17.
Sparrow, Charles, burgess, 190, 205, 230, 268.
Spelman, Henry, killed by Indians, 52.
    Sir Henry, K't, 24.
Spencer, Nicholas, burgess, 318, 349; secretary, 393, 394, 398.
Spicer, George, servant, 21.
Sprigge, Thomas, 221.
Stafford, Sir John, 274.
Standish, Capt. Miles, 95.
Stanley, William, 221.
State House needed at Jamestown, 138, 221.

INDEX. 443

Stebbins, Luke, widow of, marries Ralph Wormeley, 415.
Stegg, Capt. Thomas, 135, 136; fined, 151; speaker of Assembly, 167; seizes a ship at Boston, 179; Parliament commissioner, 218; lost at sea, 219; will of, 219.
Thomas, Junior, 219: councillor, 317.
Stephens (Stevens), Frances, widow of Samuel, 341.
George, burgess, 186, 189, 226, 230.
Richard, 66, 69; councillor, 78, 88; fights a duel, 88; his widow marries Gov. Harvey, 152, 415.
Samuel, 341, 415.
Stevens, Major Philip, 207, 417.
William of Accomac, 221, 417.
Somerset, 207, 417.
Stillwell, L't Nicholas, 188.
Stoakes, Robert, an insurgent, 374.
Stone, Capt. John, rough mariner fined, 91, 95; killed, 96; mention of, 410.
Matthew, 221.
Maximilian, servant, 16.
Verlinda, wife of Gov. William, 416.
William of Northampton Co., first Protestant Governor of Maryland, 201, 416; letter from Lord Baltimore, 212; brother-in-law of Francis Doughty and John Rozier, clergymen, 406, 416.
Story, Thomas, Quaker preacher, 361.
Stoughton, Samuel, burgess, 194, 198, 236.
Strachey, William, servant, 16.
Strange, William, servant, 16.
Stringer, John, burgess, 221, 267, 269, 300, 497.
Stephen, 221.
Stuteville, Sir Martin, K't, 74.
Stuyvesant, Governor, 232, 272.
Symes (Simes, Symmes), Benjamin, founds a school, 71, 112, 113.
Symonds, Dorothy, wife of Harrison, the non-conformist minister, 202.
Samuel, 202.
Swan, Thomas, burgess, 189, 205, 261, 349, 353.
Swedes of Delaware River, 138, 139.

T.

Tabernor, Thomas, burgess, 262.
Talbot, Sir William, Sec. of Md., 327.
Taverner, Capt. Henry, 128.
Robert, 42.
Taylor (Tayler), James, 410.
Philip, burgess, 121, 168, 410, 416.
Thomas, burgess, 194.
William, burgess, 168, 198, 221; councillor, 225, 212.
Silas, engineer, notice of, 322.
Tegger, Richard, 223.
Thomas, Edward, Quaker, 364.
Nathaniel, servant, 23.
William, burgess, 230.
Thompson, Ann, servant, 16.
George, servant, 40.
L't., burgess, 74.
Maurice, 217.
Paul, 74.
Richard, associate of Claiborne, 108.
Roger, 16, 71.
William, 40.
Thornbury, Thomas, burgess, 233, 234.
Thoroughgood, Adam, burgess, 74, 90, 133, 134, 318.
Sir John, K't, 134.
Thomas, as to Maryland charter, 307.
Thorpe, George, 19.
Otto, 383.
Thurston, Capt. Richard, 419.
Mary, Quakeress, 299.
Quaker preacher, 252.
Tilney, John, 221.
Tobacco trade, 27, 47, 55, 56, 91, 121, 145; excessive planting, 287, 291, 304, 316, 317.
Riots, 394, 397.
revenue, 403.
Toleration in Religion, 197, 250, 311.
Tompson, Nicholas, servant, 17.
Thomas, 57.
William, minister from New England, 167, 184.
William, Roman Catholic, 167.
Tottopottomoy, Indian Chief, killed, 245; family neglected, 246; mention of in Hudibras, 420.
Town organization desired, 30.
Towns, building of, a failure, 310.

INDEX.

Townsend, Richard, servant, 39; burgess, 73; councillor, 132, 157, 184, 186.
Traverse, Raleigh, burgess, 318.
Col. William, 349; speaker of Assembly, 385.
Travis, Edward, burgess, 184.
Tree, Richard, burgess, 73.
Trelawney, Robert, 123.
Troops arrive from London, 372.
Truman, Thomas, 221.
Major Thomas, of M'd., harsh toward Indians, 347.
Trussell, John, burgess, 206, 236, 239.
Tuchin, Simon, suspected, 36.
Tucker, Daniel, 34.
Elizabeth, 40.
Mary, 40.
William, councillor, 38, 40, 78, 88, 90.
Turner, John, insurgent, 374.
Martin, servant, 17.

U.

Underwood, William, burgess, 230.
Upton, John, burgess, 23, 90, 189 199.
William, 133.
Urwick, Rev. Doctor, alludes to Doctor Harrison, formerly of Va , 202.
Ute, John, burgess, 73, 78, 88, 92, 117, 119.

V.

Vane, Sir Henry, Kt., 102.
Vassalls, Samuel, 76, 97.
Vaughan, Richard, 22h
Vernald, Mary, bequest to, 220.
Verney, Lady, letter to, 109.
Sir Edward, 108.
Thomas, 108, 111.
Vicaredge, Robert, merchant, 290.
Vincencio, the Italian, 18.
Virginia Company, 33, 85, 159,164.
commissioners, 11, 12, 13, 85, 217.
population, 26.
university projected, 27.
church government, 167.
submissive to Parliament, 221.
land ceded, by the King, 289.
urged to imitate New England, 292.

Virginia continued.
presents silk to King, 328.
remonstrance, 382, 395, 421.
Von Twiller, Governor at Manhattan, 95.

W.

Waddelove, Nicholas, 221.
Waleford, John, 221.
Walker, Capt. Edward, 127.
John, burgess, 185, 190, 194, 205, 242; councillor, 261, 268, 353.
Peter, burgess, 221, 236.
Thomas, burgess, 297.
Walklett, Gregory, an insurgent, 375.
Wallings, George, burgess, 297.
Waltham, John, 406.
Ward, Captain, 408.
Mary, 241.
William, 221.
Warne, John, bequest to, 70.
Thomas, burgess, 189.
Warner, Augustine, burgess, 222, 267 ; councillor, 353.
Augustine, Junior, at Merchant Tailors' School, London, 419.
Mildred, wife of Lawrence Washington, 420; her second husband, 420; buried in England, 420.
Ralph, councillor, 68.
Warnet, Thomas, merchant, 69; will of, 70.
Warren, Ratcliff, 120.
Thomas, burgess, 184, 266, 297, 318.
William, 116.
Warwick, Earl of, 31, 176, 179, 197, 200.
creek, 178.
the ship at Potomac Falls, 92; wrecked, 92, 104.
Washington, Augustine, father of the President, 420.
Eleanor, 257.
George, President, ancestor of, 256; taught by a convict servant, 329.
John, the immigrant complains of the hanging of a supposed witch, 258; warden, 259; burgess, 318; harsh toward Indians, 347.
son of Mildred, 420.
of Barbadoes, 257.

Washington, Henry, 257.
Lawrence, brother of John, 259.
   son of John, 420.
   brother of George, 257.
   Mildred, 420.
   daughter, of 420.
   Richard, 257.
   of Barbadoes, 257.
Waters, Edward, 410.
   Grace, 410.
   Nathaniel, 388.
   Susanna, 388.
   William, 407, 410.
Waterhouse, Mr., 25.
Watkins, Rice, 41.
Watson, Abraham, burgess, 232, 236.
   James, servant, 23.
Weale, John, burgess, 155.
Webb, Giles, burgess, 261, 266, 269.
   Stephen, servant, 18; burgess, 167, 184.
   Wingfield, burgess, 236.
Webster, Richard, burgess, 261, 413.
Wells, Richard, burgess, 190, 198.
Wentworth, Earl of Strafford, 67, 68.
Werden, Sir John on Va. insurgents, 371.
West, ancestor, 15.
   Francis, brother of Lord Delaware, 15, 37, 43, 51, 52, 55, 59, 78, 88.
   Frances, widow of Nathaniel, 15, 49, 405.
   John, Governor and councillor, 15, 72, 78, 88, 118, 129, 130, 155, 186, 198, 225, 242, 267, 271, 349, 364.
   John, Junior, 271.
   Nathaniel brother of Lord Delaware, 15, 49; his widow marries Abraham Peirsey, 49.
   Nathaniel, Junior, 405.
   Richard, Attorney on Va. suffrage, 330.
   Toby, 271.
   William, an insurgent, 374.
Weston, Capt. Hugh, 127.
   Sir Richard, 11.
Westrop, John, burgess, 185, 241.
Wethrall, Robert, burgess, 189, 226, 230.
Weyre, John, burgess, 267, 269, 297, 314, 318.

Whaly, Major Thomas, insurgent, 372, 375.
Wheatley (Wheatliff), David, 221, 238.
Wheeler, Clasen, a fiddler, 376.
Whitaker, Alexander, minister, 406.
   Jabez, councillor, 38, 406.
   William, burgess, 205, 206, 232, 236, 266.
   William, D.D., 406.
Whitby, William, burgess, 226, 230, 232, 237.
White, Andrew, Jesuit missionary, 187, 201, 415; Va. minister, without orders, 126.
   Francis, D.D., 12.
   Jeremy, 41.
   Major William, 349.
Whitehand, George, servant, 16.
Whitehead, John, 221.
Whitmore, Robert, 41.
Whittington, William, 221, 417.
Wiggins, Capt. Edward, 348.
Wighcomoco River, 121.
Willrahan, Sir Roger, Kt., 61.
Wilford, Thomas, executed, 369, 376.
Wilkins, John, his widow, 407.
Willcox, John, burgess, 262.
Williams, Pierce, servant, 23.
   Robert, surgeon, 219.
   Roger, surgeon, 21.
   New England minister complains of Councillor Ludlow, 136.
   Thomas, 42.
   Walter, 221.
Williamson, Dr. Robert, 297, 318.
Willis, Ann, servant, 16.
   Francis, burgess, 226, 230, 267, 269, 349.
Wilmore, George, 12.
Willoughby, Elizabeth, 157.
   Francis, 157.
   Henry, 157.
   Thomas, 46; councillor, 134, 157, 186, 188, 193.
   Junior, pupil in Merchant Tailors' School, London, 157.
   William, Colonel, 157.
Wilson, George, Quaker, letter of, 285.
   James, sentenced to death, 373.
   John, early minister, 146.
Windham, Edward, burgess, 158, 168.
Wingate, Roger, Colonial Treasurer, 146, 156.

INDEX.

Winslow, Edward, 33, 52.
Winthrop, Gov. John, of Mass., 97, 103, 136.
Wise, John, 221.
Witch, woman hung as a, 257.
Witchcraft, 239, 257.
Wollaston, Capt., 113.
Wolstenholme, Sir John, Kt., 12, 85.
   John, Junior, 85.
Wood, Abraham, burgess, 185, 190, 193, 194, 231, 236, 245, 261, 263, 268, 279, 327.
   Thomas, dies among Indians, 328.
Woodhall, John, 37.
Woodhouse, Henry, burgess, 102, 103, 199, 230, 247, 281.
Woodliffe, Captain, burgess, 230.
Woodward, Christopher, burgess, 72.
   John, 229.
   Thomas, assay master at London mint, 229; in Carolina, 307, 317.
Worleigh, George, burgess, 158.
   Margaret, taken by Indians, 188.
Worlich, William, burgess, 206, 236, 269, 270.
Wormeley, Agatha, 210, 386.
   Christopher, Senior, 132, 156, 415; marries widow Stebbins, 415.
   Junior, 349; marries the widow Aylmer, 363.
Worsley, Benjamin, 217.
Wos, William, burgess, 185.
Wraxall, Capt. Peter, 419.
Wright, William, under sheriff, 340.
Wrote, Samuel of London, 12, 45, 50, 79, 85.
   Sir Thomas, 11.
Wyatt, Anthony, burgess, 14, 156, 190, 232.
   Edward, 271.
   Eleanor, 14.
   Francis, Governor of Va., 13, 14, 20, 28, 37, 44, 60, 85, 145, 151, 155.
   son of Governor, 156.
   George, father of Governor, 13, 37.
   George, son of Governor, 13, 155, 156.
Wyatt, Hawte, brother of Governor, 13, 69.
   Henry, son of Governor, 156.
   Margaret, wife of Governor, 13, 14, 155, 159.
   Nicholas, 349.
   Ralph, 14, 94, 156.
   Richard, 156
   Thomas, 13.
   William, 156, 271.
Wynd, Sir Humphrey, Kt., 61.
Wynne, Capt. Robert, burgess, 261, 268, 287, 293, 297, 317.

Y.

Yates, Captain, voyage of, 19.
   Edward, servant, 16.
Yeardley (Yardley), Argall, 48, 157; councillor, 186, 189, 221, 225, 242.
   Elizabeth, 48.
   Governor of Va., 16, 27, 28, 38, 44, 47; will of, 48; house in Jamestown, 68.
   Ralph, brother of Governor, 48, 50.
   Temperance, wife of Governor, 16, 48.
Yeo, Leonard, burgess, 186, 190, 297, 318.
   Hugh, burgess, 298, 318.
Young, Gregory of London, grocer, 105, 378.
   Capt. Thomas, 106, 107, 108, 152, 378.
   Susanna, 105, 378.
   Thomas, son of Captain Thomas, 152; executed as an insurgent, 152, 373, 377, 378.

Z.

Zouch, Sir John, Kt., 85; visits Va., 118; letter to, 118-120.

CORRECTIONS.

Owing to the distance of the author, from the press, while the pages were printed, the following corrections are necessary.

Page 14 Muster of Sir *Thomas* should read Sir Francis.
    47 *Sanisbury*, " " Sainsbury.
    68 *Manefie*, " " Menefie.
    69 *was* the grounds, " " were.
    77 *Bolton*, " " Button.
    79 Foot note erroneous, reference to the hero in a Spanish romance, see page 408.
    86 *Dillingham*, should read Bellingham.
    88 *Warwick*, " " Maverick.
    91 *Harman*, " " Harmar.
    93 " " " "
    99 *Sir Philip* of Erwarton, " " Sir Philip Parker.
    113 *Kingston*, " " Kiquotan,
    120 Ratcliff *Warner*, " " Warren.
    " Charles *Harney*, " " Harmar.
    126 *Rabent*, " " Rabnet.
    139 *vicesino*, " " vicesimo.
    " *placits*, " " placito,
    168 *Edward* Scarborough, " " Edmund.
    198 Thomas *Petters*, " " Pettus.
    202 *Warwick*, " " Urwick.
    " 1834, " " 1634.
    205 October, 1644, " " 1649.
    209 *Edward* Scarborough, " " Edmund.
    230 William *Gonge*, " " Gouge.
    232 John *Bushopp*, " " Bishop.
    233 William *Melliu*, " " Mellinge.
    " holding *officer* " " office.
    288 John.
    328 *Last eight lines of text*, " " as the first 8 lines.
    342 165-, " " 1650.
    345 *vindicative*, " " vindictive.
    349 Col William *Bull*, " " Ball.

www.ingramcontent.com/pod-product-compliance
Lightning Source LLC
Chambersburg PA
CBHW020527300426
44111CB00008B/565